PSYCHOLOGY IN PROFESSIONAL SPORTS AND THE PERFORMING ARTS

The relationship between sport and exercise psychology and the realm of professional sport and performance has grown exponentially in recent years. Elite athletes increasingly see the value in seeking psychological advice and expertise, while consultants now work in a wider range of elite performance environments.

Psychology in Professional Sports and the Performing Arts: Challenges and Strategies is a unique and timely collection that brings together the experiences and knowledge of a range of applied psychologists working in these exciting industries. The book begins with a section outlining the core skills that practitioners require in the field, before chapters discussing individual sports, team sports, and the performing arts. Each author looks at how theoretical principles can be applied within a particular professional context, delineating how performers may benefit from working with a psychologist, as well as the ethical and cultural challenges that they faced.

Assessing the role of applied psychologists across a truly unique range of activities, from polo to motor racing and ice hockey to modern dance, *Psychology in Professional Sports and the Performing Arts: Challenges and Strategies* offers unrivalled insights into how sport and exercise psychology can be put into practice in challenging professional environments. It will appeal to anyone studying sport and exercise psychology or working in the field.

Robert J. Schinke is the Canada Research Chair in Multicultural Sport and Physical Activity, and a professor at Laurentian University, Canada. He is both a mental training consultant to Olympic and professional athletes and an active researcher.

Dieter Hackfort is a Professor for Sport Psychology and Head of the Department for Sport Science at the University FAF Munich. He has served as a counselor for professional performers and athletes of various sports at the Olympic Centers in Germany. His research has been published in 27 books and edited volumes and in more than 150 contributions in national and international journals.

International Perspectives on Key Issues in Sport and Exercise Psychology

Series Editors: Athanasios Papaiouannou and Dieter Hackfort

International Perspectives on Key Issues in Sport and Exercise Psychology is a series of edited books published in partnership with the International Society of Sport Psychology. Each title reflects cutting-edge research in the psychological study of high-level sport, written by key researchers and leading figures in the field of sports psychology.

Books in this series:

Athletes' Careers across Cultures
Edited by Natalia B. Stambulova and Tatiana V. Ryba

Routledge Companion to Sport and Exercise Psychology:

Global Perspectives and Fundamental Concepts
Edited by Athanasios Papaioannou and Dieter Hackfort

The Psychology of Sub-Culture in Sport and Physical Activity:

Critical Perspectives
Edited by Robert J. Schinke and Kerry R. McGannon

Psychology in Professional Sports and the Performing Arts:
Challenges and Strategies
Edited by Robert J. Schinke and Dieter Hackfort

PSYCHOLOGY IN PROFESSIONAL SPORTS AND THE PERFORMING ARTS

Challenges and strategies

Edited by Robert J. Schinke and Dieter Hackfort

Routledge
Taylor & Francis Group

LONDON AND NEW YORK

International Society of Sport Psychology

First published 2017
by Routledge
2 Park Square, Milton Park, Abingdon, Oxon OX14 4RN

and by Routledge
711 Third Avenue, New York, NY 10017

Routledge is an imprint of the Taylor & Francis Group, an informa business

British Library Cataloguing in Publication Data
A catalogue record for this book is available from the British Library

Library of Congress Cataloging-in-Publication Data
Names: Schinke, Robert J., editor. | Hackfort, Dieter, editor.
Title: Psychology in professional sports and the performing arts : challenges and strategies / edited by Robert J. Schinke & Dieter Hackfort.
Description: Abingdon, Oxon ; New York, NY : Routledge, 2016. | Series: International perspectives on key issues in sport and exercise psychology
Identifiers: LCCN 2016003130 | ISBN 9781138808614 (hardback : alk. paper) | ISBN 9781138808621 (pbk. : alk. paper) | ISBN 9781315750569 (e-book)
Subjects: LCSH: Sports—Psychological aspects. | Professional sports—Psychological aspects. | Athletes—Psychology. | Professional athletes—Psychology. | Performing arts—Psychological aspects. | Sports psychologists—Biography.
Classification: LCC GV706.4 .P6844 2016 | DDC 796.01/9—dc23
LC record available at http://lccn.loc.gov/2016003130

ISBN: 978-1-138-80861-4 (hbk)
ISBN: 978-1-138-80862-1 (pbk)
ISBN: 978-1-315-75056-9 (ebk)

Typeset in Bembo
by Apex CoVantage, LLC

CONTENTS

BIOGRAPHIES

Co-editors

Robert J. Schinke, EdD, is the Canada Research Chair in Multicultural Sport and Physical Activity and a Professor of Sport Psychology in the School of Human Kinetics at Laurentian University in Canada. As a Canadian Sport Psychology Association registered practitioner, Schinke has extensive experience working with national teams and professional athletes of North America, South America, Europe, Asia, Africa, and the Caribbean. Robert has authored more than 100 refereed publications and co-edited 15 textbooks, including the *Routledge International Handbook of Sport Psychology*. His research has been supported by the Social Sciences and Humanities Research Council of Canada, the Indigenous Health Research Development Program, and the Canadian Foundation for Innovation. In addition, Robert served as an associate editor for *Psychology of Sport and Exercise*, and he is presently the co-editor for the *International Journal of Sport and Exercise Psychology*, and associate editor for *Case Studies in Sport and Exercise Psychology* and with the *Journal of Sport and Social Issues*. He is also on several editorial boards off other peer-reviewed journals. Robert is also the current Past-President of the Association for Applied Sport Psychology and serves as a member of the Managing Council for the International Society of Sport Psychology. He, his wife Erin, and their two sons, Harrison and Pierce, reside in Sudbury, Ontario, Canada.

Dieter Hackfort, PhD, is a professor for sport psychology, Head Department for Sport Science, at the University FAF Munich. In 1986 he was a visiting professor at the Center for Behavioral Medicine and Health Psychology at the University of South Florida. From 1991 to 2004 he was the Head of the Institute for Sport Science at the University FAF Munich. From 2004 to 2009 Dr. Hackfort was the founding Dean of Aspire the Academy for Sports Excellence in Doha, Qatar. From 2009 to 2010 he served as a founding Director of the Sport Science Program at Qatar University. He has served as a counselor for professional performers and athletes of various sports at the Olympic Centers in Germany. His research has been published in 27 books and edited volumes and in more than 160 contributions in national and international journals. From 1996 to 2008 he served as a co-Editor-in-Chief for the *International Journal of Sport and Exercise Psychology*. He led projects in Quality Management and successfully managed ISO 9000 and EFQM certifications in educational and sports organizations in Germany and Qatar. From 2005 to 2009 Dr. Hackfort served as the President of the International Society of Sport Psychology (ISSP). He received the Carl-Diem Plakette Award in 1984 from the German Sports Federation for his outstanding research and leadership. In 2001 Dr. Hackfort received the Honor Award of the ISSP in recognition of significant contributions to national and international sport psychology through leadership, research, and personal service. In 1999 he was appointed an Honorary Professor of the Wuhan Institute of Physical Education in China. Dr. Hackfort has consulted extensively in tennis, golf, and car racing (Formula One, GT, Ralleigh) for more than 20 years.

Authors

Sharon A. Chirban is a seasoned clinical sports psychologist. She has maintained her private practice, Amplifying Performance Consulting, for more than 20 years. In private practice, Dr. Chirban works with clinical eating disorders, athletes with disordered eating, and individuals with depression, anxiety, and adjustment issues. She consults with executives and medical professionals around performance issues. Her sports psychology expertise translates well into the high-performance world. Sharon has also treated hundreds of athletes through her sports psychology clinic at the Division of Sports Medicine at Boston Children's Hospital. She has developed expertise in the psychology of injury rehabilitation, management of post-concussive syndrome, and prizes herself as a comeback specialist. Consulting with the Boston Ballet in different facets over the years, her practice is a Boston Ballet Health Alliance Partner, providing workshops and individual consults to the company and staff. Dr. Chirban is a Certified Consultant with the Applied Association of Sport Psychologists and is on the Olympic Registry of Sports Psychologists. She also serves as the Mental Health Advisor of *Women's Health Magazine* and is frequently interviewed in national news media.

Stiliani Chroni, PhD, has an educational background in sport sciences and sport psychology. Currently, she is a professor at Hedmark University College in Norway, teaching and conducting research. She has two research lines: one focuses on the safety and well-being of female sport participants, while the second explores performers' on-field lived experiences that influence persistence and performance. At present she is focusing her research on the psychology of elite coaches. She is a Certified Consultant both in Greece (HSSP) and the United States (AASP), and presently Chroni is a member on the board of the Norwegian Sport Psychology Association. She has consulted in the sport of polo for more than 15 years.

Dr. Stewart T. Cotterill is a Reader in Sport and Performance Psychology at the University of Winchester. Dr. Cotterill is the author of several books, including *Team Psychology in Sports* and *The Psychology of Cricket*. He is the inaugural editor of the Association for Applied Sport Psychology (AASP) Case Studies in Sport and Exercise Psychology (CSSEP) journal, and serves on the BPS Sport & Exercise Psychology committee. He has extensive applied experience across a range of team sports at the elite level, including cricket, soccer, and rugby union. He has also worked with individual athletes across a broad range of sports.

Paul Dennis recently retired after a 20-year career with the Toronto Maple Leafs men's hockey team. As the Leafs' Player Development Coach, he assisted athletes in their professional and personal development. He also consulted with the Toronto Raptors of the National Basketball Association (NBA) and Toronto FC of Major League Soccer. He was the mental skills coach to Canada's World Junior hockey team in 2002 and 2003 and Canada's National Sledge hockey team in 2012. Dennis recently left his position as the High Performance coach at York University to return to the University of Toronto, where he lectures in sport psychology.

Edward F. Etzel, PhD, serves as a Professor in the Department of Sport Sciences within the West Virginia University College of Physical Activity and Sport Sciences. Ed is a Licensed Psychologist in the state of West Virginia. He is listed as a consultant on the U.S. Olympic Committee's Sport Psychology Registry. He serves as Chair of the Association of Applied Sport Psychology's Ethics Committee. Ed is a Fellow in the AASP. He received the APA Division 47 Distinguished Contribution to Education in Sport and Exercise Psychology Award in 2009. Ed was the Gold Medalist at the 1984 Olympics in rifle shooting.

Leslee A. Fisher, PhD, is an Associate Professor of sport psychology at the University of Tennessee. She holds a PhD in Sport Psychology from the University of California, Berkeley. Leslee has published more than 55 academic and applied articles and has presented at numerous national and international conferences. Her research focuses on cultural sport psychology and can be found in *The Journal of Sport and Exercise Psychology, The Sport Psychologist, International Journal of Sport and Exercise Psychology*, *International Journal of Sport Psychology*, and *Women in Sport and Physical Activity*. Leslee also served as the Secretary/Treasurer of the Association for Applied Sport Psychology (AASP) and is an AASP Fellow and an AASP-certified sport psychology consultant.

Frank L. Gardner, PhD, ABPP, is Associate Dean and Professor in the School of Health Sciences at Touro College in New York City. He earned his PhD in Clinical and School Psychology from Hofstra University and is board certified in clinical psychology. With more than 30 years of experience as a practicing clinical and sport-performance psychologist, Frank's specialties include the evidence-based psychological treatment of anger and violence, and interventions for performance enhancement and performance dysfunction. He is co-developer of the Mindfulness-Acceptance-Commitment (MAC) approach to performance enhancement and psychosocial well-being, and he was the founding Editor-in-Chief of the *Journal of Clinical Sport Psychology*.

Richard Gordin, PhD, is an Emeritus Professor at Utah State University. He has been at the university for 35 years. He was a Professor in the Department of Health, Physical Education and Recreation and was an Adjunct Professor in the Department of Psychology. He was the department's graduate coordinator for 15 years. Dr. Gordin has published 95 scholarly articles and book chapters and has made 370 professional presentations at state, regional, national, and international conferences. He has been a sport psychology consultant for numerous athletic teams at his university, USA Gymnastics, USA Track and Field, US Ski and Snowboard Association, and several professionals on the PGA and Champions Tours. He is the former chair of the certification committee of the Association for Applied Sport Psychology (AASP). He is listed on the sport psychology registry of the U.S. Olympic Committee for the 2012–2016 quadrennium. He was the sport psychology consultant for the USA Women's Gymnastics Team in Seoul in 1988 and a sport psychology consultant for the USA Track and Field Team for the 2004 Olympic Games in Athens. He recently served as the sport psychologist for the USA Nordic Combined Ski Team in Vancouver in 2010 and in Sochi in 2014.

Chris Harwood, PhD, is a Reader in Applied Sport Psychology at Loughborough University, where he is leader of the Sport and Exercise Psychology Research Group. His academic interests focus on the psychological development and environments of youth athletes as well as the professional development of practitioners. A registered practitioner psychologist, former national standard tennis player and coach, he has provided consultancy services in tennis for more than 20 years. He worked as lead psychologist for the Lawn Tennis Association from 2010–2013 and serves on the Women's Tennis Association (WTA) tour sport science advisory panel.

Yoichi Kozuma, MPE, is a Professor in the Department of Competitive Sports of the College of Physical Education at Tokai University in Japan, where he teaches undergraduate and graduate courses in applied sport psychology. He received his masters of physical education at Thukyo University in Japan. He is a nationally (in Japan) certified Mental Training Consultant in Sport and is also Director of the Applied Sport and Mental Training Psychology Lab at Tokai University. In addition, he is the founder of the Japanese Society of Mental Training and Applied Sport Psychology (JSMTASP). He works with professional, national, and Olympic athletes, as well as junior and senior high school teams. He holds a sixth-degree black belt in karate and is a former All-Japan Champion. Professor Kozuma is widely published in Japan and is pleased to have this opportunity to share his information with English readers.

Charles A. Maher is Professor Emeritus at Rutgers University and Sport and Performance Psychologist/Senior Director of Personal and Organizational Performance for the Cleveland Indians. He is a licensed psychologist, a certified consultant of the AASP, and has practiced sport and performance psychology for 30 years in Major League Baseball (Cleveland Indians, Chicago White Sox, New York Yankees, Detroit Tigers); the National Football League (Cleveland Browns, New England Patriots, New York Jets); the National Basketball Association (Cleveland Cavaliers, San Antonio Spurs, Oklahoma City Thunder); and the National Hockey League (Minnesota Wild; New York Rangers); and with professional athletes in tennis, golf, boxing, and horse racing.

Stephen D. Mellalieu, PhD, is a Professor in Applied Sport Psychology in the Cardiff School of Sport at Cardiff Metropolitan University, UK, where he is Associate Dean for Research. He has published more than 70 research papers in a wide range of international sport psychology journals and texts. He is Editor of the *Journal of Applied Sport Psychology* and co-founder and Network Editor of the *World Rugby Science Network*. Stephen is a Chartered Psychologist of the British Psychological Society, a registered Practitioner Psychologist and Partner with the Health and Care Professions Council, and a British Association of Sport and Exercise Sciences accredited Sport Scientist. He has 20 years' consultancy experience in Olympic and professional sport, working predominantly within professional rugby union for the past 7 years.

Jean Francois Ménard, MA, is the founder and president of Kambio Performance. Jean François Ménard is an internationally recognized mental performance consultant and speaker. J. F. Ménard has worked for several years with world-class performers at Cirque du Soleil, an internationally acclaimed entertainment company that showcases the true meaning of expertise. His practical and hands-on signature techniques have been taught to numerous sport psychology university programs across North America. This University of Ottawa graduate also shares his knowledge regularly on the national French Canadian sports channel RDS. His clientele ranges from Olympic/Paralympic athletes to professional performers to circus artists to successful business corporations and beyond. He is based in Montreal, Canada, with his wife and two kids.

Angus Mugford is the Director of High Performance for the Toronto Blue Jays, where he leads a team of specialists across Sports Medicine, Sport Science, Strength and Conditioning, and Mental Performance. Prior to this role, he served as the Director of the International Management Group (IMG) Institute, serving junior student-athletes, as well as athletes across the NFL, NBA, MLB, and WTA and ATP tennis tours. In 2015, he was elected by his peers as the President for the Association for Applied Sport Psychology (AASP). He is a certified consultant and is listed in the United States Olympic Committee (USOC) registry.

Zella E. Moore, PsyD, is Associate Professor and Chairperson of the Department of Psychology at Manhattan College in New York. She received her PsyD in Clinical Psychology from La Salle University. Zella is co-developer of the Mindfulness-Acceptance-Commitment (MAC) approach for enhancing human performance and psychosocial well-being, and was the founding Senior Associate Editor of the *Journal of Clinical Sport Psychology.* From a clinical perspective, Zella has worked extensively with individuals with depressive disorders, anxiety disorders, and schizoaffective disorder, and specializes in the treatment of anger dyscontrol and its behavioral manifestations.

Mark S. Nesti, CPsychol., AFBPsS, is an associate professor in psychology and sport, and a specialist in applied sport psychology, especially in relation to professional sport including football. He has written on existential phenomenological psychology, counseling, identity, anxiety, spirituality, and peak performance in sport. Mark leads the MSc sport psychology programme at Liverpool JM University. He has worked in Premier League football with players and staff at Everton, Chelsea, and a number of other clubs, and was formerly first team counseling sport psychologist at Bolton Wanderers 2003–2007, Newcastle United 2007–2008, and Hull City 2008–2009. The work involved helping players develop their psychological skills and qualities, and acting as an organizational psychologist to support the coaching and sports science staff. Mark was based at these clubs four to five days each week. His most recent books, published by Routledge, focus on delivering applied psychology and English Premiership football (2010) theology, ethics and transcendence in sport (2011), and elite European football youth academies (2014). Mark was Executive Director of the Centre for the Study of Sport and Spirituality at York St John University, and is Research Lead at the John Paul II Foundation for Sport. A British Psychological Society chartered psychologist and Reader in Sport Psychology in the School of Sport and Exercise Sciences at Liverpool John Moores University, Mark has been a BASES accredited sport psychologist since 1990 and has worked with a range of sports at different levels of performance, from club to Olympic standard.

Robert M. Nideffer, PhD, has been a professor, a researcher, a service provider, and a business developer. He is best known in the field for his research and writing on the integration of concentration skills, emotional arousal, and performance. His first book, *The Inner Athlete*, provided a conceptual bridge between theory and practice that both professionals and the coaches and athletes that they work with could accept and understand. *The Inner Athlete* provided a compelling rationale for the use of psychological techniques to enhance performance, thereby adding to the credibility of the field.

Lois Butcher-Poffley, PhD, has her MEd and PhD in sport and exercise psychology from Temple University in Philadelphia, PA. She is a Certified Consultant through the Association for Applied Sport Psychology (CC-AASP) and a member of the United States Olympic Committee's Sport Psychology Registry. Her performance enhancement consulting practice includes work with professional performing artists (musicians, singers, rock, classical genres), conservatory students, and dancers. As a sport psychology consultant, her clients include Olympic, NCAA Division I and Division III, and USGF nationally ranked athletes. Dr. B has also worked extensively in gymnastics as both a psychological skills trainer and a dance coach.

Miriam R. Rowan, MS, is a clinical psychology doctoral candidate at the PGSP-Stanford PsyD Consortium. Her clinical interests include evidence-based anxiety, trauma, and eating disorder treatments for adolescents and young adults. Miriam's research activities have focused on cognitive-behavioral and mindfulness approaches to treating social anxiety and the prevention of eating disorders in athletes. Over the course of 20 years, in addition to her psychology background, Miriam trained at the School of American Ballet and danced professionally at the San Francisco Ballet. Combining her passions, Miriam looks to support dancers in healthful pursuit of their goals.

Christian Smith, MA, joined IMG Academy in February 2007 and serves as Lead Golf Mental Conditioning Coach. Christian has developed the mental games of many golfers, from young beginners to NCAA DI champions, USGA champions, and Symetra, LPGA, and LET players. From Nottinghamshire, England, Christian enjoyed amateur success and played DI college golf at Coastal Carolina University while completing his BA in Psychology. He earned his MA in Kinesiology (Exercise and Sport Psychology) from San Diego State University, while serving as volunteer assistant men's golf coach. An AASP member, Christian has presented at professional conferences, consulted with golf federations, and been featured in golf publications and on domestic and international television networks.

Rebecca Symes, MA, runs a thriving consultancy, Sporting Success, working full time as an applied Sport Psychologist. She is Chartered with the British Psychological Society and a registered Practitioner Psychologist with the Health and Care Professions Council. Rebecca has almost 10 years' experience within elite sport and currently works with pro mixed martial arts (MMA) fighters preparing for British and World Title fights, as well as extensively within professional cricket and Archery GB. Rebecca has worked at European and World Championships as well as working as an accredited Psychologist at the London 2012 Paralympic Games. When time permits, Rebecca also works as a performance coach in the corporate sector.

Jack C. Watson II, PhD, is a Professor of Sport and Exercise Psychology and Chair of the Department of Sport Sciences at West Virginia University. Dr. Watson is a past president of the Association for Applied Sport Psychology (AASP), a Certified Consultant with AASP, is listed on the United States Olympic Committee's Sport Psychology Registry, and is a Licensed Psychologist in West Virginia. He is the Head of Public Relations for the Russell Bolton Center for Sport Ethics at West Virginia University, has written extensively on the topic of ethics, and is a past Chair of the AASP Ethics Committee.

1

EMBARKING ON SPORT PSYCHOLOGY WITH PROFESSIONAL LEVEL ATHLETES

Dieter Hackfort and Robert J. Schinke

If you have yet to work with professional performers as a sport psychology consultant, you likely know, or have heard, about someone who is or who has worked with these clients. As sport psychology becomes a more visible and reputable profession in various action fields in sport and beyond, we are beginning to find sport psychologists and mental training consultants working with many teams and in many performance contexts, regardless of the performance discipline. When thinking of what these contexts might be, they include team sports, such as football, cricket, ice hockey, rugby, and polo. There is also a breadth of individual sport disciplines, such as mixed martial arts, boxing, golf, and sumo wrestling. Though these sport contexts are known to be places where sport and performance psychology professionals engage in their craft, performance contexts also hire our professionals. Ballet and modern dance are two such contexts, and then there are performance environments, such as Cirque de Soleil, and there are also music contexts, such as rock and classical, where people with sport psychology training have found a home and earned a wage. We are only beginning to understand that the breadth of possible environments receptive to this sort of professional practice is as wide and deep as we venture to explore and chart. Common issues and strategies which might be transferable between various action fields can be detected in numerous contributions to this volume, as well as very specific ones which play a key role in an engagement in this sport or action field. It was one of the initial ideas for this kind of compilation of chapters to set the groundwork to reveal commonalities as well as specificities with regard to certain issues, approaches, and strategies or even mental techniques for performance enhancement.

As far as we know, this international book project on sport psychology in professional sport and performing arts is the first of its kind. We were not able to secure every sport and performing art, which were only attempts in vain. In several cases, these chapters were secured and then withdrawn at various stages of development. One such occurrence related to a team sport where the author sent a final version of the chapter to management to ensure its authenticity before publication. The author was then notified by the sport organization's attorney that the chapter needed to be withdrawn or the author would risk litigation. Then there were cases where authors who were full-time practitioners could not complete their commitments because their employment was in peril. These fluid aspects in relation to this book reveal the very nature of professional sport and performance psychology contexts. Practitioners are employees of large organizations, and their commitments can change at the drop of a hat, with little to no notice. From the vantage point of the co-editors, these losses are unfortunate, but they are not insurmountable. From another perspective, many of the authors contributing to this book are full-time practitioners, and we have been truly fortunate that they were able to meet our commitments over and above their own. There are nuggets in each chapter and symmetries that we refer to in our concluding chapter that might be regarded as consistencies across professional contexts. The nuances of contexts are highly important, and yet, the professional approaches that follow are also to some extent transferable skills that might be modified, though with basic elements, such as professionalism, ethics, humanity, and organization, left intact.

Purpose

We have enlisted a broad scope of contexts representing highly relevant and interesting professional performance environments. The reader will find that the authors we secured are at the very top of their game. These people were handpicked because they have substantial experience which is of significant value for the next generation and/or longevity in professional performance contexts. All of these people have been honing their craft for several years, and they have become specialists in their respective sport and performance contexts. These authors were encouraged to share the uniqueness of the contexts where they work, and what we have found is that aspects of professional practice are unique to the context; there are sub-cultures to consider. Practitioners will not work with a boxer as they would a drummer, using the same language, negotiating the same physical space, or using theoretical approaches in the same manner. Nuances come with each context, and practitioners need to observe these and pick up on social cues in order to navigate effectively in their environments, becoming one with the sub-culture. Despite the uniqueness you will find in relation to each context, common threads unite these world-class authors. What have we found these commonalities to be? All of these people are generous with their time and their knowledge. In some environments there are said to be trade secrets, and yet the authors in this book have chosen to hold nothing back. They share with you the challenges they have experienced, how they honed their skills, and why they have succeeded in their worlds. There is little meant to mystify you in this book. Instead, all of the authors agreed to peel back the onion in their contexts and try to anticipate the questions someone might ask, before embarking on performance psychology work in professional contexts.

Therefore, the purpose of this book is to provide the opening to discussions about how one might engage in professional sport/performance psychology practices. Meanwhile, many people in the world are doing these sorts of jobs, and they are doing it well! Our goal is to provide a window into what good-quality work might look like and how it might be structured, while also revealing some of the characteristics of what it takes to be a successful professional in this field. In addition, the contributors have looked within themselves and considered some of their pitfalls – lessons we might learn form their experiences. There are enough unique lessons to be learned and mistakes to be committed as we enrich our practices. We can avoid some mistakes by gaining a jump on common mistakes through this reading. Our hope, as the editors, is to try and anticipate some of the questions you might wish to have answered and feature answers to these from within and across contexts. Examples of these questions that will be answered include the following: (a) How does one prepare for practice at the professional level and what sorts of skills are needed? (b) How does a professional develop an effective application for a job at this level by context? (c) How does one embark in one's work once being hired? (d) What are the sorts of rookie mistakes that typically transpire at the beginning of a career at this level of practice? (e) How does one develop effective practice within the sub-culture and context? (f) What does it take to become rooted within a contract or employment position? Our shared goal with the authors is to promote further dialog in our professional community, with more consistently creditable work being done, which can only benefit generations to come. The development of our field is dependent on the exchange of useful information. This book has been developed to help you build a better knowledge of what might be needed in order to thrive at the professional level.

Structure

This book has been divided into sections. Each of these sections will be introduced in turn. The sections are as follows: (a) core knowledge, (b) individual sports, (c) team sports, and (d) the performing arts.

Section I: core knowledge

This book opens with core knowledge. Core knowledge refers to some of the basics that span contexts. Within this section, Angus Mugford, a former employee for a sport management group, who is now employed by a professional baseball franchise to lead their analytics, considered how to prepare athletes for the career stage of becoming a professional athlete in chapter two. Mugford also opens up discussions about the importance of cultural knowledge and athlete holistic development. Robert Nideffer, a world expert on attention, has spent many years working with professional athletes and corporations. He focused his chapter on how to effectively build a consulting business. You will find in chapter three that Nideffer shares many of the mistakes he experienced and also, how to avoid these same pitfalls. Frank Gardner authored chapter four about how to overcome resistance with clients. Gardner brings lengthy experience working with National Hockey League (NHL) and National Basketball Association (NBA) teams to his chapter. From his experiences, one begins to see how he partners so effectively with professional sport teams. Zella Moore was invited to write about her experiences working with transnational professional athletes in chapter five. Within many professional sports, athletes relocate from one country to another, often temporarily, to pursue their sport careers. Moore explores the emerging discussion relating to athlete acculturation, and shares strategies of how to support this stressful process to the athlete, derived from her work with NHL players. Jack Watson and Edward Etzel are well-known ethicists in the field of sport psychology. They authored chapter six, focusing on the various challenges that practitioners will likely encounter when working at the professional level. At this level, performance is a business. Watson and Etzel recognize this situation and offer suggestions of how to work ethically and how to avoid the pitfalls that might compromise one's work and credibility.

Section II: individual sports

Section II comprises seven sports where athletes perform as individuals. Though these athletes could be well surrounded by a working team, especially as they progress in their careers and improve their rankings, the performance within the confines of the field of play is an individual effort. Within this section, Chris Harwood authored chapter seven. Harwood works with all stages of elite tennis players, beginning his work with them when they are juniors and continuing consultation when they transition forward into world-ranked professionals. Embedded in the tennis chapter, the reader will find some of Harwood's well-respected work on athlete reflection. Reflection is indeed a central part of what needs to be inculcated in aspiring athletes from our field. Richard Gordin authored chapter eight and focused on his long-standing work with male athletes competing within the Professional Golf Association (PGA) Tour. Gordin reveals a highly humanistic approach in his work, and he also identifies some of the necessary requirements for practitioners interested in gaining entry into PGA Tour work. There are specific standards asked by the tour, over and above those expected by a sport psychology accreditor. Christian Smith, who works for International Management Group (IMG), authored chapter nine pertaining to his work in the Ladies Professional Golf Association (LPGA). One finds within Smith's chapter, one pathway through which our professionals begin to specialize in a preferred sport – some grow up in the sport they eventually become specialists in. From Smith's first experience with sport psychology from the vantage point of being an athlete, he recognized the importance of connecting with his athletes and understanding the sport's sub-culture. Much of the knowledge Smith draws on is based on his personal exchanges with athletes over the course of a season, leading to major tournaments such as the US Open. In addition, Smith does what a sound consultant should do: he engages in collateral discussions with coaches, caddies, family members, and the various other people central to the client. This sort of approach has permitted Smith, and likely most every author in this book, a 360-degree understanding of each athlete, situated in her training and performance context. Dieter Hackfort authored chapter ten based on his experience working with some of the best German Formula One (F1) drivers in the world, including several world champions. The reader will find that Hackfort is scientific in his approach to applied practice. He must be in order to reinforce effective mastery and coping skills in this high-risk sport. Hackfort's prevailing messages are that mental skills training should be based on systematic assessments, and not only practitioner intuition, though both approaches are necessary. Hackfort's words return the reader to one prevailing message pushed throughout this book and by both co-editors – that a science-to-practice link is central to work at the highest level. Robert Schinke focused on professional boxing in chapter eleven. Schinke introduces a few novel approaches that he has utilized over nearly 20 years of working with professional world championship boxers. Within the chapter, Schinke considers the importance of contextual understanding and belonging within the sub-culture. This author, who is also a researcher specializing in cultural sport psychology, provided suggestions on how to become culturally astute. Also found within chapter eleven is a skill set referred to as psychological profiling. Schinke uses profiling to discover the tendencies of his boxers' opponents and then brings this information to the client to facilitate much quicker psychological adaptation leading up to critical matches. His profiling work is framed within resilience scholarship and explanatory patterns. Rebecca Symes is an emerging practitioner who works within the field of sport and also in the corporate sector. She is one of the few practitioners working with professional mixed martial artists (MMA). In chapter twelve, Symes discusses how she gained a foothold in this emerging sport and also the interest her work generated within a local MMA group. Symes' work is built from a cognitive behavioral framework, though her use of skills is something she regards as "eclectic". Within this chapter, we learn about the MMA culture, where little is presently known from the vantage point of our field. Yoichi Kozuma from Japan was asked to share his work with sumo wrestlers in chapter thirteen. To my knowledge, there is little contribution from authors who write in English about this most interesting Asian sport. Kozuma began serendipitously with this sport, and after some initial success became known for his exemplary work with a notable athlete. Since then, he has worked with several sumo athletes. Kozuma uses psychometric assessments to guide his work, and he also advocates for athlete education, often asking his athletes to read up on skills and engage in various workbook tasks before their next session with him. Kozuma proposes that all of his athletes should develop seven key mental skills: goal-setting, arousal control used in two different programs, visualization, concentration, positive thinking, and psychological tournament preparation. Kozuma's emphasis is on mental skills, and he clarifies that athletes must practice these as part of a daily training routine.

Section III: team sports

Section III includes seven chapters that are focused on team sports. The focus within these sports extends to the coordination of athletes' efforts, in addition to working with coaching staff, management, and ownership. Stiliani Chroni, the author of chapter fourteen, has worked for many years within professional polo contexts, most often in the United States. Her entry into the sport began when she was a graduate student working with the University of Virginia Polo Team. From there, she progressed to working with professional polo players as a result of working with the team in Florida during their competitive season. Chroni's attraction to polo was guided by suggestions from her then-supervisor to choose a sport that could afford her skills. Chroni became a student of her sport, similar to the authors before and following this one. She asked many questions early on of grooms, family members, and athletes in order to expedite her learning curve. The level of commitment from Chroni, though, in terms of taking Spanish courses, reminds the reader of the extreme level of commitment needed when working with athletes, with skills sometimes extending beyond mental and psychological skills training. Paul Dennis authored chapter fifteen based on his concentrated work within the NHL. Dennis gained entry into what was a long-standing role, working with the Toronto Maple Leafs. Earlier in this chapter, we identified the importance of longevity in a single sport context, and Dennis exemplifies this message very well. He gained his entry into professional ice hockey through his work as an elite junior coach for the same sport. Dennis knew his sub-culture well, at least in relation to elite junior performers within the sport where he evolved. He then transitioned into the role of video coach for the Toronto Maple Leafs and then expanded his role over time from there. Dennis's story reminds the reader that longevity is often the result of beginning in one role and then either expanding that role or branching out into a role that becomes one's "home". Another takeaway from this chapter is the necessity to stay current with scientific research. Finally, Dennis recognizes that each athlete and team is its own boutique operation, with uniqueness that influences how a sport psychology consultant ought to work. Mark Nesti authored chapter sixteen focusing on the sport of football (termed soccer in North America). Nesti is a renowned qualitative researcher from the area of phenomenological psychology. His skills, as both a person who listens well and as an introspective service provider, likely tie back to his research skills. Nesti shares in common with several of the authors an athletic background gained in the sport where he became a practitioner. Nesti centralizes the importance of cultural understanding within his work, as many of the authors in this book have. In relation to cultural context, Nesti recognizes that sport psychology work is offered in a context that includes not only athletes, coaches, and management but also a demanding media, sport agents, and contractual negotiations over salary. All of these demands infuse into what a sport psychologist must understand as additive to an athlete's and a team's stress load. Stephen Mellealieu, a psychologist and renowned scholar from the area of stress and performance, authored chapter seventeen about his work in professional rugby. The professionalization of rugby is a relatively recent development. Similar to many of the authors, Mellealieu brought an extensive athletic background as a junior international level rugby player to his practice, and as such, he understood the sport's culture (i.e., its physicality and demonstrations of aggression) before beginning to hone his professional skills in a formal role. Within this chapter, the reader finds that it is useful for practitioners interested in professional sport contexts to have a mentor, also with such experiences to share. A prevailing message from Mellealieu is that the sport psychology consultant needs to form alliances with all staff, to become part of an integrated support team (IST). Stewart Cotterill considers professional cricket in chapter eighteen. Cotterill, a former multisport athlete, believes that athletes should leave no stone unturned, including their mental game. Cotterill entered into cricket by working with youth athletes in an academy. His approach was to develop his contextual knowledge with promising young athletes before he transitioned by word of mouth to professional cricket. He, unlike some of the authors, though consistent with the two co-editors, came from a sport background that was not where he eventually established himself as a professional provider. This beginning as a non-cricket player or coach, he feels, has permitted him to ask questions about the sport in a way where his inquisitiveness was not regarded as judging. Cotterill suggests that sport psychologists can integrate many approaches in order to do their work, as opposed to specializing in a particular methodology. Charlie Maher has practiced in a vast number of professional sports, especially professional team sports, including American football, the NHL, and in Major League Baseball (MLB), his focus in chapter nineteen. Maher, a psychologist by trade, began as a guidance counselor and coach, and then as a university professor. He found that his diverse experiences have all influenced the way he does his work as a practitioner. Maher gained formative experience within baseball as a high school and then as a collegiate coach. A professional baseball team initially approached Maher to assist with mental training programs for athletes and staff. Since 1995, Maher has worked with the same baseball team, a true sign of longevity. Moreover, Maher's role has expanded beyond sport psychology. Now his work includes managing a department of personal and organizational services. Within chapter nineteen, where this section concludes, Maher provides several key characteristics that need to be understood in terms of baseball as a business. Maher also provides a series of useful personal characteristics that will assist not only with the sport psychology consultant gaining entry but also with the longevity of one's role in a MLB team.

Section IV: the performing arts

Sport psychology consulting has slowly expanded beyond the world of sport to the performing arts. This section only features three chapters – examples of the professionalization of sport psychology into contexts where it is a recent and accepted resource. Leslee Fisher and Jean Francois Ménard are featured in chapter twenty. Fisher is an academic with considerable expertise within the emerging topic area of cultural sport psychology. She was invited by Ménard to assist him with the development of his chapter, due to the time commitments posed by his work with Cirque de Soleil. Ménard, a mental training consultant, has worked with Cirque since 2008, first as a full-time employee and more recently as a contractor. Examining this chapter, the reader will find that Ménard is highly reflective in terms of who he is as a person and how his background has contributed to his practical approach. He also shares with the contributing authors a desire to remain current within his field, by attending conferences and remaining an avid reader of scientific and practical approaches from his field. Ménard approached the circus context with little contextual knowledge about his environment. He asked many questions, watched Cirque shows and documentaries, and was mentored by another staff member early on, in order to understand and then become immersed within the performance context. Similar to a few of his colleagues who worked in multicultural contexts, with athletes form various nationalities, he took language courses in the most common dialect spoken in Cirque other than French and English – Russian. Ménard's approach, as the reader will find, echoes the importance of holistic athlete support. His work developed form mental training onward to stress management, time management, and acculturation. Sharon Chirban and Miriam Rowan authored chapter twenty-one about their work in classical ballet and modern dance contexts. Chirban is a clinical psychologist with more than 15 years' experience working with dancers. She became involved in dance work as a result of familial interests. Rowan is a former professional dancer, who more recently is completing her doctorate in clinical psychology. The reader will find in this chapter a balance of mental training and clinical topics that are encountered when working with dancers, such as overly involved parents, fear of losing one's place in a dance company, a heavy performance schedule, physical injury, and eating disorders. One will also find within this chapter the importance of contextual knowledge, such as the life demands posed by being a dancer, who is to some degree isolated from a typical life existence. Chirban refers to herself in relation to this context as a comeback specialist – someone who can help performers return to performance with sound body and mind. Lois Butcher-Poffley, a former dancer and singer, authored chapter twenty-two. Butcher-Poffley is highly aware of the demands posed on performance artists, such as how they might be critiqued in the media, with extreme highs and lows. Over the course of an extensive career as a mental training consultant, Butcher-Poffley has become known and respected in terms of her work with musicians, especially rock musicians. When working with rock musicians (Butcher-Poffley works with musicians of all types), she has come to realize that her approach in order to fit within the context necessitates being relaxed and laid back. Some of her focus when working with these performers is to assist them to develop and deepen an internal focus that can buffer the performers from particularly harsh critiques. This sort of work necessitates an understanding of resilience and how to assist the performers with re-attributions. Throughout much of Butcher-Poffley's chapter, there is an undercurrent of cultural sport psychology. She outlines some of the basic characteristics of rock musicians, such as the importance of spontaneity and performing within a fluid structure. She, similar to Chirban and Rowan, also appears to be very effective in supporting comeback stories within her clients.

In chapter twenty-three, the conclusion, the co-editors will try to point out key messages and substantial learnings growing out of the various single contributions and coming from across the entire book. In addition, the co-editors will engage in emerging issues relating to professionalism and the execution of one's skills, which might be essential for the advancement of sport and performance psychology. These discussions to come will not only be written in relation to established professionals, but of equal importance, for the young generation of emerging professionals who are enthusiastic to become involved and motivated to develop competencies needed to become accepted and effective in this challenging action field.

Without further ado, we wish to welcome you to this first edition of *Psychology in Professional Sports and the Performing Arts: Challenges and Strategies*. We wish to thank Routledge and the International Society of Sport Psychology for the opportunity to bring you this compilation of professional performance contexts.

SECTION I
Core skills

2

CONTEXT IS EVERYTHING

Working with the transitioning athlete

Angus Mugford

'It's not the best player who wins, but the player who plays the best'. This idea captured my attention as a child and channeled my curiosity into the mental and emotional side of competition. It's perhaps no surprise then that I have found my chosen career in applied sport psychology, although I am one of a fortunate few that have been able to consult and coach the mental game in a full-time role.

Born and raised in the United Kingdom, but a resident and citizen of the United States for the last 15 years, I have benefited from a combination of cultural perspectives and opportunities both academically and professionally. One of the significant moments of my early career was on my first day in my chosen undergraduate field of psychology and sport science. Expecting to be inspired and hear the pearls of wisdom from our lead professor, he told us there was simply no such thing as a sport psychologist. While many of us felt dejected and confused, it's certainly true that there's not a clear career track or large number of salaried jobs in the field. Nonetheless, it was a rude awakening to someone with a passion and fascination for mental performance.

'Transition' is not a new concept for young professionals who are busy trying to make sense of the options in front of them, yearning for a crystal ball that will tell them the right answer and what the future holds. This was true of my experience, and I somewhat blindly persisted in what I felt most passionate about, not necessarily in what had the best chance of success or return on investment. It wasn't until undergoing an internship at IMG Academy that I had a series of 'Eureka!' moments and finally understood that mental skills, like setting effective goals, mental rehearsal, and self-talk, were just as effective in my own performance as a mental coach, as well as for my clients. This realization helped me make significant strides in my development.

As the saying goes, "experience is the best teacher". The trouble is that for the athlete or performer in transition, the quality and quantity of experience can be limited, and the ability to maximize learning is a game changer. The business theorist Arie de Geus (1998) was quoted saying, "The ability to learn faster than your competitors may be the only sustainable competitive advantage" (p. 128). In many respects this concept holds true in elite performance as well. To climb the rankings in professional or elite junior sport, like our clients at IMG, athletes must continue to learn and develop. However, the stark reality is that they also need to win. This pressure to win can ironically prevent young athletes from focusing on development, and this is perhaps one of the biggest challenges and paradoxes for athletes in transition. They need to develop in order to win, but they need to win in order to continue to have access to resources and support to develop.

A by-product of my self-discovery and performance in my internship at IMG resulted in a full-time job offer just one year later, after completing my PhD. As a performer, this was another lesson in practicing what you preach, since I achieved my dream outcome goal by focusing all of my energy on achieving daily process goals and being the best consultant I could be. I would also add that timing and a little luck helped, too.

IMG Academy has also been a dream factory for many athletes over the years. One thousand student-athletes from ages 10 to 18 years old are enrolled across eight sports (tennis, golf, basketball, baseball, football, lacrosse, track and field, and soccer), ranging from 80 different countries; it is truly a utopia for developing athletes. Andre Agassi, Maria Sharapova, and a multitude of tennis Grand Slam champions grew up at the academy, and many others in different sports made it to Division I scholarships and the professional tier. Many of those 1,000 students enrolled now are aiming to follow in those footsteps.

IMG Academy is in the business of transition. All of these athletes face transition, specifically coming into the academy environment, many with professional dreams and aspirations, to those transitioning out of the academy and into their college, professional, or other domain. The role of the staff, and especially the 10-person mental conditioning department, is to help support the mental and emotional component to developing these athletes' capacity to make successful transitions.

Gaining an understanding of the sport and subculture

Learning from others' experience with transition is a helpful start to understanding the demands and what research there is in this area. While much of the academic study in transition research has focused on career termination and transition out of sport, the International Society for Sport Psychology (ISSP) took a holistic position to identify the multiple transitions in the athlete career cycle and that support and planning for balancing demands were recommended (Stambulova, Alfermann, Statler, & Côté, 2009). My time and experience with athletes is typically in the early stages as these individuals transition from a developmental to mastery stage.

Wylleman and Lavallee (2004) proposed a model that's received a great deal of support with a holistic view of the transitions faced by athletes. The four phases of the athletic life transition from initiation to development, and for those who make the next level, mastery, and ultimately a fourth and final phase of discontinuation.

The transition from developmental to mastery stages is where IMG Academy sees more than their share of clients. The prototype student is an aspiring junior athlete transitioning into the senior and even professional levels. What's interesting is that these individuals are not just going through transitions in their sport. For many of these youngsters, this is also a transitional time for their psychological development (from adolescence to adulthood), psychosocial development (living with family to living independently), and academic/vocational development (from school to college or a job).

IMG Academy is in the business of helping maximize the potential for student-athletes to make the transition to the next level. Whatever that level is, the goal is to help maximize the person's resources to 'make it'. For the vast majority, of course, this is to the college level, not the professional arena. In fact, it is estimated that over the last 5 years, IMG may have as many as 2% go straight to the professional ranks, with 98% that go on to compete in sport in college with some kind of scholarship support. Of that group going to college, 60% of that group will play at an elite Division I level program (IMG Academy, n.d.). Of the student-athletes going directly into the professional ranks, many of these are in tennis, and in reality they are already identified at an early age and placed into the academy pro tour group. There are exceptions to this rule, but it does affect the culture of each training group and the expectations of the student-athletes.

Research from the wider scope of transition into the professional levels highlights some important implications. In one 5-year study looking at the elite junior to elite senior transition, Vanden Auweele, De Martelaer, Rzewnicki, De Knop, and Wylleman (2004) observed only 17% making a successful transition from elite junior to elite senior sport. There are many reasons for the attrition involved, but the bottom line is that in elite competition there is always going to be attrition by the very nature of competition. A study looking at the specific sport of men's tennis even saw that with juniors reaching the top 10 (under 18 years old) in the world, just 58% of them reached a professional ranking inside the top 100 on the men's tour (McCraw, 2011). Sport is a competitive industry and making it at the next level is a complicated and taxing process.

Given this is such a hard transition, the question of how we help these athletes make it is the million-dollar question. Stambulova, Franck, and Weibull (2012) have done significant work in the realm of career transition, and they define successful transition as ultimately being able to cope with a set of transition demands. This is a dynamic balance between the coping resources individuals have, like competence, skill, knowledge, social support, and the perceived barriers they may have, which might be a lack of the skills, financial, or social support. Their success will largely depend on how well they are able to balance these demands. Battochio, Stambulova, and Schinke (2015) recently shared insights into the stages and demands in the careers of professional male hockey players, highlighting similar such transitions and the basis for career assistance and support based on these career stages. While we may determine some of these stages as a somewhat predictable experience, it remains a personal and individual journey for each player. The role of the coaches and support team for these athletes can have a great deal of influence in preparing for and navigating the transition.

The little fish in a big pond

While there are many highly talented youngsters in this program, it's also important to state that the competence and skill level of many athletes attending IMG Academy are not actually elite. Indeed, one of the key transitions for many student-athletes we see is that individuals are among the best for their age in their local town, school, or district and see enrollment at IMG as their ticket to a Division I scholarship or the fast track to the pro level. The reality when they arrive and begin training alongside some of their peers is that they are no longer the strongest, fittest, smartest kid. They may have never lost in practice before. In fact, they hadn't lost at much ever. Experiencing failure for the first time or seeing the benchmark they thought they'd achieved can be traumatic.

Gaining insight into this culture was not hard, because in our environment it is almost palpable. The first few weeks of the academy semester uses competition as a way to help assess the ability level of each student-athlete. For some of these students, losing for the first time is a shock, and for others the stress of being evaluated and being selected to a lower group than they perceive their level to be can create tension and stress. Returning to Stambulova and colleagues' concept of demands and resources, these students are experiencing high demand, but critical to this equation is having an understanding of their resources. What IMG put in place to help this situation is a team of specialists in a department called Athletic and Personal Development. This department is made up of world-class staff in physical conditioning, sports medicine, nutrition, and mental performance who deliver programs in leadership, mental conditioning, and cognitive-perceptual training. All students get exposure and support in all of these areas, specifically to help support these youngsters deal with the pressure and focus to develop.

A tale of two cities

For the purpose of this chapter, I wanted to share two examples of supporting transition but in two very different contexts where I have spent a great deal of my professional career. The first context is in the realm of elite junior tennis players, who make the transition to playing professional men's or women's tournaments, which have the interesting feature of being able to play both junior and adult concurrently – often from one level to another and back again. The second example is a new group of athletes each year, who are preparing to enter the National Football League (NFL) draft. These individuals are among the best and most talented American college football players, whose agents pay for them to participate in our intensive training program in order to maximize their draft stock to prepare for what some herald as the toughest interview in professional sports. Our goal is not just to help maximize their performance for the event of the NFL combine, but to also help them transition from being an amateur college player to being a professional athlete.

The culture of elite tennis is an interesting one. At the pro level on the men's Association for Tennis Professionals (ATP) tour and Women's Tennis Association (WTA) tour, it's estimated that it costs up to $200,000 (Finch, 2009) a year in expenses to pay for a full-time coach and cope with the travel, training, room, and board. In 2014, according to official ATP and WTA records, the 100th ranked player on the ATP tour made $170,000 in prize money (Filip Krajinovic) and the 100th ranked player on the WTA tour made $130,000 (Saisai Zheng). Of course, endorsements and sponsorships add to that amount, but it doesn't take long to realize that the majority of players are at best breaking even and at worst are losing money. While the very top of the pro tennis ladder can make millions both on and off the court, the reality sets in for many players on the proverbial bubble as to how long they can financially stay on tour and pursue their dream. Reaching a pro ranking of 500th in the world in itself is a remarkable feat; however, when looking at an actual sum of prize money, on the ATP tour this was $8,582 (Ivan Nedelko) and on the WTA tour $6,847 (Isabella Holland). In order to achieve these points and prize money, the travel schedule crosses the globe and the season spans 11 months of the year, so many players are forced to be extremely thrifty, and the competition for resources becomes intense.

The economic impact on the culture of elite tennis means that, for many, they leave no stone unturned to maximize their investment. It's also important to emphasize the role of the agent, who is trying to predict success and invest in young talent, knowing many will not make it. The payoff is when a player like Maria Sharapova comes along. Maria arrived at IMG

Academy with big dreams at the age of 9, and ultimately she received a scholarship and signed with an agent, turning pro at age 14, and won Wimbledon at 17. Her meteoric rise to success lead to becoming the highest paid female athlete in the world and now enjoying a career spanning more than a decade.

Leaving no stone unturned in that investment can mean intensive tactical and technical coaching, strength and conditioning, sports medicine, nutrition, and mental performance. All of these factors come in as pieces of the puzzle to increase the chances of tour success. At some point though, the pressure to leave the sport through debt and burnout can be tremendous. The opportunity to play collegiate tennis at schools in the United States can be extremely attractive, by removing the financial burden for many of these youngsters to continue to develop their game at a competitive level. For some in the tennis culture, even playing at the Division I collegiate level can be seen as a failure that you can't make it on the professional tour. As some players are having more success on tour after college, like John Isner and Kevin Anderson, and the average age in the top 100 is 27, this shift in the pressure to win and win now is palpable.

Life as a professional football player is very different. Fifty-three players make each NFL team roster, which across 32 teams makes 1,696 players in total. The minimum salary for these players is $420,000, although the average is closer to $1,900,000 (Burke, 2012). While the average career length is around 3 years (Statista, 2014), this paints a remarkably different picture than the world of professional tennis. Having said this, it has been estimated that within 5 years of retirement, 78% of NFL players are either bankrupt or in financial distress (Torre, 2009), which is consistent with research conducted in this population (Coakley, 2006; Koonce, 2012). While money is not everything, there is an emphasis on getting the best first contract as a rookie, knowing that second contracts are not guaranteed. The NFL designed an ingenious system for league parity and growth, as well as something that has become a fan experience all in itself: the NFL combine and the NFL draft.

The NFL combine is a showcase and opportunity for the top 330 college players to be invited to Indianapolis to be tested medically and psychologically, interviewed, and finally measured for strength, speed, and with a series of position- and sport-specific skills. It allows apples-to-apples comparison, overcoming the challenge of trying to compare talent across the collegiate landscape with different locations, strength of schedule, and teams. It didn't take long for player agents to identify the value of the 8-week window of time between the end of the National Collegiate Athletic Association (NCAA) season and the NFL combine. In fact, Sierer Battaglini, Mihalik, Shields, and Tomasini (2008) identified significant differences in drills like the 40-yard dash between drafted and non-drafted players, along with other drills that varied by position, helping NFL decision makers use predictors of success and return on investment.

Financially, contracts are dictated by where a player gets drafted in that process. The difference between being drafted at number 1 ($22 million) versus number 10 ($12 million) is $10 million over 4 years (Fitzgerald, 2014). If a player's stock value moves him to the second round, starting with the 33rd pick, then he is likely to make in the region of $5 million over 4 years. The implications for players are all about draft stock and value. A lower-stock player can dramatically increase his value by a strong combine performance if he was initially projected as a sixth round pick, to elevating his status to a second or third round pick. Conversely, someone with a high stock coming out of college who does not perform well in the combine may lower his earning income by dropping from the first round to the second, third, or fourth.

For the NFL prospect, this means that in the 8-week window of time between the college season and the NFL combine, a lot of earning potential is at stake. For the performance team at IMG, this means that we provide an intensive focus on maximizing not only players' ability to recover from the season but also their physical, technical, mental, and emotional ability to perform in those key moments for their draft stock. In huge contrast, the aspiring tennis pro at IMG is often actually a junior player who signed a contract with a professional agency at the age of 16 or 17, and who plays a combination of junior tournaments along with low-level professional tournaments against fully grown men and women. While there is pressure, it is more of a pressure cooker that burns slowly over an 11-month season, year after year. The developmental window for the human performance team (strength and conditioning, sports medicine, mental conditioning, and so on) is much longer, so there is often better continuity and relationships. However, especially in the case of the mental performance coach, players are at the academy or their home base for training blocks, but they spend the greater part of the year playing tournaments, often up to 25 weeks a year. This means distance communication is key, whether that's through phone, skype, or texting, and through the coach, assuming they have coaching support.

Keeping the big picture in mind

While a picture has been painted with the economic impact of the NFL and professional tennis landscape, the question of defining success is key. For the NFL prospects, maximizing their performance and exposure before the NFL draft is the goal, although the ultimate draft pick made by a team becomes very subjective, based on team needs as well as a host of different factors. The long-term success of the IMG team, however, is establishing the habits that will help athletes to make a successful transition in and earn a second contract, extending their career.

For tennis players, their ultimate ranking and tournament success is also the focus, and this takes time. Grand Slam tournament success is the dream, and achieving ranking goals are directly related to players' financial stability, automatic qualification for tournaments, as well as respect among their competition. Of a common average of 25 tournaments a year, achieving strong results in 5 to 10 could be considered by many to be very successful. It's most definitely the marathon compared to the sprint.

Overcoming challenges to access and developing trust

Working in professional tennis and football is much like the rest of elite sport, in that reputation and the network of relationships are crucial. This is especially true when looking at coaching mental performance, something that is still not commonplace in the coaching team, and particularly rare with NFL teams. At IMG Academy, we have a unique – and in many ways optimal – setup, because the athletes are coming to us primarily for the more comprehensive purpose of sport-specific coaching and holistic performance training.

For professional tennis players, there is a focus on drilling and match play on court, but also a broad selection of à la carte support, including access to sports medicine, strength and conditioning, and mental conditioning services as desired. At the elite junior level, the integration of physical and mental training, along with sports medicine support, is simply part of their schedule and coaching team. The same is also true for NFL prospects, where players opt into our program, which prioritizes mental training as a mandatory part of the IMG NFL combine preparation program. The key to developing this proposition is through internal credibility and buy-in into the culture. Specifically, buy-in is developed into the importance of training the physical, mental, technical, and tactical aspects of being football players, and looking at every resource and specialist to be able to do this and maximize their chances of doing well at the combine. The athlete's time training in this environment is an investment in holistic human performance training. Our collaboration and work together is about helping the clients achieve their goals, rather than each division receiving individual credit.

The development of trust impacts many of the stakeholders involved. In the professional arena, whether that's tennis or football, agents play a significant role. Often they are picking up the tab, and while they will typically do what the players ask them to do, they have perhaps the clearest sense of return on investment and what true investment costs are worthwhile. For many athletes, family also play a major role in decision making, especially if the relationship is new and investment has to be made in either living somewhere new, or the cost of training is also high. Parents stereotypically play a large role in the sport of tennis, many having acted as the player's coach at one time or another. As players become veterans in their sport, they often become much more savvy and are likely to approach you out of reputation or referral. Indeed, in our experience the higher status the client, the more likely they are to come to you, rather than you successfully lobby them to become your client. Being independent from a team or organization sometimes increases trust level, because players know that you do not have influence with the front office, contracts, and personnel decisions.

In the sport of tennis, coaches carry a great deal of weight in deciding where to train and whom to train with. Being a coach at this level can be considered a stressful occupation. Between living on the road the majority of time, living and working with their client 24/7, as well as riding the roller coaster of wins and losses, injuries, and emotional ups and downs, players can expect to have multiple different coaches throughout their careers. As one coach is fired, they typically stay on the tour and move on with another player. While IMG Academy coaches have stability and often work with the same elite junior players until they have enough income to take someone on the road with them full-time, we develop relationships with traveling coaches that end up bringing different players and clients back to us.

Last, but not least, are the athletes themselves. Without trust here, there is no relationship. Certainly nothing long term can be mandated, even if an agent and coach want it to happen. Establishing boundaries and how communication and collaboration can work with clients and their support team is paramount. Some players may want a coach or agent to be integrally involved, and some may be the opposite. The key to a successful relationship in this respect though is to have the discussion and understand the client's goals and expectations and then to be impeccable with your word and ethical conduct. Trust can take a long time to develop but a matter of seconds to lose.

Developing a contextual philosophy

A consultant's philosophy will typically not change from client to client, but the consultant's role and context most assuredly will. Males, Sappington, and O'Shea (2015) shared a great article on 'What Sport Can Learn From Business'. One of the primary takeaways was acknowledging the complexity of factors that applied sport psychology consultants work with in the multidisciplinary environment, and that it is hugely important to develop 'contextually intelligent consultants'.

As a consultant, my philosophy is generally shared across the mental performance team at IMG. Specifically, that we take a humanistic perspective, understanding the person across a holistic set of needs, outcomes, and collaboration across our support teams. We typically use cognitive-behavioral tools and educational methods to develop people's self-awareness and ultimately help them coach themselves and manage their thoughts and behaviors. Beyond this, the IMG team has also developed a team-based purpose statement and set of values consistent with this approach (IMG Academy, 2014). Specifically, our mission is 'to help people excel by training a high performance mindset'. There are four team values that we see as behaviors that exhibit our commitment, which are: (1) we are passionate about helping others; (2) we are committed to a growth mindset; (3) we are impeccable with our word; and (4) we always find a way. These values help us stay on the same page and keep a foundational perspective when context does shift.

There are perhaps three main areas where context and our role shift on a regular basis. The first is relative to the team around the client(s), including the coaches, interdisciplinary team staff, and performance context for that client. The specific performance needs of the client will be relative to the training block with us at IMG. For example, are they in pre-season training? Are they coming off an injury? How long will they be training with us? Are they invested in their goals and ready to collaborate? Have they trained with us before, and have they had exposure to formalized mental training? There are many questions to consider.

The second area is to understand the specific mental performance needs of the client. In tennis, the needs are typically consistent, although the individual game style and player personality will be different. American football, however, increases its complexity, not just to an individual level, but also the demands of each position, background, experience, and acknowledgement of the different team and coaching culture they are coming from. In terms of transition, this is particularly relevant for the player going into the NFL, where part of the remit for our mental performance education is helping them understand and prepare for a change of context. The ability to reflect and understand the core of what has helped them be successful to this point is central, knowing that many factors may be outside of their control. While this is a fact, it's important to understand the basics of what they can control and how to better leverage their new environment and factors that can help them continue to learn and develop.

For the NFL predraft training group, the context is grafted around the weeks building up to the NFL combine. We have developed an 8-week program that is delivered in a group program across multidisciplines, specifically position-specific football coaching, mental training (branded 'NFL mindset'), perceptual-cognitive and biofeedback training (branded 'Mindgym'), psychological testing (branded 'test prep'), nutrition (branded 'fuel for performance'), strength-conditioning and movement training, and interview and communication skills training. Each week, themes are laid out based on the timeline of experiences they go through, including preparation for invitational bowl games (e.g. Senior Bowl), the combine, and pro-days. This is the formalized process, although there is a great deal of informal and individualized work, often beginning with medical treatment and any other individual needs and contexts for specific players.

The third context we keep visible goes to the humanistic part of our philosophy. Our team's members are not licensed psychologists, so we collaborate with mental health specialists when we need to focus on that as a need. We understand that humans are not binary, meaning we're either mentally sick or healthy, but our team takes a focus on education and developing tools that provide a proactive game plan to enhancing mental performance. Physical and mental health is a priority, so the resources need to be in place. However, the analogy is true that it's also not necessary for everyone to visit your medical staff every day. Our athletes are here to be coached, but we also know that everyone at some point has felt depressed or anxious, so we need to keep perspective on the context of the client, especially when people are going through potentially life-changing and high-stakes transitions. As such, these considerations are very much at the individual level and are treated as such.

We have talked a lot about context here, but something that is worth mentioning is also what we know about managing change. There is a reason why 'change is hard' is a popular colloquialism. As individuals go through transition from one level to another, whether that's from junior to professional, or rookie to veteran, change is inevitable. What makes these particular changes different is that you are typically talking about very successful individuals who are making a transition because they have already been achieving success. Sometimes it can be hard for an athlete to see the changes they need to make, or anticipate what some of the new challenges can be, whereas others may see the transition or change as extremely intimidating and stressful.

The context of what stage individuals are at with their transition can bear a significant impact on their success. DiClemente and Prochaska's (1998) transtheoretical model can be useful to highlight that there are stages of readiness for change. Athletes in a pre-contemplation stage are often not ready to hear coaching and preparation for change and transition. Helping an athlete shift from not being ready to contemplating a change could be a monumental achievement. I have shared experiences with coaches in tennis where a supremely talented young player was the best player in the world for his age, but he had a poor work ethic and a terrible attitude toward preparation and training. Despite this, he could walk on the court against just about anybody and beat them handily. This ability drove his coaches crazy, but it was hard to break through to him, because he was in a pre-contemplation stage since what he did already worked. It took facing some adversity for the first time and consistent messages and support from the entire coaching team before this player began contemplating and moving toward change. As he became more successful against higher level opponents, it was easier to establish buy-in, and sequentially he was more prepared to make changes, take action, and ultimately maintain his behavior. This flow can be seen in Figure 2.1.

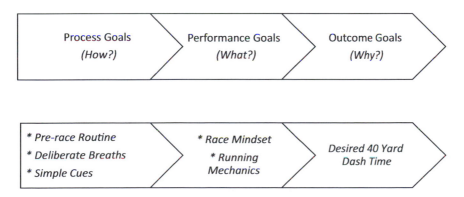

FIGURE 2.1   Simplified sample of a goal-setting profile for a National Football League draft prospect.

Being effective

Coaching legend John R. Wooden famously said, "don't mistake activity for achievement". While he was talking about his student-athletes, the metaphor is clearly relevant to a broader scale. To be effective as a consultant, being sensitive to individual context is at the heart of the debate between 'being active', doing a lot, versus 'achieving' and making progress and change with a client.

While we have formalized group education for the NFL predraft group and elite junior tennis players, the reality is that developing a relationship and trust at the individual level is one of the keys to being effective. Listening to the context of the individuals going through these important transitions fosters understanding and the conditions necessary for collaboration. Their perception of their experience and expectations of what they are going through determine a great deal of their success in bridging the gap. Simply delivering a one-size-fits-all approach to education may provide good content but fail to make the connection and application. For this chapter, we wanted to share a couple of practical examples of strategies used that have been effective tools for these athletes in each respective context.

In the case of the professional, or elite junior tennis player making the transition, winning is everything. Lose in the first round, and there is no consolation. There is no ATP or WTA points that help bolster your ranking, no prize money, just expenses. Winning matters. While this is a simple truth of professional life, this single fact can trigger a great deal of negativity for a player. In terms of achievement motivation, the emphasis often shifts to an ego orientation and can easily threaten a player's status. For some players this can positively tap into their competitiveness, but many struggle in certain situations, and finding this balance is key. As a way of introducing players to this concept, and to understand more about their perspective, expectations, and understanding of themselves is to ask them two relatively straightforward questions: (1) How do you define success? (2) How do you define failure?

Almost without fail, the definition of success from an aspiring or professional tennis player is to win. There is no doubt that their livelihood is directly tied to winning, but it's soon clear that the answer is not quite as simplistic and straightforward. Winning is an important outcome: ask any medical physician, airline pilot, or soldier, and they will tell you winning matters. However, a couple of fundamental follow-up questions can help open some deeper levels of thinking and discussion: 'Is it possible to be successful, and still not win the match?', conversely, 'Can you win the match, but not be successful?'. Ultimately we can get to a discussion about the difference between long-term success and short-term failures. Indeed, taking a concept like growth mindset (Dweck, 2006) allows us to reframe 'failure' into 'feedback' and that losing becomes a temporary setback and opportunity to learn and grow. There is always a commitment to excellence, but it's the acknowledgement of what 'perfect' actually is in the professional arena.

A specific example of 'perfect' in the sport of tennis can be obtained by looking at a breakdown of point statistics. A study conducted on men's Grand Slam results of just the top 16 players in the tournaments of 2007 and 2008 revealed some interesting data (Cross, 2010). Broadly speaking, there are three kinds of ways to win a point: (1) hit a 'winner', which is a shot that is too good and your opponent is unable to touch it; (2) make a 'forced error', which is when a player hits a good enough shot that the opponent is forced into making a mistake; and (3) make an 'unforced error', which is when a player makes an easy mistake without any pressure applied. The statistical breakdown is roughly the same for players who won or lost their matches, and across tournaments it roughly shows the distribution is equal. With the exception of the French Open, which is played on clay (a significantly different surface), approximately 33% of points are winners, but also the same for forced errors and unforced errors. The reason that this is a powerful set of statistics to share in this context is that players are often completely unrealistic about the game. In fact, players often focus so much on hitting winners and eliminating unforced errors that they find it hard to bounce back and let go of those errors. Part of this exercise is really about redefining success and what perfect actually is, and that actually coping with errors and setbacks is part of being successful.

While the research is pretty clear on the positive impact on performance of effective goal setting (Cerasoli, Nicklin, & Ford, 2014; Kleingeld, van Mierlo, & Arends, 2011), it's amazing how many athletes do not like setting goals or don't set effective goals. One of the signature techniques that we have employed at IMG is really an extension of the previous discussion on defining success and failure. While it's very easy to capture attention and focus on winning, developing a model to understand the relationship among outcome, performance, and process goals can create an important shift into understanding how people see the value in each and how it drives their behavior.

Using the NFL pre-draft players as an example, there is a propensity for many to look at their 40-yard dash time as the largest individual milestone that will influence their draft stock and long-term goals of security and employment. While this outcome focus can provide the drive for them to motivate their attention and mobilize effort, it can also become a source of great anxiety and doubt if they focus on the result too much and the ramifications of running that time or not. Figure 2.1 is a teaser, with some examples that apply to each of these steps. One particular feature to pay attention to is the importance of the flow from process to performance to outcome (left to right). When talking with the players themselves, the attention and discussion automatically goes to the right and the outcome. By instead shifting the discussion to clearly defining the key process goals, it's soon apparent that these behaviors lead to high performance, and that high performance leads to results. In addition, when focusing primarily on the result, there is no guarantee that we perform the actions necessary to achieve it. In fact, we're probably more likely to not perform those key process goals, and our performance actually suffers as a result.

While it is a simple educational process, using video and examples from current NFL veterans are invaluable. While we create the framework, having a respected NFL veteran speak to his experience more than reinforces the point. We are also fortunate to have a world-class track and field training group and are able to cross-utilize athletes to speak to each other. We have often used Olympic champions to talk about their pre-race preparation and understand the pressures and mental preparation that has helped them be effective. By creating buy-in and clearly signposting steps and why they are effective, this helps us get to the point where players begin to create their mental game plan. Ultimately, we work with each player to develop a series of checklists of process goals that we work with on the field turf in training and they laminate for use at the final combine performance in Indianapolis.

Thoughts and recommendations for the aspiring practitioner

When defining 'transition', we are talking about the process or period of changing from one state to another. This could technically describe any athletes at any time of their careers.

Acknowledging the importance of where clients are during their careers and where they want to be is a hugely important contextual question. The same can be said for the consultant, also as a 'performer'. Taking a moment to reflect and consider where you are, as well as your strengths, weaknesses, and priorities for your development, are important questions to begin with before you can hope to maximize your impact on others.

Develop yourself as a performer

There are many areas to consider when developing yourself as a consultant (Cremades & Tashman, 2014; Mugford, Hesse, & Morgan, 2014; Taylor, 2014), but we will focus on three areas to develop your contextual intelligence. The first critical skill that is sometimes taken for granted is that of listening. When hired as a consultant, there is sometimes a perceived pressure to come in and deliver solutions and share the knowledge, insights, and examples you have. This mistake is often made by consultants who lack experience and the confidence to listen and observe before intervening. When going from an individual to a team sport or organization, the layers of complexity can broaden. However, even an individual sport – like the example shared with elite tennis – can include a range of coaches, agents, parents, human performance and medical staff, let alone the actual players themselves. It may not be what is said, but sometimes what is not said that is noteworthy. Likewise, actions speak louder than words, so developing a full picture of the context can help you be much more impactful when understanding the context and where athletes are in their preparation to transition to a higher level.

The second skill is that as a consultant you are a learner. Ironically, consultants who participated or coached in the sport for which they're consulting sometimes struggle to do this. While they may have a massive wealth of personal and sport knowledge, this can create blind spots into context and with regards to the client's own experience. Continuing to be a student of the game, the culture, and the athlete can be a valuable skill to develop and focus on. If the sport is not as familiar, as was my case with professional tennis, I relied heavily on tennis coaches, experienced players, and human performance staff to help educate me. I would watch games and listen to commentators, as well as listening to players themselves, and hear the sticking points and pay attention to the things they would celebrate or agonize over.

Learning the dynamics of a sport is a priority, but it is also important to anticipate and learn about the issues specific to the stages of a career. Assuming that as a consultant you did not experience your own transitions in the culture of that sport, you can develop a picture of the needs and issues faced by listening, observing, and leveraging people already in that industry in different vantage points. In the case of the NFL, ask what issues are faced by rookies entering the league and their initial experience. Veteran players can provide valuable insights, but it can be fascinating to hear different vantage points from agents, coaches, team front office staff, athletic trainers, strength coaches, family members, and a host of people who experience their transition as a part of that support network. These individuals are also key stakeholders, so understanding expectations, benchmarks, and performance indicators provides important insight. Organizations like the National Football League Players Association (NFLPA) are set up to specifically look after the players' interests and provide some valuable resources and insights in this area. While we have a particular emphasis on the entry into the NFL, there are unique and additional issues mid-career and also during the transition out.

Being aware of the pitfalls and understanding there is always a next level or transition on the horizon can help you be that much better prepared to anticipate the support and resources that could make a difference.

Third, and a final consideration for your contextual intelligence, is that there is sometimes a temptation to be all things to all people. As people in a service industry, many consultants simply want to help, but with good intention they will sometimes overstep their areas of competence. Understand your role and the required skill sets that go into the overall concept of seeing yourself as a performer. Not only undertake self-reflection, but also seek mentoring or coaching, which will help you develop greater insight into your competencies and how to grow these areas.

The client in these situations can also vary in complexity. While the person who is paying the bill may be the agent, organization, or even parent, the welfare and primary concern for the athlete is always paramount (AASP Ethics Code, 1996). Therefore, clarity over expectations on your interactions, measures of effectiveness, communication, reporting, and the breadth and limitations of your role will help both you and the client(s) set the stage for success. Without clear discussion, both you and the various stakeholders are left to their own assumptions; while every eventuality can't be forecast, you will generate more rich discussion and develop greater insight and clarity.

Getting work, and keeping it

Developing a philosophical viewpoint on yourself as a consultant and business is important. Getting paid to deliver your services is an important part of work, not just because you need to pay bills, but more importantly because your services should provide value. There's an interesting expression often shared in the sport psychology business, and it's the idea that consultants should work themselves out of a job. By this, it's often meant that the consulting is helping clients to develop the skills to manage their thoughts and behavior effectively themselves. By definition they are working to become independent and autonomous. If this is your viewpoint, you have to know and understand your business model and how you continue to grow and develop your business. It also depends significantly on your role with a client or organization. An independent contractor has a different situation than a salaried employee within an organization. In both of these contexts, they can still share a similar philosophy about developing autonomy in clients. The key is to understand how this outcome works with your business plan. Great work and word of mouth are often the best marketing and sales mechanisms a practitioner can have, but a host of ethical and professional considerations should go into the thought process.

Some of the most common questions that come up from aspiring mental coaches who want to work with the NFL or tennis professionals are how to gain access. Developing relationships is without a doubt the best way to do this. Professional communities are typically small and, in our experience with the NFL, organizations have already done their homework on you and will ask around their peer group to validate your reputation. The stakes are high and time is valuable for most professional sport personnel, so consider their side of the table. The performance and coaching market is saturated with people pitching things and wanting to be associated with leading brands. As a result, the 'b*ll sh*t' detectors are often high, and it's important to be able to create a good impression: be concise, deliberate, and meaningful with your message.

Once key decision makers are on board, relationship building does not end. In fact, identifying your buy-in strategies for relevant audiences is a very important process. For clients, this might include processes to be engaging, clear, and use tangible ways to work together. This can come in the form of technology, assessment, or on-field or on-court collaborations with other coaching staff, too. Be creative, but consider the opportunities and ways that you can continue to develop buy-in and the relationships.

If they are set up in the right way, the expectations for yourself as a practitioner and what is expected of you by the clients and/or key stakeholders allows you clarity over your deliverables. For example, the expectation may not be to come into a situation and deliver X number of training sessions; it may be to come and observe training and provide feedback and recommendations. Working with a tennis professional, this might be a realistic way to get to know the player's 'team' and build a rapport and get to know everyone and how they work. However, in our NFL pre-draft training program, there is a curriculum and clear deliverables that are unique to that program. There is also a wider scope to individualize and develop more and different offerings over time, but the minimum expectations are met with distinct deliverables. One saying that rings true for some of the most effective consultants I've been fortunate enough to know is that they have a strong sense of providing value to their clients, but also to "under promise, over deliver".

References

AASP Ethics Code. (1996). Accessed at http://www.appliedsportpsych.org/about/ethics/ethics-code/

Battochio, R. C., Stambulova, N., & Schinke, R. J. (2015). Stages and demands in the careers of Canadian National Hockey League players. *Journal of Sports Sciences*, Published online June 18, 2015. doi:10.1080/02640414.2015.1048523

Burke, M. (2012, December 7). Average player salaries in the four major American sports leagues. *Forbes*. Retrieved from http://www.forbes.com/sites/monteburke/2012/12/07/average-player-salaries-in-the-four-major-american-sports-leagues/

Cerasoli, C. P., Nicklin, J. M., & Ford, M. T. (2014). Intrinsic motivation and extrinsic incentives jointly predict performance: A 40-year meta-analysis. *Psychological Bulletin, 140*, 980.

Coakley, S. C. (2006). *A phenomenological exploration of the sport-career transition experience that affect subjective well-being of former National Football League players*. Unpublished doctoral dissertation. Accessed at http://libres.uncg.edu/ir/uncg/f/umi-uncg-1099.pdf

Cremades, J. G., & Tashman, L. S. (2014). *Becoming a sport, exercise, and performance psychology professional: A global perspective*. New York: Psychology Press.

Cross, R. (2010, September 1). Five ways to win a point. Retrieved from http://www.physics.usyd.edu.au/~cross/GrandSlamStatistics.htm

de Geus, A. P. (1998). Why some companies live to tell about change. *The Journal for Quality and Participation, 21*(4), 17–21.

DiClemente, C. C., & Prochaska, J. O. (1998). *Toward a comprehensive, transtheoretical model of change: Stages of change and addictive behaviors*. New York: Plenum Press.

Dweck, C. (2006). *Mindset: The new psychology of success*. New York: Random House.

Finch, S. (2009, April 17). The costs of being a pro tennis player. *The Insider*. Retrieved from http://thetennistimes.com/costs-of-being-a-pro-tennis-player-complete-breakdown/

Fitzgerald, J. (2014, May 11). 2014 NFL draft rookie contract and salary cap estimates. *Over the Cap*. Retrieved from http://overthecap.com/nfl-rookie-salary-cap-2014.php

IMG Academy. (2014). *Mission statement & values for the IMG Academy Mental Conditioning Team*. Bradenton, FL: Author.

IMG Academy. (n. d.). Academic achievements. Accessed at http://www.imgacademy.com/prep-school-program/academics/academic-achievements

Kleingeld, A., van Mierlo, H., & Arends, L. (2011). The effect of goal setting on group performance: A meta-analysis. *Journal of Applied Psychology, 96*, 1289–1304.

Koonce Jr., G. E. (2012). Role transition of National Football League retired athletes: A grounded theory approach. *Marquette Sports Law Review, 23*, 249–338.

Males, J., Sappington, R., & O'Shea, D. (2015, Spring). What can sport learn from business? Consultant, student and educator perspectives. *AASP Newsletter, 30*(1), 17–19.

McCraw, P. D. (2011). Making the Top 100: ITF Top 10 junior transition to Top 100 ATP tour (1996–2005). *Coaching & Sport Science Review, 55*, 11–13.

Mugford, A., Hesse, D., & Morgan, T. (2014). Developing the 'total' consultant: Nurturing the art & science. In L. Taschman & G. Cremades (Eds.), *Becoming a sport, exercise, and performance psychology professional: International perspectives: Approaches and techniques in supervision* (pp. 268–275). New York: Routledge.

Sierer, S. P., Battaglini, C. L., Mihalik, J. P., Shields, E. W., & Tomasini, N. T. (2008). The National Football League Combine: Performance differences between drafted and nondrafted players entering the 2004 and 2005 drafts. *The Journal of Strength & Conditioning Research, 22*(1), 6–12.

Stambulova, N., Alfermann, D., Statler, T., & Côté, J. (2009). ISSP position stand: Career development and transitions of athletes. *International Journal of Sport and Exercise Psychology, 7*, 395–412.

Stambulova, N., Franck, A., & Weibull, F. (2012). Assessment of the transition from junior-to-senior sports in Swedish athletes. *International Journal of Sport and Exercise Psychology, 10*, 79–95.

Statista (2014). Accessed at http://www.statista.com/statistics/240102/average-player-career-length-in-the-national-football-league/

Taylor, J. (2014). *Practice development in sport and performance psychology.* Morgantown, WV: Fit Information Technology.

Torre, P. (2009, March 23). Why and how athletes go broke. *Sports Illustrated.* Retrieved from http://www.si.com/vault/2009/03/23/105789480/how-and-why-athletes-go-broke

Vanden Auweele, Y., De Martelaer, K., Rzewnicki, R., De Knop, P., & Wylleman, P. (2004). Parents and coaches: A help or harm? Affective outcomes for children in sport. In Y. Vanden Auweele (Ed.), *Ethics in youth sport* (pp. 179–193). Leuven, Belgium: Lannoocampus.

Wylleman, P., & Lavallee, D. (2004). A developmental perspective on transitions faced by athletes. In M. Weiss (Ed.), *Developmental sport and exercise psychology: A lifespan perspective* (pp. 507–527). Morgantown, WV: Fitness Information Technology.

Other recommended reading

Bruner, M. W., Munroe-Chandler, K. J., & Spink, K. S. (2008). Entry into elite sport: A preliminary investigation into the transition experiences of rookie athletes. *Journal of Applied Sport Psychology, 20*, 236–252.

Cannon, J. J. (2012). *"When are you going to get a real job?": An experiential sport ethnography of players' experiences on the men's pro tennis futures tour.* PhD dissertation, University of Tennessee, Knoxville.

Cosh, S., LeCouteur, A., Crabb, S., & Kettler, L. (2013). Career transitions and identity: A discursive psychological approach to exploring athlete identity in retirement and the transition back into elite sport. *Qualitative Research in Sport, Exercise & Health, 5*, 21–42.

Gordon, S., & Lavallee, D. (1995). Career transitions in competitive sport. In T. Morris & J. Summers (Eds.), *Sport psychology: Theory, applications and issues* (pp. 474–501). Brisbane, Australia: Jacaranda Wiley.

Hollings, S. C., Mallett, C. J., & Hume, P. A. (2014). The transition from elite junior track-and-field athlete to successful senior athlete: Why some do, why others don't. *International Journal of Sports Science and Coaching, 9*, 457–472.

Morris, R., Tod, D., & Oliver, E. (2015). An analysis of organizational structure and transition outcomes in the youth-to-senior professional soccer transition. *Journal of Applied Sport Psychology, 27*, 216–234.

Park, S., Lavallee, D., & Tod, D. (2013). Athletes' career transition out of sport: A systematic review. *International Review of Sport and Exercise Psychology, 6*, 22–53.

Park, S., Tod, D., & Lavallee, D. (2012). Exploring the retirement from sport decision-making process based on the transtheoretical model. *Psychology of Sport and Exercise, 13*, 444–453.

Poczwardowski, A., Diehl, B., O'Neil, A., Cote, T., & Haberl, P. (2014). Successful transitions to the Olympic Training Center, Colorado Springs: A mixed-method exploration with six resident-athletes. *Journal of Applied Sport Psychology, 26*, 33–51.

Pummell, B., Harwood, C., & Lavallee, D. (2008). Jumping to the next level: A qualitative examination of within-career transition in adolescent event riders. *Psychology of Sport and Exercise, 9*, 427–447.

3

HOW TO BECOME A CONSULTING BUSINESS

Robert M. Nideffer

It was both an honor and a shock for me to be asked to write a chapter on "How to become a consulting business." I have never considered myself a businessman. I can promise you that sales, marketing, and business administration are not my strong suits. For that reason, the notion of becoming a consulting business as opposed to developing a consulting business is a very apt description of the way Enhanced Performance Systems (EPS) evolved. If I had been a businessman, or if I had the money to hire someone who was, I might have developed my business in a couple of years. Instead, it took some 18 years for the business I envisioned to develop.

I began trying to develop a product and services business in 1977. The focus of that business was on helping individuals perform up to their potential under highly stressful and/or competitive conditions. I will be the first to admit that a great deal has changed over the past 38 years, both with respect to what it takes to be successful in business and with respect to where the field of sport psychology is today. Technological advances, for example, have changed the way we market, sell, distribute, and provide services. The credibility of sport and performance psychology has increased considerably from what it was in 1977. Today, more professional teams are employing sport psychologists than ever before. More sports governing bodies and more colleges and universities are incorporating sport psychologists and sport psychology techniques into their programs.

At the same time, a lot has not changed. There are still far more people seeking to make a living in sport psychology than there are jobs to go around. Thus, those of you who do not land one of the available jobs will have to create your own business if you want to work in the field. Today, as it was when I started out in the field, graduates are competing in the consulting marketplace with professionals in academia who offer their services for free or for a fee that an independent consultant cannot live on. Today you are not only competing with others trained in sport psychology, but also with psychologists from other disciplines as well. Today, as it has always been, you still have to: (1) differentiate your services from others in the marketplace; (2) establish your credibility and expertise; (3) communicate in a language that your client understands; (4) network to get and keep yourself in front of potential clients; (5) provide a service that makes a difference in the coach and athlete's bottom line and/or in their feelings of self-worth; and (6) make sacrifices in other areas of your life. Today, as it was when I entered the field, the chances are extremely high that, for awhile anyway, you are going to have to "get a real job" if you hope to survive while you attempt to build your consulting business. Take a look around and you will see that a great many of the successful consultants in our field's primary support comes from the fact that they hold an academic position.

In this chapter I am going to share some of the mistakes I made and some of the lessons that I learned along the way to building a self-sustaining consulting practice. Hopefully, you will be able to learn something from my mistakes, and thereby shorten the length of time it takes to create the kind of consulting business you dream of.

Why sport psychology?

If you haven't already dug down deep to try and understand what is motivating you to become a consultant to high-level athletes, you need to do so. People enter the field for a lot of different reasons. Those reasons, whatever they are, are important because they provide you with the strength and drive and motivation you need to keep going when you run into problems. Those reasons will determine how you will interact with clients. They will also affect your credibility and how the athletes and coaches you work with perceive you. Some questions you might want to ask yourself include: (1) Am I financially driven? (2) Am I a fan, living my life through my affiliation with elite level performers, basking in their reflected glory? (3) Am I motivated by the belief that I can actually make a difference in the lives and performances of those I work with? (4) What is it that excites me when I think about working with elite level performers?

Whatever drives you, finding the right balance between making enough money to survive and support your family and having your needs for affiliation and/or the sense that you are making a positive difference in the lives of others is a huge challenge for most of us in the field. Depending on where that balance is, you may or may not have difficulty setting fees for your service. Depending on where that balance is, you may end up having to work (e.g., do things you do not enjoy) to survive as opposed to being able to live out the life that you dream about and that plays to your greatest strengths. Depending on where that balance is, you may be asking others to sacrifice their needs to support you and your needs.

Being of service and making a positive difference in the lives of others has always been my primary driver. As a result, when I have made bad decisions, they have consistently resulted in either my business suffering and/or my family suffering so that I could continue to indulge my need to do what I loved to do. Don't get me wrong. I have worked hard to meet my family's needs. Most of the time I have been able to do that, and at the same time meet my own needs, too. Still, when I have failed, it has either been because I was too willing to give away my services or because I have sacrificed time with my family in order to be there and make a difference in the lives of clients.[1] You will see that theme play itself out as I describe how and why my consulting business evolved.

What differentiates you from the competition?

Even though I am not a businessman, when I started out I was astute enough to recognize that to be successful as a consultant, I would have to be able to differentiate myself and the services I offered from those of other consultants. At the end of this chapter, I have listed a few consulting websites along with a brief description of each of them. As you look at them you will see that each of them tries to highlight their uniqueness. For some, it is the expertise they have in a particular sport (e.g., golf), and for others it is their knowledge and expertise when it comes to the application of a particular treatment methodology or approach (e.g., biofeedback, hypnosis, use of TAIS or the MBTI, or some other assessment and/or treatment approach).

Not very many people can differentiate themselves from the competition by the time they complete their graduate training. You usually need more experience than that. It took me 34 years to develop and to identify for myself and for others what differentiated me from the competition. From as far back as I can remember, I have always been fascinated with the question, "What would we be capable of doing if we could fully integrate mind, body, and spirit?" My life has revolved around trying to answer that question. It was through my writing that I first differentiated myself from the competition and began to establish some credibility.

In 1976 I published an article in the *Journal of Personality and Social Psychology* that presented a theory about the interrelationship between cognitive (attentional) processes, interpersonal skills, emotional arousal, and performance. That article also described the development and validation of The Attentional and Interpersonal Style inventory (TAIS). TAIS was designed to measure performance-relevant concentration and interpersonal skills or attributes (Nideffer, 1976a). During that same period, I published a book titled *The Inner Athlete*, which examined the various techniques that were being applied in the sport psychology area. In *The Inner Athlete*, I used the theory underlying TAIS to provide a performance-relevant rationale for the application of various psychological techniques to specific performance-related issues. The book also helped to identify some of the critical differences between athletes who do and do not perform well under pressure (Nideffer, 1976b).

With the appearance of those two publications, I quickly became recognized in the field as an "expert," when it came to helping athletes improve their concentration skills and their ability to perform under pressure. I was invited to give presentations at national and international meetings, to give colloquia at various schools, and I got considerable exposure in newspapers, lay journals, and on television. Depending on whom you ask, all of that exposure either gave me a false sense of security (my wife's opinion) or the courage to take a risk (my position). Whichever it was, in response to what was going on, I resigned from my associate professorship at the University of Rochester in New York and moved to California without a job.

1977 – my first big mistake

If you look at consultants within the field of sport psychology, you will see them bringing in money in one or more of these three ways: (1) they receive money for services they provide (counseling, consulting, training); (2) they receive money from the sale of products (e.g., TAIS, CDs, books), and (3) they make money by hiring other consultants and then taking a percentage of the fees that they bring into the organization.

One of the things you want to think about as you build your business is the balance you hope to obtain with respect to the different sources of income. When the only income you have coming in is fee-for-service income, you can get burned out. When the only income you have coming in is fee-for-service income, you can also find yourself hanging on to clients longer than you should and working with clients that you would rather not work with. My goal in building a business was to see the balance shift from mostly fee-for-service income to mostly product sales income. I wanted the indirect income to free me up to do the things I wanted to do, and to be able to pick and choose whom I would consult with.

Moving back to Southern California, I wasn't thinking about building a business that would involve others. Because I don't see myself as a sales and marketing person, or as a business administrator, I was content to "let the business develop itself." I naively made the assumption that my reputation and the books and test I had developed would somehow sell themselves. That was a huge mistake.

Sales and marketing are absolutely critical to the development of any organization, and that is where I have always faced my biggest challenges. Somehow, in my head, sales and marketing activities are seen as self-promotion, as placing my financial needs or personal needs ahead of the needs of the people I want to serve. That makes it very hard to set fees and to do the networking and promoting you need to do to be successful.

Just before I left the University of Rochester, a faculty member who had a business on the side called Behavioural Research Applications Group (BRAG) approached me and asked if they could market and sell TAIS. I was only too happy to let them take on that responsibility, because it meant I wouldn't have to "dirty myself" by engaging in sales and marketing and self-promotion. I completely distanced myself from the sales and marketing of products I had developed.

When it came to selling my services, as opposed to selling my products, I showed a similar "avoidance pattern." A couple of individuals were absolutely sold on the value of TAIS. Robin Pratt, a psychologist and Dean at the University of Redlands, came to me saying he wanted to learn as much as he could about TAIS and its underlying theory. He told me that the theory underlying TAIS had made sense of his research and helped him to integrate all of the reading he had been doing around performance. Robin became TAIS's biggest supporter, and over the years he has organized and provided TAIS trainings, he has written books and articles about the instrument, and he contributed to the development of computer software and test reports. Somehow I convinced myself that through my writing, and through others like Robin spreading the word about TAIS, consulting opportunities would come to me, and I would not have to go out and sell my services.

I made the mistake of assuming that by coming up with a theory, and by developing and validating an inventory, I had made my contribution. I left the task of building a business around my creative ideas to the responsibility of others. I handed off the most important parts of building a business to people who, despite their commitment to me and to TAIS, did not have the time and/or skill sets to do the job. Not only that, but by withdrawing from the things I did not enjoy doing, I made their jobs all but impossible. I was incredibly naive. I assumed money would roll in from TAIS sales and from sales of the books I was contracted to write. I thought all of the press I had received would cause the world to beat a path to my door.

First, test sales did not materialize. Oh, BRAG sold a few tests, but they were making their money off of the counseling they were doing based on TAIS results. They might sell a test for $5 and then provide interpretation and coaching services around that test for from $200 to $500. The consulting took time away from selling and marketing, and they only needed to sell enough tests to keep themselves busy consulting. It would take 20 years before BRAG began to sell enough tests to provide any meaningful income to EPS. That is why EPS began to add additional distributors in the mid-1980s. Those distributors like BRAG were also in the consulting business. As consultants, they wanted to become distributors to reduce the cost they paid for tests and to generate some indirect income for themselves through the sale of TAIS to others. The actual gain in test sales was minimal, as the consultants were marketing their consulting services more than they were marketing TAIS.

Second, writing books is not particularly lucrative, especially in the field of sport psychology. The two books I had advances on never sold enough copies to pay more than the advances. Two other books that I wrote, which became classics in the field, paid me a total of around $25,000 over the years. The potential value of the books is not in the money they bring in, but instead in the credibility they bring to you and the services you have to offer.

I was right about one thing: the exposure that I had received through my writing and through TV appearances, press coverage, and stories in lay publications did result in people knocking on my door. I was being asked to provide consulting services, but no one wanted and/or expected to pay for those services. National Governing Bodies (NGBs) of sports and the United States Olympics Committee (USOC) would pay expenses, but that was it. Likewise, many professional athletes and teams behaved as if they were doing me a favor by allowing me to work with them.

I quickly learned that the development of business requires constant networking and the willingness to actively market and sell yourself and your product. That was something I could not seem to make myself do. I was forced to realize that if I was going to develop a business, I would either have to change or I would have to hire someone to compensate for my weaknesses. I would have to pay someone to be a business administrator and to market and sell TAIS and my consulting services. I did not have the money to do that. In fact, I did not have the money to pay my own bills, let alone hire someone else. So, within 6 months of moving to California, I temporarily gave up the idea of developing a consulting business and took a half-time position at the California School of Professional Psychology (CSPP). I also started a clinical practice to supplement my income from CSPP, seeing 8 to 10 patients a week. It was not what I wanted to do, but it was paying the bills.

1977 to 1983 – keeping the dream alive

I was on the faculty at CSPP from 1977 through 1983. CSPP provided the opportunity for me to continue to conduct research on TAIS, and during this time I began to develop computerized programs to administer, score, and generate reports for TAIS. I was still very much involved in the field of sport psychology, but I was certainly not making a living from it. Services to NGBs, professional organizations, and to the USOC were provided for free. Oh, I would get expenses paid when I went to a training camp, but no salary. As for the sale of TAIS, it was being used for the most part for research, and very little money – if any – was coming in from it. You can imagine how overjoyed my wife was when I would get to travel to exotic places for training camps or competitions without getting paid, while she stayed home with a 7-year-old and a 3-year-old and tried to figure out how to pay the bills.

In 1983 things really heated up because I was selected to be one of two sport psychologists working with the U.S. Olympic Track and Field team at the 1984 Olympics. Not only would I be spending about four weeks with the team in Santa Barbara, California, just prior to the games, but I would be traveling to elite athlete development camps, to the World Championships in Helsinki in 1983, and to other major events leading up to the games.

I was wondering how I was going to be able to maintain my responsibilities at CSPP and manage all of the traveling that I would have to do. Then, one night my wife talked me into having dinner with another couple whose kids played on the same soccer team that ours did. During our dinner conversation, my wife mentioned I would be working with the Olympic Track and Field Team. That got the interest of the husband, who turned out to be a venture capitalist. He asked me a lot of questions about my background and then asked if I had ever thought about developing a business. I told him yes and mentioned the problems I had encountered and admitted my sales and marketing hang-ups. To make a long story short, he became convinced that a viable business could be developed and promised to help me raise the capital to do that.

I was given a check for $50,000 and told that his group would raise $1 million for the initial development of the business, and then move toward an initial public offering (IPO) to raise more money for the business. I would have to quit my job at CSPP, and I would have to hire someone to be responsible for sales and marketing since that was clearly not my strength. I would be giving talks, providing services, and developing TAIS and related reports. It all sounded too good to be true, but I figured with $50,000 in hand, what did I have to lose?

I resigned from my position at CSPP. I then talked a friend into quitting his job to head up sales and marketing for my new company. Then, the bottom fell out of the venture capital market. The group walked away from the $50,000 they had given me, and I never saw or heard from them again. The only bright light was that I had developed the beginning of a business plan, and I now had a name for my business should it ever get off the ground: Enhanced Performance Systems (EPS).

1984 to 1994 – moving into new areas

Much to my wife's chagrin, I took out a second mortgage on our home to pay my friend the $30,000 salary I had promised him for the first year. That decision on my part, and the feelings of insecurity that it created for my wife, placed a great deal of strain on our marriage, one thing led to another, and we eventually divorced. Once again, my lack of concern with respect to financial issues and/or my tendency to put my need to follow my dream first cost me, and more importantly my wife and my children, a great deal.

I am not telling you these things to discourage you from following your dreams. I am telling you these things so that you incorporate them into your plans. You can do that by remaining single, or by taking the time to check in with your spouse to make sure that he or she is on board with your mission. I am hoping that you will be more sensitive and thoughtful than I was.

Over the next 10 years, I spent most of my time writing, consulting, and continuing to work on the development of software for TAIS. I quickly learned that I had to expand my consulting beyond elite sport to survive. Fortunately, performance under pressure is something that most high-level performers have to do whether their performance arena is business, sport, or the military. To work with those other groups, however, I had to develop a whole new language, and I had to be able to relate my theory and my approach to a whole new set of problems. I had to speak in my clients' language and use examples they could relate to.

By the end of 1994, I found myself in a position where I was making enough money from TAIS sales and from my consulting to incorporate EPS and to hire someone to assume responsibility for business administration and business development. I need to point out that most of the money was coming in from consulting in the business arena, not from sport. Once again, my goal in moving forward with the development of a business was to generate enough indirect, not fee-for-service, income so that I could spend my time doing what I wanted to do – be that research, writing, service provision, or whatever else I might think of.

I have pointed out a couple of the mistakes that I have made along the way, so let me also point out one of the things I have done that has served me well. I have been flexible enough to adapt to changing situations, markets, and technologies. Over the years I moved from hand-scored tests and individualized typewritten reports, to the development of on-site software for administering, scoring, and generating reports, to the use of the Internet for sales, marketing, test administration, scoring, and report generation. As indicated earlier, I have also adapted to different performance arenas. That kind of flexibility will become critical for most of you reading this chapter, especially if you hope to develop your own consulting business.

1995 to 2000 – finally building a business

In 1995, I hired Marc Sagal following his graduation from the San Diego State University sport psychology program. Marc was in the right place at the right time, but he had taken the initiative to be in that place. Marc was willing to do whatever I asked in order to get a job. He had not gotten a degree in sport psychology to be a business administrator, marketer, or salesman. He had played soccer at a high level, and his heart's desire was to work directly with high-level athletes. He knew when he signed on that he would not be working with athletes for a long time.

Marc threw himself into learning how to run a business, how to market and sell. He also threw himself into learning about EPS products and software. The payoff for hiring Marc was not immediate; in fact, it would be years before he would be bringing in enough money to cover his salary. At about the same time I hired Marc, a decision was made to hire a technical support person (Dale). I knew that it was important to move our assessment service and products to the Internet, but I did not have the time or the talent to do that, and neither did Marc. Between Marc and Dale, I found myself having to cover about $110,000 in salary. I was making good money with the business consulting, but I was pouring every extra dime back into the business. Soon, we were also paying an intern from the computer sciences program at UC San Diego to help support Dale with technical challenges and customer issues related to the Internet services we were providing.

Up to this point, I was the only one providing services under the EPS name. I was on the road 60% of the time, traveling all over Europe and North America. I had remarried after my divorce and started another family. Our first child was born in 1994 and our second in 1998. Once again, family was being sacrificed for the sake of the development of the business and so I could live out my dreams.

Integrating customer knowledge with products and services

Things finally began to click for EPS, both from a test sales standpoint and from a consulting services standpoint, around 1997. Some Special Forces units in the U.S. military had begun using TAIS, and I was asked to provide training for the military psychologists who would be using TAIS with various units. Major Mark Lowry had made arrangements for the training, and I had been very impressed with both his knowledge of TAIS and his unique ability to take TAIS constructs and relate them directly to the missions and objectives of Special Forces teams. Shortly after the training, Mark left the military and took a job with an assessment company. The company hired him on the assumption that he would be able to expand the use of their instruments by the military. When that job did not work out, I asked Mark to join EPS.

Individuals like Mark are perfect fits for an organization like EPS. Mark came to EPS with established credibility in a particular area (special operations). He came to EPS with an already developed network of contacts within the Special Forces command. He had great respect and great knowledge about the relevance of the attributes measured by TAIS to the demands faced by Special Forces personnel. Within a few months of joining EPS, Mark had developed a contract with the military that more than paid for his salary and increased the sale of TAIS.

I have gone into depth in talking about Mark, because there are important lessons to be learned here. That is especially true if you hope to land one of the few jobs that are out there, as opposed to developing your own consulting business. The more you can do to develop contacts and network with others as you move through the education process, the better off you will be. The more you can develop expertise with specific tools or techniques, and the more credibility you can gain as a service provider within a given area (e.g., by speaking the language, by having competed in that area yourself), the greater your chances of landing a job. Kimberley Amirault, who is mentioned later in the section on websites, is a good example of this. So, too, is Geoff Miller.

Throughout his education at San Diego State University, Geoff continued to network with others, and in this case one of the people he networked with was Marc Sagal. While at San Diego State, Geoff did everything he could to develop skills and a reputation for working with baseball players, especially pitchers. Geoff was totally dedicated to baseball, and he began using TAIS as a tool to help him develop performance improvement programs. Geoff was hired by EPS, and because of the focus that he had maintained through his training, within a short period of time he managed to develop a consulting contract with a Major League Baseball team.

Don't expect tools and techniques to do the work for you

There is a huge difference between becoming a real expert in the use of an assessment tool or in the use of a particular approach to treatment (e.g., biofeedback, hypnosis, goal setting, attention control training) and taking a class or getting "certified" in an area and then presenting yourself as an expert. The individuals I just mentioned paid their dues and developed the expertise necessary to provide a real service to their clients; they integrated theory and practice, and because of that they could recognize and respond to exceptions to the rules.

I cannot tell you the number of individuals I have seen who somehow hope that a tool or a therapeutic technique is going to magically get them clients who will be willing to pay for their services. They pay to go to a two- or three-day certification workshop, somehow thinking that will negate any need on their part for networking, selling, and developing their skills to the point of being able to adapt their interpretation and approach to the needs of very different clients. As a result, the tools and techniques they use control them and their approach rather than the other way around. Individuals, for example, who get certified in TAIS and then fail to put in the time necessary to really understand the theory that ties the various constructs to each other and to performance. These are individuals who want to rely on a canned report that does not require any thinking or consensual validation on their part. In their minds, if something goes wrong, the problem is with the tool, and not with them.

You might get away with canned reports and with stumbling through a feedback or counseling session with someone at the youth sport level. At that level, enthusiasm and a big smile may go a long way because support and encouragement are more important than anything else. At the elite level, in sport, in business, and in the military, however, you better know the ins and outs of your business. You had better be able to communicate the relevance of the information that you have to offer to the bottom line. And, you had better be able to do that in very few words in a language that your client understands and can relate to. You cannot do that if you are not thoroughly versed in the theory that underlies your particular approach. All of that takes dedication and hard work.

2001 to 2006 – shifting priorities

After I arrived back home from an extended stay in Europe, my 8-year-old asked a question and made a statement that began to change my life: "Dad, when are you going to spend more time at home? I miss you, and I like it when you are around." I was exhausted from the trip. As I mentioned, the business was growing, but every extra nickel I was making was going back into it. I had not saved a dime for retirement, and we had not done much as a family. That fact wasn't of concern to Marc, who was running the business and had his own ideas about how best to develop it. He was putting a great deal of pressure on me to either work harder to make more money to fund an expensive marketing campaign or to borrow the money.

Marc and I began to battle over the direction the company would go in. My son's request had forced me to see the sacrifices that I had been asking my family to make. I had been so focused on building the business and helping clients that I hadn't responded to my children's needs. I did not want to risk their future by borrowing money to support Marc's ideas, and I did not want to spend even more time on the road. So, in March 2001 it was decided that Marc, Mark, and Geoff would take the customers they had developed and become a TAIS distributor. They incorporated as The Winning Mind, and over the past 13 years have helped to dramatically increase TAIS sales. With their leaving, EPS was reduced to myself and to Rich Dawes, the one-time technical support intern. Rich had been thrust into taking on all of the technical support responsibilities, when Dale found he could make a lot more money with his skill set working for a high-tech company outside of Boston.

Dale's departure, by the way, helped me realize just how lucky we were to have hired an intern. Dale's departure was a surprise and happened on very short notice. Had we not had Rich in the wings, so to speak, we would have been in a lot of trouble. Lesson to be learned. Make sure you know who is critical to your business and have a back-up plan in place.

With everyone leaving, I turned my attention toward providing some security for my family. I told my son that I would start spending more time at home in three years, but it turned out to be four. For those four years, I continued the consulting, but instead of pouring all of the extra money back into the business, I put it into retirement accounts.

2006 to 2014 – living the dream

By the end of 2006, I had finally accomplished my dream. Between the money I had put into retirement accounts and the income being generated by TAIS, I was in the very enviable position of being able to reduce and, if I wanted to, to completely stop doing any consulting. I could spend as much time at home as I wanted, I could spend as much time writing or conducting research as I wanted, and I could travel with my family for pleasure if I wanted.

EPS was still a company, but it consisted of one service provider (me) and a tech support person (Rich). Rich made sure that online administration, scoring, and report generation of TAIS continued to function properly and that new accounts got set up in a timely fashion.

Monthly billing of distributors for the tests they and their clients used was being handled by my accountant's office.

I began to do everything I could to minimize both overhead and the amount of work involved in keeping the EPS website, which was now the business, up and running. If anything happened to me, I wanted the income from the business to be able to support the members of my family pursuing their dreams, not mine. I did not want them to have to sacrifice their desires to keep my dream alive.

2015 – handing off the baton

In the last quarter of 2014, two different groups who were interested in purchasing EPS approached me. Well, they were not really interested in purchasing EPS. What they wanted to purchase was the intellectual property (IP) rights to TAIS and related materials, along with the company's "good will." Those groups saw a great deal of value in TAIS, and they wanted to update the inventory and improve test reports, customer service, etc. Through those discussions, I realized that it was time to hand off the baton. If I and/or my family continued to run the business the way I was planning, TAIS would die a slow death. On the other hand, if someone else took over, who had the money and energy necessary to continue to develop and improve the product, then everyone would benefit.

On March 26, 2015, I signed a purchase agreement that sold the IP rights to TAIS to a group who incorporated the business under the name TAIS Performance Systems Inc. I have a consulting agreement with the company, and I chair their advisory board. That board also includes Marc Sagal and Robin Pratt. EPS now acts as one of their distributors. If the new company follows through on its promise, TAIS and associated reports will be improved, and the instrument will be around for a long time.

That is the behind-the-scenes story of how I stumbled and fumbled my way to some degree of success with respect to developing or rather "becoming" a consulting business. Hopefully, you will learn from my reluctance to get actively involved in the actual administration, marketing, and sales of products and/or consulting services, so that you can accomplish your dream in a much shorter period of time. Hopefully, too, you will do a better job of managing the stress that your business development focus will cause for those who are close to you and need your time and attention.

I want to close this chapter by pointing you to some of the websites that have been created by individuals who are consulting within the sport psychology arena. I have made a few comments designed to point out some of the lessons that you may be able to learn from them and from how they present themselves. Two of the things that you will see immediately are: (1) the competition is tough; and (2) you will need to take advantage of the Internet and social media to get the exposure you need to be successful.

Examples of sport psychology consultant websites

http://drkimberleyamirault.com/index.php/drkimberley/
> If you listened to Kimberley Amirault's presentation at AASP in Las Vegas, you heard about the networking she does and about the sacrifices she has made to be successful. Kimberley's site is a testimony to her focus, her dedication, and to the way she has been able to leverage her contacts and her success to build her business.

http://www.mentaltraininginc.com/cmt.php

Robert Neff's website, Mental Training Inc., provides a great example of one of the ways consultants are trying to survive in the sport psychology arena. Having burned himself out providing fee-for-service training, and recognizing the need to develop passive income, he came up with a unique idea. Dr. Neff, like myself, had to learn business lessons the hard way. So, he decided to put together a training program designed to give others the business development skills required for success.

http://thewinningmind.com/

The Winning Mind website helps to show the importance of being able to have a corporate focus or mission – in their case it is helping individuals perform under pressure. As you look at the description of the principles, you can see how their expertise is tied to specific groups and to their corporate mission.

http://www.performancecoaching.ca/en/

Dr. Peter Jensen has developed a very successful business by applying lessons learned from coaching and consulting in sports to business. Note how skillfully he ties the two together, using his sport experience to build credibility for himself and his organization in the business world. Dr. Jensen shows the importance of being able to communicate common lessons in two different languages (business and sport).

http://www.vision54.com/html/about-us.html

Lynn Marriott and Pia Nilsson's website illustrates the fact that, as a sport psychologist, you are competing not just against other sport psychologists. You are also competing against coaches who recognize the importance of psychological factors and who believe they can help the athletes they work with manage the mental side of the game as well as the physical side.

http://www.drjimtaylor.com/3.0/

Dr. Jim Taylor is a sport psychologist who was a member of the U.S. National Ski Team. Jim, more than most, has been able to recognize and take advantage of opportunities that present themselves. Jim is extremely hard working and dedicated. He is not afraid to take chances, and he knows the importance of being willing to actively promote one's self and one's expertise.

Note

1 If you listened to Keith Henschen's Coleman Griffith speech, or Kimberley Amirault's keynote address at the 2014 AASP meetings in Las Vegas, you heard about the sacrifices that get made and the consequences of those sacrifices on others.

References

Nideffer, R. M. (1976a). Test of attentional and interpersonal style. *Journal of Personality and Social Psychology, 34*, 394–404.

Nideffer, R. M. (1976b). *The inner athlete*. New York: Thomas Crowell.

4

OVERCOMING RESISTANCE FROM CLIENTS AND STAKEHOLDERS

Frank L. Gardner

The work of a sport psychologist is, at its heart, an interpersonal interaction between a provider and client of a professional service. In the case of any psychological service, the interaction between the professional and client requires both overt and covert agreement regarding goals, timing, and effort associated with the delivered intervention, and necessitates a commitment to ethical behavior and the preservation of boundaries. Yet in the best of cases and worst of cases, sport psychologists know all too well that resistance to intervention occurs on a regular basis, and they further recognize that the manner in which resistance is handled largely determines the success of the sport psychologist's intervention efforts. Encouraging sport psychologists to reflect upon their relationships with coaching staff, sports management personnel, and athletic clientele, this chapter highlights that in order to reach and impact our unique client base, we must first and foremost attend to the professional relationship, including resistance, and further, appreciate that our influence and effectiveness are likely to be slow, evolutionary, and dynamic processes.

Defining resistance

Resistance in the context of psychological intervention may be most simply defined as a client's unwillingness to cooperate and ultimately change in response to a psychological intervention (Beutler, Moleiro, & Talebi, 2002). There are a multitude of reasons why clients may be resistant within a professional relationship. First, some clients are ordered or referred to the sport psychologist by a third party (e.g., coach, agent, management). While many such clients are eager and willing to participate in psychological services, it is also common for referred clientele to have an absence of genuine intrinsic motivation for improvement, and they thus may be reluctant to engage in the intervention process. In fact, even clients who personally seek out psychological services often manifest some resistance to the discomfort that change can bring. Interestingly, clients often oppose change, and therefore resist intervention efforts, even if it is what they desire, as change can be a difficult process even for the most motivated.

In my extensive personal experience as a clinical and sport-performance psychologist, and in educating and training doctoral-level psychologists, I have found that practitioners will most often display a tendency to view "resistance" as a function of the client and as a convenient construct by which to explain any lack of progress. Yet, resistance should not be narrowly conceptualized as a characteristic of, or emanating from, the client, but rather should be viewed as the result of an interaction between the [sport] psychologist, client, and context. Appreciating the bidirectional nature of the resistance construct, there are a number of reasons why "resistance" behaviors may be present. For instance, resistance may emerge if a sport psychologist tries to intervene too quickly without aligning goals with the client, is too forceful with intervention efforts, and/or misjudges the client's initial discussion about her/his goals and objectives as an indication of immediate readiness to change. Additionally, the context of intervention efforts is critical, as resistance may emerge as one's motivation to change fluctuates according to factors outside of the professional relationship, such as a change in the athlete's environmental situation (i.e., coach, injury, agent).

Interestingly, while the topic of resistance holds great importance in the practice of psychology in general, with empirical research suggesting that a robust 21% of the variance in clinical/counseling outcomes can be explained by the therapeutic relationship (Norcross & Hill, 2002), sport psychology seems to have neglected this exceedingly important topic (Gardner & Moore, 2006), which has vast implications for client well-being and therapeutic progress, professional ethics, and professional development of practitioners. Thus, I seek for this chapter to reflect how my 35-plus years as a clinical psychologist and 25-plus years working with elite athletes and teams in various professional and Olympic sports (including multiple championship teams) have uncovered the various forms that resistance may take in the sport milieu, its connection to the possible demise of a functional professional relationship, and its connection to specific contextual challenges.

Contextual fit

Before we can dig deeper into client (e.g., athlete, team/organization) resistance to the intervention efforts of the sport psychologist, we should first consider the contextual fit of the sport psychologist in the athletic environment. The importance of comprehending this contextual fit as a foundation to understanding resistance lies in the reality that sport psychologists do not work in a vacuum. There are numerous beliefs, pressures, and political dynamics at play, which in some cases are out of our hands. Yet if the sport psychologist can remain mindful of the above realities, while simultaneously navigating the demands associated with changes in professional roles and responsibilities, fluctuating and atypical modes of intervention, and the cultivation and maintenance of sound professional relationships, the foundation is likely to be set for a long and successful tenure with the client or organization. Understanding these nuances requires awareness, reflection, and patience. And, it wholeheartedly requires the practitioner to avoid the intellectually lazy and overly simplistic conclusion that "the player/client is being resistant," when in fact, the aforementioned realities contribute widely to the formation of resistance behaviors. So, let's embark upon a discussion of factors associated with contextual fit, namely professional roles and responsibilities, modes of intervention, and the professional relationship, which will pave the way for a deeper discussion of sources of resistance and resolution strategies later in the chapter.

Professional roles and responsibilities

A sport psychologist's roles and responsibilities tend to evolve over time within a specific team or organization, assuming that goodness-of-fit has been established and the sport psychologist has weathered her/his initial contract. Over time, professional roles tend to be subject to change based on both personal skill sets/competencies and changes in coaching, management, team record, and player personnel. While evolving roles can certainly be exciting and rewarding, the naturally occurring change in roles and responsibilities can alter the perception of the sport psychologist by staff and players alike, and can thus impact her/his professional relationships and client comfort, albeit usually for the short term. For example, early in my career as a psychologist working in professional sports, I was a holdover in my capacity as team psychologist following a change in management and coaching staff. Being a holdover is fairly atypical to begin with, as management and coaching changes often result in other staff cleansing in order to make room for a new regime. Luckily, I was able to maintain my position, with the knowledge that I would quickly need to win over the new senior management and coaching staff. Understandably, for a brief period of time following this changeover, my time with the team was reduced, and as such the ability of athletes to easily and freely come forward to work on performance and/or personal issues was impacted. In essence, the organizational changes briefly impacted when and how my work with athletes could occur, which in turn temporarily modified working relationships, subsequently leading some athletes to briefly exhibit behavior (e.g., being less forthcoming in conversation) that would generally be classified as resistance.

Modes of intervention

In addition to the fluctuation of roles and responsibilities over time, the sport psychologist must become comfortable with varying modes of intervention in order to maintain a contextual fit within the organization. Unlike typical psychological practice, which follows a more traditional session length and frequency model, sport psychology sessions can range from formal to informal meetings, brief individual sessions to longer group/team-oriented classes/sessions, and may transpire in hotel restaurants or locker facilities and on buses/planes or the sidelines. Without comfort with the unique modes of intervention delivery required in the sport domain, true contextual fit cannot be obtained, and clients will inevitably sense this disconnect. Such varied professional activities may take some adjustment for the novice or transitioning sport psychology professional, yet successful navigation cultivates both practitioner comfort and client willingness to explore intervention services.

The professional relationship

The *contextual* foundation of sport psychology practice, from the successes we have to the client resistance we face, lies firmly in the professional relationship developed with stakeholders, including athletes, coaches, management, team/organization personnel, and ownership. Those who have worked in the field can surely acknowledge that many stakeholders are suspicious, or even outright cynical, about the value of sport psychology services. Indeed, there are some good reasons for that attitude, as some sport psychologists (as with any profession) oversell the efficacy and/or certainty of their services, and others fail to accurately describing their training, education, competencies, and practice limitations. Writing that sentence actually makes me chuckle, as it reminds me of a time when I received a call from the general manager of a professional team with which I was/am employed, who joked about having received a letter from a sport psychologist who claimed that if the organization employed his services, he could *guarantee* a championship within two years! Unfortunately, such stories abound, and they only push prospective clientele further from our reach. A lack of consistent evidence-based practice in the field has been an additional contributor (Birrer & Morgan, 2010; Gardner & Moore, 2006; McCarthy, Wilson, Keegan, & Smith, 2012). While not an exhaustive list of reasons for suspiciousness, together, the culmination of aforementioned variables means that sport psychologists frequently have to overcome the confirmation biases of athletes and/or team staff before even having an *opportunity* to practice their wonderful craft.

To facilitate a sound professional relationship and minimize excessive resistance (note: some resistance is to be expected, as will be discussed later in this chapter) within sport psychology practice, the sport psychologist must first accept that until invited to "move in," our profession is a guest in the sport milieu. We are *not* imminently necessary, but we *can* be quite useful! If sport psychologists cannot accept their inherent limitations within the field, resistance is not only probable, but it is likely to be a certainty. Working in the sport environment and *minimizing* the resistance of stakeholders requires humility, interpersonal effectiveness (not salesmanship), flexibility, patience, and the ability to adapt to a reality of often rapidly changing needs of an entire organization/team. It is critical that honest communication about organizational and individual needs, and the practitioner's strengths and limitations, occur at the outset. Indeed, establishing general agreement about individual client needs and goals, and the psychologist's goals for the client, is a critical component of a sound and effective professional relationship. Whether the client is an individual athlete or larger organizational body, an alliance between the sport psychologist and the client cannot be established unless the client perceives that the practitioner understands (and can empathize with) her/him and a clear and agreed-upon alignment of goals has been established. Further, the sport psychologist must effectively communicate and maintain appropriate professional boundaries, adhere to the demands/organizational structures of the team/organization, and develop an effective rapport with management, staff, and athletic participants. This is a long list of tasks to accomplish prior to even attempting to enact substantive change with clients, yet it sets the stage for all that is to come – that is, if the sport psychologist wishes to avoid the early establishment of client resistance, personal organizational conflict, and a short tenure.

Sources of resistance

With the aforementioned foundations discussed, let's progress deeper into the topic of resistance by discussing some of the most likely sources of resistance, followed by general strategies for minimizing that resistance among the individual athletes and organizations with whom we work.

Readiness for change

On the surface, sport psychology practice aims to achieve many things – performance development/improvement, performance maintenance, the remediation of clinical/personal concerns, and rehabilitation adherence, to name but a few. Yet regardless of the type of sport psychology interventions we employ or the goals we think we seek, at the heart of all of our interventions is an effort toward some form of *behavior change*. Indeed, we are trying to change athletes' or organizational behavior in one form or another, and such change is rarely a single revolutionary event. Sometimes we may work with an athlete who, after experiencing a competitive performance crisis of some type, readily complies with strategies suggested by a sport psychologist. More often, however, we sometimes find our athletic clientele to be seemingly unable or unwilling to engage in suggested strategies or techniques (again, *behavior change*), even when they are identifiably in need or are reaching out for help. Although an evolving topic for well over a century, the construct of behavior change has welcomed renewed scientific attention within professional psychology within the past 30 years, with substantial advancement within the past 15-plus years. During this time, it has been reconceptualized as a *process*, with some theorists viewing this process in a stage-like manner (i.e., pre-contemplation/not ready, contemplation/getting ready, preparation/ready, action/engaged in change, and maintenance/maintaining change; Prochaska, DiClemente, & Norcross 1992). Whether one views change as truly a dimensional stage-like phenomenon or a more continuous process, what can be concluded is that for most individuals and organizations, behavior change occurs gradually, with clients generally moving from less interested or unwilling to engage in change-promoting behaviors to increasingly greater willingness to consider and ultimately attempt behavior change.

Resistance is often encountered when a client (either individuals or an organization/team) is pushed too hard to alter their behavior when they are not yet ready to commit to such actions. When noting "resistance" in the form of some specific overt behavior, sport psychologists are encouraged to engage in a bit of self-reflection and consider diffusing the resistance, rather than adopting the tendency to immediately view the "resistance" as a client characteristic or "problem," and instead of directly challenging the client's perspective at the heart of the behavior in question. In essence, this requires the practitioners to take a step back in their change efforts to avoid developing an adversarial relationship. Rather, the sport psychologist is advised to help the clients see the incongruity between their stated values or goals and the actions that they are choosing. This can actually be related to off-field training (e.g., wanting to be a well-conditioned athlete vs. skipping training days), utilization of pre-competitive routines (e.g., inconsistent utilization), or a myriad of other suggested beneficial behaviors that the client is or is not engaging in. When clients reach the point at which they can recognize that their current behavioral choices are inconsistent with whom they would like to be (i.e., their values) and how they would need to function in order to reach their stated goals, cognitive dissonance can occur. *Cognitive dissonance* is discomfort associated with an observed inconsistency between one's attitudes and behaviors (Festinger, 1957), which precisely promotes an individual's readiness to change. However, it is important to note that resistance is most often more than a single reaction to the intervention efforts of the practitioner, but rather, is commonly a reflection of a fundamental issue relating to the professional relationship/alliance between the sport psychologist and the client.

Ruptures of the professional relationship

It is not uncommon for professional relationships to involve a moment in which the bond between the practitioner and client is challenged. When this happens, the relationship or alliance is said to experience a "rupture" (Safran & Muran, 2003). A *rupture* of the professional relationship refers to an impairment of the quality of the alliance between the practitioner and client. Relationship ruptures can vary in presentation. In the extreme, clients may become overtly negative to the practitioners' efforts or even discontinue working together. In more minor (and somewhat more common) situations, minor changes in the quality of the relationship may occur. In any event, these ruptures present as resistance in one form or another. Over the last several decades, substantial evidence has shown the importance of relationship factors in psychological interventions (Norcross, 2002). This has led some to conclude that the practitioners' techniques are less important than the relationship aspects of their work (Wampold, 2001). However, as Barlow and colleagues have suggested (Barlow, Bullis, Comer, & Ametaj, 2013), technical and relationship factors in psychological interventions are interdependent and thus inseparable aspects of the same process.

Let's look at a number of different themes that are commonplace indicators of relationship ruptures, while maintaining the understanding that relationship ruptures are best understood as being a *bidirectional* process between the sport psychologist and the client.

Goal rejection

A very common indicator of a relationship rupture involves the client suddenly questioning or rejecting the goals or tasks of the intervention. In a very real sense, the strength of a professional relationship can be best defined by the degree of agreement between the sport psychologist and client about goals and tasks related to the intervention – in essence, the what, when, how, and why of the intervention. When intervention goals become an issue, behavior that the practitioner may define as the "resistance" is the most likely manifestation. Once again, it should be stressed that resistant behavior in response to misalignment of goals may be seen among both individual and organizational clients. It typically reflects a loss of belief in the practitioner (perhaps transient, perhaps permanent), possibly due to (a) a lack of empathic understanding of what the client needs, and instead forcing one's own agenda, or (b) an overly eager attitude toward intervention, when readiness for change has not been considered or when the foundational readiness-for-change stages have not been met.

Lack of compliance

A lack of client compliance is also a very common indicator of possible ruptures in the professional relationship. In such situations, rather than overtly challenging or being negative to the practitioner, clients may manifest their resistance by simply not engaging in tasks and exercises asked of them. Surely everyone engaged in sport psychology has experienced this situation. The client simply does not engage in the between-session/meeting exercises and activities that are expected as part of the intervention. This is the place where the novice practitioner will tend to dismiss the lack of client engagement as "resistance" and ascribe the fault squarely with the client. I suggest, however, that such noncompliant forms of "resistance" are very likely reflective of a rupture in the professional relationship. Namely, there is a lack of attunement to readiness for change, the politics of change, or simply the client's understanding of and time to engage in the intervention suggested by the practitioner.

In-session avoidance

Relationship ruptures will often manifest as resistance in the form of in-session avoidance. In such circumstances, the client may be essentially unresponsive to the sport psychologist's efforts by changing topics frequently, agreeing too readily and vehemently, arriving late and/ or cancelling/failing to show up for established appointments, etc. Another frequently seen form of resistance, these in-session avoidant behaviors very often reflect a client's anxiety or discomfort with the techniques being suggested and/or the purpose/goals of the intervention. The practitioner therefore cannot simply blast through these relational issues. Rather, one must reflect the resistance and then patiently but directly confront the underlying issue(s).

Sudden and often extreme changes in attitude and openness

This is an indicator of a relationship rupture that manifests itself in the extreme. In such cases, the practitioner is confronted with an apparent "day and night" change in the client's attitude and behavior, seemingly (and actually at times) overnight. This usually leaves the practitioner perplexed and frustrated. In fact, this particular change in interpersonal behavior is usually the result of outside forces bearing down on the athlete or organization, perhaps from agents, media, family, friends, teammates, and/or staff. There are a myriad of reasons that could lead to this outside influence, and these situations can be extreme, confusing, quite uncomfortable, and extremely difficult to alter. Once again, the practitioner is encouraged to confront this apparent change, rather than observe and hope for the best. Only by understanding the causes of the apparent change in attitude and behavior can the practitioner address misconceptions, allay fears, and/or engage in multiparty communications (e.g., meetings with player and agent together), which are most often at the heart of these dramatic changes.

Of course, this discussion still leaves us with a nagging question that cuts across themes of resistance and alliance ruptures. That is, what can the practitioner *do* to alleviate or overcome these relationship ruptures and subsequent resistance? The next section of this chapter reviews some basic foundational rules to consider when attempting to manage and repair relationship ruptures and associated resistant behavior with athletes, and follows with a parallel discussion of these issues with organizational stakeholders.

Resolving resistance and relationship ruptures with athletes

Resolving acute or chronic resistance among stakeholders can be a challenging process, and it necessitates patient diligence and a commitment to self- and other-awareness. Attending to ruptures in the professional alliance, accepting one's own role in cultivating resistance, empathizing with the athlete's experience, and dispassionately noting incongruity between the client's stated goals/values and actual behavior are all key tasks that contribute to the successful resolution of resistance behavior, and that help forge the path to a sound working alliance and intervention compliance.

Attending to ruptures in the alliance

When it comes to ruptures in the professional alliance and resistant behavior, speed of attention is of the essence. This is extremely important in that the process of resolving the issues cannot possibly begin until the problem has been noted and discussed. The practitioner must be able to recognize the pattern of behavior indicative of relationship ruptures and resistant behavior and determine the likely causes. While this first step is not a solution in and of itself, let's say that it is *necessary albeit not sufficient*. This may seem obvious and simple at first glance, yet the reality is that the practitioner in her/his zeal to intervene and be effective often closes her/his eyes and ears to the signs of resistant behavior and relationship ruptures. Mindful attention-to-the-moment and enhanced awareness to the process of the intervention, and not simply the techniques and strategies of the intervention, is essential.

Accepting responsibility

After, and assuming that, resistance and relationship ruptures have been noted, the next step is for practitioners to clarify (in their own mind and in their own words to the client) that they do not maintain the static and narrow view that this is a client-only issue. Practitioners must engage in honest self-reflection and acknowledge their roles in the formation of resistance and in any strains to the working alliance. Only through this mutual collaborative process can the relational bond be reforged, and the intervention process itself can move forward. By considering the aforementioned themes and genuinely reflecting on our overt and covert contribution to the present dilemma, we can begin the process of renewing trust in the relationship and in the interventions we seek to employ.

Empathizing with the athlete's experience

Following the acknowledgement of any possible contribution to the relationship rupture, it is important for the sport psychologist to communicate an empathic understanding of how the client experiences their work together. It is not enough to simply say, "Let's start over." The practitioner should convey a true understanding of how their relationship and the attempted intervention efforts have impacted the client. Only from seeing the client's perspective, including experiencing the professional relationship and all efforts associated with that relationship from the client's perspective, can the practitioner rebuild the stability of the professional enterprise and reestablish the collaborative working alliance necessary for successful psychosocial intervention in its variety of forms.

Willingness to dispassionately note incongruity between stated goals/ values and actual behavior

Once any relationship rupture has been resolved using the steps outlined above, practitioners will then have the opportunity to recalibrate their work with the client by pointing out how the resistant behavior (in its varied forms) is fundamentally inconsistent with the client's previously acknowledged goals and values. This is done to refocus clients on the agenda that they have adopted and away from the "resistant" behavior. In essence, this serves as a reminder of the purpose of their work together, provides an opportunity for recommitment, and reiterates what the end product of intervention efforts can hopefully be. For example, an athlete who is working on improving communication with teammates and staff will perhaps be reminded that the work together is not about the practitioner or even about techniques, but rather, is about the issues that the athlete identified as goals/values to strive toward.

Now that we have discussed resistance as a concept, and described the association between the professional relationship and resistant behavior in our work with individual athletes (although some of the aforementioned issues and concepts are relevant to team/organizational clients, as well), it is important to consider some of the most likely sources of resistance and general strategies for minimizing that resistance in the context of the organizations with whom we work.

Resolving resistance with organizational stakeholders

The first and most pernicious issue that easily and quickly creates organizational resistance is an inaccurate perception of the skills, abilities, and purpose of the practitioner. It is natural in the development of a working professional relationship between an individual and organization that preconceived expectations exist, both spoken and unspoken. The spoken expectations often include hours/frequency of work, intended length of professional work, compensation, and other important details that outline responsibilities and commitments made by both parties. Those spoken, and in most cases written (contract), expectations will often, but not always, include specific services to be provided. Quite frequently, those services are discussed and agreed upon in the most basic/general of ways, such as "psychological services," "performance enhancement services," etc. The potential problem with this approach is that there is often an incorrect assumption that both parties fully understand the briefly described professional services. Yet in fact, each party may have very different ideas about what constitutes "psychological services," "performance enhancement," "mental skills," etc. Team ownership, management, staff, and athletes often know very little about the nuances and distinctions among professional services provided by various types of sport psychologists. So, organizational staff may assume that working with players who are experiencing the emotional upheaval that frequently follows divorce is within the purview of the individual they hired for "performance enhancement," although the informed and ethically sound practitioner will understand that more counseling/clinically related concerns necessitate interventions that do not meet the spirit of the too-brief contract description, and the sport psychologist may not be trained for the provision of such services (Gardner & Moore, 2006). Likewise, an organization may have no desire for athletes' personal problems to be discussed, and may instead solely desire brief class-like lectures pertaining to mental training. In either case, the initial agreement between the sport practitioner and the organization must truly reflect and clarify expectations. This helps ward off problems both from the onset and in cases in which professional expectations shift over time due to emerging and unanticipated situations.

For instance, a number of years ago, a professional sport organization hired a mental skills coach to provide performance enhancement–related interventions, yet when a team crisis later emerged unexpectedly, clinical services were immediately needed. As reports go, the team simply did not understand these professional nuances, and in fact were quite angry when they learned that an additional psychologist would need to be brought on board (who at that point had no involvement with the team) to help address the significant and time-sensitive issues. Describing this previous experience to me, the team's general manager later stated, "How was I supposed to know there were different *types* of sport psychologists?"

The above example, and the issue in general, reflects a major problem that was actually exceptionally easy to prevent simply by allocating the time and energy to explicitly clarifying roles, responsibilities, and services both within and outside of one's training/education. Indeed, there is little that can injure a professional relationship, create resistance, and prevent the overcoming of resistance from an organizational perspective more than unmet (and usually unspoken) expectations. And, explicitly clarifying expectations is not simply related to types of service provision – falling short on time commitments reflects another major obstacle. While time and compensation are typically outlined, it is not uncommon for teams to have certain time periods in which their current needs are far beyond what was agreed upon. Such is the nature of the sport milieu! The unspoken expectation is that the sport psychologist will demonstrate her/his commitment to the organization even if it is above and beyond what may have previously been discussed. An inability or refusal to respond in these circumstances is likely to seem disloyal, unprofessional, and/or uncommitted. The end result? Well, such a situation is likely to create a circumstance that makes it difficult for the practitioner to work in the short term, and may call for an end to the professional partnership with the team/organization in the long term.

A second problem that can lead to organizational resistance occurs when the practitioner oversteps her/his role and/or boundaries. This obstacle may be particularly likely to occur (although it is certainly not limited to) during those times in which practitioners are feeling confident and comfortable with their role, and thus attempt to extend their work, or express their thoughts/ideas, in contexts/to people where/to whom it does not belong based on competence, organizational expectations, or inter-professional boundaries. Examples of this are voluminous, but for the sake of this chapter, consider the practitioner who provides opinions to an athlete regarding game tactics, even to the point of it being integrated into her/his performance efforts. While this might in rare cases be acceptable in very specific circumstances, and if it occurs with the consent of and very close consultation with the coaching staff, such an effort at extension of one's role could create massive resistance within the organization and may lead to rapid termination. As another (albeit extreme) example, consider the actual story of a practitioner who crossed appropriate boundaries by *asking* to wear a full team uniform and engage in pre-game practice. While extreme examples are plentiful, a final extreme example would be a practitioner who begins expressing opinions/ideas to the local media, which can inadvertently be construed as representative statements of the team in general or even specific team personnel (this latter issue will be discussed in greater detail in the coming pages).

In less extreme examples, providing advice related to injuries and taking an overtly supportive position (to a player) regarding playing time complaints are recipes for internal conflict and organizational resistance. In such cases, once such practitioner-induced resistance occurs, it is difficult, or in some cases impossible, to overcome. If the practitioner survives the misstep, overcoming the resistance and relationship rupture that often follows requires patience and persistence. The practitioner must patiently allow the alliance to be repaired, first by being aware and accepting responsibility (as noted earlier in the chapter), but also by patiently allowing time and ongoing professional behavior to frame the practitioner apart from the previous unfortunate action. Of course, self-induced obstacles such as these are never comfortable. Yet, the practitioner must persist in these efforts despite one's own anxiety and resist efforts toward a quick fix, as no such quick repair is likely. The take-home message here is to act in a manner that will avoid such unnecessary resistance, for the sake of the organization, its athletes, and oneself, as repair (if possible) is a slow, challenging, and emotionally taxing endeavor.

Aside from the aforementioned self-induced issues, in my experience, one of the greatest sources of organizational resistance can be found within the idiosyncratic internal dynamics of any given team/organization. Probably the most frequent internal dynamic that is likely to cause resistance, and that the practitioner is very likely to face, is the natural tension between many coaches and senior administrators, whether that be a general manager (professional team), athletic director (collegiate team), or some version of these titles. While a discussion of the natural push–pull of these two positions is well beyond the scope of this chapter, simply put, coaches' thought processes mostly reside (appropriately) at the nexus between the last game and the next game – that is, a short-term, immediate focus on wins and losses. On the contrary, the senior administrator must take a broader and more long-term view of the team/organization. As someone who has lived through more than his share of the trials and tribulations of this internal dynamic, I can assuredly say that it can be highly stressful for everyone involved. In most cases, the senior administrator controls the purse strings and thus broad access, and the coach runs the day-to-day functioning of the team and thus controls the practitioner's functional access to team personnel. Typically, the practitioner is hired by one or the other, and thus will inevitably be seen as that person's "guy" (a euphemism that transcends gender). Suspicion and thus resistance by the other party is often inevitable. The practitioner must be open, honest, ethical, and above all professional in her/his work to survive and thrive in such circumstances. One must have a degree of empathy and understanding for each, and must be fully professional in not only what they do, but in how they do it, in order to achieve success. Ultimately, overcoming this rather pernicious resistance requires that, in time, the practitioner is seen as being there first and foremost for the athletes and team, regardless of who brought her/him into the organization. Now, this does not mean that this particular internal dynamic will not be a source of ongoing stress, as it certainly may; and it is a type of stress that can be expected to have a naturally occurring ebb and flow. But, if the practitioner can remain focused on task, and not get pulled into the cauldron of the dynamic between these individuals (or staffs), especially during times of team stress (most often centered around losing), then they can overcome resistance and even foster a collaborative relationship that can last for many years.

Yet, dynamics between senior administrators and coaches are not the only internal dynamics to consider. There are similar internal dynamics within professional relationships that serve as resistance pathways: coach and conditioning staff; conditioning staff and medical staff; medical staff and coach, to name but a few. As for the previous dynamic, the sport practitioner must maintain a diligent focus on the professional tasks for which one was employed, remain out of the interpersonal struggles of organizational staff, and therefore gain a reputation as a professional and collaborative partner (not triangulator) among athletic colleagues and participants. While this may not necessarily *avoid* resistance, which is often a natural component of professional relationships, it will allow the athlete or organizational client and the persistent practitioner to more quickly overcome any resistance and thrive in what are often difficult situations.

Finally, I would like to briefly touch on the topic of professional ethics and its relationship to resistance, both from an individual and organizational perspective. By nature of the profession, sport psychologists will, on a regular basis, be faced with issues of boundaries and professional behavior. Sport psychology interventions are likely to be performed both in formal and informal settings (e.g., sidelines, locker rooms, training rooms), and invitations to team events and holiday parties will likely be forthcoming. The manner in which one fulfills professional obligations and activities needs to be carefully thought out, as do boundary issues associated with details such as accompanying teams on road trips, eating at team meals, and where to sit on charter plane flights and bus trips (Moore, 2003). The ability to interact as part of the team, while maintaining professional boundaries, requires the utmost contemplative professionalism, as casual behavior that accompanies the sport milieu can lead to a slippery slope of unprofessional behavior.

Indeed, in such an atypical field, it is far too easy for unprofessional behaviors to manifest; in fact, even professional behaviors can be taken out of context in an environment flooded with fans, professional competitors, and media! For instance, the notoriety that sport psychologists may achieve by their work with sport organizations, especially professional, Olympic, and other high-profile sports, can bring about tricky professional situations that can result in client resistance and compromise professional relationships. Practitioners working with high-profile athletes or teams may be sought out for newspaper, magazine, and television interviews regarding issues that have relevance to sport psychology. Yet, even if the news piece has nothing to do with the athlete(s) or team(s) with whom the practitioner is working, the potential for obstacles is great, for two main reasons (as I see it). First, as previously noted, athletes/teams are frequently a bit cynical and suspicious of "strangers" in their midst, which is what sport psychologists often are, regardless of how long they are employed. As such, athletes and organizations may be hypersensitive to the motivations of even the most well-meaning sport psychologists. Is the sport psychologist really just a fan who happens to also be a professional? Is the sport psychologist looking to attach themselves in some way to the athlete or the team in order to get something, such as tickets, team merchandise, etc.? Is the sport psychologist seeking personal fame? The aforementioned public interview and even a casual conversation with an interested stranger can be misconstrued, even if one's commentary is not directly about the athlete or team with whom the practitioner works. The misconstrual, as one can imagine, has the very real potential to trigger significant problems in the professional relationship, and can lead to overt and covert resistance.

Second, practitioners should be wary of attempting to seem the expert on topics they know little about, and should remember that anything they say in public will be assumed by the public to be in reference to one's client. Thus, the best-case scenario, albeit challenging, would be for us to refrain from speaking about other athletes or teams (public: "Might this mean the team is about to make a *trade*?") and news of the day as it relates to sport. To expand upon this latter point, consider this example: The sport psychologist is asked by the media to comment generally on intimate partner violence (IPV) across sport, yet due to the practitioner's affiliation with an organization, connect-the-dot conspiracy theorists may assume that she/he is actually alluding to a domestic violence act committed by an athlete on the team with which she/he works. In fact, since IPV is a specialty of mine, actually, might I right now be sending *you* a message? (Of course, I'm laughing as I write this sentence, but you see what I mean!) It's a battle that honestly cannot be won, and therefore, it is best to remain expertly mindful of such fascinating dynamics and potential pitfalls. While surely not altogether avoidable, careful attention to such issues will help preserve professional relationships and avoid/minimize a myriad of resistant behaviors that can emerge if these instances are handled poorly or thoughtlessly. In the end, *competence*, not publicity or notoriety, will result in the longest tenured sport psychologists.

Conclusion

As a dynamic interpersonal interaction, resistance is, and will remain, an obstacle to the excellent services that sport psychologists provide. Whether its emergence is gradual or immediate, and whether its presence is overt or covert, it reflects some basic truths: relationships are often hard, and change is often difficult. The ability to be mindful of one's own contribution to the professional relationship and to accept client behavior as being in part dependent on the context of that relationship is an important, yet often under-discussed, skill for the sport psychology practitioner. As the manner in which resistance is resolved widely determines the success of the sport psychologist's intervention efforts, this chief construct necessitates careful consideration and thoughtful decision making.

References

Barlow, D. H., Bullis, J. R., Comer, J. S., & Ametaj, A. A. (2013). Evidence based psychological treatments: An update and a way forward. *Annual Review of Clinical Psychology, 9*, 1–27.

Beutler, L. E., Moleiro, C. M., & Talebi, H. (2002). Resistance. In J. C. Norcross (Ed.), *Psychotherapy relationships that work: Therapist contributions and responsiveness to patient needs* (pp. 129–144). New York: Oxford University Press.

Birrer, D., & Morgan, G. (2010). Psychological skills training as a way to enhance an athlete's performance in high-intensity sports. *Scandinavian Journal of Medicine & Science in Sports, 20*, 78–87.

Festinger, L. (1957). *A theory of cognitive dissonance.* Stanford, CA: Stanford University Press.

Gardner, F. L., & Moore, Z. E. (2006). *Clinical sport psychology.* Champaign, IL: Human Kinetics.

McCarthy, P., Wilson, M., Keegan, R., & Smith, D. (2012). Three myths about applied consultancy work. *Sport & Exercise Psychology Review, 8*, 3–16.

Moore, Z. E. (2003). Ethical dilemmas in sport psychology: Discussion and recommendations or practice. *Professional Psychology: Research and Practice, 34*, 601–610.

Norcross, J. C., & Hill, C. E. (2002). Therapists' contributions and responsiveness to patients. In J. C. Norcross (Ed.), *Psychotherapy relationships that work* (pp. 3–16). New York: Oxford University Press.

Prochaska, J. O., DiClemente, C. C., & Norcross, J. C. (1992). The transtheoretical approach. In J. C. Norcross & M. R. Goldfried (Eds.), *Handbook of psychotherapy integration* (pp. 300–334). New York: Basic Books.

Safran, J. D., & Muran, J. C. (2003). *Negotiating the therapeutic alliance: A relational treatment guide.* New York: Guilford Press.

Wampold, B. E. (2001). Contextualizing psychotherapy as a healing practice: Culture, history, and methods. *Applied & Preventive Psychology, 10*, 69–86.

5

WORKING WITH TRANSNATIONAL PROFESSIONAL ATHLETES

Zella E. Moore

By the time athletes reach the professional level of sport participation, they have experienced just about everything – rabid fans, intense scheduling demands, tremendous physical challenges, contract disputes, and draft/selection anxieties, to name but a few. Yet, for most professional athletes, there are at least a few calming truths. Most athletes largely train and perform where their own language dominates and in a culture they generally understand. But what about the thousands of professional athletes worldwide whose talent and determination take them to unfamiliar lands? This chapter is dedicated to precisely those issues – namely, performance and personal challenges that transnational professional athletes face, and how sport psychologists can help such athletes develop and maintain enjoyment and success in the face of such challenges.

It's not uncommon to overhear a fan exclaim, "What a life . . . these athletes just have to show up and play a *game*!" Yet by its very nature, professional sports is an extremely complex and highly stressful working environment. Thus, before one can understand the challenges that transnational athletes face in professional sports, some of the common on- and off-field challenges faced by elite athletes in general, including those from dominant cultural groups, should be understood in order to establish an appropriate context.

From the obvious overt competition with an opponent to more covert and ongoing competition with teammates (albeit at times unspoken to maintain the façade of a "team first" attitude, for whom it applies), justification for playing time, preferred roles and responsibilities, and notable contracts that are commensurate with those opportunities represent very real and often underappreciated chronic stressors. Of course, most elite athletes are motivated to "be the best they can be." Yet the combination of intrinsic motivation and the allure of a big contract with a lengthy term, increased status, and tangible (e.g., product endorsements) and less tangible (e.g., fame, adoration) recognition, can easily contribute to a clouded mind – one that motivates athletes to perform their best while also navigating the inevitable intra-team politics between the coach and athlete, junior and senior players, starters and reserves, administration and athlete, administration and agent, etc. It is unusual to meet an athlete who does not believe, "If only I had the chance to . . . I would produce more," and with that desire often comes the perhaps unspoken assumption that such changes would increase the athlete's contract/endorsement value.

While the aforementioned struggles are inherent in the professional sports milieu, such challenges can be even more complicated for the transnational athlete. As Berry (1997) has posited, athletes who are born in countries other than where they presently live, train, and perform often express that *acculturative stress* is a distinct component of their sport experience. Transnational athletes are indeed outsiders in the technical sense, and in many cases are considered to be outsiders in a figurative sense as well, especially if participating in a Eurocentric sport culture (Parham, 2005, 2008) or for a team that is monocultural at its foundations (Ryba & Wright, 2005). Brought onto teams/organizations from distant lands, these individuals frequently harbor divergent expectations regarding intra-team roles, competition, and coach relationships. Furthermore, as these athletes often represent a small percentage of the team/organization, they may be alone or among a small number of compatriots in terms of language, traditions, customs, and even style of play (Schinke & Moore, 2011). Yet, the playing surface shows no sympathy for the struggles that accompany these differences, as transnational athletes must not only consistently perform to a level commensurate with their salary and professional status, but must simultaneously navigate significant cultural challenges on and off the field. Smooth transitions and seamless integration are therefore difficult, at best.

Interestingly, the discussion of cultural factors within sport psychology remains in its infancy, as it has only been a bit over 10 years since notables such as Wrisberg, Fisher, and Wright began the long-overdue consideration of the complexities surrounding the sport-culture intersection (see Ryba & Wright, 2005; see also Schinke, Hanrahan, & Catina, 2009). Their work paved the way for this immensely valuable dialogue, and soon other notable researchers and practitioners such as Robert Schinke and Stephanie Hanrahan furthered the discussion (see Schinke & Hanrahan, 2008), stressing to the field that cultural competence within sport psychology practice is not a choice; it is a requirement. Yet, before embarking upon a discussion of how sport psychologists can positively impact the lives of transnational athletes (e.g., adjustment, acculturation, performance, well-being), let's consider this brief case vignette highlighting a few of the aforementioned struggles:

An Eastern European ice hockey player has signed a contract to play in the National Hockey League (NHL). Physical relocation has actually been a smooth process, and although he misses his fiancé, family, and friends (all of whom continue to reside in his home country), he is nonetheless feeling energized to start workouts, attend training camp, and begin the new season. In a very short period of time, the season is upon him, and he hits the ice in his first NHL game. His excitement is palpable, as he's waited for this moment for most of his life! Yet over the course of a few weeks, as he desensitizes to his initial emotional and physiological arousal associated with this grand achievement, he begins to notice a feeling of disconnect, both professionally and personally. He has struggled to adjust to the smaller ice surface and somewhat different rules used in North American hockey, and he has physically struggled to keep up with the faster pace of the game and a more physical style of play. While he is convinced that these skills-based adjustments will simply take a little time and concerted effort, he finds it difficult to focus on on-ice sport adjustment due to a myriad of off-ice obstacles. Specifically, he is *physically fatigued* due to differences in training expectations (weight training during season vs. off season only), feels *emotionally depleted* from his efforts at establishing new interpersonal relationships and gaining the respect and friendship of staff and teammates (many of whom correctly view the transnational athlete as competition for playing time), and feels *mentally drained* because all communication efforts are compromised by a significant language barrier.

Of course, everyone in the general population faces transitions that require adjustment. Whether transitioning from the adolescent years to adult life, experiencing relationship termination, tackling a new job or job loss, or adapting to parenthood, adjustment is a natural process that is an inevitable and fluctuating part of human existence. Yet, when most of us face a new or altered situation that requires adjustment, we typically gain empathy, support, and understanding from others, because those around us face similar life situations. Professional sport culture is rarely that understanding – teams, endorsers, and fans have a lower tolerance for athletes' transitions and associated struggles. Although the adjustment process, in both time and intensity, may be well beyond the normative adjustment experience, there is often little tolerance for an adjustment period in a professional athlete's expected level of performance. Transnational athletes may be venturing into an unknown land with a different dominant language and a myriad of cultural differences, yet the whirlwind of on-field and off-field adjustments are expected to remain behind closed doors while the athlete immediately performs at the most elite level, against some of the best athletes in the world in the respective sport. Added to the above struggles are the performance expectations that transnational players have placed upon them by their parent organizations. Are they expected to be the star from day one? Are they seen as being in a support role to the better/more dominant athletes on the team? Is that what the athlete expected when signing her/his contract to come and play? Is she/he familiar and comfortable with that role?

Additionally, transnational players' relationships with teammates, coaches, trainers, and other team personnel are often challenging and underappreciated as a source of stress. First, for many, would be a language barrier. It is difficult to participate in day-to-day banter, understand common colloquialisms used by teammates and staff (which can also vary by sport), and accurately understand tactical/strategic/training instructions without a good support system in place. In some cases, teams have multiple transnational team members who share the same or very similar language/nationality, yet most teams do not. The latter situation is particularly complicated and can be fraught with challenges. Further, from a cultural perspective, the role/position of coach can differ across nationalities. For example, one culture may value the formation of the coach–athlete bond. In such cases, the coach may serve a formative leadership role, while also interacting with players in a somewhat social and informal manner. Another culture, however, may promote a strict authoritarian coaching role in which bidirectional communication is less likely to occur. Venturing into a different cultural context, the transnational player may seem guarded and quiet, which can be misperceived as distant, unemotional, or even disengaged. The possibility of misunderstanding, discord, and further stress is therefore quite high, with its obvious subsequent impact on roles, responsibilities, and ultimately, performance. Relationships with teammates can reflect similar challenges, especially if the dominant or team culture is not one of support, mutual encouragement, and acceptance. It is therefore easy to surmise how a transnational athlete may come to feel alone and without valued support (and thus possibly struggle with some level of depressivity) in an environment that is in many ways harsh and unforgiving due to the intense spotlight and ongoing pressure to perform optimally. But what of the non-sport pressures experienced by professional athletes? How does one maintain friendships and a semblance of a normal life (e.g., socializing with friends) while being easily recognized and having to always consider nutrition, sleep, and energy management? How does one manage a family/personal life with frequent travel? How does one balance a need to rest when not playing/practicing and the realities of family time? How does one develop a pregame routine to help maintain focus, while dealing with ever-present life issues such as laundry that needs cleaning and a car that needs repairs? Such challenges are difficult enough for the most committed and responsible professional athlete, but they can be additionally taxing for the transnational athlete in a foreign land, perhaps with a non-native language, a (very often) vastly different culture and lifestyle, and separated from most (if not all) family/friends and trusted support systems.

With an appreciation for the unique demands of the transnational athlete in mind, the remainder of this chapter adds to this basic context by considering (a) what sport psychologists can do to be in a position to help transnational athletes; (b) how sport psychologists can assist transnational athletes with both on- and off-field challenges and demands; and (c) what challenges and obstacles sport psychologists face in their efforts to get buy-in from transnational athletes.

Getting in: how to be in a position to help the transnational athlete

Because professional sports are massive international businesses in which extremely highly paid athletes are considered substantial assets to be carefully selected, developed, and protected by their parent organization (Gardner, 2001), over the last several decades sport psychologists have become increasingly called upon by professional sport organizations to aid in talent selection, development, and maintenance. Indeed, sport psychologists engage in a wide range of psychological services with elite organizations, including such diverse activities as performance enhancement intervention/consultation, clinical/counseling interventions for the promotion of overall well-being and the remediation of psychological distress and dysfunction, psychological testing as part of the player selection process, and neuropsychological consultation (Gardner, 2001; Gardner & Moore, 2006). In fact, a quick perusal of this text demonstrates the myriad of services and resources that sport psychologists can provide at various levels of sport participation.

To be honest, in the best of situations, the world of professional sports is a closed and often paranoid system (Gardner, 1995). Individuals wishing to become part of the closed system of professional sports will usually be heavily scrutinized and evaluated by team personnel and athletes alike, and ultimately they are judged as either being an "insider" or an "outsider." While those judged to be outsiders can at times gain entrance, they typically remain on the periphery of influence and decision making, and often maintain short tenure within an organization. Clearly, earning trust and becoming accepted as a valued member of the organization (both from the perspective of team personnel and athletes) are remarkable challenges, in and of themselves. As such, before being of any real service to transnational athletes, they will likely need to view the sport psychologist as a valuable and trusted member of the organization, one that is a regular and visible part of the team fabric. Gaining visibility and the trust of transnational athletes can be particularly challenging, as such athletes may not be quick to ask for assistance for fear of perceived weakness, may not understand the reporting structure, may struggle with the language, may not actually know what services are available, etc. To make these connections and develop a professional relationship with transnational clientele, the sport psychologist will therefore need to be seen as accessible, trustworthy, valued by the organization, and (often) "vetted" by more tenured members of the team (to be discussed later).

Before venturing to help any professional athlete, including transnational athletes, the sport psychologist must be fully cognizant of her/his place in the organization's reporting structure. Namely, to whom does she/he directly report (Gardner, 2001)? Is it the coach, the general manager, the team physician, or even the owner of the organization? In cases in which the sport psychologist provides multiple services within an organization, the sport psychologist's direct report may even be determined by the specific role of the sport psychologist at any given moment. For example, when working on performance-based issues, the sport psychologist would likely maintain a direct reporting structure to the coach, whereas the reporting structure for clinical issues may very well include the coach, general manager, and team physician. Further, psychological testing as part of a pre-draft selection process would most certainly involve a direct report to the organization's general manager. Working with injured players, however, would likely necessitate a direct reporting line to the training staff and team physician. Understanding reporting structures is an important, ethically responsible, and often overlooked aspect of sport psychology practice that is not only critical from an organizational perspective but also has profound implications for one's work with athletes.

Yet, the establishment of trust is imperative if athletes are to seek out and adhere to sport psychology services, and in order for athletes to develop trust in the sport psychologist, athletes need to believe that the practitioner is invested in the athlete's best interest and does not simply serve as a vehicle for the coach and/or team management. One can anticipate that transnational athletes, who are far from home, may not have a mastery of the dominant language, have few trusted resources, may not even be familiar with the form of sport psychology services offered by the organization, and may be hesitant to seek out or engage in such services. It is completely understandable that individuals of nearly all kinds would be less trusting in unfamiliar lands and when the professional stakes are high – and thus, sport psychologists cannot simply appear to be another person of authority. Portrayal of one's genuine commitment to athletes' best interests, whether performance or personal, is a tremendous necessity.

Related to the issues of role and organizational fit is the degree to which the sport psychologist is embedded in the day-to-day workings of the team/organization. This is in part related to trust (as previously described), yet also relies upon the perception of accessibility. Athletes not only need to trust, but also need to see the sport psychologist as part of the fabric of the team/organization so that conversations with her/him are no different than those with any other staff member. Once again, this is particularly true for the transnational athlete who may not want to ask for or even receive unrequested help in a culturally/linguistically challenging milieu. Contact at a very kind and friendly level can promote comfort simply by frequency. In essence, what is being described is a desensitization process of sorts, as once the issues of trust and accessibility are achieved, the sport psychologist can be of help to the transnational athlete and add value to the organization.

Making a difference: how sport psychologists can assist transnational athletes

There are two broad ways in which sport psychologists can be of help to transnational athletes. The first is simply to be present, allow a relationship to grow, and increasingly (with a great deal of patience) allow oneself to become a naturally occurring support system. The sport psychologist should be someone who can, either via the athlete's minimal to moderate facility with the language or through an interpreter, be spoken to about off-field struggles, family concerns, and cultural challenges, and additionally who is a source of safe information about the realities of the league, team/administration culture, and/or the nuances of staff personalities and staff–player interactions (these efforts can help prevent or mitigate unnecessary misunderstandings). Of course, depending on the sport psychologist's skill sets, educational background, and role with the team, she/he could provide performance enhancement work, or more structured psychological services such as clinical/counseling interventions, as well (Gardner & Moore, 2006). Interestingly, regarding performance enhancement work and clinical services, much has been written in the sport psychology literature about varying techniques and theoretical models to use in one's work. In fact, as an aside, I am a major proponent of such dialogue, as I have long contended that we have an ethical and moral obligation to practice in the most empirically informed, evidence-based manner possible. Yet, little has been written about the importance of the professional relationship, and relationship skills in general, for effective professional practice (Andersen, 2005). Further, it is even more disappointing that in the decade since we have allotted more attention to aspects of culture, there appears to be a unidirectional imbalance in the discussion. Namely, variables of cultural importance are often talked about in reference to the transnational athlete, yet rarely do the cultural variables of the practitioner gain attention (McGannon & Johnson, 2009), with an exception. As Robert Schinke and I stated in our 2011 article, "it is not only a matter of understanding the other, but also one's self as a cultural being" (p. 284).

The importance of relational skills, both personal and professional, cannot be overstated when working with transnational athletes. The sport psychologists must overcome language barriers, cultural barriers, and mistrust that at times can border on (non-clinical) paranoia. The sport psychologist must navigate this with her/his relational skill set, first and foremost. How can she/he relate as one human being to another, with true empathy and concern for the struggles and challenges not only as a professional athlete but one that faces the disorienting reality of being in a relatively foreign land, with foreign customs, and a foreign language? For the transnational athlete, whether alone or with family, the sport psychologist can take a role of support personnel and environmental normalizer, someone who can explain, discuss, and problem solve in the safety of a professional human-to-human relationship. I have previously discussed the importance of understanding professional roles and boundaries in a sport setting, and that it is equally important for the sport psychologist to be able to carefully and honestly explain her/his role in the organization and describe the limits, if any, to confidentiality (which is expected of psychologists; Moore, 2003). Readers interested in a discussion of ethics in sport psychology are referred to Moore (2003) for a comprehensive discussion of this important topic.

In my own experience and the experiences of those with whom I have consulted, working with transnational athletes very often includes discussion of family issues such as the loneliness of a spouse, schooling of a child, and concern for ailing parents, and single athletes often report loneliness and the challenge of forging a "normal" life away from both home and the playing surface. Clearly, there is no manual on how to address these issues. Each transnational athlete will possess a unique circumstance based on age, nationality, level of language proficiency, family circumstance, location of team/organization, sport, and individual differences in personality and psychological stability. Indeed, the provision of a genuine and empathic ear, by a professional who can appreciate the cultural challenges while serving as a catalyst for effective problem solving, is essential.

Certainly, on-field challenges are no less important. Based on the sport psychologist's education and experience, her/his role with the team/organization, and direct expectations of the organization, assistance with performance-related issues may be requested or required. For example, let's consider a transnational football (American soccer) player who worries immensely about his young family, who still resides in his home country. His ruminative worry follows him both on the road and even during practice/training sessions, and that "cloudy head" negatively impacts both practice intensity and competitive performance. A gradual and targeted development of regularly practiced meditation can promote greater in-the-moment attention and can be helpful in breaking the rumination and distraction associated with worry. It will not change the stressful realities of a challenging home situation, but it can offer a successful way to maintain and promote more effective performance-related focus. If the sport psychologist has truly been accepted as part of the team fabric and culture, and if the sport psychologist has developed her/his role to the point that she/he is trusted and her/his opinion on issues is sought out and respected, he/she is then in a position to offer organizational suggestions to improve the transitions and ease the adjustments experienced by transnational athletes.

Once again, it is important to point out that there is no absolute or set way that the sport psychologist can or should assist the transnational athlete. Rather, the take-home message is that the sport psychologist working in professional sports that consist in part of transnational athletes must look beyond simple knowledge of and comfort with diversity, but rather, understand the necessity to engage, listen, support, and be prepared to offer direct service at the individual level or advocacy at the organizational level. This, of course, necessitates avoidance of the slick trap of *sensitive stereotyping* (see Andersen, 1993; Kontos, 2009; Terry, 2009), which can easily occur if the sport psychologist oversimplifies cultural nuance so much that information is condensed into gross overgeneralizations (Andersen, 1993; Schinke & Moore, 2011).

Challenges to getting buy-in from transnational athletes

The discussion in the previous sections indirectly highlights some of the challenges and obstacles that can arise when attempting to get buy-in from transnational athletes. Yet, sport psychologists working in professional sports must be aware of some more subtle pitfalls. The first of these involves the sport psychologist's role and entry point into the organization. For the most part, when a sport psychologist is brought into a professional sport organization by a coach, the primary, if not exclusive, goal is usually performance-related work. In such cases, a transnational athlete may be seen as just another athlete with whom to work, and the greatest challenges facing the sport psychologist are likely to be (a) the language barrier, (b) a very common lack of experience with sport psychology (or a different type of experience), and (c) the perception/belief/fear that the sport psychologist is simply an arm of the coaching staff. These three factors alone or in combination can result in guardedness (at best) and suspiciousness or outright rejection (at worst). Complicating this situation is the reality that head coaches have a very short lifespan in most professional sports, and thus, when the coach is the one bringing a sport psychologist onboard, the sport psychologist is also likely to have a very short tenure with the team. As a consequence, working relationships are more difficult to foster patiently.

When the sport psychologist is brought into the organization by upper management (e.g., general manager or team ownership), the sport psychologist is likely to have a somewhat longer tenure with the team (generally speaking), and thus, the practitioner has a greater opportunity to establish sound working relationships and enact positive change. However, depending on the culture and personal experience of the transnational athlete, suspicion and mistrust will commonly occur at the onset of the sport psychologist's work, typically until most or all of the team (especially transnational athletes) clearly understand the role and reporting structure of the sport psychologist and become comfortable with the independence of the practitioner (assuming this is the case). In a very real sense, buy-in challenges for transnational athletes are no different than with all other professional athletes, except that they may be magnified due to cultural and language-related issues.

One last point in this regard: just as an individual cannot force a friendship or romantic involvement, as relationship development involves a slow and gradual process that includes adequate personality matching of individuals, so too is the process of creating a sound working relationship with athletic clientele. Some clients will come around sooner than others, and some may never desire the establishment of a sound and trusting working relationship; nevertheless, patient persistence is essential. One has to patiently, and without pressure, persist in efforts at being present, interact in a civil and appropriate manner, allow the athlete to see the sport psychologist "in action," resist any temptation to force oneself on the team, and over time, become just another part of the team and overall organization. In particular, transnational athletes need to feel heard, respected, and valued, but not treated differently simply because the practitioner thinks she/he "should." Even then, for the professional relationship to take hold and lead to positive outcomes, there should be a good match between the sport psychologist's skills and the player's needs. For instance, if the sport psychologist is not trained in clinical or counseling psychology and the athlete requires guidance for a personal problem, a relational problem, a problem of her/his child's adjustment, etc., the skills–needs mismatch is likely to prevent the establishment of a sound working relationship (although the professional will hopefully recognize professional limits and serve as an appropriate referral source).

Expectations of staff

Expectations and opinions of the professional organization's staff (e.g., general manager, coach, owner, team physician) with regards to the sport psychologist's role with the team also necessitate great consideration. Expectations and opinions can range widely – based on cautious trust in a new sport psychologist due to a general manager's previous bad experience with a former sport psychologist; to an organization's owner who forces sport psychology on the coaching staff and athletes; to full buy-in and trust by all. As much as expectations and opinions can vary, so can one's role in an organization. While a sport psychologist's role can remain set and inflexible, roles can also shift to meet the demands of any particular player, team, year, team/athlete outcomes, personnel changes, etc. For this reason, sport psychologists who possess a variety of competencies and skill sets are particularly likely to thrive in professional sport organizations. For instance, a transnational athlete may have personal transitional/adjustment issues that impact overall well-being, while another transnational athlete may have difficulty adapting to changes in rules, playing surface, practice expectations, and travel requirements. Whichever competencies and skill sets one possesses, it is imperative to state them clearly and adhere to them firmly, while understanding that transnational athletes may require additional description and discussion of the sport psychologist's roles, especially if language or cultural differences are present.

It is also not uncommon to find that a coach is very concerned about whether the message that the sport psychologist is providing matches the message that the coach wants athletes to hear. At its foundation, I believe that this is usually a concern about giving up control. Nevertheless, it can surely be an obstacle, as such an attitude can impact what, when, where, and how the sport psychologist is allowed to operate. In such instances, the coaching staff may structure one's role so that the sport psychologist works with groups of athletes rather than with individual athletes, and as such, a particular downside is that transnational athletes may have a diminished opportunity to establish the kind of trusting professional relationship noted throughout this chapter.

Conversely, if the sport psychologist has greater autonomy and professional leeway (which is more common when one is brought into the organization by upper management), the challenge is to not be *perceived* as an arm of upper management, where conversations/issues are often not kept in confidence. Quite obviously, no matter what one says to the athlete about confidentiality, trust is slowly earned and can be quickly lost. If, for any reason, accurate or inaccurate, the *perception* of conversation with those in authority occurs, athletes tend to shut out the professional or even "test" them by making up an issue to see how far the information travels (I personally know that this has happened to sport psychologists on a few occasions, and it ended poorly in each case). This issue of perception is all the more critical in working with transnational athletes who, by reason of culture, language, or personal experience, may enter into interactions with the sport psychologist already fearing this to be the case.

Organizational structure and placement of the psychologist

Organizational fit involves more than simply who hired the sport psychologist and what function she/he serves; it also speaks to the influence that she/he may have in advocating for the athlete's specific needs. As previously mentioned, there are times when what the transnational athlete needs is not a direct service or intervention strategy, but rather, an advocate for the athlete's (and/or one's family's) specific needs. These needs may entail advocating for the organization to locate and utilize an appropriate translator, or locating someone who can assist the athlete and her/his family in finding appropriate neighborhoods in which to live, schools for their children, or even social contacts that might help aid the cultural transition into a new part of the world. This advocacy role cannot happen easily if the sport psychologist is marginalized by labels, whether they are "performance enhancement coach," "mental health worker," "shrink," or any other narrow box. I do not think the broader and more flexible service delivery model is the norm within North American sport psychology at this time, but as I have stated elsewhere (Gardner & Moore, 2006), a more inclusive and comprehensive practice model offers great value – and possibly the greatest value to transnational athletes. The absence of a more comprehensive model of sport psychology is more than likely going to present massive obstacles to effective work with transnational athletes.

Unsupportive outside forces and their staff

An obstacle to working with professional athletes as a whole, but particularly with transnational athletes, which is seldom discussed (if at all) in the sport psychology literature, is the unsupportive outside force. This term is used here specifically to refer to the player's agent and the agent's personnel. In the professional sports milieu, the agent is not only seen as the vehicle for the athletes to solidify the contract (i.e., compensation) that they see themselves as deserving, but also protects their interests in every way – whether how they are utilized by a team, how they are treated by coaches and support staff, how their off-ice activities are perceived, and often how their money is handled. It is therefore not surprising that agents are increasingly maintaining a team of financial, personal training, nutritional, and even sport psychology personnel to work for their client-athletes. As such, it is not uncommon for players to seek an okay from their agent before working with a team-hired psychologist. This sole step has an unspoken (or even possibly directly stated) message to the player, which is, "Be careful, she/he works for the team and not you." A full and comprehensive discussion of this issue, and the growing reality of its significant implications for the practice of sport psychology in professional sports, would require a chapter in and of itself, as it is a significant potential obstacle that sport psychologists (and teams) must navigate. Sport psychologists who are known in league-wide circles, agents who have better relationships with the team management, and players who are more independent minded are the variables that in some combination must be present for this obstacle to be bypassed.

Otherwise, when working with transnational athletes, this relationship can become quite problematic, in several ways. First, the agent is likely to have more influence and be more involved with the athlete. On one hand, this can be positive, in that the agent is likely to be more involved in some of the off-ice issues that have been noted throughout this chapter. Yet, on the other hand, the agent is more likely to be suspicious of the team's motivations and has greater influence to nix any work that the sport psychologist may want to offer the athlete. Second, and of importance, if the agent happens to be transnational (not at all uncommon), then the issues become more complex, and the suspicion and guardedness on the part of the agent is likely to be even greater. A general suggestion is that the sport psychologist working in this arena, especially those with limited experience in professional sports, always be mindful of this issue and never ignore its vast potential to be a significant challenge.

Lack of patient persistence

The final obstacle to gaining necessary buy-in from the transnational professional athlete is the sport psychologist her/himself. I, of course, begin this brief discussion with the assumption that respective practitioners will be appropriately trained and comfortable with dealing with diverse clientele. I am not referring here to the knowledge base, skill sets, and professional attitudes that emerge during graduate school training, but rather, I am referring to the understanding and implementation of "patient persistence." The patient persistence approach to one's work can in large part determine success or failure, and this is especially true when one's clientele includes transnational athletes. Sport psychologists working in professional sports need the *patience* to accept that trust is not instantaneous, overcoming language barriers can be a lengthy and taxing process, and adjusting to cultural dissimilarities does not occur instantly. Working with athletes who face these challenges requires time, concerted effort and engagement, and a willingness to allow the athlete to comfortably move toward accepting professional service. Being pushy, subtly pressuring the athlete, or being "sticky" in one's approach to the athlete will have deleterious effects on the establishment of the professional relationship, and can quickly end one's tenure with an organization. As is the case with any budding relationships, an excessive "in your face" approach is likely to push individuals away rather than draw them toward you. Sport psychologists are therefore encouraged to be mindful of this concept and to develop the capacity to comfortably make one's services known while patiently waiting for athletes to express interest.

Simultaneously, the sport psychologist needs to be *persistent*. By this statement, I certainly do not mean "pushy." Rather, I am speaking of maintaining an attitude of not giving up. Let's face it: professional athletes very rarely give up. Take Rich Peverly, a professional hockey player for the Dallas Stars in the NHL. Last season, Rich's heart *stopped* in the middle of a game, and he collapsed on the bench. The doctors and trainers were miraculously able to revive him in the locker room, and Rich insisted on being allowed to continue the game! (Of course, the medical staff declined his request.) Sport psychologists who make it into the world of professional sports, and certainly those who *stay there* for 10, 20, or 30 or more years, inevitably learned what it takes along the way: (a) persistence to become elite at what they do and striving to remain life-long learners within their profession, (b) not over-responding to a seeming lack of interest or the cold shoulder, and (c) persistence in their basic human civility (e.g., saying "hello" each day, genuinely asking "how are you?", stating "have a good game tonight," etc., are powerful beginnings of a personal connection). Stated succinctly, these three suggestions refer to how to get good and stay good, keep from over-responding to challenges, and maintain your kind and meaningful nature. When this genuine patient persistence is observed and experienced by athletes, the foundation of a working relationship can be established. When that new working relationship evolves into culturally informed practice that considers the manner in which cultural differences (of both the practitioner and athlete) influence our ability to disseminate interventions, and the transnational athlete's ability to receive those interventions, positive change can really take hold (Schinke & Moore, 2011).

Conclusions and recommendations

As Robert Schinke and I stated in our 2011 article, "Sport contexts are naturally occurring cultural contexts where athletes and psychologists bring their own unique and respective cultural identities to the table" (p. 291). If sport psychologists are appropriately mindful of the myriad of struggles that frequently accompany transnational athletes through their professional endeavors, maintain cultural competence, strive to foster sound working relationships, and implement the most evidence-based interventions (when applicable), then they can significantly help such athletes develop and maintain enjoyment and success in the face of their unique, multifaceted, and complicated performance and personal challenges.

References

Andersen, M. B. (1993). Questionable sensitivity: A comment on Lee and Rotella. *The Sport Psychologist*, 7, 1–3.

Andersen, M. B. (Ed.). (2005). *Practicing sport psychology*. Champaign, IL: Human Kinetics.

Berry, J. W. (1997). Immigration, acculturation, and adaptation. *Applied Psychology: An International Review*, 46, 5–68.

Gardner, F. L. (1995). The coach and team psychologist: An integrated organizational model. In S. Murphy (Ed.), *Sport psychology interventions* (pp. 147–175). Champaign, IL: Human Kinetics.

Gardner, F. L. (2001). Applied sport psychology in professional sports: The team psychologist. *Professional Psychology: Research and Practice, 32*, 34–39.

Gardner, F. L., & Moore, Z. E. (2006). *Clinical sport psychology*. Champaign, IL: Human Kinetics.

Kontos, A. P. (2009). Multicultural sport psychology in the United States. In R. J. Schinke & S. J. Hanrahan (Eds.), *Cultural sport psychology* (pp. 103–116). Champaign, IL: Human Kinetics.

McGannon, K. R., & Johnson, C. R. (2009). Strategies for reflective cultural sport psychology research. In R. J. Schinke & S. J. Hanrahan (Eds.), *Cultural sport psychology* (pp. 57–75). Champaign, IL: Human Kinetics.

Moore, Z. E. (2003). Ethical dilemmas in sport psychology: Discussion and recommendations or practice. *Professional Psychology: Research and Practice, 34*, 601–610.

Parham, W. D. (2005). Raising the bar: Developing an understanding of culturally, ethnically and racially diverse athletes. In M. Andersen (Ed.), *Practicing sport psychology* (pp. 211–219). Champaign, IL: Human Kinetics.

Parham, W. D. (2008). African-descendent student athletes: An invitation to respond to their invisibility. In E. Etzel, A. P. Ferrante & J. Pinkney (Eds.), *Counseling college student athletes: Issues and interventions* (pp. 215–238). Morgantown, WV: Fitness Information Technology.

Ryba, T. V., & Wright, H. K. (2005). From mental game to cultural praxis: A cultural studies model's implications for the future of sport psychology. *Quest, 57*, 192–212.

Schinke, R. J., & Hanrahan, S. J. (2008). *Cultural sport psychology*. Champagne, IL: Human Kinetics.

Schinke, R. J., Hanrahan, S. J., & Catina, P. (2009). Introduction to cultural sport psychology. In R. J. Schinke & S. J. Hanrahan (Eds.), *Cultural sport psychology* (pp. 1–12). Champaign, IL: Human Kinetics.

Schinke, R. J., & Moore, Z. E. (2011). Culturally informed sport psychology: Introduction to the special issue. *Journal of Clinical Sport Psychology, 5*, 283–294.

Terry, P. (2009). Strategies for reflective sport psychology practice. In R. J. Schinke & S. J. Hanrahan (Eds.), *Cultural sport psychology* (pp. 79–89). Champaign, IL: Human Kinetics.

6

ETHICAL PRACTICE CHALLENGES OF CONSULTATION IN PROFESSIONAL SPORT

Edward F. Etzel and Jack C. Watson II

Would you rather consult with a local Little League team or a Major League Baseball (MLB) franchise? Many students and professionals would likely gravitate toward the professional realm for a variety of reasons. Why not? This seems like the work of dreams. One would most likely be getting paid rather well, get to rub shoulders with high-profile people, maybe help some stars, perhaps be recognized for one's work, and network, which may lead to new consultations with high-level clients.

But wait a minute. Why consult with professionals? What *is* your purpose? Are you seeking personal dream work and the things you imagine come with that? Do you really know what you *might* be getting into? Are you truly well prepared and capable of doing this kind of work in the culture of professional sport – are you "fit" to practice competently (Hays & Brown, 2004)? As one might imagine, sport psychology consultation in the world of professional sport presents some unique, predictable, and unpredictable challenges to high-quality, ethical consultation. You need to be ready to practice in a way that is consistent with the principles and standards of ethical practice to benefit clients who may seek your help and to avoid doing inadvertent harm to them, and maybe yourself, your work, and the evolving profession of sport psychology.

Professional sport

Before going too far, it would seem timely to consider what professional sport seems to mean. We will be approaching this topic from the perspective of North American sport, which differs from sport in other parts of the world. Professional sport in the United States and Canada can be thought of as an extension of various forms of informal play and organized sports, which are characterized by rules and teams for the purpose of providing opportunities to be active and competitive, versus money, media, and power-driven corporate sport (Sage & Eitzen, 2013). Thus, the neighborhood sand lot baseball game would be seen as informal, Little League as organized, and MLB as corporate sports.

Professional or corporate sports include familiar media-friendly sports such as professional baseball (MLB), basketball (NBA), football (NFL), hockey (NHL), golf (PGA/LPGA), and soccer (MLS), as well as other sports such as NASCAR, boxing, track and field, horse racing, cycling, mixed martial arts (MMA), and the X-Games. Corporate sports also consist of minor league athletic activities (i.e., minor league baseball) and ostensibly amateur Olympic level athletics and intercollegiate athletics (i.e., National Collegiate Athletics Association [NCAA], Canadian Interuniversity Sport; Sage & Eitzen, 2013). For the purpose of this chapter, we will focus on corporate, professional sports, excluding the latter settings.

Values of pro sports and sport psychology

What is the raison d'etre of pro sports? In a nutshell, they exist to make money – as much as possible. As suggested by the term *corporate*, professional sport is an industry – typically *very* big business (e.g., Federation Internationale de Football [FIFA]; Major League Baseball [MLB]; National Football League [NFL]). Professional sport is commercialized, for-profit, and structured around attracting money from large audiences of fans who pay to watch, in person or via other media forms, and to attract financial support from sponsors who use games, matches, and other events as a platform for advertisement (Coakley, 2014). Those athletes and coaches who started playing for fun in the backyard, frozen-over pond, or sand lot become valued performers – commodities with talents, skills, and experiences that sell tickets. Success in professional sports may involve gamesmanship – practices that support rule bending to obtain competitive advantages, as well as disregarding the welfare and safety of players (Hansen & Savage, 2012). Together, the athletes, coaches, and other persons who may be clients of sport psychology professionals may get lost in a culture of winning (perhaps at all costs) for profit.

Central issues impacting ethical practice in professional sport

As the reader might imagine, several practice-related issues must be considered when entertaining ethically sound work in professional sport organizations and/or with individual professional athletes. Within this chapter, we will focus upon ethical issues within the practice of sport psychology within professional sport. We will differentiate ethical issues from moral issues, with moral issues being those issues that influence behavior in everyday social life (e.g., the golden rule), and ethics being the critical positions taken by professional organizations with regard to how professionals within that organization should behave during their professional lives (Hackfort & Tenenbaum, 2014). Given the space limitations of this chapter, we have chosen to discuss those ethical issues that appear most salient and common to the setting of professional sport. These issues are not necessarily novel. For example, consultants who work in the realm of intercollegiate athletics experience many of these same issues in that unique milieu (Etzel & Watson, 2007). The issues discussed below are: (1) sport psychology professional values and pro sport organizational values; (2) confidentiality; (3) competence; and (4) multiple role relationships.

Sport psychology professional values and pro sport organizational values

It is clear that the business-oriented values associated with professional sports do not always appear to be in line with the values associated with the profession of (applied) sport psychology. Even a brief look at the introductions to human service–oriented ethics codes of the

International Society of Sport Psychology (ISSP), the American Psychological Association (APA), the Canadian Psychological Association (CPA), the Association of Applied Sport Psychology (AASP), and other allied helping fields such as the American Counseling Association (ACA), reveals an apparent disconnect of stated professional principles from those of the professional sport industry (e.g., Canadian Psychological Association, 2013). Taken together, those helping profession ethical codes are based on values such as: (1) doing good work for others (beneficence); (2) doing no harm (non-maleficence); (3) respecting the autonomy and independence of clients; (4) following the Golden Rule (to be fair, objective, and respectful); (5) caring and compassion; and (6) responsibility and accountability (Koocher & Keith-Spiegal, 2009). In contrast, sport ethics codes, if articulated, tend to be quite general and not easily transferable to professional practice. For example, FIFA's ethics code preamble discusses the organization's responsivity to protect the image, integrity, and reputation of football worldwide and loyalty to FIFA and playing fairly (FIFA, 2012). Thus, a sport psychology practitioner's values and ethics may be challenged, because the values of professional cultures and those who hire practitioners differ.

Disconnects between organizational values and professional ethics

Professional sport teams are first and foremost, business enterprises. They place a primary emphasis upon the mission of winning (Gardner, 2001). With performance success, it becomes easier for them to be successful at selling tickets and merchandise, attracting sponsors, and generally making more money. As such, when they employ a sport psychology consultant to work with their organization, this is done with the aim of improving the performance quality and consistency of individual athletes, and hopefully the team, and is likely looked at from a direct cost-benefit perspective (Ravizza, 1990). However, there are times when the business-oriented values of the team conflict with the professional ethics of the consultant. In such situations, it is essential that professionals understand how to manage themselves and how to effectively deal with the conflicts that arise. Such strategies may include setting clear boundaries, protecting confidentiality, dealing with conflict, engaging in deliberation, developing personal trust and integrity, and effectively disseminating appropriate information that may be shared in an ethical manner (Eubank, Nesti, & Cruickshank, 2014). When these situations arise, it is important to have a sound appreciation for the ethical principles and standards within which we are expected to operate, to have a clear understanding of the goals and values of the team, and to work to maintain professional boundaries between the two (Gardner, 2001).

With the goals of making money and winning contests in mind, organizations may indicate that they have the best interests and welfare of their athletes in mind, but such statements may not always be demonstrated by their actions. Players can be exploited, overworked, traded, demoted, replaced, and have their personal lives infringed upon – whatever it takes for the team to be successful and profitable. Two prime examples of this behavior are playing injured athletes and forcing concussed athletes back to play prematurely. While these similar strategies may be used in other businesses, in pro sport, the product being sold is actually people and the entertainment value of their performances.

Contained in the Ethical Standards for the AASP, Principles D and E relate to "Respect for People's Rights and Dignity" and "Concern for Other's Welfare," respectively (AASP, n.d.). Based upon the values of these core principles, sport psychology professionals are encouraged to take steps to respect others, reduce the impact of bias or unfair and discriminatory treatment of people, and attempt to positively contribute to the welfare of those with whom they work. In other words, do good work for others and avoid harming them. While not black-and-white statements, these underlying principles exist to guide the work-related behaviors of sport psychology professionals.

Related ethics codes also contain specific ethical standards that speak to the challenges listed above. Ethical Standard 3.11 of the APA ethics code refers to the provision of services through organizations. According to this standard, practitioners should provide specific information to management and employees about the nature of the services to be provided, identify the intended recipient of services and who is perceived as the client, clarify relationship expectations with all involved, outline who will have access to information, and overview the limits to confidentiality (APA, 2010). Further, AASP Ethical Standard 24 (AASP, n.d.) and ACA Standard I.2.d (ACA, 2014) relate to dealing with perceived or real conflict between professional ethics and the demands of an organization with which one is working. According to these standards, it is important for practitioners to clarify the nature of the perceived conflict and then act in a way that allows them to address the situation and follow the ethics code. In such instances, it is prudent to consult with competent others on a case-by-case basis. The ethical standards from the AASP ethics code that are most likely to come into conflict between the organizational values of a professional team and the ethics of a sport psychology practitioner include Standard 4 (Exploitation and Harassment), Standard 18 (Maintaining Confidentiality), and Standard 9 (Multiple Relationships) (AASP, n.d.).

Exploitation

Ethically, sport psychology practitioners do not exploit or take advantage of their clients, and they take steps to protect their clients from such practices. This is important to remember when situations arise where there is a potential conflict between the athlete's best interests and the organization's goals. For instance, an athlete who is central to the success of a team receives a hard hit and is believed to have suffered a concussion. Coaches and leadership may not notice the effects of the concussion on the athlete's behavior and actions and wonder why he is not able to return to normal team activities. They take steps to work around or avoid following the normal concussion protocols in an effort to help the athlete return to play faster, even though the athlete is experiencing some lingering concussion-related symptoms. However, they feel justified in doing so, because the athlete has expressed some desire to return to team activities, and the team is in the middle of a crucial series of games that will determine their playoff standing. However, in meetings with you, the athlete has expressed fear and frustration about the situation. He wants to return to help his team and feels guilty that he is not able to be on the field with his teammates, but he realizes that he is not at 100% and has heard many stories about the debilitating effects of concussions later in life. Moreover, he may also feel the pressure to continue playing so as to maintain his position on the team and the viability of his career. In these situations, it is important for the consultant to be willing and able to accurately represent the athlete's needs to coaches and management. Recognizing the inherent conflict in these situations, it is important that the consultant have the trust and respect of the coaches and management to facilitate the discussion and help others understand the athlete's best interests (Gardner, 2001). In the end, these decisions will not be made by the sport psychology practitioner. However, it is the ethical consultant's job to represent the athlete's best interests to those who do make the final decisions.

It is possible that the confidentiality of one's work with an athlete and the nature of that work is the ethical standard most likely to come into conflict for a sport psychology practitioner working with a professional team. In fact, coaches have indicated that confidentiality limits the value of the services provided by sport psychology practitioners to teams (Pain & Harwood, 2004). These coaches appear to have trouble understanding the importance of trust associated with confidentiality and why sport psychology consultants are not able to keep them totally abreast of their clients' concerns. Coaches are certainly used to having full or nearly full access to information about their athletes, as provided by other staff members. Addressing disconnects with the values and ethical practices of consultants – such as the importance of confidentiality with management, coaches, and others such as sport medicine staff – at the time of hire is an important task for practitioners, and a step that would be best to readdress periodically (Gardner, 2001).

Confidentiality

Confidentiality is one of the cornerstones of effective, ethical work – built on the establishment and maintenance of trusting relationships over time. Sport psychology consultants are clearly directed by the ethics codes of their professions (e.g., APA, AASP) and bound by individual informed consent agreements with clients to protect their identities. Consultants must not share any referral-based information about their work with players (even that they are seeking assistance) without voluntary releases of information (preferably written).

Unfortunately, in a sense, a professional athlete is owned by his/her organization. As noted above, the professional sport organizational culture is typically closed, characterized by extraordinary oversight and control of work-related behavior and player information. Management controls much of the time of the athletes on their team and often pay very well. In particular, during pre- and in-season times, athlete's hours are tightly scheduled with involvement in a wide range of pre-participation, training, competitive, travel, and recovery activities. Players are under the intense external scrutiny of media and the internal eye of management and their staff. Information about strengths and shortcomings, health status, personal-social issues, and business endeavors appear to be fair game. Along with perception of intense control over the athletes on their team comes the assumption that athletes' lives in professional sport are somehow an open book.

This must not be the case in sport psychology practice if one is to obtain referrals, be helpful to new clients, and avoid harming them. However, overcoming the life as an open book perception may be a difficult task and an ongoing process fraught with uncomfortable interactions with those who may believe they have a need and right to know about the nature of one's work with players. Given athletes' common mistrust of management, who may have hired the consultant, it may be challenging to build strong working relationships with professional athletes. One may be mistrusted merely through perceived association with management, when athletes assume that open book information about work will be somehow shared with inquiring third parties. If afforded the opportunity to begin work with an athlete, it is crucial to work to assure the athlete client and third parties that information will in fact be kept private and why, unless the athlete wants specific information revealed to any third party, such as a coach or medical staff member.

There is some risk for consultants to get personally caught up in the ethical-legal bind associated with fitting into the professional sport culture. One may be tempted to compromise the confidentiality agreements to make advantageous professional connections with management, start and continue to make money, and/or to be trusted by those who call the shots. A consultant may be asked things like "Are you working with X?" "How are they doing?" "Should we play her this Saturday versus another player?" "Do you think Z is mentally ready to come back from his injury?" While these are all legitimate questions from third parties who are likely interested in the player's readiness to play, it is risky practice to engage in such discussions that likely involve information obtained in confidence. Thus, a useful practice is to have a clear and fair agreement with those who hired you, indicating the importance and implications of keeping any details of work with athletes confidential.

Competence

Sport psychology professionals need not only be interested in work within professional sports, but more importantly they must be especially capable of delivering consistently high-quality services and interventions in an ethical manner. They must be competent to work in a unique, sometimes uncomfortable, dynamic environment characterized by frequent personnel changes and the pressure to help others perform consistently at a very high level (Gardner, 2001). To do so, one clearly needs to be well-trained, possess accurate contextual knowledge, and have experience working with a range of athlete and perhaps team or other third-party (e.g., management) presenting concerns in the context of professional sport. As the result of the varied aspects of this setting, Zaichowsky and Stonkus (2014) indicated that many licensed and unlicensed sport psychology consultants have entered into the professional sports world who have not been sufficiently competent and prepared to work with such organizations, causing a mismatch between the needs of the organizations and individuals and that may undermine the profession as a whole.

Determining that one is competent and a good match is a challenge in itself. This is true because there are no established, generally accepted training models for sport psychology professionals. So, a rather daunting initial task is to self-assess competency for performing this work. Fortunately, some general guidance exists in resources like APA's Sport Psychology Proficiency (APA, 2003), which outlines requisite knowledge domains, skills, and procedures that can be used, and may help identify people who may be competent sport psychology professionals. The APA and AASP ethics codes provide some guidance on competence. Taken together, those documents tell their members to realistically assess and understand their limitations and to work within these limits. Sport psychology professionals must be aware of the nature and scope of their professional capabilities as well as the unique characteristics of those persons to whom they provide professional services. This challenging task should not be taken lightly, as determining a good consulting professional fit takes considerable thought and effort (Hays & Brown, 2004).

Beyond general sport performance psychology, it may be rather difficult to assess sufficient perceived competence to work in professional sport. Accordingly, given no road map, it would seem useful for the professional interested in this challenging path to consult with one or more experienced peers who may be willing to discuss their work in professional sports and what competencies are perceived to be useful for expert service provision. One author did just this when preparing to work with a professional sport organization. He touched base with several peers in the field to inquire about these matters, as well as other business–related issues (e.g., fees, liability insurance, contracts and travel). APA Ethical Standard 2.01 concerning competence boundaries also suggests that it is prudent for those new to them (i.e., pro sports) to seek "relevant [continued] education, training, supervised experience consultation or study" as best they can (APA, 2010).

Cultural competence

As is true with effective, ethical work with clients from diverse backgrounds, sport psychology professionals need to have an understanding of the population and culture of those with whom they work. They need to be culturally competent of the general professional sport realm – and even better, the unique world of baseball, hockey, or golf (Hanrahan & Schinke, 2011). What does a sport psychology professional need to know about the lifestyle and culture, customs, and language of those working in professional sport? Regrettably, relatively little has been written about these matters over time, which makes this question somewhat difficult to answer. What has been shared is similar to some contextual features that have been written about in other high–performance cultures, such as intercollegiate athletics, Olympic level sport, and the military (Aoyagi & Portenga, 2014; Arnold, Fusinetti, & Wilson, 2014; Etzel & Watson, 2007; Gardner, 2001). As observed by these and other authors, professional sport and other cultures tend to be closed to others – inaccessible to people who are not seen as part of the team (e.g., the football family). What is discussed and what goes on is highly protected information, related at least in part to maintaining a competitive advantage over other organizations or competitors. Consequently, trust and acceptance of a sport psychology professional is essential – crucial to entry, acceptance, and any work over time. Clearly, it takes professional credibility and some time to establish confidence and trust in a competent outside consultant. For example, the first question that was asked of one author who was contacted on the telephone by an NBA team was "Who else do you work with?"

Stigma about psychology, psychologists, and sport psychology is common in society and sport organizations. Attitudes and behaviors associated with psychological stigma are likely to be encountered in work with professional athletes, management, and others in professional sport societies. Understanding who seeks help, who is referred for consultation, how these things are done, or how a sport psychology professional is employed is knowledge that is part of one's cultural competence. These issues must be discussed at the outset of any consultation. While some professional sport organizations may hire a sport psychology professional, views about the person, her/his services, and even if they are used is important to know. It may be that given the limitations of player trust in management, they may not use services internal to an organization. Rather, athletes may be more inclined go through agents to seek help for performance or personal-social reasons.

Furthermore, to be culturally competent in this milieu, it is beneficial to understand the often complex dynamics of the team or organization one is working with and their history of working with sport psychology professionals (Gardner, 1995). To facilitate a good consulting fit, Gardner suggested that developing a good sense of an organization's past, its values, goals, rules and regulations, chain of command, etc. (as best one can) is useful to fitting in and developing opportunities to do good work with its members. So, if a professional team wants to bring a sport psychology consultant on board, s/he needs to learn as much as possible about them and that team's culture – as soon as possible.

Professional athletes

Although it is prudent to not make many assumptions about professional sport athletes because of numerous individual differences, there appear to be some generalizations about them and their lifestyles that relate to ethical practice. These generalities may help the would-be sport psychology consultant work more competently. For example, Grange (2010) shared several observations about some features of this population, to include (a) being under constant scrutiny and personal accountability from the media and controlling management; (b) owning idiosyncratic, perhaps extremely competitive cultural norms associated with their [closed] sport communities and gender; (c) having considerable travel and free time along with extraordinarily large sums of money associated with the potential to engage in irresponsible, risky behaviors; (d) being seen as public role models; and (e) having limited career life spans associated with uncertainty and constant transitions and life change. Pro athletes would also seem to normally own strong athletic identities, be cautious of work with those perceived as outsiders, be suspicious of ownership and management, and have a limited circle of trustworthy confidants.

Multiple role relationships

While not inherently unethical in practice, multiple role relationships need to be dealt with very carefully in psychology practice. Multiple role relationships can be defined as a psychologist entering into a professional relationship with a person (1) with whom they already have a relationship with; (2) with whom they already have a relationship with a person closely connected with them; or (3) promising to enter into a future relationship with a client or person closely connected with them (APA Standard 3.05; AASP Standard 9) (APA, 2010; AASP, n.d.). Because of the nature of sport, particularly professional sport, multiple role relationships appear to occur more commonly and be more accepted in these settings versus more traditional psychology service provision.

Within the professional sport setting, consultants often interact with many members of the sport organization on a regular basis, including athletes, sports medicine personnel, coaches, staff members, and management (Zaichowsky & Stonkus, 2014). Sport psychology consultants often travel with the teams, meaning that they may interact with all of these individuals across multiple settings, such as on planes and buses, at meals, before and after team meetings, at practices and games, in social settings, and may even share a hotel room with a member of the organization. Further, many practitioners working in professional sport provide services to the athletes on the team, but may also consult with members of the organization other than the athletes (Gardner, 2001; Zaichowsky & Stonkus, 2014). For example, consultants may provide services to coaches, managers, and sport medicine personnel, and at other times are invited into important meetings with these individuals.

These many and varied interactions with all members of the sport organization certainly present opportunities for practitioners to learn about the team and its culture and provide services to their clients, but also bring many opportunities for boundary crossings to occur that may result in harmful multiple role relationship dynamics to develop. For instance, the development of a strong relationship with a non-athlete member of the team could easily result in the formation of biases about an athlete's performance, their standing on the team, or how they are treated. While some of these boundary crossings may be easy to identify and avoid (e.g., speaking about a player's work without a release of information), others may create problems that are not readily apparent to the consultant or third parties. Therefore, it is crucial for sport psychology practitioners to always focus on their specific role and to clearly keep in mind who their client is.

A clear boundary crossing may occur if a consultant is asked for advice about the psychological readiness of athletes on the team. Without a signed waiver to release such information or opinion, sharing this information with coaches or management would create an ethical breach. If such an ethical breach was identified, it would likely result in significant damage to the relationship between the athlete(s) and consultant, and could result in serious professional and legal ramifications to the practitioner (i.e., malpractice). However, it would be tempting for a practitioner to get wrapped up in feeling important when a coach asks their opinion about playing time or an athlete's readiness to play. Therefore, it is important to remember issues of confidentiality and scope of practice before answering such questions. Obviously, this requires a delicate balancing act for the practitioner who wants to be viewed by coaches and managers as important to the team, but also respectful and ethical to the athletes.

While the effects may be less obvious, athletes on the team may have concerns about their ability to trust a sport psychology consultant if they observe frequent interactions between the consultant and coaches or front office personnel. They may perceive that the focus of the conversations is somehow about the athletes and what they have spoken about with the consultant. While these interactions may occur while traveling on planes or buses, at team dinners, or other team-related events, such interactions with individuals who make playing time and contract decisions can result in a lack of trust among athletes out of a fear that the private information they share with the consultant will not remain confidential. This lack of trust may actually permeate throughout the team subsequent to the hiring of a consultant if the team members believe that the consultant was hired to learn more about the issues that are affecting athletes on the team. As noted earlier, it would not be entirely outside the realm of possibility for professional athletes to go through their agent to find a private consultant outside of the team if they feel as if they need confidential services.

Conclusion

It should be apparent from the information presented above that sport psychology consultations at the professional level share more similarities than differences with consultations with athletes at other levels of participation. However, it is important for practitioners to identify those factors that make consultations at the professional level unique and challenging. Working with professional athletes and other organization members, such as coaches, sports medicine staff, and management, clearly requires unique cultural competence and organizational knowledge beyond those that are often required for work with other athletes. Professional organizations have a great deal of control over athletes and expect a return on their investment from service providers. These challenging expectations often mean that the organization's values may conflict with the professional ethics that guide the consultant's practices, and may bring issues of confidentiality into question. Further, the demanding training, game, and travel schedules of professional teams increases the opportunities for complicated relationships to form, which can have a negative impact on the judgement of practitioners.

In short, effective sport psychology consulting within professional sports requires practitioners to maintain a firm working knowledge and understanding of the ethical principles and standards that govern their work. According to APA Ethical Standard 3.11, it is important for practitioners to clearly articulate with organizations at the onset of service delivery several issues that will affect the provision of services (APA, 2010), such as the objectives of your services, who will be the recipients of your services, who you perceive to be the client, what information from your consultations will be made available and to whom, and any limits to confidentiality. Beyond these central ethical issues, it is certainly beneficial for practitioners to develop and maintain strong professional relationships with team administration and develop effective skills for dealing with conflict and adversity.

References

American Counseling Association. (2014). *ACA code of ethics.* Accessed at http://counseling.org/Resources/aca-code-of-ethics.pdf

American Psychological Association. (2003). *APA sport psychology proficiency.* Accessed at http://www.apadivisions.org/division-47/about/sport-proficiency/index.aspx

American Psychological Association. (2010). *Ethical principles of psychologists and code of conduct.* Accessed at http://www.apa.org/ethics/code/

Aoyagi, M., & Portenga, S. (2014). Five ring fever: Ethical considerations when consulting with Olympic athletes. In E. Etzel & J. Watson II (Eds.), *Ethical issues in sort, exercise and performance psychology* (pp. 61–74). Morgantown, WV: Fitness Information Technology.

Arnold, T., Fusinetti, M., & Wilson, K. (2014). Ethical considerations for mental skill trainers working with soldiers in the United States Army. In E. Etzel & J. Watson II (Eds.), *Ethical issues in sport, exercise and performance psychology* (pp. 111–122). Morgantown, WV: Fitness Information Technology.

Association for Applied Sport Psychology. (n.d). *AASP ethical principles and standards.* Accessed at http://www.appliedsportpsych.orgabout/ethics/code

Canadian Psychological Association. (2013). *Code of ethics for psychologists.* Accessed at http://www.cpa.ca/aboutcpa/committees.ethics.codeofethics/

Coakley, J. (2014). *Sports in society: Issues and controversies* (11th ed.). New York: McGraw-Hill.

Etzel, E., & Watson, J.W. (2007). Ethical considerations for psychological consultations in intercollegiate athletics. *Journal of Clinical Sport Psychology, 1*(3), 304–317.

Eubank, M., Nesti, M., & Cruickshank, A. (2014). Understanding high performance sport environments: Impact for the professional training and supervision of sport psychologists. *Sport and Exercise Psychology Review, 10*(2), 30–36.

Federation Internationale de Football. (2012). *FIFA code of ethics.* Accessed at http://resources.fifa.com/mm/document/affederation/administration/50/02/82/codeofethics2012e.pdf

Gardner, F. L. (1995). The coach and the team psychologist: An integrated model. In S. Murphy (Ed.), *Sport psychology interventions* (pp.147–175). Champaign, IL: Human Kinetics.

Gardner, F. L. (2001). Applied sport psychology in professional sports: The team psychologist. *Professional Psychology: Research and Practice, 32*, 34–39.

Grange, P. (2010). Professional athletes. In S. Hanrahan & M. Andersen (Eds.), *Routledge handbook of applied sport psychology* (pp. 396–404). New York: Routledge.

Hackfort, D., & Tenenbaum, G. (2014). Ethical issues in sport and exercise psychology. In A. G. Papaioannou & D. Hackfort (Eds.), *Routledge companion to sport and exercise psychology* (pp. 976–987). London: Routledge.

Hanrahan, S., & Schinke, R. (2011). Culture in sport psychology. In T. Morris and P. Terry (Eds.), *The new sport and exercise psychology companion* (pp. 533–566). Morgantown, WV: Fitness Information Technology.

Hansen, K., & Savage, M. (2012). What role does ethics play in sports? Markkula Center for Applied Ethics. Retrieved June 16, 2015 from http://www.scu.edu/ethics/publications/submitted/sports-ethics.html

Hays, K., & Brown, C. (2004). *You're on! Consulting for peak performance.* Washington, DC: American Psychological Association.

International Society of Sport Psychology. (n.d.). *Code of ethics.* Accessed at http://www.issponline.org/p_codeofethics.asp?ms=3

Koocher, G., & Keith-Spiegal, P. (2009). *Ethics in psychology and the mental health professions: Standards and cases* (3rd ed.). New York: Oxford University Press.

Pain, M. A., & Harwood, C. G. (2004). Knowledge and perceptions of sport psychology within English soccer. *Journal of Sports Sciences, 22,* 813–826.

Ravizza, K. (1990). Sportpsych consultation issues in professional baseball. *The Sport Psychologist, 4,* 330–340.

Sage, G., & Eitzen, D. (2013). *Sociology of North American sport* (9th ed.). New York: Oxford University Press.

Zaichowsky, L. D., & Stonkus, M. (2014). Ethical issues in professional sport. In E. Etzel & J. Watson II (Eds.), *Ethical issues in sport, exercise and performance psychology* (pp. 49–60). Morgantown, WV: Fitness Information Technology.

SECTION II
Individual and pair sports

7

TWENTY YEARS' EXPERIENCE WORKING WITHIN PROFESSIONAL TENNIS

Chris Harwood

Introduction

The aim of this chapter is to provide personal insights into a range of professional work representing 20 years of experience delivering psychological services within tennis. First, I will discuss my personal and academic background, noting how this facilitated both my entry into the sport as well as elements of my consulting philosophy and models of practice. Second, I will then outline the various work and career-related progressions that I experienced in service delivery and reinforce the range of formal and informal roles that exist for a tennis consultant working in a national organization. Drawing from this experience, I will outline strategies and thematic areas that I believe have underpinned my more effective consulting outcomes. Finally, I will conclude the chapter with some reflective recommendations for practitioners who are keen to gain the opportunity to work with tennis clients.

Personal and academic background

Sport psychology practitioners find routes for their professional services into a sport in a variety of manners. My involvement in tennis consulting stemmed from a combination of long-term competitive participation in the sport, professional coaching experience, and the focus of my academic studies. I was a comparatively late starter to tennis (10 years old), representative of an early diversification, multisport childhood. I experienced virtually the full performance pathway of the game as it existed in 1980s Britain, progressing from county, regional, to national levels of the game. Importantly, alongside my parents, I lived the organizational and competitive demands of the game through the weekly two-hour round trips to individual coaching and group sessions, the week-long tournaments around the country, and politics over ranking and representative selections. It is important to stress how much this long-term developmental experience of insider involvement facilitates a practitioner's work in a given sport (Wylleman & Lavallee, 2004). The ability to empathize with young tennis clients and their parents is heightened from memory, and displays of genuineness and congruence are never forced; they are simply natural and ingrained through experience of the subcultural norms of the sport. I reached a competitive level equivalent to a national senior player representing my county team (i.e., state) at senior amateur level until the age of 34, and currently continue to play in veterans events. Continued competitive participation in the game is important not only for my mental and physical health, but also to maintain currency and reputation in terms of the modern-day sociocultural and organizational 'goings on' within the national game. I built a local and regional level status as a player, and later as a coach, which enhanced my 'entry capital' as a sport psychology practitioner. On occasion I have felt an internal pressure in some way to maintain that reputation as the competitive player; that I am a practitioner who does 'walk the talk and the walk' in terms of their own 'mental game'. Whether imagined or real, this pressure has been both positive and challenging for me.

At 17 years of age I passed my first professional Lawn Tennis Association (LTA) tennis coaching award, and three years later whilst at Loughborough University I gained a more senior LTA coaching qualification that would allow me to coach players up to a national level. I engaged in part-time youth coaching while studying for a degree in Physical Education, Sports Science and Management. This degree program also contained a very strong tennis emphasis due to my mentors, Rod Thorpe and David Bunker, both of whom were the originators of the Teaching Games For Understanding (TGFU; Bunker & Thorpe, 1982) approach and who taught applied sport science and coaching modules. During this undergraduate period, I became immersed in the interdisciplinary nature of tennis and studied the demands of the sport from psychological, physiological, biomechanical, and sociocultural/organizational dimensions. The implications of court surfaces, climate, equipment, technological advancements, and ranking systems were all interesting and relevant themes with respect to impact on the human competitor. This knowledge shaped a key part of my subsequent working philosophy as a practitioner.

Worlds collided for me over the next five years as I was offered the opportunity as a player-coach to the University team while studying for an MSc in sports science, and subsequently a PhD in sport psychology. During my MSc, I read the first edition of *Motivation in Sport and Exercise* (Roberts, 1992). This career-defining text introduced me to the principles of achievement goal theory (AGT). AGT resonated with me for many reasons based on my playing experience. First, tennis is a result-oriented sport which externally rewards performance outcomes over personal improvement and offers a poverty of individualized feedback. In such a zero-sum game, players are challenged to find other sources of information to build and maintain their perceptions of competence as opposed to sole reliance on normative, opponent comparisons. Second, the emphasis on perceptions of one's ability is heightened due to being 'lonely yet never alone' on court. As an individual sport, there is personal responsibility for everything (e.g., managing one's own line calls; confronting an opponent's calls; self-coaching; dealing with setbacks; managing time and fatigue; closing out matches). Whilst there is no outside help or assistance in such matters, there are outside expectations and judgments in the player's mind either from a physically present audience (e.g., of coaches, parents, other players) or from more remote significant others (e.g., 'Did you win your match?'). With ability-based evaluations typically around factors such as match outcome, scoreline, unforced errors, and winners, tennis creates a motivational climate that is inherently ego involving (Ames, 1992). Moreover, significant others (e.g., coaches, parents, officials) can serve as co-conspirators in shaping this climate for a young player.

AGT focused my attention on how and why young people come to define success in two contrasting manners, and the value of pursuing self-improvement goals (i.e., task involvement) over purely superiority goals (i.e., ego involvement). Tennis served as a laboratory for examining AGT, and my own personal insights suggested that one's view of success situationally changed due to varying factors both before and within matches (e.g., self-confidence; match importance; ranking of opponent; flow of the match; goals/expectations of parents and coach; peer and selection pressures). Over the course of the next five years, I undertook field-based research into achievement goals in youth tennis culminating in a practical intervention program for players, parents, and coaches (see Harwood & Swain, 2002). Outside of my playing and coaching roles, this period of immersion into applied research within the sport perhaps most facilitated my subsequent work as a practitioner.

Transition to consulting and processes of accessibility

My professional work in tennis at youth and senior levels has been represented by three clear transitions or phases to date – Working with Coaches, Working with Players, and Working within an Organization – all of which were natural evolutions without any planning or forecasting. I will deal with each of these phases in turn.

Phase 1: coach education

Whilst conducting my PhD studies, I completed supervised experience and training to become an accredited sport psychology practitioner with the British Association of Sport and Exercise Sciences (BASES). On completion of my PhD in 1997, I was employed as head coach at Loughborough University in conjunction with a newly supported LTA scheme for university tennis. I had some challenging decisions to make with respect to my ongoing career, but none included working as a full-time practitioner in tennis. There were few full-time professional roles for sport psychologists at this time, and the LTA did not have a sport psychology department or strategy. Nevertheless, gaining entry into tennis psychology consulting opportunities was not a problem during this period. The central reason for this was that I had built connections with coaches and sport scientists at the LTA, who supported my research with British youth players. As my studies had informed the role of the coach and parent in creating an optimal motivational climate for players, there was interest from the LTA coaching department in presenting my work back to the Association. My contacts with fellow coaches also led to my first consulting work with players in a private capacity. Moreover, a high-level LTA coach education qualification was being developed, and I was approached to construct and deliver the psychological strand of the course. As a psychologist-coach educator, this enabled me to develop close relationships with many national coaches, support staff in the LTA coaching department, and colleagues within LTA sport science team over the coming years.

Beyond delivering to selected tennis coaches on the coaching qualification, I also developed one-day introductory and advanced 'mental skills' professional development courses for British coaches. These courses drew upon my PhD research into motivation and focused on optimizing the tennis environment whilst teaching the principles of tennis-specific goal setting, imagery, relaxation, and routines that coaches could employ with their charges. By this time in the late 1990s, I had transitioned out of my university coaching role into an academic role as sport psychology faculty member at Loughborough. Concurrent with the construction of a new tennis centre on campus was the development of an LTA high-performance player program. This enabled more direct work with players who were selected into the program. Nevertheless, the key message for practitioners from this phase is the importance of building effective relationships with coaches and demonstrating to them the value of psychology and their psychological responsibilities to players. I would stipulate this as one of the key entry mechanisms for neophyte consultants accessing the sport.

Phase 2: player education and support

The high-performance program comprising regional centres focused on the country's most talented 12- to 16-year-old players. Although sport psychology remained a more marginalized support service compared with the emergence of strength and conditioning personnel at this time, there was very little doubt amongst the more educated coaches that mental skills training was a critical component to player development. With a limited budget and time allowance for sport psychology, my model for player development combined a psychological skills training (PST) and integrative approach (see Poczwardowski, Sherman, & Ravizza, 2004). Critical for this adolescent phase is an increased awareness of the psychological demands of the game (i.e., what makes tennis psychologically tough?) and an appreciation of some of the mental skills that help elite players to conquer these demands. Group sessions would serve as a platform for junior player discussion to raise shared awareness, as I believed that the knowledge already existed within the room. Players of this level will have already experienced many mental challenges in matches, and they will have started to form ideas of how to cope (e.g., playing the difficult or 'bogey' opponent; closing out matches; responding to losing sets; dealing with line calls; breaking an opponent's rhythm). The role of the practitioner is to draw out this knowledge and awareness, and introduce strategies that players can begin to experiment with and apply. Video clips of elite players coping with varying situations, or talking about strategies they used, formed some of the material for these educational sessions.

In conjunction with enhanced awareness and education was the integration of mental skills training on court and the application of strategies in conditioned games. This work was initiated with the coach or through the coach so that players had the opportunity to practice optimal psychological responses on a daily basis. On-court work would include the refinement of between-point routines and the practice of taking time between points and rallies to cognitively and behaviorally refocus, re-energize, and commit before engaging the next point or rep in training. It is important for young players to mentally and emotionally manage time effectively, given that 70% of a match is usually 'dead time' without the ball in play. They need to 'make the dead time live' for them. Coaches would often inject simulated stress into game situations (e.g., winning three points in a row to earn one point; losing serve at 5–4 means you are 4–5 down next game). Two favorite games of mine were 'Confidence Booster' and 'Risks and Gambles'. The former game allowed players to reward themselves with an extra point if they noted an excessively negative reaction in their opponent. The latter game allowed either the server or receiver (or winner of the prior point) to decide how much the next point was going to be worth to the winner (e.g., one, two, or three points). Both of these types of games taught the players about consequences, balanced decision making, and also the processes of keeping their cool. There are many ways of crafting mental skills drills in tennis to condition a player's attentional skills and emotional discipline (see Crespo, Reid, & Quinn, 2006; Lauer, Gould, Lubbers, & Kovacs, 2010), and coaches well-versed in the principles can create exciting but meaningful challenges in their sessions.

A final element of my consulting approach in this phase was self-reflection and performance review. With players educated about mental preparation and self-management in performance, I believed that performance debriefing and self-evaluation after matches were important components to a player's self-regulation skill. I constructed both training and match review sheets for players within their mental toughness player log book. Various iterations of these emerged over the years as both the players and I evolved, and where players sought autonomy in developing their own review routine. However, based upon my academic work in AGT, they would always include a process goal-setting element and a breakdown of the key mental behaviors (e.g., body language after mistakes) that the player could focus on executing in the match. There would also be an open section for reflection by the player and by the coach (if in attendance). The goal of these review processes was to encourage greater task involvement and 'growth mindset' development (Dweck, 2006) in adolescent players who struggled with viewing the match through anything other than an 'outcome' lens. I was careful not to discount the importance of competitiveness and the need to possess a killer instinct in tennis (a point I will return to when discussing the role of philosophy). However, such review processes were relevant to help players draw on additional sources of competence information in matches and evaluate a range of controllable processes or 'winning behaviors', regardless of whether they had won or lost the match. I wanted them to learn to review their performance not their outcome, and this did not come easily to many of my young clients. Further, representative of my interdisciplinary training in sport science, these mental toughness log books also reinforced the importance of effective nutritional habits and physical routines prior to training and matches. In this respect, I was acting as the performance psychologist with intentions to ensure that players recognized the impact of other factors on their performance and devoted the appropriate psychological attention to these relevant disciplinary elements.

I noted earlier that we (i.e., coaches and myself) attempted to create an environment where players had the opportunity to practice mental skills. We could lead the horse to water, but not all players would passionately drink it. Some players took the opportunity to practice and apply themselves to mental training more than others. I can state that those players who failed to apply themselves fully never made it beyond a junior national level. One of the 12-year-olds who did apply himself made a professional career in the game, and I continued to work with him until his retirement at 27 years of age. This particular player was a psychological 'sponge', and my own experience of delivering sport psychology support to players through adolescence into the senior professional game was greatly facilitated by the opportunity of working with this player. I will discuss some of the key strategies, challenges, and approaches that I feel are central to the junior-to-senior transition later in this chapter. Nevertheless, a culmination of my coach education work, playing and academic background, and consulting experience led me towards the most recent phase of providing psychological support to the national governing body (i.e., federation).

Phase 3: managing services within an organization

Fast forwarding to 2010, and I was now a senior academic at Loughborough University. In tandem with my applied experiences in tennis and professional football over the intervening years, my research interests had diversified to the psychological aspects of coaching and parenting in youth sport. However, my academic role limited my available consultancy time, and I primarily focused my energies on (i) support to my professional client, (ii) mentoring young practitioners-in-training, and (iii) occasional contributions to coach and parent education in the sport. During this time, the LTA was going through a restructuring process, and I was approached by the Player Development Director to provide support services to the men's and women's elite player teams at the National Tennis Centre in London. This was a challenge I embraced, and assisted by yearly negotiations with Loughborough, I subsequently spent the equivalent of two days per week for the next three years working with the national governing body.

Whilst not a full-time appointment, the opportunity to work more intensely within an interdisciplinary support team and national federation steepened the learning curve in ways that helped me grow further as a practitioner. Most notably, as a federation psychologist the scope of formal and informal roles and services can increase exponentially, and it becomes a matter of managing time effectively and organizing priorities with the Performance Director or Head of Sports Science. Below are some of the key inputs, services, and initiatives that may accompany your role in a national tennis organization should you gain such an opportunity.

Targeted support to senior coaches and players

Senior coaches and players may be interested in psychological inputs that will offer them the 'marginal gains' to their game. Whilst some players continue to resist psychology due to a misplaced stigma or poor prior experience with a consultant, many now recognize the value of a specialist contribution to their team. Some of this work may be more counselling-focused with respect to the external demands and organizational pressures of the game on identity, relationships, confidence, and overall mental health; whilst more performance-based work may focus on excellence in goal setting, tournament planning, quality of training, pre-match preparation, positive thinking and self-management behavior, match debriefing, and recovery processes. Performance-based psychological support entails match observations, video-based work, and a close working relationship with the coach. Indeed, it can also include supporting the coach-player dyad by profiling their relationship and providing advice to optimize relationship functioning. A psychologist's support isn't limited to the player, and many psychologists will directly work with the coach, as well as 'through the coach' and 'for the coach'. Hence, there are often multiple roles to manage in terms of being counsellor to a coach's needs as well as a supervisory educator to the coach in reinforcing important plans and messages to the player.

Referral network and SP-client fit

The sport psychologist (SP)–client fit is important, and it is unreasonable to believe that every player will want to work with you, or that your approach and background will suit every player. In my experience at the LTA, some players favored my more technical, tennis-specific background, whilst others felt more comfortable seeking support from both outside the organization and outside tennis, where there was perhaps a greater sense of detachment. The role of a federation psychologist is to provide support service options to players and coaches, and that doesn't mean that you are automatically the best option. Developing an appropriate referral network is a key role, and this means sourcing clinical and counselling psychology professionals who are able to support players in areas that are beyond the sport psychologist's competence and training (e.g., depression, eating disorders, addictive behaviors). It also means being fully open to directing players to other professional colleagues who don't occupy the close, insider role that you naturally occupy as the federation lead.

Interdisciplinary support

Working within an interdisciplinary sport science team is an important feature of federation employment. You are one member of the 'Team around the Player', both when the elite player is on site during a training block or off site for a series of tournaments. The role of the sport science team is to help keep the player injury free and in optimal physical and mental condition. Assessments of training load, stress, recovery, well-being, hydration, sleep, and diet are but a few of the areas that a sport science team will monitor. Psychologists work closely with physical trainers in optimizing training and adherence, as well as with physiotherapists on injury prevention routines. Injury can be a distressing experience for a player, and it is important to develop a protocol with physiotherapists, trainers, and coaches so that necessary steps are taken to provide positive psychological support alongside an appropriate, agreed-upon plan for treatment and recovery.

Performance lifestyle management

Adolescent players attempting to make the transition to the senior game may have sacrificed a normal education and social life in the pursuit of a tennis career. Additionally, there may be individual differences in the degrees of independence and life skills possessed by players, particularly in instances where everything has been taken care of for them. Managing and organizing travel on their own, handling the media, understanding budgets and finance, cultural awareness, education about gambling and doping are but a few examples of lifestyle management themes. In contemporary UK sport, performance lifestyle advisers are employed to work with athletes on these areas, and my experience is that sport psychologists can make an effective team with such an adviser in order to provide more holistic support to a young player coming through the ranks.

Parent education and support

In a federation psychologist role, building effective relationships with parents is an important and often challenging task. At this level, parents are typically highly concerned about their child's future and demanding of the best support for them. While some tennis parents become less involved as their child moves more independently through adolescence, my experience is largely counter to this pattern. Parents can be highly present in a surveillance type role, take on the more managerial duties, and be in contact with agents about their child's sponsors, program, and options. My experience is that parents want to leave no stone unturned, and this passion and motivation for supporting their child is perhaps the psychologist's strongest card in helping them to understand how they can play an optimal role (as opposed to an overinvolved role) for the child and coaching team. Working with parents on role delineation and the quality of their involvement is an important, early-stage initiative. The stress that an overinvolved parent can consistently cause a coach and sport science team is both negative and remarkable. Everyone suffers when roles aren't clarified from the start, but the player tends always to be the ultimate victim.

Organizational culture and environment

The performance departments of national federations (and high-performance tennis centres) benefit from a working environment where there is an agreed-upon performance mission and vision, alongside clear, agreed-upon values and objectives for staff. An informal role as a psychologist may be to monitor the quality and health of the organizational environment and determine if there are ways of improving team effectiveness and job satisfaction. As a psychologist you will be more empathic and attuned than most to the quality of group processes and levels of communication between staff. In conjunction with men's and women's team managers, you may be asked to facilitate team building and management sessions that permit discussion and consensus around core staff values and qualities, as well as the behaviors that enact and represent such values. In addition, it is important to ensure that the training facility and venue is a motivating and inspiring place for players. Therefore, your role as a psychologist may extend to design psychology and the use of past achievements, current successes, motivational phrasing, elite player photos, and colour to highlight and invigorate the tennis environment.

Integrated mental skills education for juniors

When working with older junior players in transition to the senior game, or senior players (i.e., progression to ITF and ATP Challenger Circuits) moving up, I believe it is important not to forget your responsibility to younger age groups. These are the next generation of players who may benefit from (and be more receptive towards) more bespoke support, and developing a clear strategic plan for the mental skills education of adolescent juniors (e.g., 12–16 years) is pivotal in my opinion. You may be involved with off-court and on-court educational inputs on age group national and regional training camps. At the very least, you should be responsible for ensuring that sport psychology and mental skills training is well-represented to young players and, as noted earlier, that players have an awareness of the psychological demands of the game. In my time with the LTA, I worked on numerous 2- to 3-day training camps or longer training blocks where psychological skills and outcomes formed elements of the camp. It is important to integrate on court with coaches so that players see mental skills and strategies as natural extensions to their training and conditioning as a player.

Performance education outreach and grass-roots communication

When acting as sport psychology lead for a national federation or high-performance centre, it is literally your responsibility to lead the discipline and ensure that stakeholders in the game know all about sport psychology. No one else is going to do this for you. In tennis, the key stakeholders (i.e., players, parents, coaches, officials, sponsors, media, and agents) are generally warming to the value of performance psychology and mental health services in the game. Ironically, the recent high-profile stress, depression, and suicide cases in other sports are piquing interest in psychology. Whereas in the past, the mental health and clinical face of psychology almost unequivocally fuelled the stigma and negative derogation that held back the efforts of performance, developmental, and humanistic psychologists, the global 'mental health in sport' agenda is now making psychology more relevant and attractive. There is a responsibility on a federation psychologist to capitalize on this interest, even if not to focus overly on the clinical side of the game. In a leadership position nationally, there may be an opportunity to communicate and outreach to local tennis communities, as well as the general public in some instances. Written contributions to coach and parent education on a federation's website, or through tennis member magazines, help to spread the message on tennis psychology. Regular tennis enthusiasts (like mid-handicap golfers) are always eager for tips on improving their mental game, so titles such as "Getting tough when it's getting tight", "How to close out matches", "Dealing with your bogey opponent", and "The smart player's guide to playing a cheat" are going to resonate with anyone who has picked up a racquet.

All of these latter subsections reflected elements of my work with the national governing body, and it enabled me to appreciate the wide scope of the tennis psychology role. In this penultimate section, I'll shine a more intense light on my consulting philosophy and examples of strategies that I have found impactful at various levels of the game.

Consulting philosophy and signature strategies

My philosophy as a practitioner blends humanistic, holistic, and cognitive-behavioral principles in respect of empowering tennis clients to reach their potential. I aim to be client-centred in helping players to recognize their own strengths in an unequivocally tough sport, and reflect on potential areas of growth and development, as well as solutions to challenges. However, my experience of tennis and young tennis players reinforces how (i) managing the quality of thinking, emotion, and behavior is a critical, ongoing process, and (ii) the quality of the environment around the player should facilitate self-development in ways that prepare a player for any career, not simply a potential tennis career. This experience has informed me that young players (10 years and above) require a more proactive cognitive-behavioral approach to awareness and education about their thoughts, feelings, and behavior before, during, and after matches. I have consulted with a number of technically strong mid-to-late adolescent players (e.g., 15–18 years) who have paid little ongoing attention to mental skills and strategies, and are now finding competitive tennis a mentally and emotionally difficult place to be. Additionally, with an excessive emphasis on results and a limited percentage of invested players who do not transition successfully (i.e., do not make the grade professionally), I believe that federations, coaches, and parents need to be jointly responsible for the holistic development of the player as a person. As a psychologist, I am therefore interested in how players are developing their social skills and independence, as much as their ability to 'handle a lefty' or 'keep a lid on their anger'. On this basis, the reader will already appreciate that my models of practice can include a counselling focus (as necessary), an educational and integrated psychological skills training (PST) focus, and an interdisciplinary sport science focus. As a social cognitive scholar, my achievement goal research informs me that thinking processes and behavior are subject to substantial social influence. Parents, grandparents, coaches, peers, and officials can shape the way a player thinks and acts within competitive tennis contexts. Therefore, my work with an individual takes account of the relevant behavior, involvement, and interactions of others in the ecological system of the player. The section below draws upon a few of the key strategic or technical areas that have formed effective components of my practice.

Shaping the competitive performance mentality

A key piece of advice I want to share with practitioners is to be careful not to discount the importance of competitiveness and application of a killer instinct in tennis. Talented players and experienced coaches switch off when people suggest that winning doesn't matter and tennis is just about trying hard, or having fun. Such messages do not resonate well in the more professional tennis world because they grossly discount the personal, social, and emotional challenges that the game places upon the player. There is a tendency for parents to protect their children from pressure and disappointment by using language that can provide excuses for children not to compete or battle for victory (i.e., winning and losing doesn't matter = competing unconditionally doesn't matter either). I feel that a key strategy for a tennis psychologist is to help talented young players understand what tennis is demanding of them and develop a personal philosophy for how they will approach the test of a competitive match. Through my PhD work in achievement goal theory, I have focused on educating players about a Competitive Performance Mentality (CPM; Harwood, 2004; Harwood & Swain, 2002).

Players with a CPM acknowledge and tackle two simple tests that the sport of tennis will always set up for contestants – the self-challenge and the game challenge. The *self-challenge* reflects the opportunity to strive to the best of one's current capacity in skills that are under the player's control. The *game challenge* reflects the test of competitively overcoming the opponent that tennis presents them with on that particular day. These two challenges exist in every single match, whatever the situation or level of opponent, and either, both, or neither of the challenges may be met successfully. After *every match* it is important to review and appraise the self-challenge first (i.e., unconditional consistency of effort, discipline, composure, application of tactics, and levels of technical skill execution relative to personal expectations). This is the 'Me versus Me', self-referenced performance debrief that should highlight positives as well as firmly draw out any areas for self-development and practice. Appraisal of the game challenge includes time to reflect on the competitive flow of the match, the strengths and weaknesses of the opponent, elements that tested the athlete's resources, and ultimately what they learned about themselves and their opponent from the challenge today.

A CPM draws from research demonstrating the positive outcomes of high-task/high ego-goal profiles in athletes (Hodge & Petlichkoff, 2000) as well as self-reflection. It engages players to value striving to the best of their 'controllable' abilities, whilst depersonalizing the battle with the opponent and reducing an extraneous focus on others' expectations. Players direct their attention solely towards the competitive processes that will help them 'in battle' and 'to learn fully from the battle'. The development and application of a CPM requires players and coach to habituate pre- and post- match routines where process goals are openly discussed, agreed on, written, and reviewed. Commitment to performance review and match logbooks facilitates the growth of this mindset in tennis, a mindset that I believe helps players to maintain long-term motivation and confidence through rough patches and temporary slumps in form.

Body language and emotional control

How players choose to manage themselves physically and emotionally on court is both a determinant of how they will perform at key moments, as well as how their opponent may perform (i.e., remember the 'Confidence Booster' game). Working with players on their physical presence, body language, and emotional self-regulation is like working with actors or artists in a performing role. My approach typically starts with a version of Jim Loehr's quadrant approach to energy – hi-lo positive/hi-lo negative (Loehr, 1986; Loehr & Schwartz,

2003) – to help players become aware that a match is about energy management and conservation. When visually presenting the quadrants with different emotions representing directed energy (e.g., lo-positive = relaxed, hi-positive = pumped, hi-negative = anger, lo-negative = dejection = 'tanking'), young players can articulate their emotional range and identify why and when they shift quadrants. They can also tell you that Rafael Nadal spends most of his time 'between here and here', whereas Roger Federer or Maria Sharapova 'are a little bit lower down' (i.e., more relaxed and composed). This exercise in emotional awareness is a light bulb moment for many young tennis players looking to master the 'red mist' or rather 'fog' that emerges during adolescence. They can see the emotional map and how certain emotions are the pathway to behavioral problems. It can lead to the discussion of colors or words for different emotions and strategies that assist in managing emotions and available energy levels. Work on body language and physical presence starts with gaining video footage of players in competition and working with players on identifying the micro behaviors that players feel are optimal to their confidence and energy management. Such work begins to inform between-point routines that players can begin to practice on court with coaches. Through the introduction and experience of imagery, breathing exercises, and rational self-statements, players begin to harness the components of their emotional control skills in dead time periods. They also cultivate the power to look like they are physically in control of themselves, rather than charging the battery of the opponent. Observing players through the journey of the match (or via video footage) whilst charting their body language and emotional control can be a powerful feedback and reinforcement process.

Sensory awareness and attentional control

Tennis is a sport that physically embodies power, grace, finesse, agility, and dynamism, as well as speed of perception, anticipation, decision making, and reaction. Few sports offer such lengthy, complex, and pressured tests of the body, the mind, and the mind-body connection. Due to these challenges, players need to practice being in touch with their body and mind in order to reproduce such connections effortlessly in a match. Tennis players strive for that sense of rhythm and flow in matches where time begins to slow down, movement is automatic, and ball striking feels 'clean . . . centred . . . inevitable'. A player's senses are heightened in this state: breathing is calm and rhythmic; visual attention is narrowed; acute kinesthetic (i.e., feel) and auditory (i.e., sound) feedback allows players to adjust spin, velocity, height, and angle of ball strike with greater ease. Being in the zone is quite a chilling and exhilarating experience, episodes of which I believe players are able to master more frequently with practice.

Sensory awareness and attention practices are part of the effective coach's manual, where players are instructed to narrow attention purely to the spinning ball and its trajectory. Perception, reception, and anticipation drills apply the visual sense to develop psychomotor skills from a young age. However, attention can also be directed purely to breath awareness and exhalation on contact, as well as kinesthetic sensations of 'loading the legs' and 'finishing through the strike'. Andy Roddick provided an excellent model of breath exhalation on ball strike in addition to exhalation on his opponent's contact. I encourage coaches and players to practice isolating and heightening the senses for brief periods (e.g., 60 seconds) in drills so that they can maintain or strengthen neural connections between a particular sensory mode and effective shot making. My experience is that tennis players don't often intentionally practice 'heightened sensory awareness' or attentional control, yet tennis is a sport that will brutally cajole the mind into task-irrelevant thinking traps and distractions. Therefore, on-court and off-court techniques that help players to condition task-relevant or neutral attentional states should be a staple diet of a player's program at whatever level.

Rational thinking and identity management

The sections above begin to reveal some of the key foundations to coping with the demands of tennis from a psychological perspective. One of the personal attributes that I believe tennis challenges in aspiring players is self-concept. When tennis players invest themselves in the sport, their perceptions of competence and identity can become tied, narrowed, and defined to their achievement on court. Self-concept can be fragile when it is based on irrational beliefs (e.g., 'I'm a failure if I lose this match'), a lack of recognition of strengths and virtues, and a unidimensional view of the person behind the player. With this in mind, a progressive exercise that I employ with elite junior players is to construct a more holistic, competitive identity through the process of developing a four-quadrant poster.

For quadrant one, players are asked to create their 'Rules of Engagement' based on collaborative discussion around questions such as 'What adversities and challenges that you may face in competition are you going to accept?'; 'What expectations do you have of yourself as a competitor?'; 'What choices do you want to make in the way that you behave on court?'. Such discussion stimulates thinking around rational and less rational beliefs, and challenges players to think more smartly about match play. For example, 'I know that to deal with adversity (e.g., poor line calls), I have to experience it'; 'I will make brave decisions that 'stretch' my level without fear of mistakes'; 'I will be an unconditional competitor throughout the match'.

For quadrant two, players profile their specific strengths from a technical, tactical, physical, or psychological perspective. Discussion stems from questions such as 'What skills do you enjoy doing/executing most in matches that sends a message to the opposition?' 'What attributes can you depend on in a tough situation?'. Responses might include, for example, an explosive forehand, exceptional reactions, and 'hands' at the net, dominating second serve returns – quick footwork and anticipation.

For quadrant three, discussion focuses on the specific mental tools that the player will use in matches (pre-match and during performance). Stimulus questions might include: 'What do you do before or during competition that helps you to optimize your strengths and meet your rules of engagement?'; 'What mental strategies and actions pull it all together for you?' An example from one player included: 'Body language – I project a strong and confident image; I give them no energy at any time'.

Finally, for quadrant four, discussion focuses on the notion that one's strengths and qualities as a person are far broader than what one has the opportunity to demonstrate on court. The 'Real YOU' cannot be defined by the result of a match, and it is critical to explore and acknowledge those qualities, values, and experiences that make up the strengths of the Real YOU away from tennis. Discussion questions therefore focus on these qualities, and 'What would you like other people to say about you behind your back?'. This latter quadrant serves an important assessment of the players' sense and breadth of identity, and it may be that further identity-based work is required to help them understand that they are more than just a tennis player. Clients have noted personal qualities such as trustworthy and dependable, finds good in people, honest and respectful, a strong family character, and a great team player. My belief is that when players recognize and attend to the strengths, qualities, and dimensions of their 'Real YOU', it helps their on–court 'Competitive YOU'. No matter what the match situation, intrinsic knowledge of their Real YOU allows their Competitive YOU greater freedom to express itself in a match without fear.

This process can take a number of sessions and builds up progressively over time as player and practitioner build a relationship with each other. Ultimately, the poster enables players to see a more rounded, bigger picture guiding their mental approach to the game. They can then offer a code name or identity to themselves that represents this approach. Components of the poster may, of course, be useful material to guide imagery work with the player, as well as observation and performance debriefing of mental tools, strengths, and rules of engagement.

Autobiographical, team magazine, and video-based work

A selection of final strategies that have been well received by players and coaches revolve around allowing them to create stories and reflective accounts of their experiences in the game. My long-term work with the professional player noted earlier offered several examples of such strategies. Firstly, when recovering from injury at 12 years of age, he kept himself immersed in the game by writing a small book for aspiring young players. These included brief chapters on psychology, diet, support, travel, physical fitness, managing friendships, and schoolwork to name but a few. Later in our relationship when he was 18 years old, I developed a Team Magazine where the player, coaches, physical trainer, and parents could contribute review sections with humorous elements that had occurred during the preceding period. This also sparked the idea to ensure that we gained video footage of physical sessions and drills where mental strategies were being practiced. Such material became useful for self-confidence building through highlighting performance accomplishments in different elements of the game (see Harwood, 2009). Most recently, these techniques were effectively used in another injury rehabilitation program, whereby the player kept a video diary of his goal setting and commitment to sessions and his ongoing reflections of progress. This paralleled support from his coach and physical trainer to videotape sessions on court, in the pool, and in the gym. All of this footage allowed us to create a DVD of his journey through recovery and return to play on the ATP tour. Such a project can be highly effective in terms of motivating players while they are injured and offering them involvement and responsibility in producing the storyline of their recovery.

Conclusions and recommendations

The aim of this chapter has been to offer insights into one practitioner's professional experience of working in tennis. In so doing, I have attempted to show the connections between my background and my philosophy and models of practice, as well as how they relate to the contextual nature of tennis. I have described the factors that enabled access to working with players, coaches, and the national organization, and some of the key roles and strategies that I believe are important for effective consulting. The development and journey of this chapter leads me to several summative recommendations for young practitioners.

1. Do your interdisciplinary homework

The most effective consultants understand the demands of tennis from a multidisciplinary sport science perspective, and they can integrate into an interdisciplinary team. They can also help to integrate a team around the player. Therefore, spend time in tennis environments at junior and senior level, and accumulate an understanding not only of the technical intricacies of the game, but also of how you can help sport science and how it can help you.

2. Manage your identity and the SP-client-coach fit

Psychologists with a coaching or playing background perhaps have an advantage in more confidently integrating psychological drills on court with coaches. In contrast, psychologists who stand by a counselling model of practice function better as the detached outsider, supporting players away from the on-court environment. Individual players and coaches may want different types of practitioner, and practitioners should reflect on their models of practice and how much they are comfortable and competent on and off the court. There are ethical matters around confidentiality and competence here, with certain types of practitioner being more visible and integrated than others. The psychologist should pay careful attention to any conflicting dual roles and consider how they want to manage the visibility of their relationship with player, coach, and support staff.

3. Watch, learn, debrief

Notwithstanding the above point, I believe that a psychologist learns most about his/her client by observations under pressure in match play. Ultimately, your role is most probably performance-focused, and therefore it is important that you gain opportunities to evaluate clients in the heat of battle as part of any psychological assessment, formulation, or intervention plan. As a private practitioner, I would have no hesitation in costing up observations as part of your service to players, as it is the context where both the player and yourself may objectively learn the most.

4. Educate early with a psychosocial agenda

The scope for working as a professional psychologist in tennis extends from supporting the local junior through to consultations and clients on the ATP and WTA tour. Nevertheless, the junior player market is substantial, and much can be gained from offering services to parents and tennis centres that illustrate the mental journey ahead. Parents want the best support and education for their children in a sport where uncertainty of the future is a consistent worry. Provide educational services that help parents and players to understand the developmental challenges, as well as the qualities and life skills that can be gained through long-term participation. Figure 7.1 provides a schematic representation of the varying demands of tennis and the individual skills and environmental processes that can influence player performance and development. I use this schematic as a tool to remind myself of the varying philosophies (i.e., holistic, humanistic, cognitive-behavioral) that may matter when best serving clients.

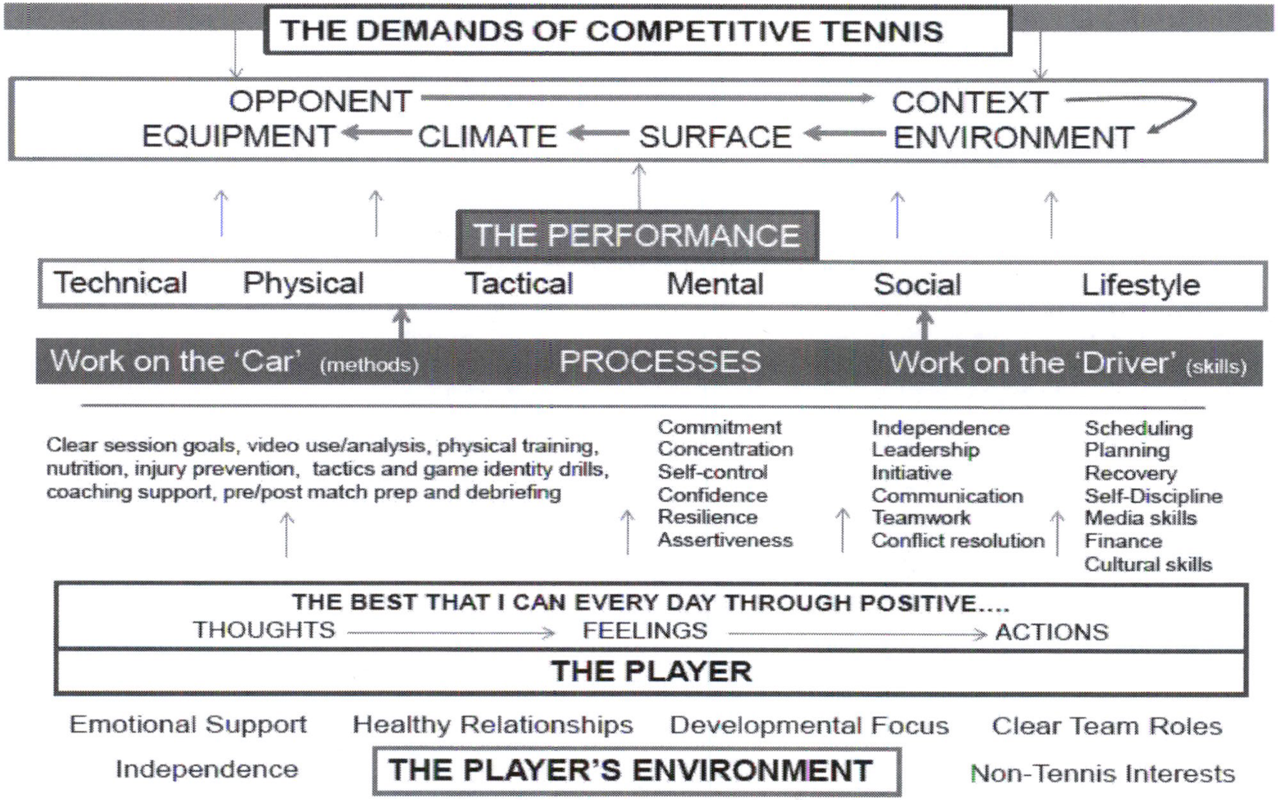

THE DEMANDS OF COMPETITIVE TENNIS

OPPONENT → CONTEXT
EQUIPMENT ← CLIMATE ← SURFACE ← ENVIRONMENT

Technical | Physical | Tactical | Mental | Social | Lifestyle

THE PERFORMANCE

Work on the 'Car' (methods)   PROCESSES   Work on the 'Driver' (skills)

Clear session goals, video use/analysis, physical training, nutrition, injury prevention, tactics and game identity drills, coaching support, pre/post match prep and debriefing

Commitment
Concentration
Self-control
Confidence
Resilience
Assertiveness

Independence
Leadership
Initiative
Communication
Teamwork
Conflict resolution

Scheduling
Planning
Recovery
Self-Discipline
Media skills
Finance
Cultural skills

THE BEST THAT I CAN EVERY DAY THROUGH POSITIVE....

THOUGHTS → FEELINGS → ACTIONS

THE PLAYER

Emotional Support   Healthy Relationships   Developmental Focus   Clear Team Roles

Independence   **THE PLAYER'S ENVIRONMENT**   Non-Tennis Interests

FIGURE 7.1   A holistic schematic of key processes and considerations in competitive tennis.

In closing, I hope that this chapter has gone some way toward educating you about the contextual and organization-related issues to consider when working in tennis, as well as enhancing your confidence in introducing strategies and themes that are relevant to stakeholders in the sport.

References

Ames, C. (1992). Achievement goals, motivational climate, and motivational processes. In G. C. Roberts (Ed.), *Motivation in sport and exercise* (pp. 161–176). Champaign, IL: Human Kinetics.

Bunker, D., & Thorpe, R. (1982). A model for the teaching of games in secondary schools. *Bulletin of Physical Education, 18*, 5–8.

Crespo, M., Reid, M., & Quinn, A. (2006). *Tennis psychology: 200+ practical drills and the latest research*. London: The International Tennis Federation, ITF Ltd.

Dweck, C. S. (2006). *Mindset: The new psychology of success*. New York: Random House.

Harwood, C. G. (2004). Goals: More than just the score. In S. Murphy (Ed.), *The sport psych handbook* (pp. 19–36). Champaign, IL: Human Kinetics.

Harwood, C. G. (2009). Enhancing self-efficacy in professional tennis: Intensive work for life on the tour. In T. Holder & B. Hemmings (Eds.), *Applied sport psychology: A case-based approach* (pp. 7–32). Wiley: Chichester.

Harwood, C. G., & Swain, A. B. (2002). The development and activation of achievement goals within tennis II: A player, parent, and coach intervention. *The Sport Psychologist, 16*, 111–137.

Hodge, K., & Petlichkoff, L. (2000). Goal profiles in sport motivation: A cluster analysis. *Journal of Sport and Exercise Psychology, 22*, 256–272.

Lauer, L., Gould, D. R., Lubbers, P., & Kovacs, M. (2010). *The USTA mental skills and drills handbook*. Monterey: Coaches Choice.

Loehr, J. (1986). *Mental toughness training for sports: Achieving athletic excellence*. Lexington, MA: Stephen Greene Press.

Loehr, J., & Schwartz, T. (2003). *The power of full engagement: Managing energy, not time, is the key to high performance and personal renewal*. New York: Free Press.

Poczwardowski, A., Sherman, C. P., & Ravizza, K. (2004). Professional philosophy in the sport psychology service delivery: Building on theory and practice. *The Sport Psychologist, 18*, 445–463.

Roberts, G. C. (1992). *Motivation in sport and exercise*. Champaign, IL: Human Kinetics.

Wylleman, P., & Lavallee, D. (2004). A developmental perspective on transitions faced by athletes. In M. Weiss (Ed.), *Developmental sport and exercise psychology: A lifespan perspective* (pp. 507–527). Morgantown, WV: Fitness Information Technology.

8

MY CONSULTING LIFE ON THE PGA TOUR

A 25-year experience

Richard Gordin

Author's background as a guide to sport context and understanding

I grew up in a family of athletes surrounded by sport on a daily basis. My father was a coach and university professor and my mother raised a family of three boys. I played every sport imaginable and was literally "in the locker room" as a young boy. I am absolutely convinced that this type of environmental exposure was instrumental in my development as an applied sport consultant. The world of golf is a small one. My father was a collegiate golf coach for 39 years, was an inaugural member of the Golf Coaches Hall of Fame, and knew many people in golf. Although I was not a golfer, I played football (through the collegiate level), basketball, track and field, baseball, and every other sport. Both of my brothers were excellent golfers and played at the university level. Needless to say, we lived and breathed sports in our family. Moreover, my vocation in sport was a foregone conclusion.

I officially trained as a physical education teacher and coach in my undergraduate degree work. For the next several years, I taught high school and coached various sports. Many important lessons were learned by coaching, attending workshops to listen to successful coaches, as well as trying various mental training techniques with my teams. By learning in a trial-and-error fashion, I was able to pull the lessons from various successes and failures to form a philosophy of service delivery. I discovered that performance success and failure was dictated not only by physical aptitude but also by mental toughness. As a player, I knew this, but at the time there was no formal training or service delivery in applied sport psychology. The players learned to be mentally tough without formal instruction. Having had high school teaching and coaching experience acted as a springboard for my formal study in the field of applied sport psychology.

I attended graduate school from 1978–1981 and was awarded a doctoral degree in the field. During my doctoral work I had the opportunity to work with a collegiate gymnastics team as a consultant. Needless to say, I was trying new things at the time and was fortunate to have a very supportive head coach, who was my advocate with his athletes. I also was exposed to the USA national team by contacts from within the world of gymnastics and was officially made the team mental consultant for the Olympic games in Seoul. Coincidentally, this was the first Olympic games when the United States Olympic Committee (USOC) in Colorado Springs sent an officially appointed sport psychologist to the games. During these times, my journey was facilitated by a great working relationship with coaches, athletic trainers, and to some degree National Governing Body (NGB) personnel. The timing of my career was facilitated by a sense of being in the right place at the right time.

The field of applied sport psychology was also emerging on the Professional Golfers Association (PGA) Tour. Dr. Bob Rotella and Dr. Dick Coop were making a significant impact with the touring professionals throughout the 1980s. Both were applied sport psychologists who did an excellent job representing our field on the Tour. Both colleagues were highly successful in introducing the field in an excellent fashion. They were nonintrusive in their approach, and they were cooperative with the teaching professionals already established (PGA Class A professionals). Rotella and Coop made presentations at coaching conventions as well and were instrumental in opening the doors to more consultants to enter the exciting world of the PGA Tour.

About this time, I was approached by an agent of one of the professional athletes to help him with a few performance issues he was experiencing. I flew to his residence and spent two days working with him on focusing skills and composure under pressure. He returned to the Tour the next week and finished second in a PGA event. He immediately started to spread the word to others professional, and within a short period I had eight clients on the Tour. This type of referral is best, as it comes from athlete-to-athlete, not from brochures placed in lockers or advertising. In the field of service delivery to athletes or athletic teams, it is crucial to understand the sport and all of its demands in order to be an effective consultant.

Even though I was not a golfer in my adolescent years, I managed to get an adequate exposure to the sport because of my father's role as golf coach. I would watch him coach his team, and I was introduced to the culture of golf. I learned the proper golf terminology, etiquette, tempo of the game, and language that one would need to converse with the athletes in an enlightened fashion. Although not necessary for success, talking the lingo of the sport (i.e. specific golf terminology such as "fade the ball", "move it from right to left", "hole out") can be an advantage to service delivery. I also played the sport reluctantly as a child, as both of my brothers were excellent golfers (since I am the oldest child, I did not relish losing to them on a consistent basis!). I, therefore, chose football, basketball, and track and field as my sports to avoid sibling rivalry. Another advantage of having experience in playing many different sports is that professional athletes often learn and connect best when using examples from other sports to make a point. My own experience playing golf was also advantageous to my understanding of the intricacies of the game. There is some controversy in our field regarding the extent of one's sport knowledge required to be a good consultant. Some consultants are very good consultants despite never having been an active athlete in the sport in which their consultations occur. However, I have always believed that having experience playing the sport might be advantageous to the consultant's knowledge base. There are some things you cannot learn from reading or observing the sport as your only form of understanding what the athlete is experiencing. Likewise, it has been possible for me to actually play a round of golf with my clients from time to time, and this has proven to be helpful in establishing a better rapport with the player. I am not suggesting that these experiences are a necessity, just that they might be an additional form of information that might enhance competency.

The game of professional golf is like a "travelling circus". Everyone goes from site to site every week. The actors in the play are the players, the coaches, the caddies, the sports medicine personnel, the equipment representatives, the agents, the translators for the foreign players, the strength and conditioning specialists, the family members, and the sport psychologists. Each player has his support team around him, and everyone knows everyone else on tour. Each player is an individual agent playing for a purse of $6–7 million per week. If you are fortunate to win one of golf's four major tournaments (Masters, US Open, British Open, PGA Championship), your entire career is changed in a dramatic fashion. Any win on the PGA Tour is monumental as it is very difficult to win a tournament. Every week 132–156 professional athletes are vying for a victory. Some will never win in an entire career, and often a player might only win once or twice in a 10–15-year sojourn on tour. If you are not a tour winner, then you are actually at a disadvantage financially, as well as falling well down in the pecking order for future tournament invitations to participate. The PGA tour invites a certain number of players to be participants each week, and the tour winners are given preference over non-winners. I worked with one player who won 14 collegiate tournaments in his college career and only won once in his 20-year PGA tour career. Although he made a very nice living, the stigma of not having multiple wins on tour diminished his reputation and status with the other players, as well as limited his opportunities to gain entry into tournament fields over his career.

Golf is a game of humility and embarrassment as the spectators scrutinize every shot. It is a unique game in that spectators play the same equipment as the professionals, and they can therefore directly compare themselves to the performance of the professional athlete. There are no referees to influence the course of the competition, and players call penalties on themselves. The performance of the player is directly related to the paycheck. If you do not play well (missing cuts, etc.), then you do not get paid that week. However, your expenses are always payable. The average player spends about $100,000 per year just in travel expenses. There are minor leagues in golf, such as the Web.com Tour, the Canadian Tour, as well as a senior tour called the Champions Tour. If you are a good player, you can make a nice living in this profession (players on tour can make anywhere from $500,000 to $1 million and never win during a specific year), but many young aspiring players spend their entire life being called a "journeyman player". Many players spend their entire careers making cuts and making money but always returning to the Qualifying School or dropping down to the minor leagues of golf. I have found it a challenging and exciting life to be a part of the Tour over the past 25 years. I believe a young sport psychologist would enjoy this ride very much, but it does come with pressures that can be challenging. I will discuss some of these pressures later in the chapter.

Initial challenges to access and trust

The initial challenges to access and trust are substantial, and gaining entry to the PGA Tour as a consultant is limited. Golf is a "closed shop", and the new consultant must earn his/her trust on tour. Everyone will inquire about who you are and what you do, even in casual practice rounds. When I first got involved in 1990, sport psychological service provision was still somewhat of a novelty. No one really understood this service completely, and many were still suspect of the delivery model provided. Fortunately, Rotella and Coop were great models for success with the players and coaches, but some who claimed to be sport psychologists were not. Coming from an academic background, I did not have the urgency to make a living in my consulting on tour. Some colleagues were trying to make a living at this time and were placing materials in players' lockers, such as books they had authored, and consulted using questionable ethical practices. One of my players was coerced by a colleague to take a psychological inventory at the US Open Championship and was provided with his profile results without adequate explanation. I had to do a significant debriefing to assure my client that all was well with him, as some of his profile results indicated some attention and focus difficulties, and of course he was concerned. This type of behavior (i.e. soliciting clients, ambulance chasing, etc.) can and still does occur. However, the tour does require a credential to practice on tour, including a $3 million liability policy for each occurrence of malpractice. This requirement has alleviated some unethical methods but has not completely solved the problem of misrepresentation of qualifications. A number of so-called sport psychologists still proliferate on tour and often give the field a bad reputation.

In order to be effective in your work, one must gain the trust of the players, caddies, and coaches. In order to do this, I have found that to be inclusive and collaborative is essential. The player is the client, but the cooperation among the support team actually helps to create a good working relationship. In this regard, the teaching professional (golf coach) is an excellent source of pertinent information about the player and concerning golf in general. If this person is a trusted ally, then this collaborative relationship can benefit the player tremendously. However, one must be careful regarding how much information to share, as with all confidentiality issues. Information of a personal nature and information that is specifically pertinent to a player's request for confidentiality should never be shared. I have very seldom found a player who is reluctant to encourage this type of collaborative relationship, as he knows he will benefit in the long run when the sport psychologist and coach work together. However, a coach and sport psychologist should never confuse a player with conflicting information. Confusion can occur when one or both parties breech their area of expertise and delve into instructing in areas where competence does not exist. If a coach attempts to be the sport psychologist or vice versa, then a conflict can arise and the player can become confused and conflicted.

As far as the caddie is concerned, it is a fact that these gentlemen know the Tour. Many have been on tour for years and know the players well. Players and caddies are in close contact with each other for the entire golfing experience, as they are "inside the ropes" together when most things happen. I often tell players to select the caddie with care because of the delicacy of the circumstance. I have also found that when I am not present on tour, the caddie can be a wonderful source of valued information to help me assess the player's performance. Generally, the athlete is cognizant of the fact that I might engage the caddie in conversation regarding the player's performance – and sometimes this is done with the player present – but I caution any future practitioners to always ask permission to share information. As one might expect, sometimes the player's evaluation of his performance is biased to protect his ego (using self-serving attributions) and therefore not always as forthright as it could be. For example, professional golfers are perfectionists by nature and always are hypercritical of their performances. Also, the players are often so perfectionistic that their evaluations are biased toward destructive rather than constructive analysis. The consequences of hypercritical tendencies and inaccurate analysis are an eroding of confidence and a fixed mindset rather than a growth mindset.

Another important aspect of establishing trust is to provide professional athletes with a valuable insight when initially starting the consultation. The athlete is seeking help from you with some sense of urgency. I accomplish this by utilizing some psychological inventories, such as the Test of Attentional and Interpersonal Style (Nideffer, 1976), the Competitive Styles Profile, and the Learning Styles Profile (Ogilvie, Greene, & Baillie, 1997), as well as a structured interview. With the help of these information-gathering methods, I am able to connect immediately with the athlete in order to assure him that I have the requisite knowledge to understand his needs. I develop a rapport immediately using this method, and as with any consulting relationship, the first session (impression) is of the utmost importance. The typical dialog revolves around my explanation of each factor on the profile, with the athlete's consensual validation driving the conversation. In this way, rapport is established and a plan can be formulated to aid in performance enhancement. Without establishing this trusting relationship, the success level of the consultation is in jeopardy. A professional athlete has a sense of urgency unsurpassed in all of consulting. The athlete must know that he trusts you implicitly and that you have some way to help him immediately. The urgency comes from the fact that one is making a living by playing golf. This is not a hobby but a financial livelihood for them.

One suggestion I would make to any future consultant on the PGA Tour would be to use caution regarding coaching. Sometimes the athlete will attempt to draw you into the instructional process. That is, asking technical questions regarding swing mechanics or practice routines. It is my recommendation to refrain from making suggestions in this domain for three major reasons: (a) the swing coach might take umbrage with this behavior; (b) you might give the wrong advice; and (c) it is not expressly written in your contract of service delivery. Even if you have significant expertise in swing mechanics and practice theory, it is dangerous and unethical to make this leap in service delivery. These interactions and requests usually come from the player in times of duress rather than during normal interaction.

When a sport psychology consultant is trying to gain entry to the Tour, it is important to fit into the existing culture. The dress code is strict on tour and, in fact, it expressly states in the credential application that it must be followed. A great asset for the young professional consultant is to observe and practice all golfing etiquette when first arriving on tour. For instance, no jeans or improper footwear are tolerated. These demands are expressly spelled out on the PGA Tour application that must be completed before a credential is issued. Consequently, the consultant must adhere to the dress code or be subject to revocation of the credential. It is also important to blend in and not be considered a distraction on the practice range, the golf course, or in the locker room. The general rule is to speak to players only when the player addresses you. The practice range is "their office", and all of the athletes appreciate normal, courteous office behavior. A bad reputation might be developed if the consultant becomes too gregarious with players you do not work with currently. I have witnessed this behavior many times from some of my colleagues, and it poorly represents all consultants. That is not to say that one should be impolite to others, but appropriate decorum is required when working on the PGA Tour. As mentioned earlier, everyone understands these norms and appreciates adherence to them. Another behavior that merits discussion is the "pecking order" on tour. The professional athletes are the reason the Tour exists; therefore, as one might expect, they are the reason people come to the tournaments. All of the rest of the team members are there at the discretion of these professionals and should understand that "we are not the show". The sport psychology professional is a consultant and should act as one. The professional athlete is the reason for people to patronize the event.

Be prepared and ready to help in any way possible to clear the path for the performance demands of your clients. Your working day may be exhausting at times. It is important not to be part of the problem but part of the solution during long and arduous days on tour. One more caution regarding life on the Tour is gaining the trust of the players. It is important to be on time, stay in the background, do not demand extra treatment or attention from the player (such as asking for tickets), and generally be a professional. If you follow these suggestions, you will be readily accepted as one of the Tour's family.

Consulting philosophy

My consulting philosophy has been developed over a 35-year career in applied sport psychology. I believe that athletes are ordinary people accomplishing extraordinary physical achievements. I also believe that my consultation involves the whole person, not just the athlete. By this I mean that all aspects of his life influence his performance on the golf course. Although my focus on service delivery is always performance driven, I am keenly aware of the many aspects of life that can influence performance, such as travel demands, family pressures, professional obligations to sponsors, and demands on an athlete's time. Determination, drive, and discipline are the essential qualities for excellence. If an athlete is lacking in any one of these personality components, it will be very difficult to accomplish great things. The *mental skills* of focusing, refocusing, maintaining composure, developing mental toughness, and utilizing persistence must also be considered when you develop a plan for each professional athlete.

When you begin a relationship, an adequate assessment of where the athlete lies on mastery of each skill is essential. As I interact with the athlete, I enjoy hearing the athlete's story about his emergence as a professional. It is within this story that I can formulate the most effective plan to add the requisite tools to the athlete's toolbox. Every consultation is a unique blending of all that this person has developed over time. Respect for the athlete and his past becomes an important part of relationship development. As a consultant, you are being invited into the athlete's life as a guest, and therefore you should respect the invitation by treating it with respect. Do your homework, so that you can understand the journey that has brought him to this point in his career.

There is nothing truly separate or unique in working with golfers over clients from other sports, except that golf is a game of failure. It is a game of mishits and misdirected shots. The athlete must learn to evaluate himself by assessing performance improvements, not just by tournaments won. As mentioned earlier in this chapter, golf is a sport where you do not win every week. The philosophy of service delivery that I adhere to contains the following aspects: (a) it is about the athlete, not about me; (b) the consultant should be off stage not on stage; and (c) it is about *education* not problems. When problems do arise, it is important to explain that "it is a situation with which *you* have a problem" not an insurmountable problem. The problem then becomes educational.

Some of the plausible dangers of the consulting relationship are getting too close to the client, becoming a cheerleader, promising results, expecting huge gains too quickly, not establishing a timeline for improvement, setting inappropriate fees, travel demands, and taking on too many clients. Each one of these dangers must be analyzed and planned for before they become a problem. Each player with whom I have worked has his own idea of need. One might want more attention than the other or want me to be physically present on the Tour more often. Consultation can take place in person, by cell phone, FaceTime, email, Skype, or any other form of communication (yes, even text messaging!).

Fee setting is important to establish at the beginning of the consultation and can be accomplished in many ways. Some players prefer hourly rates, some prefer retainer fees, and even others like incentive fees. The caddies on tour are paid a weekly stipend plus a percentage of the purse. Swing coaches usually are on retainer fees, whereas physiotherapists and strength and conditioning personnel are on hourly wages. I have found it useful to stay away from incentive payment for several reasons. The greatest problem would include becoming too dependent on the player's performance. This concern ties back into my advice: do not allow yourself to become involved in promising results that are tied to fee setting, as this might add to your own stress. The hourly arrangements as well as retainer fee payment methods have worked for me for the past 25 years in an efficient way.

Travel is also a concern as an entire competitive season lasts all year and might involve travel from Hawaii to the United Kingdom. Depending on the player demand, it is possible to spend as many as 100 days on the road during any given competitive season. Travel expenses are always part of my contractual agreement with the players, and these expenses are charged and reimbursed in addition to my consultation fee by either the player directly or by his agent.

Effective strategies

Most of the effective strategies that have been employed revolve around developing a positive relationship with the athlete. Not all of my consultations have been successful, as any consultation depends on developing a good working relationship with the athlete. Two important principles must be established: (a) the athlete must trust you implicitly; and (b) he must believe that you have something useful to give him in order to improve his performance. Also, I have found that the best approach is to treat the athlete holistically. If you meet these relationship requirements, then a successful outcome is not assured but is likely. The first important task is to get to know the athlete in a timely fashion without a lot of time wasted in idle chitchat. I have accomplished this by utilizing appropriate psychometric inventories that are sport specific and information rich. Next is a consensual validation of the results with a feedback session that involves the athlete disclosing more information to expand upon what has been gleaned from the inventory results. More effective communication can be developed in a short period of time, and the professional athletes appreciate your effort in letting them know that you understand them and that you can provide solutions, including proper training in the mental game.

The next step is to arrange a follow-up session to formulate a plan of action with a timeline. I do not promise results, but I imply that if the required effort is put forth, then some positive results can be expected. My emphasis is on the *mental training* necessary, as no immediate or magic results occur in performance gains without working on skill development. One of my most effective methods is to utilize relaxation and imagery, including focusing practice, to develop a "script of excellence" outlining great performances. I have the athletes remember the most memorable and efficient performances and sometimes have them verbally record these rich descriptions into an audio script. This technique is complimented by using the athlete's own voice in the audio recoding. I also encourage the athletes to do their imagery while in an athletic position rather than lying on a bed in a prone position. This is a much more powerful way to re-experience performance excellence. Most of these professionals are athletic geniuses and are simply seeking ways to unlock their potential to perform in "the rhythm of the game of golf". Other common areas of concern are lack of adequate game plans for the golf course, putting too much pressure on themselves to perform well in every tournament, not accepting the vagaries of the game (golf is played outside on uneven surfaces with bad bounces and inclement weather), comparing themselves with others while playing the game, and perfectionism.

To be effective as a consultant on the PGA Tour requires close observation of behaviors, not only on the course but also off the course. Attention should be paid to daily habits required for success, such as adequate rest, functional practice sessions, appropriate commitment to sponsors and golf outings, time management expertise, good relationships with caddies and swing coaches, and generally adequate handling of life on the tour. Rookies are often spending a large portion of their first year on tour trying to understand where to stay, where to eat, routing to and from the golf course, courtesy cars, adulation of fans, handling the "awestruck syndrome", and trying to fit in and believe that they truly belong on tour. My most effective consultations have involved helping these men adapt and feel accepted and comfortable in their new careers. Most have been highly successful golfers at the collegiate level, but life as a professional is an entirely different experience. It incorporates the development of support groups, travel demands, loneliness, and establishing daily routines. I sometimes take on the role of confidant, as agents and well-meaning family members do not always understand the rigors of playing at such a high level week upon week. Most professional golfers play between 24–30 tournaments a year, and getting into the flow of a week on tour takes some adaptation in the various areas already mentioned.

Some of my most meaningful contributions come from helping young professionals understand and plan for the disruptions and distractions of tour life. Not often discussed openly is the strain put upon relationships by the life on the PGA Tour. Players are often torn between their love of golf and following their dreams and obligations at home with family and well-meaning friends who are living vicariously through their performances. Perspective provided in the aforementioned areas is often the best service provision provided. Many of these athletes can become confused and are not able to concentrate for long periods of time (4-hour rounds over four days) because of added concerns off the course. Compartmentalizing is a skill that the great golfers have perfected, and this is a requirement for great performance in golf. It takes total focus on every shot to be a contender on tour; if your mind wanders at the wrong moment, disaster can be imminent.

Finally, my own commitment to consultation is a major factor in a successful consultancy. This commitment requires a tremendous amount of time and effort by the consultant, and he/she must be present and effective on tour. The pressures of the consulting process can accumulate over time and have a deleterious effect on the consultant. It is important for the sport psychologist to stay in top physical condition, practice some form of mindfulness on a daily basis, rest and recuperate consistently, and understand that you can and will be fired by the athlete at some point in your career. One of the perils of a career as a consultant on the PGA Tour is that longevity of employment for these professionals can be relatively short term. Turnover of the coaching staff is often used because these professionals believe that change may result in better performance. One can be dismissed for almost anything, including lack of an athlete's notion that a consultant has given inappropriate time to the relationship, a "flight to health" reaction because of immediate gains in performance, and the added expense required for consulting services.

Summary

Twenty-five years on the PGA Tour has been an exciting and rewarding endeavor and one that has provided me with many valuable and irreplaceable lessons and joyful experiences.

I am often asked what I do and why I do it. My answer to why is because of the relationships with the players, coaches, and others committed to pursuing excellence in life. Victories will be experienced, poor performances and disappointments endured, and lifelong relationships created. I have been fortunate to attend the Champions dinner given on the evening of a Masters Tournament victory as well as a "riding out" of a major championship in the car with a client who shot 80 in the final round. I have been in the room when a prospective Ryder Cup player was informed he was not chosen for the team, as well as being with a player who was experiencing the exhilaration of a first-time victory on the PGA Tour. Also I have shared in the joy of a client making it through the Qualifying school or playing onto the PGA Tour because of his success on the Web.com Tour. All of these feelings that only a professional athlete can describe, including euphoria, depression, and anger, are examples of the powerful emotions that are part of the sporting experience in professional golf.

The privilege of contributing a small part to these experiences is an indescribable benefit for those of us who do what we do. Most of the time on the PGA Tour, it is life as usual, "grinding it out" week by week to make a living and striving to pursue a dream of achieving excellence in one's chosen profession. To be able to share the ride is a rare privilege. To those of you who are considering this sport discipline as part of your consulting career, I wish you the best and hope that this chapter has given you some insight into what is required to be a sport consultant of the PGA Tour.

References

Nideffer, R. M. (1976). Test of attentional and interpersonal style. *Journal of Personality and Social Psychology, 34*, 394–404.

Ogilvie, B. C., Greene, D., & Baillie. (1997). *The interpretive and statistical manual for the competitive styles profile and learning styles profile.* Unpublished manuscript.

Suggested resources

Albaugh, G., & Bowker, M. (2006). *Winning the battle within: The perfect swing is the one you trust.* Placerville, CA: Kele Publishing.

Coop, R. H. (1993). *Mind over golf: How to use your head to lower you score.* New York: Wiley Publishing.

Gordin, R. D. (2002). Special feature: *Dr. Rich Gordin's golf tips.* Accessed at www.mikeweir.com

Gordin, R. D. (2012). Dr. Rich Gordin. In M. Aoyagi & A. Poczwardowski (Eds.), *Expert approaches to sport psychology: Applied theories of performance excellence* (pp. 37–49). Morgantown, WV: Fitness Information Technology.

Nilsson, P., & Marriott, L. (2005). *Every shot must have a purpose.* New York: Gotham Books.

Parent, J. (2002). *Zen golf: Mastering the mental game.* New York: Random House.

Rotella, R. J. (1995). *Golf is not a game of perfect.* New York: Simon & Schuster.

Rotella, R. J. (2004). *The golfer's mind: Play to play great.* New York: Free Press.

Rotella, R. J. (2008). *Your 15th club: The inner secret of great golf.* New York: Free Press.

Rotella, R. J., & Bunker, L. K. (1981). *Mind mastery for winning golf.* Englewood Cliffs, NJ: Prentice-Hall, Inc.

Unestahl, L-E., & Gordin, R. D. (1995). *Mental training for golf: A 16-week audio mental training program.* Orebro, Sweden: Veje.

Utley, S. (2006). *The art of putting.* New York: Gotham Books.

Valiente, G. (2005). *Fearless golf.* New York: Random House.

9

HOW A PLANT POT LED ME TO PERFORMANCE PSYCHOLOGY IN WOMEN'S PROFESSIONAL GOLF

Christian Smith

I was a golfer long before I ever decided to become a mental conditioning coach for golf. The game has been a part of my life for as far back as I can remember. My connection began when I was roughly 18 months old in my grandparents' garden with a very small metal golf club, an airflow ball, a plant pot for a cup, and a cane used for supporting plants for a flagstick. No one in my family played golf. I was introduced to the game by my grandfather, who caddied in his youth at a private course in my hometown in England, where I am currently a member. Growing up I always saw myself playing golf, and not once did I consider my future would involve anything other than me chasing a little white ball for a living.

Unlike many modern-day junior golfers, although I picked up the game at a young age, I did not specialize early. During my late childhood and early adolescence, I participated in a variety of sports and represented my school in both individual and team sports. It wasn't until I won my age group championship (U14) in a national golf tournament and my family petitioned the school headmaster that I was allowed to use sport time to practice golf.

Growing up, I lived on the golf course both literally and figuratively. My parents took positions as caterers at three golf clubs, and each time the assigned living quarters were annexes of the clubhouses. I could get from my bedroom onto the practice area or first tee in less than a minute. When I wasn't practicing, playing, travelling for competitions, or doing homework, I would show my appreciation for the sacrifices my parents made to make it possible for me to pursue my passion by helping them in the clubhouse kitchen.

As a junior golfer, I learned about the history, values, culture, language, etiquette, and rules associated with the game over time through my relationships with older club members, club professionals, professional golfers, and elite level coaches. I grew up reading golf magazines and instruction books, as well as watching instruction videos and professional golf tournaments both in person and on television. I was constantly searching for things to help take my game to the next level.

I watched the pros play and often wondered what made them capable of doing what they did. I worked continuously on "perfecting" my technique, as well as on the other more tangible parts of the game – course management, physical conditioning, and nutrition. That said, the value of the mental game was not lost on me. I can vividly recall the pressure I felt standing on the first tee with a large crowd watching me in a local qualifier for The Open Championship at my home course. I can also recall playing in a one-day, 36-hole event shooting a course record 5 under par 66 in the morning followed by a lackluster 81 in the afternoon on the same golf course. These are just two of many experiences that I have had over the years that served to educate me on the impact the mental game can have on performance. Over time, I learned how important the mental game was but didn't know how to go about improving it.

There were a couple of occasions I sought help with the mental game. Firstly, I met with a sport psychologist on my club's practice area, but I remember not connecting on a personal level and not being able to make sense of what he was telling me to do. I also remember having one session with a licensed clinical hypnotherapist, but he wasn't a golfer, and yet again I had a hard time connecting what he was saying with what I was experiencing both as a young person and as a golfer. The first book specific to the mental game of golf I ever read was *Golf is Not a Game of Perfect* by Dr. Bob Rotella (Rotella & Cullen, 1995). I recall reading it and feeling that Dr. Rotella had shared *what* I needed to do but not necessarily *how* to do it, and consequently I was left with more questions than answers.

In 2001, I received an athletic scholarship to play collegiate golf in the United States at Coastal Carolina University near Myrtle Beach, South Carolina. After going two years undeclared, I decided on psychology as my major, which led me to my first undergraduate sport psychology class. It was while I was playing on the men's golf program that I first heard of the David Leadbetter Junior Golf Academy in Bradenton, Florida. Three of my former college teammates had trained there full time. In my senior year, I decided that I would inquire about job openings and sent letters to both the golf and mental conditioning (MC) departments. Chris Passarella wrote back on behalf of Team MC and informed me of the summer internship program open to students in graduate school pursuing sport psychology. With graduation on the horizon, I looked into graduate schools and finally decided on San Diego State University (SDSU). After arriving on campus, introducing myself to Head Men's Golf Coach, Ryan Donovan, and expressing my interest in using the last year of my NCAA eligibility, I instead accepted the position of volunteer assistant golf coach. Dr. Jay Brunza (a former clinical psychologist for the U.S. Navy turned sport psychologist, who has worked with Tiger Woods) was brought in to consult with the golf team, and I was able to build a relationship with him. I applied for the 2006 summer internship at IMG Academies and was one of four applicants accepted. I spent the summer working in Bradenton alongside Team MC, "drinking from the fire hose" and learning many of the ins and outs of applied consulting. It was in the Fall semester, after I had returned to San Diego, that I was again contacted by Chris Passarella and offered a full-time position. My first official day working for IMG as a mental conditioning coach was February 1, 2007.

International Management Group (IMG) is a global sports, fashion, and media business, which was founded by Mark McCormack in 1960. IMG purchased Nick Bollettieri Tennis Academy in 1987, and in 1993 it acquired the youth division of the David Leadbetter Golf Academy. The IMG Academy golf program has a rich history of developing elite junior and professional golfers, both male (Sean O'Hair, Casey Wittenberg, Peter Uihlein, Emiliano Grillo) and female (Yani Tseng, Michelle Wie, Paula Creamer, Julieta Granada). IMG Academies was rebranded as IMG Academy and subsequently sold to William Morris Endeavour Entertainment, LLC (WME), a talent and literary agency, in its acquisition of IMG Global in 2013. IMG Academy offers multiple training modalities to Academy students, Camp athletes (youth and adult), and specialty populations (collegiate athletic programs and professional athletes and teams). At the center of IMG Academy is a co-educational, college preparatory school for students focused on academics, sports, athletic and personal development, as well as social responsibility.

How the sport context and sub-cultural understanding were gained

My first-ever experience coaching female athletes came during my summer internship at IMG Academy. My experience increased significantly after I was hired full time to work primarily alongside the golf program. Interacting in both groups and on a one-on-one basis, attending golf tournaments, talking with the young women in the program about their experiences at the junior, amateur, and professional levels, as well as staying in contact with alumnae who have graduated and gone on to play college and professional golf, have all added to my understanding of female competitive golf.

Since working at the Academy, I have been fortunate to work alongside a group of world-class coaches who have shared with me their own coaching experiences and whose coaching relationships with elite female golfers have allowed me to establish my own connections with some of their players. David Leadbetter, David Whelan (Director of Instruction, IMG Academy golf program), Larry Marshall (former Director of Post-Grad golf program), Kevin Collins (Senior Certified Instructor), and many other David Leadbetter Golf Academy (DLGA) and IMG certified instructors, as well as Chris Passarella (former Head of Mental Conditioning), Trevor Moawad (former Director of Athletic and Personal Development), Dr. Angus Mugford (Head of Personal and Organizational Performance), Dr. Taryn Morgan (Assistant Director of Athletic and Personal Development), Dr. Vanessa Shannon (Mental Conditioning Coach), and former physical conditioning coaches for golf, Corey Stenstrup and Trevor Anderson, have all been integral to my work with Ladies Professional Golf Association (LPGA) Tour players and have all positively shaped my understanding of working effectively with elite female athletes.

Over the years, I have forged relationships with LPGA players who have trained at IMG Academy either as full-time students or after having turned professional. In more recent years, I have been able to travel with players to support them while competing on the Symetra Tour, in LPGA qualifying school, in regular LPGA Tour events, and in major championships such as the Kraft Nabisco Championship and the US Women's Open. Being on the road has allowed me to learn not only by observing and interacting with other players and coaches but also from my own firsthand experiences inside the ropes. My presence has allowed me to have conversations with golf coaches, caddies, managers, agents, the players' families, and members of the media, all of whom have graciously shared their insights about life on tour.

Being around young players just picking up the game to those who compete and have won at the very highest level has helped shape my appreciation for the challenges the game presents. Some challenges are universal, while some are unique to each environment, such as the LPGA Tour. That said, at its core, golf is golf. No matter where or what level it is played at, it involves hitting a ball using a club into a hole, the overall goal being to get the ball in the hole in the fewest strokes possible.

Initial challenges to access and trust and how these were overcome

Just as a golfer faces challenges that are both universal and unique, so too does a mental conditioning coach. Two specific challenges that need to be navigated are gaining access to athletes and developing trust.

It is fair to say that I would not have had access to the thousands of golfers (junior, amateur, collegiate, and professional) that I have worked with over the last 8 years without holding the position of lead mental conditioning coach for the IMG Academy golf program, the brand-name recognition of David Leadbetter and WME | IMG, as well as the relationships I have developed with world-class golf instructors and staff whom I work alongside on a daily basis.

The female professional golfers I have had the opportunity to work with since starting at IMG Academy fall into one of two categories – those who have come *through* the system (trained as a full-time student and turned professional) and those who have come *to* the system (trained with us after having turned professional).

Coming through the system

Access is most certainly less of a concern as a mental conditioning coach at IMG Academy than for most sport psychology professionals since athletes coming through the system are already enrolled in sport programs on campus. The full-time Academy program begins in late August and ends in early June. The IMG Academy golf program is currently home to approximately 120 golfers. The Academy golf program includes core mental conditioning sessions on a weekly basis. We have chosen to use the term "mental conditioning" to draw a relationship in the athletes' minds to physical conditioning. Although the mind is not a muscle, we believe, like muscles, it can be strengthened with consistent exercise over time.

As lead mental conditioning coach for the golf program, I see every student each week in a small group session (15–20 students), which takes place inside a classroom, out on the practice area, and from time to time on the golf course. For those students who are so inclined, we also offer one-on-one coaching at an additional cost, if they would like more individualized attention.

Outside of delivery time, my schedule allows for observation time out at golf. The students also see me around campus – in the cafeteria, in the school classroom, observing workouts, walking or riding a tram between East and West campus, in the lobby area of the dorms, riding on the bus to and from the golf course, or occasionally sitting in on other Athletic and Personal Development classes such as Nutrition and Leadership. Being able to see them in a variety of contexts allows me to cultivate relationships by getting to know the athletes as people as well as golfers. The quality of these relationships allows me "access" to the athletes' eyes, ears, hearts, and minds.

While access is certainly less of an issue, there is still the matter of trust. One phrase my colleagues and I use a lot is "they don't care how much you know until they know how much you care." I think these words summarize a fundamental part of our team's philosophy when working with people to help them develop the High Performance Mindset (HPM).

Developing trust relates to both the players and their coaches, given the influence the coaches can have on their students. The connections I have developed with golfers have always been facilitated by my relationship with the golf coaches and other staff members here at IMG Academy. I have found that if the golfer trusts the coach and the coach trusts me, then the golfer typically trusts me, even if I haven't had the chance to develop a strong connection with her. This transference of trust also applies to friends of the golfers and other golfers they look up to. If you help their friend or someone whose game they respect to get better, this too can help create rapport. My preexisting relationships with returning Academy golfers also helps to foster relationships with new student–athletes. My ability to develop trust has also been facilitated by my work with other professional golfers. When the students have become aware of my involvement with professionals, this too has helped create the conditions for buy-in.

Trust is much easier to lose than it is to build. Earning the trust of a person can take time. I don't believe that you can have a long-lasting, positive impact on people without first establishing a trusting relationship with them. Some of the challenges to trust I have encountered in my work with golfers include not knowing them/them not knowing me, the golfer's perception that the mental game is not important, them having had a previous negative experience working on the mental game, their golf coach not valuing what I do, and their belief in the stigma behind working on the mental game (e.g., asking for help is a sign of weakness as opposed to believing, as I do, that you don't have to be sick to get better).

In an effort to earn the trust of the golfers I interact with, I have found myself focusing on four key areas: availability, approachability, utility, and authenticity. Being available to golfers and coaches in the sport environment, as well as online, are both ways to establish trust, particularly with respect to today's generation of golfers. Being approachable encompasses what you say, and how you say it, as well as nonverbal communication such as facial expressions, gestures, and posture. These factors can either encourage or dissuade people from interacting with you. Utility refers to adding value by going outside your job description to serve and help others without devaluing yourself in the process. As one of my colleagues recently put it, "you can give them water but don't become the water boy." Lastly, being authentic speaks to practicing what you preach, being yourself, and doing what you say you are going to do.

Coming to the system

While some of the female professionals I have had the opportunity to work with began their journey to the professional ranks in our full-time program, some have come to us after turning professional. IMG Global has a division called IMG Golf, and one area it focuses on is client representation. Some professional golfers have been referred through this network of agents to the Academy for our services.

One of the main challenges to access regarding working with LPGA professionals who are not already affiliated with IMG is that I am not out there on the LPGA Tour week in and week out to make the connections and to maintain the relationships. Access, as far as my experiences with LPGA professionals are concerned, has come about as a result of the IMG brand and connections through my work at the Academy.

Those who come to the system are not likely to spend extended periods of time on campus, which comes with its own challenges. With respect to developing trust, I believe it is important to know as much about the person as possible prior to the first face-to-face interaction. Doing your homework before you meet the golfer involves researching background information on the Internet (e.g., biography, past results, blog posts, and articles written about her) and talking to your point of contact (e.g., agent, golf coach) to better understand the reason behind the introduction and to determine whether the golfer has had any agency in the decision to meet. I also feel it is better to have the person introducing you be present to make the initial introduction. After the initial meeting, follow-up with the player is imperative. Building trust from a distance can be a challenge and requires a consistent investment of time and energy. It is important that you don't unintentionally do something (e.g., over-promising and underdelivering) that might diminish the trust a player has in you as a coach. Having a conversation with a player about what she might perceive as a breach of trust can alleviate the potential for problems down the road (Nilsson & Marriott, 2014). It is also important to establish effective communication practices with the player and to begin the process of connecting with the team that surrounds her (e.g., coach, caddie, agent). Just like with players coming through the system, the success of the relationship with those coming to the system is also down to being available, approachable, valuable, and authentic.

The consulting philosophy developed for the context

When thinking about my own personal consulting philosophy with professional golfers, I am reminded of a conversation I had with a world-renowned golf instructor and the question he posed to a mental coach working with one of his players, specifically: "Are you in the business of helping them feel better when they under-perform or in the business of helping them perform better?" I believe my role involves helping golfers perform better on and off the golf course; I consider myself to be an action-based consultant who is both needs-focused and performance-oriented. I believe that better people make better golfers; I believe that people who make birdies off the course make birdies on the golf course. I believe that "You don't have to be sick to get better!" I believe that improvement is a never-ending process. I believe that results matter.

I will always remember what a veteran caddie who has helped steer a number of male players to major victories once told me: "Tell the players what they need to hear and not what they want to hear because they are often surrounded by people who tell them the latter." I believe that honesty and authenticity are integral to the success of any consulting relationship. I believe I am only part of the picture; I don't take credit for success nor accept responsibility when things don't go as planned.

I believe that progress can never precede trust; you need trust to have access to another person's ears and eyes and to ultimately reach their hearts and minds. I believe there is a distinction between performance-related issues and clinical issues experienced by athletes. Although these issues may converge in an athlete's life, I believe my scope is clearly defined, and when I identify issues outside of my scope, I make the appropriate referral. I believe that I am doing my job when the athlete no longer needs me; my goal is to help the athletes become their own mental coaches through a framework of Education, Application and Support (EAS).

A few examples of effective strategies when working with professional athletes in the context

Through my work with golfers, I have developed a framework of delivery I refer to as EAS. Education involves introducing the concepts of what, why, and how to the golfers. Application involves helping the golfers put tools into practice, ideally in an environment similar to one they perform in (practice area, golf course). Support focuses on helping the athletes in the performance arena. When it comes to Support, there are two aspects – when just the golfers are on the road and when I am also out on the road with them.

Education

In my experience, one of the foundations to education is the discussion of controllability and helping the golfers recognize what they can control, what they can influence, and what they have no control over whatsoever. As a professional, it is easy to focus too much on results (e.g., score) and results of results (e.g., winning, money list, world ranking points, playing privileges, sponsors) at the expense of what helps them perform at their best. Sharing videos of lucky and unlucky bounces and golfers playing in bad weather conditions and tough course conditions can all start the conversation relating to focusing on the process and "controlling the controllables".

Based on a book titled *How to Really Stink at Golf* (Foxworthy & Hartt, 2008), which was shared with me by a former student, I have found that asking the question "If you wanted to stink at professional golf, what would you do?" is a novel and insightful way of brainstorming and improving a player's self-awareness. This counterintuitive approach to improvement inevitably leads to players recognizing what specific areas of their mental game might need attention.

I sometimes use statistics to help create a compelling case for how small things can make a big difference in the game of golf. For example, in 2014, Stacy Lewis was first in scoring average on the LPGA Tour with 69.532 strokes per round, Na Yeon Choi was 10th with 70.536, Jessica Korda was 34th with 71.550, and Chie Arimura was 92nd with 72.532 (LPGA, 2015). The separation that is evident at the highest level of the game because of one single stroke per round reinforces the relative importance of the small things that all add up to being the difference you see between the average and good tour players, the good and great tour players, and the great and greatest players ever to play the game.

All that said, not all of the tour players I have had the opportunity to work with speak English as a first language, and communication can be a challenge. From an education perspective, when working with golfers for whom English is not their first language, here are a few strategies I have adopted to help reduce the impact of the language barrier:

- Live translator – utilize a bilingual person who can translate for both you and the golfer
- Google Translate – enter words in English and translate to the foreign language
- Video feedback – record the golfers practicing, playing, or competing and show them afterwards
- Video clips – show them someone modeling the desired behavior; I have also used TED Talks since they sometimes have either a transcript in a foreign language or can be streamed with foreign language subtitles
- Keep it simple – simple words, talk slower, use nonverbal communication (physical actions and hand signals)

Application

Interacting with golfers on the practice area or on the golf course can give you valuable insights into their mental approach to the game of golf. One putting exercise, called the tornado, is an effective way of learning a lot about a player and opens the door for discussion about many topics related to the mental game. Tornado involves setting eight tees around the hole each 45 degrees apart. The closest tee is 3 feet from the hole and each tee is progressively farther from the hole in 1-foot increments, with the last putt measuring 10 feet. Tornado is a drill, which incorporates both rewards and consequences. The basic version of the drill involves starting at the closest tee and staying at each tee until the putt is made before progressing to the next tee. There is no consequence associated with missing the putt. The second version introduces the idea of moving forward one position when a putt is made and moving backward one position when a putt is missed. In the last version of the drill, the player moves forward one position when a putt is made and starts over returning to the closest tee (3 feet) when a putt is missed. I have found tornado to be particularly useful as a conversation starter with respect to the performance cycle – Preparation, Execution, Reaction, Regeneration (C. Passarella, personal communication, February 15, 2007), as well as mental tools such as goals, self-talk, breathing, and mental rehearsal. Filming the exercise not only adds pressure but can also be used for video review to help golfers with self-awareness, helping to create consistency between what the golfers think they are doing and what they are actually doing.

Support

As previously stated, there are two aspects to support –(1) when just the athletes are on the road and (2) when you are also on the road with them.

Given my primary role as lead mental coach for the IMG Academy golf program and associated responsibilities, the majority of my time is spent supporting the professionals I work with from the Academy. This involves staying on top of their schedules, results and statistics, reading any articles written about them and interviews they give, and watching television coverage and recording them competing. Recording television footage is helpful for later use, either as a means to review and debrief or as potential material for making a video. Videos can be either motivational or educational in nature, depending on the athlete's needs at that time.

Effective long-distance consulting requires that you determine the player's preferred means of communication. There are a variety of options, including, but not limited to, phone calls, text message/iMessage, Whats App, FaceTime, Skype, e-mail, Direct Messages via Twitter, and Facebook Messenger. Some of the above are more personal, while some are less so. I have found that when working with players for whom English is not their first language, miscommunication is made more likely when exchanging ideas in writing or when you cannot see the other person's body language.

The preferred method of communication is not just related to the player but also to the team that surrounds the player. When you are not able to be present, getting an accurate picture of what is going on day-to-day, week-to-week is particularly important. For this reason, it is imperative to establish and cultivate a positive working relationship with the eyes and ears who are with the player most often, including the coach, caddie, agent, trainer, etc. As a result of these relationships, in particular with caddies, I have been able to indirectly impact a player and her performance by helping one of the team members around that player (e.g., helping a caddie understand how a player is thinking and what she can do to better support the player during the round on the course).

I truly believe there is no substitute for spending time with golfers and getting an inside look into their life. A typical week on the LPGA Tour is very busy and involves travel days, practice rounds, and pro-ams, followed by three or four tournament days. When out on the road, there are multiple opportunities to consult between the cracks. Below is an example of a typical tournament day and what I see as my role during the different timeframes.

A typical day might begin by observing a physical warm-up in the gym, where I might present a simple key message for the day (e.g., focus on what you can control), reinforced by sharing either a video clip or a short personal motivational highlight video. When travelling to the golf course in the car and/or eating breakfast/lunch (depending on the tee time), I will typically engage in general conversation or take the opportunity to reinforce the key message. Prior to the round, I observe and note any variations in the pre-round routine. I will also interact with the caddie to get a sense of how they are doing, how the player is doing from their perspective, and to reinforce the key message with them as they will be side by side with the player during the competitive round.

During the round, I follow the player's group around the golf course, making either written or mental notes of anything that I feel is important related to the performance cycle – before the shot (Preparation), the swing/stroke (Execution), after the shot (Reaction), and between the shots (Regeneration). I also use this time to connect with team members, such as family members, agents, and physical trainers. With certain players, I have also found it very useful to cultivate relationships with members of the media, in particular those who are bilingual, and I will often use this time to talk with them about their observations, especially when working with foreign players. Since members of the media are present week in, week out on the Tour and interview the players after their rounds, I have, on occasion, learned a lot about a player from post-round comments made in their native language, which I would otherwise not have been privy to simply because I don't speak the language.

When the player has finished her round, I typically talk with the caddie to get their first impressions while the player takes care of her scorecard and/or media obligations. Once all that is over, I will circle up with the player and caddie to debrief the round and solicit their thoughts on what went well, what was learned, and what can be better. This feedback can often be factored in when developing a post-round practice session. The post-round practice routine ideally might involve working on long-term maintenance drills as well as something based on the day's performance that will help with tomorrow's round. Typically, when traveling back to the hotel and/or eating dinner out with a player, my goal is to help her feel normal away from the golf course, and we often don't talk too much, if at all, about golf.

Whether on the road or not, some specific strategies that have helped players perform include keeping track of process points and identifying tangible reminders to keep an idea in the forefront of the players' minds. In golf, where the challenge is to score the lowest, creating a secondary game based on having the player score the highest often helps the player to shift her focus away from results (e.g., one point for positive visualization prior to execution of the shot). In competition, players can benefit from reminders about simple things. One player I work with now writes 100 on the palm of her glove to signify the idea that putting the left hand on the golf club is consistent with being 100% committed to the shot she is about to hit. Cue words can also be written on the ball, the scorecard, the yardage book, or the underside of the brim of a hat (anywhere the player is likely to look throughout the round), to serve as a constant reminder of what is important to help the players perform at their best.

Recommendations for aspiring practitioners

Given the relatively small number of professional golfers in comparison to the number of people who play golf in the world, the opportunities to work with LPGA pros are somewhat limited. That said, two things to bear in mind are that the majority of pros recognize the impact the mental game can have on performance, and there are people out there working with professional golfers. Therefore, it is important to appreciate that gaining access to and working effectively with athletes will not happen either by accident or overnight. It comes about as a result of creating the right conditions. There is no one way to go about it, and in some respects it depends on where you are at in your career – a graduate student or a young professional who is out in the real world looking to work with professional athletes.

Graduate student

As a graduate student with aspirations of becoming a sport psychology practitioner, I believe it is important to first acquire the relevant, formal education in psychology, sport psychology, and/or related fields. Formal education is certainly not the be-all and end-all but instead serves as a foundation for the future. While the graduate-level classes you take are designed to either introduce you to or to build on the theories of sport psychology, the challenge you will face as a mental conditioning coach is being able to present this information in a way that is both practical and easy for your audience to understand.

I would highly recommend that graduate students reach out to and connect with experts already established in our field, seek out mentors and shadowing opportunities, get involved in sports (if they are not already), and volunteer their time in exchange for experience.

I believe it is important to shadow people in the field, be it other graduate students working with athletic teams or individuals on and off campus, professors consulting with athletes and teams, or applied sport psychology consultants already doing what it is that they want to do.

It is also imperative to gain your own practical consulting experiences. Should these opportunities not exist through your graduate degree program (as was true for me at SDSU), you may find yourself having to create your own opportunities, requiring you to investigate paid and unpaid internships, part-time positions, volunteer positions associated with on-campus (e.g., intercollegiate, intermural) and off-campus (e.g., local sport organizations, high schools) athletic programs. IMG Academy Mental Conditioning no longer offers spring, summer, and fall unpaid internship opportunities but instead summer paid positions for those looking to get experience working with athletes and alongside a team of full-time mental conditioning coaches.

Joining the Association for Applied Sport Psychology (AASP) in the United States and attending the regional and annual AASP conferences with the intention of listening to and speaking with other graduate students and established practitioners can also help build your networks. Given the obvious costs associated with membership and travel to the conference, should this not be feasible, I would suggest that you read books and use the Internet and social media to follow and connect with the best minds in the field of sport psychology. Actively seeking out networking opportunities is a must for people looking to advance their careers. In addition to practitioners, building relationships with sport coaches is also important. I would also encourage seeking out continuing education opportunities aimed at sport coaches as a means to build your network within a particular sport.

With the real world waiting for you beyond graduation, an important point to consider is in what capacity you see yourself working with athletes. Do you hope to work for someone else (employee) or for yourself (entrepreneur)? As a future employee, time must be dedicated to searching for prospective employers and job openings, writing and submitting cover letters and resumes, and following up on job opportunities. As a future entrepreneur looking to start your own business, time must be dedicated to researching the market, creating a business plan and model, as well as networking and leveraging your contacts. Either way, I would recommend that while in graduate school you enroll in some classes to give you an introduction to basic business principles and/or entrepreneurship.

Young professional

As a young professional you might have recently graduated or currently be working in another performance psychology arena (e.g., military) and wanting to transition into working with athletes as a sport psychology practitioner. If this is the case, you might consider looking for job openings, starting your own business, or beginning to offer performance psychology services to athletes in addition to your current services.

With respect to working effectively with athletes and sport organizations, it is first important to consider what "effective" looks like. To me, effective is synonymous with concepts such as helping, change, getting better, making a difference, improvement, results, and ethical. In 2012, I spoke on the topic of "The 6 C's of Consulting" at the AASP Southeastern Conference hosted by Barry University and discussed the concepts of credentials, credibility, connection, communication, confidence, and creativity as a means to becoming more effective as a sport psychology practitioner (Smith, 2012).

Credentials are the letters after your name, based on the formal education you have completed (e.g., BS, MS, PhD) and any professional accreditations and affiliations you have acquired (e.g., CC-AASP, USOC, APA). The athletes I interact with and strive to help rarely ask me about my credentials. Credentials alone don't make a great practitioner but instead can serve as a foot in the door when it comes to working with athletes.

Arguably more important than credentials is credibility. Credibility is a product of many things, including who you work/have worked for, who you work/have worked with and their past results, who you know and who knows you, knowing your bounds of competence as a practitioner, your personal image (e.g., do you look the part?), your own athletic experiences, and your knowledge of the sport (e.g., history, rules, language, culture).

Beyond credentials and credibility is connection, which speaks to one's ability to make a positive first impression and to answer the question people are often asking when meeting someone new, specifically "Can I trust this person?" Connection involves building rapport, conveying your value, and creating buy-in by selling people on what you do, why you do it, and how their engagement with your guidance can make a difference. As a practitioner who believes that people "don't care how much you know, until they know how much you care", listening, sharing, and identifying what you have in common are all examples of ways you can establish a strong connection with your audience.

Effective communication between a practitioner and an athlete is essential to a productive relationship. Getting the message across to an athlete is part art, part science. Communication begins with knowing your audience. Things to consider include whether they speak English fluently, as a second language, or not at all, as well as understanding the vernacular associated with a particular sport, and being able to translate well-researched academic concepts to the real-world experiences of an athlete.

The last two C's are confidence and creativity. Confidence speaks to the level of trust you have in yourself as a practitioner and in what you are saying. To be an effective consultant, you must believe you are valuable and that you can deliver and help people produce results. In consulting, one size doesn't fit all, and therefore the last point, creativity, is about finding a way (e.g., using articles, videos, activities, images, songs, memes, hashtags) to get your point across and make your message stick with your audience.

Like anything, you are not going to become an effective sport psychology practitioner overnight. If you go about things the right way, you are, more than likely, going to become yet another "10-year overnight success". You won't start out as a great practitioner, but instead it will take time and you will inevitably evolve through your experiences, both good and bad. Working effectively with athletes is a result of years of repetition, feedback, and practicing what you preach.

As Steve Jobs (2005) once said, "You can't connect the dots looking forwards; you can only connect them looking backwards." As an 18-month-old in my grandparents' garden, I had no idea that my plant pot experiences would blossom into my working with LPGA golfers. Reflecting back on my career to date, my growth, both personally and professionally, is a result of planting seeds in the garden and then working to create ideal growing conditions by pursuing formal education, surrounding myself with experts in related fields, and focusing on learning and getting better at my craft every day. In my case, I guess you can't connect the pots looking forwards; you can only connect them looking backwards.

References

Foxworthy, J., & Hartt, B. (2008). *How to really stink at golf.* New York: Villard Books.

Jobs, S. (2005, June 12). How to live before you die [Video file]. Accessed at http://www.ted.com/talks/steve_jobs_how_to_live_before_you_die

LPGA. (2015, January 1). Scoring average. Accessed at http://www.lpga.com/statistics/scoring/scoring-average?year=2014

Nilsson, P., & Marriott, L. (2014, October). Art of coaching – Creating trust. Presentation at Titleist Performance Institute World Golf Fitness Summit, Park Hyatt Aviara, Carlsbad, CA.

Passarella, C. (2007, February 15). Personal communication.

Rotella, B. R., & Cullen, B. (1995). *Golf is not a game of perfect.* New York: Simon and Schuster.

Smith, C. A. J. (2012, February). The 6 C's of consulting. Presentation at AASP Southeastern Regional Conference, Barry University, Miami, FL.

Suggested Readings

Morgan, T., Mugford, A., & Smith, C. (in press). Applying approaches and techniques in supervision. In J. G. Cremades & L. S. Tashman (Eds.), *Global practices and training in applied sport, exercise, and performance psychology: A case study approach*. New York: Taylor & Francis.

Mugford, A., Hesse, D., & Morgan, T. (2014). Developing the 'total' consultant: Nurturing the art and science. In J. G. Cremades & L. S. Tashman (Eds.), *Becoming a sport performance psychologist: A global perspective* (pp. 268–275). New York: Psychology Press.

Mugford, A., Hesse, D., Morgan, T., & Taylor, J. (2014). Now what do you do? How to develop a consulting business. In J. Taylor (Ed.), *Practice development in sport and performance psychology* (pp. 59–80). Morgantown, WV: Fitness Information Technology.

10

THE STRATEGIES AND METHODS FOR WORKING WITH PROFESSIONAL MOTOR RACING DRIVERS

Dieter Hackfort

Consultancy, coaching, and all kinds of professional psychological interventions (the term is used as a superordinate term/category for various kinds of measures and methods like counselling, training, and modification programs) are based on intentional organized behaviour, which means actions in a specific, tangible action situation. Even though such actions are conscious and rational, to a large extent action regulation is influenced essentially by affective processes and run in some parts by developed experience. For a report on personal experiences and to uncover strategic and operational directions for professional engagement in professional sports, this has to be kept in mind. In the preparation and development of this contribution, I took the occasion of thinking about some most relevant strategies and methods I used in recent years when working in professional sports with professional performers, especially drivers in car racing, to bring it to the attention of the reader. In doing so it became very obvious that the practical measures of its selection or elaboration are largely based on (hopefully sound) theoretical reasoning, which the reader should also be aware to learn about. In front of the development of strategies and conceptual knowledge, there are influences which originate from the personal career in the action field – in my case the two fundamental action fields are sports and science – and specifically with respect to science, psychology, and sport science, the two parent disciplines of sport psychology (no matter who is the father and who is the mother) from my point of view.

The structure of this chapter will turn the order of these reflections upside down and thus follow a developmental logic. The purpose of my endeavour is to highlight some significant insights, to provide key messages for professional psychological performance enhancement, and to give examples of strategies and methods for a sophisticated approach in car racing which might be transferable in some cases.

Personal/consulting background

When I first began practicing, my initial contacts with sport psychology made it very clear to me that this discipline opens the door for interesting learning experiences, exciting research, and valuable application of knowledge and skills for my future career. Building up expertise and competencies by studying sport science and psychology following previous experiences as an athlete and coach (artistic gymnastics) and early involvement in the combination of experimental and applied research, and by completing counselling projects when I was a research assistant in sport psychology at the German Sport University (Cologne), helped me develop the conviction that the combination of research in sport psychology and experiences in the application of sport psychology is most fruitful for both the advancement of the discipline and the action field as well as the development of expertise and competencies as a sport psychology consultant. Looking for effective techniques of self regulation, psyching down and psyching up, coping and stress–control, etc. for athletes in elite sports resulted in the idea to investigate mental strategies and measures that are self-made by elite athletes and coaches for performance enhancement and to ensure that the performance potential can be realized in competition (see Nitsch & Hackfort, 1979). During these studies, stress, coping with stress, anxiety, emotion, and emotion control turned out to be key topics in the interviews and discussion with athletes and coaches. Hence, these topics were the focus of my research in that period of time (see e.g., Hackfort, 1991; Hackfort & Spielberger, 1989).

As a consequence of the less successful 1984 Olympic Games in Los Angeles, the German Sports Federation initiated the establishment of Olympic Centres, and I was involved in the development of the concept for such centres. My engagement as a consultant for the German Sports Federation was especially focused on two areas, namely sport psychology services and career counselling. In 1986 the centres (eight at that point in time) had been set up, and I started to provide services. My involvement at that point in time was at one of these centres in Heidelberg based on cooperation between that centre and the Institute for Sport and Sport Science at the University of Heidelberg. The first sport I became in touch with was weight-lifting. The coach of the national team asked me for support and invited me to work with a young athlete in super heavy weight, who was world class in training but suffered failure in significant competitions at that time. It was his understanding that this athlete should have a high potential for the 1988 Olympics in Seoul, and mental training might contribute to take advantage of his potential. Already in a short period of time, I detected that this athlete was focused on weaknesses instead of strength and competencies and suffered from a lack of self-confidence. The athlete, the coach, and I talked about certain strategies to improve self-esteem and direct attention. Other athletes in the group became aware about the cooperation and joined us in mental training sessions, consultations in various situations, and with regard to an increasing scope of issues, so they made me a regular member of the (service) team. The 1988 Olympic Games became the most successful Olympics for the German weightlifting team ever up to that point in time (one silver and two bronze medals, one for the athlete mentioned before).

A similar story happened when I moved from Heidelberg to Munich to take the position of the founding Professor for the Institute of Sport Science at the University FAF Munich in 1991. The Olympic Centre of Bavaria in Munich, amongst others, hosted the national team (female) in alpine skiing, and the national sports director asked me to become a member of his service team. At that point in time there was only one world champion (in 1992) in the group. In the following five years, we had world champions in all of the alpine disciplines and various (including gold) medallists at the 1994 Olympics in Lillehammer. Experiences in further Olympic sports (e.g., speed skating, figure skating, judo) were also very exciting and successful during the time of my involvement, and I started to turn to professional sports like tennis, golf, and racing (car and motor bike) due to various requests. My motivation to turn to professional sports essentially was founded in finding out about differences in the circumstances and key issues of service delivery in this area of business, and the interest was to learn about sport and performance psychology applications in professional action fields, including the management and staff responsible for performance enhancement.

All of the experiences in applied sport psychology emerge in parallel to discernments growing out of various research projects. The most significant insights from these endeavours consist in the following facts:

1   Psychological (that is science/evidence-based) interventions like progressive muscle relaxation or mental training always have to be based on a systematic assessment and diagnostics.
2   Testing always should be linked to training as closely as possible, especially for the athletes' understanding.
3   Explanations and recommendations which are based on data and experience are more convincing than interpretations and suggestions based on subjective impressions. Especially at the beginning of a professional relationship, the usage of objective mental performance measurements like computer-assisted tests are more persuasive than paper-and-pencil instruments or questionnaires only. An appropriate combination of tools and a proper strategy for assessment is essential for a convincing design of an intervention, mental training, or performance enhancement program to be accepted and induce commitment by the athlete.
4   Considering the subjective ("naive" = not science/professionally based) understanding of the athlete and/or coach is necessary to be able to select an appropriate starting point for mental coaching or mental training. By and by, it has to be complemented or substituted by science-based concepts and strategies to select the most relevant and effective approach for the psychological service and mental performance management.
5   Mental coaching, counselling, and mental training for mental performance enhancement always is embedded in a broader, systematic approach, which is the reason for me to prefer to talk about performance enhancement management to describe this kind of service.

In consequence, my education and training for mental performance enhancement management is based on self-organized research as well as applied hands-on experiences, feedback from and discussions with colleagues, assistants, and staff involved in some kind of cooperation, and, last but not least, the comments and evaluations by athletes, coaches, and officials. The body of my experiences was developed over 30 years and started at a time when no systematic, specific education and training existed for this action field. The situation fundamentally changed, and I have been engaged and involved very much for advancements in this respect and for our discipline (see Hackfort & Kuhn, 2014).

Contextual and sub-cultural understanding

On the one hand, the broad scope of experiences in Olympic sports created a solid basis of understanding and knowledge about fundamental mental and social issues of elite athletes and coaches and strategies how to handle them. It also became very clear to me that the various sports often don't know a lot about certain common issues and useful strategies developed in one sport which might be transferable to other sports. For example, when I was working with the shooting federation, I learned from coaches and athletes how important it is for performance in the sport to control breathing and how essential it is for performing well to use a special breathing technique. They developed and practiced effective strategies which are easy to adapt (e.g., by golfers, especially to optimize the procedure in putting, or for drivers) (see the following section on "intervention methodology").

On the other hand, the context and culture in professional sports like car racing is significantly different from Olympic sports and has to be considered to be special. For example, the organization of the sport is embedded in the car-producing industry, the promotion, marketing, etc. of the cars (product of that industry) and the brand; that is, the sport is instrumental for industry purposes. It is also argued that racing is a kind of laboratory for the car industry as developments for racing cars, with racing cars and tests by racing cars contributing to the advancement of knowledge and technological enhancements in favor of series vehicles. Maybe the culture can be regarded to be a composite of a sport and business. For sure it has a decisive impact and constitutes a specific behavior setting, not only for the drivers but for all members of the racing team, including engineers, mechanics, physicians, physiotherapists, managing staff, etc. The athlete/driver is, much the same as the other team members, an employee of the company/racing team. The ranking of the drivers is closely associated with the success of the racing team, and the driver's track record determines his/her salary. Such insight and the understanding of the specific context and culture is of fundamental meaning to be able to organize professional consultancy behavior accordingly and to be accepted in the environment and integrated into the team and to cooperate with the driver and other members of the team. This is not only true in racing, but particularly in this sport and context, performance is a team product and performance enhancement is like a puzzle, managing all elements to bring it toward a perfect fit.

In terms of developing context and sub-cultural understanding, as well as engendering respect from the team, it is essential to get access and learn from cutting-edge expertise in the sport. It is not necessary (at the very beginning) to be an expert in the idiosyncrasies in that specific sport (e.g., in the various areas of technology and engineering), but to convince the client and the team to have sufficient background and knowledge not only in psychology but also in sports, sports performance, and especially in sport performance enhancement to built rapport and earn respect, as well as for an incremental integration into the business processes and the teamwork. Generally speaking, it is crucial on the one hand to develop as fast as possible a certain body of knowledge and specific understanding of the sport, the work of the team (e.g., service team, pit crew), and the driver and on the other hand to demonstrate special expertise, to provide evidence for its relevancy, and to adopt and present a cooperative attitude. Especially in the context of an individual sport, it is important to share the attitude that peak performance is always a team effort.

Challenges to trust and access

The people who work in motor sport racing, and especially those who are very closely working with the drivers, mechanics, and engineers, are technically oriented and technology-driven experts. Most of these people trust in hard facts and data only, so for mental issues there is a very limited understanding or acceptance in this social setting. If someone (e.g., a driver) expressed concerns about a mental issue (that was not necessarily already a problem), this person would be regarded to be a bit of a wimp. Moreover, to be a doctor or professor coming from a university intending to tell the experts in this field of praxis something useful is associated with an additional task. The combination of these two specificities build up a most challenging setup to start working and become accepted.

One efficient strategy to convince people that mental and social issues are very similar to tasks or problems they are facing or familiar with is to bring to their attention the fact that in order to improve physical skills, power, or endurance in a systematic way, regular, continuous, and long-term training or exercise is needed, and this is also true for mental skills. Furthermore, the setup of the car is developed by a combination of numerous details and can be understood to be an optimal fit. To develop the optimal setup for the driver is similar, and to create the best fit it is dependent on key elements which refer to the person (e.g., the individual driver with his special profile of skills, style, etc.), the task at hand (e.g., qualifying or race), and the given environment (e.g., track, climate etc.). Mental power and toughness from this point of view are very similar to physical power, whereas communication and cooperation processes are very similar to finding the best social (instead or in addition to the technical) setup between people. Finally, to manage all of this in a most meaningful way, it is not only useful but necessary to have a model, a strategy, and instruments/measurements to do so, that is, to have a theory. I believe that a theoretical basis and approach is not luxurious; nothing is more helpful than a well-founded systematic, and by reflected experience elaborated, conceptually structured theory.

Consulting philosophy

The idea that there is nothing more practical than a good theory is attributed to the well-known German psychologist Kurt Lewin and can be regarded to be a conviction for my approach in applied sport psychology. Theories provide both a cognitive map for meaningful mental orientation and sophisticated navigation on the one side and on the other side an elaborated frame for systematic classification of observations and experiences. Moreover, for performance enhancement, knowledge is needed; not only more but also better, more specific insights have to be elaborated by systematic experiences (empirically founded), which is created on the basis of a structured conceptual and sophisticated methodological strategy. Appropriate strategies in elite sports are at least sometimes (if not often) different from other more common or widespread methods in usual/normal action fields, and they are largely based on an ipsative methodology, narratives, and single case studies because there are only very few subjects in elite sports or peak performance. Due to the exceptional sphere of human peak performance, it seems logical that we also have to expect and consider differences and discrepancies from general concepts. The common understanding of the value-expectancy theory on achievement motivation might be a good example to explain this point: As we are restricted to a very small population or single – and most of the time exceptional – cases in this field, the question is how valid and viable are findings and insights based on generalizations of results from large group studies and how an appropriate transfer or usage takes place in such a specific action field. Whereas it is proven by empirical research with normal populations that failure-oriented (more appropriate: failure-avoidance-oriented) subjects choose very (too) high or very low levels of aspiration and success-oriented subjects prefer a medium level of aspiration (Heckhausen, 1980), repeated personal experience shows that elite athletes (e.g., in tennis, weightlifting, golf, and in this context especially car racing) express an aspiration level for future performance and success which sounds illusory for average athletes.

A concrete example is Sebastian Vettel, who is at present the four-time Formula One (F1) World Champion, who at the age of 18 expressed in a personal interview that he wanted to become the fastest driver and that he had the potential to overcome the world champion at that time. In such a case, a very high level of aspiration, expressed in goals which seem to be unrealistic for normal people, are not indicators for a distinct tendency for fear of failure but rather closely connected with a strong tendency of hope for success, and the vision is associated with the mission of striving for excellence and the willingness to organize the whole life toward this goal. In consequence, it would make sense to distinguish achievement motivation (need for achievement = nA) and peak performance motivation (ppM) of elite athletes.

A psychologist in professional sports has to be aware that senior athletes are experts in their sports. The psychologist can learn a lot from an athlete, not only about the sport but also maybe most relevant for an understanding of a particular athlete, about his/her understanding including focus, his/her definition of the situation including potential obstacles or problems, his/her philosophy, and his/her strategies when the athlete is asked to explain the sport and situation. Furthermore, it is essential to notice the individual subjective concept ("implicit" or "naive theory") of the acting subject (see Hackfort, 2001), that is, the athlete or the driver. To organize efficient strategies for counselling, coaching, and mental training, it is essential to learn about the definition of the action situation (defined to be a person–environment–task constellation) by the acting subject, the athlete/driver him- or herself. His/her understanding of the task, maybe a problem at hand, the environment (e.g., supportive, challenging, or disturbing and obstructive factors), and self-concept (with regard to abilities, skills, attitude, motivation, willpower, etc.), as well as his/her assumptions about mental and psycho-physiological processes (e.g., functional meaning of affective processes and emotional arousal, attention and concentration, goal setting) provide key information for reflections on the most promising or necessary interventional measurements. The subjective intra-individual point of view of the athlete is building a reference point for the evaluation of further information (e.g., from team members, inter-individual or objective points of view, and the evaluation of variations and/ or discrepancies which might indicate the orientation and direction for required modifications). The analysis can be organized like a SWOT analysis to detect strengths, weaknesses, opportunities, and threats for an intervention. For a first step, it has proven to be favorable to indicate some strengths and not to begin immediately with weaknesses. When the communication is focusing on weaknesses and threats, the final part of the conversation should emphasize opportunities; this structure of the conversation can contribute to a constructive orientation, motivation, and good relationship to the athlete. In principle, the athlete should not be regarded to be a patient but rather a client. He or she should also be considered to be an expert and, thus, to be a partner in the endeavour of performance enhancement.

In conjunction with a consulting philosophy, it is not rare to emphasize a humanistic approach, and it is assumed that what is meant is common currency and generally accepted. For sure, the design of my consulting philosophy also comprises a basic humanistic setting for me, and this means to me substantially to accept the athlete as a highly respected person (client and in a way a partner) and to trust in the ability of a human subject to reflect. This view is associated with the overall orientation toward the welfare of the client and the endeavour to improve his/her well-being. According to this approach, it is my understanding that the learning experience in sport in principle is useful for life in general. This attitude und mind-set is associated with an action theory approach (see Nitsch & Hackfort, 2015), considering actions (intentionally organized behavior) to be characteristic for human subjects in an action situation which is defined by the acting subject. For performance enhancement, principles of performance management are utilized as well. This approach is not only referring to personal factors but also to environmental and features of the task at hand, thus, it can be understood to be an action-oriented system approach, appropriately referred to as Peak Performance Management (PPM).

For a sound philosophical foundation, ethical considerations have to be included. Standards for working ethically in professional sport are discussed in a separate chapter (seven) in this book. In my reflections, key ethical issues (for more detail, see Hackfort & Tenenbaum, 2014) refer to (a) competence (a practitioner can only offer and conduct services for which he or she has acquired a sufficient level of competency), (b) confidentiality (closely associated with privacy and consent, handling personal information including data from assessment or tests, information about intended aims, methods, and means to be used), (c) responsibility (conduct of affairs in such a way that it will contribute to the welfare of the person and avoid harm), (d) respect (with regard to the experience, insight, and knowledge of the person as well as in terms of individual differences including culture, ethnicity, nationality, religion, education, gender, socio-economic status, and mental capacities), and (e) integrity (inter alia formed out of honesty, accuracy, openness, and social trust).

Methodological procedure

The method of choice, in terms of problem analysis as well as for intervention, depends on the objective. In case of talent identification or an assessment of mental capacities and weaknesses, the procedure is quite different from a case of analysing an individual problem or developing an efficient strategy for mental performance enhancement or the design of an individual mental training program for specific purposes (e.g., improvement of decision making, concentration, or acquisition of an action program or rehearsal of motor skills). Independent of various purposes, in my general approach I am looking for information by interviews (verbal data), by observation (behavioural data), and by tests (performance and/or objective data). The latter are of particular meaning in the cultural context of racing, as drivers are used to discussing subjects on the basis of objective data. Hereafter, this chapter will focus on the assessment procedure and diagnostic purposes, as I believe a solid assessment is the basis for subsequent measures and the design of intervention programs or methods. Training without testing is blind, and testing without a training concept or program is purposeless. Testing and training have to be in a composite. The more general procedure is explained with special emphasis on talent identification and selection. Second, examples for intervention procedures and mental training with senior drivers will be explained.

Assessment methodology

Essential for any of my assessments is the data-based (subjective, observational, and objective/performance) and multiperspective-multimethod approach. Following my experiences based on interviews and observations in the sport and with drivers and further experts (e.g., team manager, engineers, mechanics) in Formula One (F1) or the German masters for touring cars (DTM), I designed a special set of tests for talent identification and selection. An important criterion for the test selection was the requirement that the individual test can also serve for psychological aligned training programs, as it is my understanding that a sport psychologist or mental coach should only use tests which are in conjunction with an intervention program or training, building a system. Such a system is built up with the Mental Test and Training System (MTTS; see Hackfort, Kilgallen, & Hao, 2009).

Having worked more than 15 years in racing sport, several teams, team managers, and drivers know about me and my work, and in consequence in recent years talent evaluation from a psychological point of view complementary to technical (e.g., driving style) and physical (e.g., endurance, strength) aspects became increasingly requested by the teams. One reason for the increase of this request is the enormous amount of money a racing team has to calculate for the development of a young driver and the high risk of spending this money in vain or, the other way around, saving the investment, which can be used more efficiently based on the decision by the selection strategy. When I tested a group of prospective drivers some years ago for a special talent program, I was able to predict all of the three winners (only the ranking of the second and third was the other way around) by using my mental test system. This was somewhat sensational for the team and got around in the field very fast.

The test system designed for this purpose is computer based, consisting of tests with regard to reaction time and decision making (Movement Detection Test [MDT]; see Hackfort, Herle, & Debelak, 2010), movement anticipation, psycho-motor accuracy and speed, risk taking, and a special test for the diagnosis of achievement motivation. While taking those tests (in a first step, the situation is neutral, no stress), the athlete is videotaped, and then at the end of the test he is confronted with questions like: "What do you think about your performance and the result of the test?", "Is your performance result average, below average, or above average?", "Do you think you can do better, and how would it be possible?". The analysis of the answers and information/data leads to a first profile of the athlete with regard to his strengths and weaknesses in action organization and action regulation/control, stress-/emotion control, motivational orientation, and, beyond this, potential areas for improvement.

From my point of view, a single factor, trait, or skill is not the key for the identification of a potential, or a problem, or a program for performance enhancement. More often it is a certain combination and constellation of various elements/traits (personal characteristics). In addition, for the design of intervention programs, it is also frequently necessary to consider environmental factors such as the people in the team, including engineers, mechanics, the agent, team manager, further service staff, and the family and/or peers who might provide certain motivational, emotional support. This point of view is a significant issue in the coordination among the team, other service providers, and especially in the case of prospective drivers with the family. Special meetings or sessions for parent information, education, and coordination – with the role and tasks of the parents described – are useful at the beginning and between such (training, developmental) programs. Insofar the orientation towards constellations (profile, group) is suitable to a system approach.

The second step is initiated by some recommendations, usually with regard to the organization of the test behaviour and suitable modifications in action regulation (tension/activation control, focus/orientation, etc.) and hints for better pre-test preparation. Such a procedure is providing useful information on learning capacity and coachability. The second test run is executed under stress conditions (e.g., noise, flashlights). It is an interesting experience to observe that most of the top drivers obviously are not ready to enable their potential until experiencing some challenge and/or being inspired and/or activated by some kind of stress. This is regularly confirmed by the result in a special category of the achievement motivation test, which refers specifically to this aspect. Noise and flashlights are representing non-meaningful disturbances, which are suitable to induce activation and force to concentration, focusing on the task hand.

Furthermore, after this test run, many top athletes want to know more about the tests, the results, the interpretation, and strategies for improvement. On the one hand, this is a significant signal for interest and ppM; on the other hand, it is a perfect starting point for future counselling and mental training. The evaluation and recommendation in this talent identification and selection process is based on the profile built up by the driver's test results, the observed behaviour (action organization and regulation), performance variation in the stress situation, his/her comments (especially self-appraisals and attributions, e.g., explaining what is regarded a success or failure by internal or external factors), and the impression of his/her coachability. We (the expert team) track these impressions of the prospective driver in further test situations about his physical fitness or his/her driving skills.

Intervention methodology

For a strategic alignment in peak performance management (PPM), three pillars of success (POS; this abbreviation is chosen to provide a positive/constructive perspective and is taken up and explained in more detail in the following) may serve for a general orientation: (1) personality, (2) organism, and (3) social support. With regard to personality, the individual profile of psychological characteristics, with an emphasis on strengths and factors of mental fitness, is decisive. With regard to the organism, it is about the physical fitness on the one hand and the awareness and self-confidence in this fitness and the trust in the ability to be able to control the body to a large extent on the other hand. It is also about the psycho-physiological arousal, the activation level, and how to monitor it. Social support refers to the micro-system (team, family), the meso-system (friends, sponsors), and the macro-system (fans, media). Again, it is essential that this is also integrated into the consciousness of the athlete/driver to give him/her emotional backing and social safety. The development, enhancement, and enforcement of positive elements in these systems are the essential tasks for PPM, and the most significant objectives are positive/constructive (no Don'ts) thinking, feeling and attitude (optimism), power of self-regulation skills (e.g., developed by biofeedback methods), and emotional, motivational, as well as instrumental support, which encompasses knowledge as well as tangible goods. From a systemic perspective, the various elements build a complex interplay. However, in practice, it is not possible to control or to always have influence on everything, even though, for the design and organization of an efficient intervention program or method at least, the complexity should be remembered and taken into consideration. In terms of mental performance enhancement in car racing and with a focus on counselling and mental coaching with drivers, emphasis will be given to some specific methods, as they have been proven effective in the preparation for the three tasks at a race weekend, which are (1) free practice, (2) qualifying, and (3) the race.

The fundamental issue in free practice is to find the optimal setup. In a broader understanding from a PPM perspective, this is the technical setup of the car, the mental setup of the person, and the social setup of the team. Whereas the technical and social (including working atmosphere, communication, and cooperation) setup is neglected here, the mental setup is subdivided into cognitive and emotional issues. With regard to cognitive aspects, the development of an action plan is essential. The action plan consists of a clear picture of the entire track, including identified cues for key sections (most often turns/curves, difficult parts of the track like chicanes) and an awareness of how to drive. For instrumental coping with these sections, action-oriented self-instructions are created (like "break here", "full throttle now", etc.) and included in the action plan. Up to that point, the action plan consists of a "cold image", that is, the constellation of cognitive elements or the rational architecture of the track and instructions for internal self-instructions. Such instructions are considered to be "cold cognitions", which should be affectively enriched and advanced to "hot cognitions". This is done by progressive driving experiences and affective feedback (feelings) from the car and the track, thus complementing emotional aspects. By progressing experience with the track and the action plan, it becomes more and more decisive how the instructions are displayed (modality, tone of inner voice/self-talk). Cold cognitions are created for the "what to do" and the hot cognitions are designed for "how to do it". Furthermore, the action plan also includes cues for phases of relaxation (e.g., by deep breathing, muscle release) and short-term regeneration or readjustment. Associated therewith the "cold image" of the track is switching to a "hot image" when a rhythm for the track is coming up, and driving the lap is including affective associations like dancing with the car. Each track has its own rhythm, and the driver has to find it and develop it in consideration of the given circumstances, like weather conditions. By working with imagination in mental simulation sessions, further emotional experiences (e.g., in conjunction with affective memories) will be integrated, and in consequence the imagination is more than a driver can see. The structure of such an action plan is developed from a (1) rough set of instructions via a (2) more elaborated and differentiated set of instructions to a (3) as simple as possible structured action plan emphasizing key parts and orientations for the driver. This action plan, in combination with the image of the track, is building the basis for mental preparation by mental simulation (see Hackfort & Munzert, 2005). Mental simulation has to be distinguished from training in a simulator, which is an increasingly significant tool in the training regime and preparation for competition with the drivers and can be used for technological and conceptual advanced mental training as well.

In the simulator, like in the test situation explained above (testing under stress), non-meaningful disturbances (e.g., noise) can be used to increase arousal and concentration, and meaningful disturbances (e.g., by a second task; (dual task situation can be used to modify action regulation in the way that a focus (cognitive processing) is given to the secondary task (backward counting) and the primary task is operated automatically (by automatisms), in this context that is a kind of instinct or natural driving. From an action-regulation point of view, sensory-motor processing is closely linked to movement-/driving-feelings which, in some situations, may induce a flow feeling. Concentration on the second task also is associated with intermediate meta-cognitions in case of mistakes which are detected by the driver. In this way, he/she is able to develop meta-cognitive strategies (e.g., how to navigate cognitions). This is useful to avoid failure in stressful situations or situations of monotony (e.g., when driving numerous laps in competition over a huge distance behind, right in the middle, or ahead of his/her competitors) and to monitor emotions.

Training in the simulator is building a link between pure mental training based on the image of the track and the action plan including self-instructions. Simulator training is very useful not only to check out the most appropriate driving style but also to practice mental techniques like self-talk, especially to explore variations and to find the best way of self-talks – that is, how to do it, the most appropriate intonation to use, rigour, etc. The way the driver is talking to him-/herself is monitoring the driving style (e.g., an aggressive intonation is inducing an aggressive driving style). For focusing on certain aspects and cognitive navigation, the

Thinking Out Loud (TOL) method is also effective and especially useful for adopting the best coaching approach, as the psychologist learns about the driver's direction of attention, what is going on in his/her mind, and how he/she is handling it (e.g., using instructions for orientation or shaping self-talks in a manner to induce self-confidence and conviction or influencing nervousness and stress symptoms).

Less advanced simulators which do not require a huge financial investment are already sufficient to serve for the development and support of implementing mental strategies. Furthermore, training in a simulator setup can be used to establish and enforce pre-performance, during-performance, and post-performance routines (see Lidor, Hackfort, & Schack, 2014), such as checking the psycho-physiological state when seated in the car and the seatbelts are fastened, deep breathing when crossing the start line, closing the eyes and visualizing the track when entering the box, and talking about driving experiences and giving feedback to the engineers.

To complete this chapter, it should be noted that mental coaching with drivers covers various methods that are well known in sport psychology, which can be subdivided by different criteria, such as by the three phases: (1) prior to competition (e.g., mental preparation and/or relaxation methods), (2) between competitions (e.g., methods for mental rehearsal) and (3) after competition (e.g., debriefing methods). An alternative criteria is the function in action regulation: either the method is skill oriented and for the improvement of psycho-motor control (e.g., mental training, visualization, etc.) or the method is for the improvement of the regulation of psycho-vegetative processes, that is, for tuning purposes including mental regeneration (e.g., progressive muscle relaxation, biofeedback training, etc.). Both of these approaches in action-regulation are usable in the three phases mentioned before. In a comprehensive approach like PPM, strategies and measures can focus on the three factors of the action situation – that is, the person (athlete, driver) emphasizing self-management, the task emphasizing task management (e.g., action program and plan), or the environment emphasizing team management. Even though professional sport above all is a business, educational processes play an important role, not only but especially in the development of a professional mindset, attitude, and essential qualities for striving for peak performance like determination and motivation (ppM), discipline and efficiency, self-efficacy, and self-confidence.

Summary and recommendations

For the establishment of professional sport psychology, it is crucial to learn about various experiences in different sports and about various conceptual and methodological approaches with regard to a broad scope of mental issues. The present book serves this concern, and this chapter adds my experiences and reflections and highlights some consequences for the next generation and further discussion with colleagues. We are only at the beginning of professional sport psychology, but there are a growing number of colleagues to share experiences with professional athletes and work in professional sports. When questions are posed about the required competencies and qualifications for a sport psychologist working in professional sports and if he or she needs to have special expertise in professional sport in general and/or the special sport he or she is involved with, based on my experiences I can say that a sport psychologist needs to have competencies in both sport and psychology. For an appropriate professional socialization, both of the parents/parent disciplines, father and mother (sport and psychology), are needed due to their specific input. In case a professional athlete is suffering from a mental problem, psychological competencies are needed and may be additional sport science competencies are not requested. In case of a task like mental performance enhancement, psychological knowledge is needed, but it is not sufficient. Knowledge about the kind of task, the action situation, and the specific requirements are also necessary. Furthermore, for effective communication in a professional sport setting like racing, a sport psychologist or mental coach needs to gain acceptance, and for this it is crucial to know and to be able to use the specific terminology and to be familiar with the jargon. Therefore, a sound professional education for sport psychology in professional sport should encompass psychological and sport science expertise.

For a meaningful, systematic, and efficient approach in applied sport psychology, an appropriate theory is needed. Such a theory provides structure for the development of diagnostic as well as intervention strategies and methods, and has the capacity to bridge gaps between various disciplinary views. The action-theory perspective (see Hackfort, 2001; Hackfort & Kuhn, 2014; Nitsch & Hackfort, 2015) focuses on the action situation, the structure and organization of actions, and action regulation processes like cognitive and affective processes and their interrelation and interplay. In the professional development, it is a first and fundamental step to learn about theories, their relevance, and viability (see above: example of ppM) and a second and necessary step to learn how to use theories in an applied setting for practical purposes in a most meaningful and functional manner. Thus, to gain practical experiences in various sports – if possible before an engagement in professional sports – does make sense and will increase the probability of recognition and success.

For an engagement in professional car racing, knowledge and skills from other sports are helpful, and the other way around, experiences from car racing could be transferable to other sports or even generalizable for mental performance enhancement in sports. Mental coaching in professional sports is embedded in performance enhancement management, thus, competencies for interdisciplinary cooperation in a professional, organized performance-oriented system is essential to be accepted, to be able to contribute, and to be effective. It is crucial for the driver/athlete as well as for the team and mental coach to understand the meaning of WIN (What is Important Now) and to adopt a proper mindset, which implies focusing on those factors which can be influenced (try to control solely what is controllable) by them and taking opportunities exclusively when there is a reasonable option.

References

Hackfort, D. (Ed.). (1991). *Research on emotions in sport*. Köln: Sport U. Buch Strauss.

Hackfort, D. (2001). Experiences with application of action-theory based approach in working with elite athletes. In G. Tenenbaum (Ed.), *The practice of sport psychology* (pp. 89–99). Morgantown, WV: Fitness Information Technology.

Hackfort, D., Herle, M., & Debelak, R. (2010). *Manual MDT Bewegungs-Detektions-Test, Version 21* (Manual for the MDT Movement-Detection-Test, Version 21). Mödling: Schuhfried.

Hackfort, D., Kilgallen, C., & Hao, L. (2009). The action theory-based mental test and training system (MTTS). In E. Tsung-Min Hung, R. Lidor & D. Hackfort (Eds.), *Psychology of sport excellence* (pp. 9–14). Morgantown, WV: Fitness Information Technology.

Hackfort, D., & Kuhn, M. (2014). Sport performance psychology service delivery process: A German perspective. In J. G. Cremades & L. S. Tashman (Eds.), *Becoming a sport, exercise, and performance psychology professional – A global perspective* (pp. 200–209). New York: Psychology Press.

Hackfort, D., & Munzert, J. (2005). Mental simulation. In D. Hackfort, J. Duda & R. Lidor (Eds.), *Handbook of research in applied sport and exercise psychology: International perspectives* (pp. 3–16). Morgantown, WV: Fitness Information Technology.

Hackfort, D., & Spielberger, C. D. (Eds.). (1989). *Anxiety in sports: An international perspective.* Washington: McGraw-Hill, Hemisphere, Harper & Row.

Hackfort, D., & Tenenbaum, G. (2014). Ethical issues in sport and exercise psychology. In A. G. Papaioannou & D. Hackfort (Eds.), *Routledge companion to sport and exercise psychology* (pp. 976–987). London: Routledge.

Heckhausen, H. (1980). *Motivation und handeln [Motivation and action].* Berlin: Springer.

Lidor, R., Hackfort, D., & Schack, T. (2014). Performance routines in sport – meaning and practice. In A. G. Papaioannou & D. Hackfort (Eds.), *Routledge companion to sport and exercise psychology* (pp. 480–494). London: Routledge.

Nitsch, J. R., & Hackfort, D. (1979). Naive Techniken der Psychoregulation im Sport [Naive techniques for the regulation of psychological processes in sports]. In H. Gabler, H. Eberspächer, E. Hahn, J. Kern & G. Schilling (Eds.), *Psychologie in der Praxis des Leistungssports [Psychology in the praxis of top athletics]* (pp. 299–311). Berlin: Bartels & Wernitz.

Nitsch, J. R., & Hackfort, D. (2015). Theoretical framework of performance psychology: An action theory perspective. In M. Raab (Ed.), *Performance psychology – beyond domains* (pp. 11–29). Oxford: Elsevier.

11

CONSULTANCY WITH ELITE PROFESSIONAL BOXERS AND THEIR WORKING TEAMS

Robert J. Schinke

I begin this chapter with a story that captures the earliest moments in my work with professional boxers. My initial hope when transitioning to practice at the professional level was to work with a National Hockey League (NHL) team. In fact, I went through two rounds of interviews with an NHL team, meeting first the owner and then the general manager. Though these people told me that I had something to offer their team, they questioned my ability to work with ice-hockey athletes based on whether I could play golf with them during their recreation time. My response, arrogant upon reflection, was that golf is irrelevant to sport psychology consulting – that is, unless you are working with golfers. I expanded and tried to make my case that especially when athletes and teams aspire to lengthen their season through post-season play, shortened off-season activities would not exclude me from entering into the context. Beyond being arrogant, and perhaps overstating my position, what I failed to understand is that each sport has its own sub-culture and entry points (Schinke & McGannon, 2014) – I failed miserably. Sport psychology consultants must become one with the cultures and sub-culture in which they work or risk extinction and obsolescence in the applied realm (Martens, 1987; Ryba, Stambulova, Si, & Schinke, 2013).

Boxing has always been a sport where I seem to fit, and we will speak about why in the next section. The athletes and coaches are often from tough family backgrounds, single-parent upbringings, youth gang affiliations, and life on the streets (Weinberg & Arond, 1952), and several are also transnational in their origins (Schinke, Yukelson, Bartolacci, Battochio, & Johnstone, 2011). Though I do not share this background, it seems that not having the same lived experience is not a barrier to entry. Having already worked for six years with the Canadian National Boxing Team before the aforementioned interview with the ice-hockey team (see Schinke, 2007), it was foreseeable that I would eventually be invited to cross over to professional boxing. One of the first professional boxers I was asked to work with in my early years was a veteran, already with three world-title fights on his record – all were losses, all by stoppage. He met with me, having already tried three other practitioners, each for only one session before severing ties. Even with three earlier unsuccessful attempts at forging an athlete-practitioner relationship, the athlete remained open to trying with a fourth in the hopes of finding the mental edge he felt was missing from his approach. We sat together and sipped our coffees after one of his early-morning runs. The athlete had seen me for several years working with a large number of international level amateur athletes, many of whom achieved medals at major tournaments. As such, I had some credibility in my favor. As we sat together, the athlete revealed to me that his next fight would be his fourth attempt at a world title, with the next match serving as a rematch against an opponent who previously stopped him. What weighed in the balance was whether he would continue as a professional athlete. A second question was whether the boxer was of world championship caliber, and moreover whether he would have the resilience to approach this next bout with adequate confidence to withstand the pressures associated with general training, and thereafter, the next big fight looming progressively closer (see Bandura, 1997).

The aforementioned uncertainty facing this boxer is encountered by many contenders at one point or another. Some of these athletes have the resilience to break through and become world champions, and others do not, many of whom are more physically talented than the eventual champions. In boxing it is inevitable that the client will eventually encounter an opponent who is equally tough, resilient, and wanting of success. Furthermore, at a certain point it becomes impossible to protect any boxer from encounters with equally competent adversaries; these match-ups are expected by the television networks, which pay the athletes' purses. Hence, the goal becomes to help build (or rebuild) the boxer so that he can withstand, not only the opponent in front of him, but also in some instances a history of faltering.

I wish to focus this chapter on the backdrop of professional boxing, and within one boxing context, situate my own work. My applied work in the sport of professional boxing continues to grow, suggesting that I am slowly gaining the necessary skills to carry me forward from the theoretical and methodological to the practical (see Martens, 1987). This chapter begins with a discussion of my own background and attraction to boxing, and then proceeds to describe the sub-culture of professional boxing and how I gained such knowledge, followed by initial challenges as a boxing consultant, the consulting philosophy that I have developed, a few practical strategies that are central to my work, and recommendations for aspiring practitioners who are interested in boxing and the combative sports, more generally.

The situation

Personal consulting background

I have consulted in high-performance amateur and professional boxing for nearly 20 years; in addition, I work with a broad range of athletes from the combative sports, including boxers, kickboxers, and mixed martial artists. I was initially attracted to professional boxing because of its violent nature (see Early, 1994). There is no better place to test one's work with clients in their mental game than in a sport where a loss is suffered on one's record and also to one's body. Some might argue, perhaps correctly, that it is unethical to support an athlete in the development of a game plan where success manifests in the dismantling of a physical opponent and the mental and physical levels (e.g., Lane, 2009). However, in reality, these athletes choose the path of becoming fighters – not from the encouragement of the mental training consultant. My attraction to this sport – termed the sweet science – was (and continues to be) to help bring a high level of understanding to the boxer and his coaching staff regarding how to prepare for, execute, and then grow from each battle as the boxer moves forward into a lucrative career. However, I must also acknowledge that not all of the clients I work with reach the pinnacle as boxers, nor do they even aspire to (Parham, 2013). My challenge and attraction to the sport, then, is the possibility of supporting a boxer in his rise from abject poverty to a career that can lead to financial independence and a better life through sport.

To present I have worked with a number of professional world champions who have fought on major television networks and earned multi-million-dollar paychecks in high-profile fights featured on global television networks – the two main global television networks that feature boxing. In addition, I have worked with the Canadian National Boxing Teams (male and female) at a number of major games and assisted more than 20 world championship medalists over the span of my involvement in amateur boxing (Schinke, 2007). I worked with the first two professional boxing clients by sheer happenstance. I was presenting a workshop at the Canadian National Boxing Championships to coaches accredited to the elite level status. One of the coaches in the audience was beginning work with a newly formed professional boxing management group, and he found my approach to boxer and coach preparation to be a good fit for his organization. At the time I was a doctoral student, so I initially declined the offer to consult in order to complete my education. Two years later, on the day I was turned away by an NHL team, I phoned him, in desperation, asking if he was still interested in working with me. The following week, my work began in earnest. I met with the aforementioned boxer and also one additional boxer, both of whom were contenders. Within six months of my start, both became world champions, and my role within professional boxing was cemented. Since that point I have worked with several world champions, some of whom became unified world champions by defeating other world champions, holding title belts in another of the four main associations: The World Boxing Council, International Boxing Federation, World Boxing Association, and World Boxing Organization. The objective for my clients now is to become lineal champions above the other champions.

I initially worked for a promoter and was paid by this person. My role was to help each athlete with the development and subsequent refinement of his mental game plan, while ensuring that resilience was built as the boxers progressed to more challenging fights, and then onward to world titles (see Schinke, Bonhomme, McGannon, & Cummings, 2012). I did this sort of work with a large stable of boxers, from which several became world champions, but others did not move beyond contender status due to an inability to withstand the sport's hardships, such as punishing fights and also chronic or career-ending injuries (Early, 1994). Since 2010, I have taken a boutique approach to my work. I work with fewer professional boxers, and I spend more time focused on a single training camp in preparation for monumental fights. Presently, I have two world-renowned clients, with each requiring at least one month per fight preparation of full-time involvement by me. These athletes both fight twice per year, and in total they require four months of my attention, in addition to the consulting time I commit to Canada's National Boxing Team and an assortment of mixed martial artists. I also have a full-time academic job as a professor and Canada Research Chair, focused on multicultural sport psychology scholarship. As such, I choose my clients selectively and all of my work in professional boxing is derived from word of mouth.

Situational and sub-cultural understanding

I began my work as a mental training coach during graduate studies. While traveling as a volunteer member on two consecutive major olympic games trips working with the Canadian Olympic Committee, I was able to forge relationships, first with the Canadian National

Shooting Team, where I served as team mental training consultant at the 1996 Olympics. While at the 1996 Summer Olympics, I met the Technical Director of Boxing Canada by strategically fetching him coffee on several afternoons in succession until he paid attention to me. We forged a friendship over this period, and so began what has become a most interesting journey into the boxing world. I was invited to my first national team training camp during Autumn 1996. The reason for my invitation had less to do with any belief from the Canadian Boxing Team regarding the potency of mental training services and more to do with the Technical Director liking my interpersonal approach, but even more so, my relentless persistence. During this initial sojourn, I ran in sprints each morning with the athletes, sat with them and their personal coaches over meals, and then met with each athlete, at least twice. I also observed every training session, held a water bottle during workouts, timed rounds of sparring, and attempted to learn my way around the sport team and sport discipline (please note that these two aspects are interrelated but also not the same; understanding sub-culture necessitates an understanding of the sport in general, the national sport system, and the team's norms and values; see Schinke & McGannon, 2014). This approach was contrasted with a previous practitioner who waited for athletes to approach him. From what I understand, his days were quite long, sitting by the pool without any consultations. Within boxing, it is the role of the mental trainer to establish rapport with the boxers, not the inverse. Trust takes time, especially when clients originate from tough backgrounds and have good reason to be wary. These people watch very carefully before they choose to engage, and then, engagement escalates to full commitment.

The transition to professional boxing was much easier in several regards as compared with amateur boxing. I already knew my way around the sport and the demographic backgrounds of the athletes and coaches. I was able to hold a conversation with the athletes and coaches regarding technical and tactical aspects of the sport, using vocabulary they felt comfortable with (Anderson, Knowles, & Gilbourne, 2004; Schinke, McGannon, Parham, & Lane, 2012). However, there were a few significant differences relating to professional boxing. The first among these was that promoters, managing groups, and corporate sponsors are involved in the boxers' careers, in addition to their personal coaches. The promoters have the objective of moving the boxer along within two to three years to the position where he can challenge for a world title. There is a pragmatic view of athletes from many a promoter's vantage point. Boxers need to move steadily forward to large purses, or they suffer a diminishing career where there is little to promote and sell to the television networks. There is little tolerance for unfocused and uncommitted boxers and no tolerance for boxers who lack resilience and mental toughness. The boxers are expected to be tough, and it is the mental training consultant's role to ensure that this is the case over the course of a career and that the meta-transitions (Schinke, Stambulova, Trepanier, & Oghene, in press) from one bout preparation, through the win and its debriefing, onward to the next positive result are carried out with intention, leading to progression. When athletes are unable to develop their mental game, they are of little use to a promoter: they lack the capacity to parlay training skills into performance on the fight night. There is no forgiveness for these athletes who experience disconnects from ability to performance; they fade into the background and then out of their careers.

Consequently, consulting in professional boxing is pragmatic. Boxers tend to come and go, much as in almost every professional sport organization, and for the most part the focus is not on the boxers' holistic development, unlike amateur sport (Stambulova, Alfermann, Statler, & Côté, 2009), but rather on their current status and promise in the near future. As a consultant, my job is to support each athlete in this process. So long as I am able to offer this sort of support, my work continues with the boxer. However, suggesting that my belonging within the sub-culture of boxing is only based on performance would be simplifying the story. As a consultant, reflexively (Anderson, Knowles, & Gilbourne, 2004; McGannon & Johnson, 2009), I am by my very role somewhat of an outsider (see Woodward, 2008). I am formally educated, and I do not box, nor coach boxing. My knowledge of boxing is somewhat less technical in terms of the physical skill sets required for performance. Each time I enter into a training camp, it seems as if I need to re-establish my relationships with the coaches and athletes, as much as I attempt to correspond between training camps, when the fighters are on vacation or in general training. For the first few days when I return to the context, I need to reintegrate into the daily lives of these people in order to become an accepted piece of the athlete's working team. There always seems to be a trust factor in the sport of professional boxing, and it takes a few days of patience and socialization in order to become one again with the context, no matter how many years I gain employment as a consultant.

So what does it mean to become an accepted part of the boxing context? The first piece to the puzzle is that I need to suspend my education and scholarship and simply become a member of the team (e.g., Halliwell, 2009), taking on house chores, running out for coffees, and contributing to a positive living environment. Indeed, as I have just suggested, I live within a house as part of the working team, where sometimes I share a room with another coach or a boxer. In these tight quarters, the working team often becomes edgy and irritable. People sometimes do not carry their weight in the household. My first job is to figure out where any irritability is originating from and pick up the slack, so that the environment returns to being positive and harmonious. Days are long, people become tired, and the people I work with in this environment often have less impulse control than one might typically encounter in the general population. Once people notice that the household climate is smoother with my attendance, I am reintegrated; only then does my focus turn to boxing-specific practice, not before.

Challenges to trust and access

Within many professional sport contexts, there is a reluctance to integrate sport psychology services. Recently I declined an interview with a high-profile professional sport organization, because the organization had just terminated a contract with another provider and from that experience was very cautious about the reintegration of mental training skills through a mental training coach. This experience has been relatively frequent in my experience. Boxing takes this concern of tampering versus contributing to the performance-related thinking of the athlete to a very high level. Boxers, by their very nature and choice of profession, choose to earn their salary and financial independence for life with their fists and their bodies. Boxers are punishers who also experience significant physical and mental torment over the course of their professional careers (Early, 1994). Many mental trainers have tried their hand at working with professional boxers, and some have worked successfully with one or a few athletes (e.g., Lane, 2009). To have longevity and ongoing access to the sport of professional boxing, the practitioner needs to allay fears that discussions will open up vulnerabilities that cannot be addressed as the athlete trains and moves ever closer to the next fight. Furthermore, I have listened to many a professional boxer who initially attempted sport psychology services with a consultant, only to experience the consultant breaching confidentiality in order to ingratiate him- or herself with the promoter or head trainer. For access to be fully realized within professional boxing, the athlete must trust in the ethical conduct of the consultant (see Harris, Visek, & Watson, 2009). Discussions will turn to frustrations with promoters, questions of salary, and possible disputes related to contract negotiations, in advance of signing with a promoter. These discussions are delicate, and the athlete must trust that his venting will go no further.

Many consultants try to serve in a dual role (Harris, Visek, & Watson, 2009), working for both the athlete and the promoter. At the beginning of a professional boxing career, the athlete will likely be unable to compensate the mental training consultant. I have experienced in several instances the promoter paying for my services and also the services of various additional sport science support personnel (Baltzell, Schinke, & Watson, 2010), such as nutritionists and strength and conditioning coaches. There are a few exceptions to this rule when an athlete launches the career with a seven-figure signing bonus, but these bonuses are few and far between. The most common chronology is for the boxer to live hand to mouth until he eventually reaches the level where a major television deal is signed with a network. During the early stages, as the promoter is paying for the services, he/she might look for updates regarding the athlete's progress, and he/she might also seek information that will inform how quickly the athlete might be moved forward into longer fights with tougher opponents. When there are dual clients (see Baltzell, Schinke, & Watson, 2010), an initial understanding must be reached with the promoter that any disclosure regarding the sessions would need to be sought from the athlete or shared at the athlete's will. Some promoters might not support this process, but the inevitable result of correct reporting measures is that the athlete will gain trust. Many of the boxers I have worked with have initially lacked trust, not in my services, but in my loyalty, until disclosure was tested and not breached a few times.

Philosophy

By my very nature as a scholar, I tend to struggle with the language I use in my consulting. The objective is always to package information in a manner so that it can be understood and then used in a meaningful way with the client and his working team (Parham, 2005). Given this tendency to overcomplicate, and by this process creating distance between my formal education and the boxers' life experiences, I initially lost several important opportunities early on in my consulting career. Though I am uncertain whether others have made the same transgression, the micro cues that I tended to pick up on indicated that my knowledge was not adequately grounded in the realities of my boxers, such as their everyday language and also their strengths and vulnerabilities. Consider the theory of self-efficacy. Granted, every boxer needs to garner this skill, and it must be cultivated with care in relation to each mounting pressure over the course of a career (Bandura, 1997). However, the way in which I initially packaged this information suggested that in some regard my athletes were mentally soft and in need of confidence, which is not a good tactic when working with athletes who are trained to fight, doling out and withstanding physical punishment for money. Perhaps this very weakness was my own inability to translate, or perhaps even understand, the basic essence of psychological theories taught to me in universities and afterward through reading.

The aforementioned weakness, and my awareness of it, eventually served as a platform to a revised philosophical approach to applied practice. I now always approach each athlete and coach as the experts of their contexts (Ryba, 2009). Though I have worked in elite boxing for nearly 20 years, I, and almost every other practitioner, am in some ways an interloper to the sport (Martens, 1987). I step in and assist amateur boxing teams with major games preparation and implementation, and I return to professional boxing working teams only after a bout contract is signed, and the next target opponent is in the crosshairs. Then, I must once more earn my way back into the working team. Doing so, I must be a person first and a practitioner second. I see what needs to be done in the context, and I fill holes without ever overstepping my boundaries of mental training. I look to develop my work as part of a coordinated plan with the coaches and athletes, and closer to the fight, I also work closely with the boxer's promotional team, ensuring that useful media questions are asked so that the client can convey the right messaging in relation to his preparation and the weaknesses of the opponent (see next section). My goal is always for the members of my team to like me, not because of my knowledge, but rather because of the ease I help inculcate in the team. A boxer and his coaching staff when put together is much akin to a pack of alpha wolves. These people travel in a pack, and yet there is always volatility. My role, as I see it, is to help ease the environment so that the pack can work as a pack without any outliers living on the periphery.

My clients strongly believe that I know exactly what I am doing. In fact, the best evidence of this external belief in me is evidenced by an allowance for me to expand my role into areas where I see gaps in an athlete's armor. Perhaps the most outstanding client I have ever worked with in professional boxing is someone I began with when he was only 16 years of age. This same athlete is now 31 – we are now in our sixteenth year working together. After watching this athlete in many world title bouts, I found that at times he would tire in the latter rounds of a fight. Other athletes have experienced similar wanes in energy and attributed this to their body type and simply to a physiological lack of stamina, but reflection was lacking (Schinke, McGannon, Parham, & Lane, 2012). With this client, I suggested a process that reconfigured how he manages the week of the fight. My belief, and now his own understanding, has taught us that he benefits from someone looking at his day from the outside in, by traveling and living with him during the week of the fight. This makes intuitive sense given that the training camp until its latter stages is undertaken with a pack mentality. I am this person – self-proclaimed, though with support from the athlete and his head coach. The present example truly illustrates what has become my philosophy within my work. I work at unusual times of day, in opportune moments as a sounding board and confidant. Though we integrate our fair share of mental training skills, I have taken the idea of being very basic in my approach to a high level. The very term *basic* tends to carry a negative connotation, but as I see it and frame my work, it is actually the highest format of practice – one where my role and information blends into the fabric of the day without too many formal calls to this work. The work is invisible and yet ever-present.

The approach

Orientation to the opponent

Each professional boxer I work with is regarded as his own boutique operation. The approaches tend to vary dependent on the various social locations that comprise the cultural background and unique identity of the athlete (Andersen, 1993). Given that my clients have been from five continents, a breadth of ethnicities, languages, families of origin, educational backgrounds, and some have also held criminal records where others have not, my approach must be tailored to these intersecting pieces of the athlete's identity (Andersen, 1993). However, each of these athletes has also come to expect certain consistencies. Among the most central expectation is that I develop a psychological profile of the opponent to assist with his psychological adaptation; part of the adaptation is garnered through learning about oneself, and the other part gained by understanding the tendencies of this next opponent. This profile is meant to reveal the underbelly of the opponent, including his familial background, amateur pedigree, preferred style, fluidities and consistencies in coaching staff, tendencies in terms of speaking about opponents through the media, behaviors at press conferences, in weigh-ins, and also during the night of the fight. These pieces of the opponent's tendencies are revealed through a careful thematic analysis of media data – something I have developed as a skill in my role as a researcher, partly based on the work of others (e.g., McGannon, Curtin, Schinke, & Schweinbenz, 2012). Though media data needs to be taken with a grain of salt, it, added to explorations on YouTube, radio interviews gathered from the Internet, and a fight record, synthesized and amalgamated, can provide useful information that contributes to effective athlete and coaching staff adaptation in advance of each important fight. Professional boxers, much like many other professional athletes, look to the researcher/profiler for useful information to draw upon in their preparation, over and above the study of fight footage.

Once the profile is developed, a process is required to ensure its complete integration. The profile is sent to the boxer and head coach one week in advance of my first-stage visit into the training camp; there are three stages of visits (general orientation, specific orientation to the fight, on-site implementation). The expectation is that the athlete, coaching, and management staff review the information on their own by reading the content once, so as to gain a general impression of the opponent. My first-stage visit is crafted with the purpose of looking generally at how the athlete and team are functioning – with this happening approximately six weeks before the fight, within the first two weeks of the training camp. During this 7- to 10-day visit, I sit with the head coach and athlete and provide an overview of what I found in relation to patterns of the opponent, and I introduce the client to the most significant fights the opponent has had and his tendencies in preparing for the fight, through to his post-bout words – especially those spoken immediately after each bout. These words within closest proximity to the fight are typically the most authentic, because there is less time to prepare and recompose, and there is also often anxiety and irritability surrounding the event. Thereafter, I pull together a summary of the opponent's strengths and weaknesses and also what the athlete and coach might expect in relation to media messaging and antics from that point in the camp through to fight week and fight night, and why the antics are being used. This process, though presented thus far as me doing most of the talking, is interspersed with discussion as we tackle each section, with the coach's and boxer's impressions. The intention is for the athlete and coach to begin to understand the psychological tactics they will encounter from the opposing boxer and his team as the bout draws closer. This understanding serves to orient my client, and thus contributes to his sense of perceived control.

Approximately 17 days before the fight, I return to the camp for 7 to 10 days and assist the staff with any interpersonal strains that are building due to the mounting stress of the bout. Within this stage, we return to the profile and discuss specific strategies for the week of the fight, keeping in mind what we know of the opponent's vulnerabilities. These vulnerabilities are to be attacked through the press conference early in fight week and then again during stare-down immediately after the weigh-in, one day before the fight. Some of the strategy might pertain to a direct attack of the opponent, and other aspects are determined in relation to indirect attacks through the coaching staff or promoter. For example, in a recent bout, the athlete attacked a questionable relationship between the opposing boxer and his coach in order to create a divide between these two people. Once these strategies are solidified, I return home for two days and then meet the working team for fight week implementation in the city where the event is being held. At this time I work almost exclusively with the athlete and reside with him in his house, or if we are out of town in the opponent's city, I have a room in his suite. Interspersed throughout the day are micro discussions relating to the next possible assault of the opponent based upon the profile. Furthermore, my living and moving with the athlete increases oversight so that the athlete is not overburdened by media requests, visits from friends and services that tend to overlap, such as an athletic therapist, massage therapist, and chiropractor. The ideal is for this oversight to assist the athlete in the implementation of a restful week in advance of the performance.

The intent through this three-stage process of profiling is to assist the athlete with his adaptation. Through my experience I have learned that, far too often, combatants, regardless of their sport, seek to adapt mostly on-site in the ring. What I have found is that psychological adaptation is far more effective when my clients adapt slowly to the challenge they are to face in the ring – not all at once. Much like the preparation of a scholar for an exam or significant presentation or interview, the adaptation in relation to the event must begin at least three weeks in advance of the performance in order for the final few days leading up to the performance to serve as implementation and on-site intuition and improvisation. Taking this format of psychological preparation permits the boxers to approach the performance with a combination of enthusiasm and confidence derived from knowledge of self and opponent as opposed to an overemphasis on the self devoid of what will be encountered outside of oneself (Hanin, 2010).

Inward focus

There is also a focus on understanding oneself as an athlete, with an identity. Within all of my work meeting with boxers, some of the discussion inevitably returns to who the athlete is as a person. Before I began my career, I read several practical sport psychology books where practitioners suggested that athletes be given identities and labels conducive to a targeted performance (these will not be referenced). For example, I recall in one instance reading about an NFL linebacker being taught to view himself as a honey badger. The honey badger is a highly aggressive animal, and in fact an animal that is known to best vicious poisonous snakes, such as the cobra. Though such strategies are interesting, and there is little doubt that athletes can take on characteristics from animate and inanimate objects and attempt to employ these within their performances, my approach is somewhat different and truer to the athlete's identity. I look to encourage and support a congruency of what the athlete is best at in general life and help guide the athlete to the integration of strategies during training, pre-bout, in performance, and during post-performance to align with the core values and tendencies of the performer, as opposed to assuming what these might be (Andersen, 1993). This morning I sat with a boxer who feels most at home engineering his warm-up. When he needs resources and support, he seeks these things out and then returns to his daily activities. This boxer's performances until very recently were inconsistent. The inconsistencies in performance, in many instances over-arousal and being a tentative starter in the ring, trace back to the day of performance and the athlete making decisions to be agreeable to the preferences of coaches and support staff. The boxer wants to be liked and yet he is conflicted, because he also has preferences for how he would like to receive his support. Though these preferences might not lead to others finding the boxer difficult, he has permitted his wishes to be secondary to being amenable to the warm-up pad strategies (for example) of his coaches. When an athlete is most comfortable being the leader in his own decisions, he must maintain this pattern in the days, hours, and minutes leading up to his performance, for that pattern to carry forward into performance from the first bell. When the bell sounds to start or resume the fight, coaches step down from the ring, leaving only the autonomous boxer.

As I have already proposed at the beginning of this section, each pugilist is his own boutique operation. When the person is most comfortable being the leader in his choices outside of the ring in life, he, and then those who support him, must engage in practices that support this format of active approach. There must be a congruency between who the person is outside and inside the ring. When this congruency is correctly engineered, the athlete is in harmony with himself – he is simply true to who he is. There is no need to take on a second – alternate – fluid persona that shifts from one moment to another, leaving him in confusion and misalignment. My role in this realm of my work is to support the athlete forward to a singular, true, and complete identity, with no conflict, and subsequently to engineer a support staff that contributes to the centralization of this identity through the various aspects of their support. For example, one of my developing clients lived several years on the streets. He and I work to take the lessons he has learned and integrate these into his ring strategy. Eventually, the approach is habitual and second nature for all concerned, contributing to an approach to supportive services that are entirely boutique and correctly formed to match with the athlete.

Recommendations for practitioners

Professional boxing is a sport where the mental trainer is a welcomed asset. I have found that consultants working within the boxing context are few and far between, for reasons of limited access, client distrust, and perhaps little to no contextual understanding regarding how to become an integrated member. I conclude with a few recommendations regarding how to effectively step into the world of boxing and have the longevity to practice with pugilists for a lifetime. The first and, I believe, most critical suggestion is for the practitioner to seek out the necessary contextual understanding in order to effectively practice within the boxing world. I achieved this early formative training by working with the Canadian National Boxing Team. I continue to work with this same team today, as the amateur boxers embark on their quadrennial preparation for the 2016 Summer Olympics (Schinke, Stambulova, Trepanier, & Oghene, in press). Working with the amateur athletes introduces the consultant to the more general sub-culture of boxing and how to speak the language (slang included) in order to fit within the context (Martens, Mobley, & Zizzi, 2000; Schinke & McGannon, 2014). Some of the athletes one meets in the amateurs will also likely become professional athletes, and when they do, assuming one is well-regarded and liked, this person will gain the opportunity to transition in consulting from the amateur to professional level, and then onward to working at an elite level.

Equally important is that the consultant be mindful of the importance of earning the trust of the athletes and their personal coaches. I have noticed that the boxing world is open to the profession of sport psychology but closed to consultants who do not have the boxers' best interests in mind. One means of gaining this trust is by ensuring that confidentiality is maintained, and a second strategy is to approach each athlete not only as a performer, but also in relation to his broader holistic development (Stambulova, Alfermann, Statler, & Côté, 2009). Discussions might extend beyond current performance enhancement strategies to the horizon of the athletic career, and also post-career plans (Park, Lavallee, & Tod, 2013), either at the next level of the sport or as one who works to produce the next generation of young boxers. One of my earliest amateur clients, who became an amateur world championship medalist, is now working alongside me on a coaching staff. We continue to define our relationship as his role in boxing evolves, with my support. Equally, a second of my clients is a renowned professional boxer, and he has just signed his first boxer to a promotional contract to manage an up-and-coming start. The client is now not only a boxer but also journeying into the administrative world of boxing, where he has a bright future as a businessman.

I would also propose that consultants in this sport should not cold call clients or promoters. Boxing is very much a grass-roots sport, where opportunities tend to happen by word of mouth, not by glitzy advertising. Though I have been witness to consultants in suits who knock on doors, who make immense promises about the potency of their work, my experience is that the best calling card is one's reputation. A good reputation is not easily earned, and it takes time and patience. At the beginning my clients were elite amateurs; I was never handed a professional world champion. I worked with many world champions, but all of these people became champions in the time of our partnership, where I attempted to be supportive of their development as boxers and as people. From champions who earned six-figure paychecks, I eventually was able to work with boxers who to this day continue to earn much more lucrative purses. These opportunities are built over time, and they require patience and years in working with the context and proving oneself as contributive.

Finally, I suggest one approaches this context as a chameleon. When I return home from a professional boxing training camp, I tend to use coarse language for a few days as I acculturate back to my regular life as a family man and scholar. The same acculturation happens in reverse when I return to a training camp. The thing is that I tend to take on the language and euphemisms of the context. Some of the boxers hold a social location within their identities as hipsters. I have come to like the music, and though one can never say I look like someone from the hip-hop culture, you will find me wearing clothes that align with the culture, which are often given to me at training camp. My language is also accessible to my clients, as I do not want people to ever believe I am above them, because this is not the case (Parham, 2005). In fact, I am the first to acknowledge that the boxers and coaches I work with all have doctorates in life education. I am slowly moving in that direction also, so that my practical experience reaches the same level as my theoretical and methodological expertise. I do not talk down to anyone; we are all equals with roles to play, part of a larger and tightly integrated whole. The practitioner who comes off as clinical and studious will not fit within the world of boxing; such people tend to be regarded as nerds and as disruptive to the ambiance of the camp and the context.

In closing, the world of professional boxing is a potential hotbed for applied sport psychology. The athletes and coaches are receptive to mental training, providing the practitioner fits well within the context. I do not wish to romanticize this sport. I have been witness to athletes with varying quality management groups. The correctly managed boxers have a well-informed and educated working team, and they can stand on the shoulders of their staff and catapult into a successful professional boxing career. However, and I have not really addressed this aspect in the current chapter, many boxers are mismanaged. The most promising boxer – turned over to the incorrect staff – can suffer a short horizon as a boxer, despite personal qualities. Due diligence rests with the boxer and personal coach to find the correct promoters and also the appropriate support staff. With the correctly chosen practitioner, the journey begins onward with each boutique boxer, integrating one's professional knowledge with an in-depth understanding of contextual sub-culture and the nuanced origins of the boxer and his working team (Parham, 2013).

References

Andersen, M. B. (1993). Questionable sensitivity: A comment on Lee and Rotella. *The Sport Psychologist*, 7, 1–3.

Anderson, A., Knowles, Z., & Gilbourne, D. (2004). Reflective practice for sport psychologists: Concepts, models, practical implications, and thoughts on dissemination. *The Sport Psychologist*, 18, 188–203.

Baltzell, A., Schinke, R. J., & Watson, J. W. (2010). Who is my client? *Association for the Advancement of Applied Sport Psychology Newsletter*, 25(2), 32–34.

Bandura, A. (1997). *Self-efficacy: The exercise of control*. New York: Freeman.

Early, G. L. (1994). *The culture of bruising: Essays on prizefighting, literature, and modern American culture*. Hopewell, NJ: Ecco Press.

Halliwell, W. (2009). Preparing professional hockey players for playoff performance. In R. J. Schinke (Ed.), *Contemporary sport psychology* (pp. 11–20). New York: Nova Science Publishers.

Hanin, Y. L. (2010). Coping with anxiety in sport. In A. R. Nicholls (Ed.), *Coping in sport: Theory, methods, and related constructs* (pp. 159–175). Hauppauge, New York: Nova Science.

Harris, B., Visek, A., & Watson, J. (2009). Ethical decision-making in sport psychology: Issues and implications for professional practice. In R. J. Schinke (Ed.), *Contemporary sport psychology* (pp. 217–232). New York: Nova Science Publishers.

Lane, A. (2009). Consultancy in the ring: Psychological support to a world champion professional boxer. In B. Hemmings & T. Holder (Eds.), *Applied sport psychology* (pp. 51–64). West Sussex, UK: John Wiley & Sons.

Martens, M. P., Mobley, M., & Zizzi, S. J. (2000). Multicultural training in applied sport psychology. *The Sport Psychologist*, 14, 81–97.

Martens, R. (1987). Science, knowledge, and sport psychology. *The Sport Psychologist*, 1, 29–55.

McGannon, K. R., Curtin, K., Schinke, R. J., & Schweinbenz, A. N. (2012). (De)Constructing Paula Radcliffe: Exploring media representations of elite athletes, pregnancy and motherhood through cultural sport psychology. *Psychology of Sport and Exercise*, 13, 820–829.

Parham, W. D. (2005). Raising the bar: Developing an understanding of athletes from racially, culturally and ethnically diverse backgrounds. In M. B. Anderson (Ed.), *Sport psychology in practice* (pp. 201–215). Champaign, IL: Human Kinetics.

Parham, W. D. (2013). The bridge goes both ways: Lessons learned on athletes searching for direction and meaning. In R. J. Schinke & R. Lidor (Eds.), *Case studies in sport development* (pp. 26–35). Morgantown, WV: Fitness Information Technology.

Park, S., Lavallee, D., & Tod, D. (2013). Athletes' career transitions out of sport: A systematic review. *International Review of Sport and Exercise Psychology*, 6, 22–53. doi: 10.1080/1750984X.2012.687053

Ryba, T. V. (2009). Understanding your role in cultural sport psychology. In R. J. Schinke & S. J. Hanrahan (Eds.), *Cultural sport psychology* (pp. 35–44). Champaign, IL: 1 Human Kinetics.

Ryba, T. V., Stambulova N., Si, G., & Schinke R. J. (2013). ISSP position stand: Culturally competent research and practice in sport and exercise psychology. *International Journal of Sport and Exercise Psychology*, 11, 123–142. doi:10.1080/1612197X.2013.779812

Schinke, R. J. (2007). A four-year chronology with national team boxing in Canada. *Journal of Sport Science and Medicine*, 6(CSSI-2), 1–5.

Schinke, R. J., Bonhomme, J., McGannon, K. R., & Cummings, J. (2012). The adaptation and maladaptation pathways of professional boxers in the ShowTime Super Six Boxing Classic. *Psychology of Sport and Exercise*, 14, 830–839. doi: 10.1016/j.psychsport.2012.06.006

Schinke, R. J., & McGannon, K. R. (Eds.). (2014). *The psychology of sub-culture in sport and physical activity: Critical perspectives.* East Sussex, UK: Psychology Press.

Schinke, R. J., McGannon, K. R., Parham, W. D., & Lane, A. M. (2012). Toward cultural praxis and cultural sensitivity: Strategies for self-reflexive sport psychology practice. *Quest, 64,* 34–46. doi:10.1080/00336297.2012.653264

Schinke, R. J., Stambulova, N. B., Trepanier, D., & Oghene, O. (in press). Psychological support for the Canadian Olympic Boxing Team in meta-transitions through the "Own the Podium" program. *International Journal of Sport and Exercise Psychology, 15,* 74–89.

Schinke, R. J., Yukelson, D., Bartolacci, G., Battochio, R. C., & Johnstone, K. (2011). The challenges encountered by immigrated elite athletes. *Journal of Sport Psychology in Action, 2,* 1–11. doi:10.1080/21520704.2011.556179

Stambulova, N. B., Alfermann, D., Statler, T., & Côté, J. (2009). ISSP position stand: Career development and transition of athletes. *International Journal of Sport and Exercise Psychology, 7,* 395–412. doi:10.1080/1612197X.2009.9671916

Weinberg, S. K., & Arond, H. (1952). The occupational culture of the boxer. *American Journal of Sociology, 57,* 460–469.

Woodward, K. (2008). Hanging out and hanging about: Insider / outsider research in the sport of boxing. *Ethnography, 9,* 536–560.

12

WORKING WITHIN PROFESSIONAL MIXED MARTIAL ARTS

Rebecca Symes

Author's background

I am interested in people and always have been, or to put it another way, I am fundamentally nosey. When I was 16, I started working at a large British high street bank in the customer services department. This initially started as a holiday job for the summer after I had completed my GCSE exams but soon became a regular holiday job for the next five years whilst I was finishing my education. I loved working there. It was a very busy branch with lots happening all the time, and there was a group of fantastic staff that socially gelled together very well, providing lots of post-work socializing. However, in the work environment, it fascinated me that for the most part, morale was very low, people didn't work together that effectively, a large proportion of the staff was stressed, and performance was often not very high (unsurprisingly, you might say). This stark contrast between how people were outside of work and within the working environment really fueled my interest in learning more about how people operate and the influence of the environment and culture. Combine this with the influence of my family background in that a number of my family worked within helping professions, and it seemed to lead me naturally into completing a psychology degree.

I undertook my Bachelor of Science at the University of Southampton, and I was always pretty clear that I wanted to become a psychologist, but I wasn't totally sure within which field. My undergraduate psychology was heavily focused on the developmental, social, biological, cognitive and clinical aspects of the area, and I gave consideration to being an educational psychologist as well as a clinical psychologist. However, I wasn't totally convinced that any of these areas were for me. My experience at the bank had made me really interested in the occupational psychology route, and this was probably where I was leaning towards when I left Southampton, although I was also applying for various graduate scheme jobs within business, mainly because that's what everyone else seemed to be doing. So when I didn't have any success getting into one of those programmes (something I am now thankful for), I got a job working in London at a business research consultancy. I saw this effectively as my gap year – an opportunity to work out exactly what I wanted to do whilst earning some money and enjoying being free from study and exams.

During this time, I attended a charity ball, working there as a volunteer. At this event I met Alan Butcher, who at the time was Head Coach of the Surrey County Cricket Club. Somehow we ended up talking about my career, or impending career, and I was explaining to Alan how I had done a psychology degree and liked the idea of being a psychologist but wasn't sure which field was for me, and we had also been talking about my love of cricket. He then simply asked me if I had ever considered sport psychology, and it was like a light-bulb moment. Why hadn't I ever thought of this? I loved sport; I loved psychology; so surely combining the two was the obvious choice.

I subsequently went on to complete my Master's in Sport and Exercise Psychology at the University of Chichester, and during this time I decided to set up my own consultancy, Sporting Success. I was very clear that it was the applied side I wanted to go into, so for the past 8 years I have been working full time as an applied sport psychologist. Throughout this time I have worked with a range of different athletes in a variety of sports, including cricket, archery, swimming, rugby, football (soccer), athletics, hockey, air pistol shooting, rifle shooting, darts, triathlon, golf, gymnastics, kickboxing, laser sailing and Mixed Martial Arts (MMA). This work has been at various performance levels from amateur to professional and has included some work within the world of business, applying the principles of elite sport to the corporate sector. The majority of my work now is within the elite and professional domains and currently focuses on MMA, cricket and archery. Within cricket, I have been on around nine international pre-season tours whilst with archery I have experienced a Paralympic Games as well as European and World Championships. My work within MMA has enabled me to work with professional fighters who have been preparing for British and World Title fights.

Sport context and sub-cultural understanding: initial challenges to access and trust and how these were overcome

When I first received a phone call about working within MMA, I was really not sure it was for me. I knew nothing about MMA, and at that point I didn't think I had much interest in it. However, as I was just starting out, I needed to be open to all opportunities, and how glad I am that I was! The phone call was from a fighter who had just taken on his first professional fight. He was studying sport science part time as a mature student, and this fueled his interest in the psychological aspects of performance. Given that he had his first professional fight coming up, and bearing in mind he had decided to skip semi-pro fights and go straight from amateur into professional, he had asked one of his lecturers if they could recommend a sport psychologist. They provided him with my details, and he made contact with me to see if I would be interested in working with him. These are often the best initial contacts, because when someone is ringing you they are already open to and interested in your help. I was really open in this phone call with the fighter and expressed that I knew nothing about the world of MMA or how the sport worked.

The pros and cons of working in sports you know and don't know is often a topic of discussion between psychologists. Ravizza (1988) even cited "lack of sport specific knowledge on the part of the consultant" as a barrier to gaining entry. However, my personal view based on my experience is that it doesn't matter if you don't know a sport, providing that you are (a) honest about that and (b) willing to find out as much as you can through the work that you do. Athletes will very quickly establish if you don't really know what you are talking about, and the worst thing you can do is use the lingo when you don't understand the context. Not knowing a sport can in fact put athletes more at ease in an initial consultation since you are sharing that you can help them with the mental side of performance, but equally you will need their help to learn about their sport and performance environment. This can help avoid the perceptions that athletes sometimes have that you are some so-called expert and are therefore potentially in a position of authority. So putting yourself in the potentially vulnerable position of admitting that you don't know the environment or sport particularly well can even out the playing field and put athletes more at ease. This can help to develop rapport and trust, which are fundamental parts of the consulting process (Andersen, 2000; Fifer, Henschen, Gould, & Ravizza, 2008; Watson & Shannon, 2010). The other benefit is that you potentially listen a lot better because you are trying to learn and you also don't make any assumption because you don't have the prior knowledge to do so. Thus, working in sports you are less familiar with can often make for a very effective consulting experience providing you are open, receptive and pick up information quickly.

MMA is one of the fastest growing sports and is steeped in the history of traditional martial arts. As the name suggests, it is a combination of martial arts, including the grappling arts (e.g. Brazilian Jiu Jitsu and wrestling) and striking arts (e.g. kickboxing and boxing). There is a culture of respect, humility, discipline and honor within MMA, and I can honestly say MMA fighters are some of the hardest-working athletes I have worked with. However, outside of the environment there can often be negative associations with MMA, mainly due to its colloquial term of 'cage fighting'. The reality though is that MMA fights take place within a 'cage' (simply a fence – no roof) due to safety reasons (to stop fighters from falling out). As opposed to MMA being the cause of street fights, MMA can actually be a really good way of helping people who might be struggling with anger issues or delinquency. Due to the sense of discipline and respect it commands within the environment, the professional fighters I have worked with are often involved in various programmes related to the rehabilitation of young offenders. Martial arts have also always promoted the connection between the mind and body, and therefore I have always found MMA fighters to be very keen on the psychological side of performance as part of an overall holistic approach to training and competition.

MMA fighters tend to firstly be associated with a gym that they represent when they fight and then to have a contract with MMA promoters. In the USA the most prominent of promoters is the Ultimate Fighting Championship (UFC) and within the UK it would be Cage Warriors Fighting Championship (CWFC) and British Association of Mixed Martial Arts (BAMMA). Championship and title fights are a maximum of five rounds, each lasting five minutes with a one-minute rest between rounds. If the fight goes to the maximum time, then the result is decided by the judges.

All of this information I have gained from working within the sport; prior to that I had no such knowledge. Having discussions with the fighters I have worked with and being around the training and competition environment have been the biggest influence on enabling me to understand the psychological demands of the sport, which is ultimately what you need in order to do your job to maximum effect. I have been fortunate that I have not experienced any challenges (aside from ensuring I am being as effective as possible) with the fighters I have worked with, and in fact, as already alluded to, I have found it to be a sport that is very open to input. Part of what helps with this is that within an MMA gym, if you have a fighter, especially a prominent one, who starts to work with a psychologist, then it tends to generate a lot of interest from other fighters. To steal a line from the movie *When Harry Met Sally*, it becomes a question of "I'll have what she's [he's] having!" Essentially that is how it worked for me; my original work with one fighter led to work with other fighters associated with the same gym.

Building up trust is crucial to any consulting work that you do, and as I often say, it doesn't matter how much knowledge you have; if you don't have a trusting relationship with an athlete, then all of that knowledge is irrelevant. Being open, honest and consistent in your support are important factors in building this trust. You have to demonstrate to athletes that you can listen, learn (about them) and offer guidance (philosophy dependent), and ultimately that you can add something to their performance. MMA fighters are very focused on performance enhancement and take their training incredibly seriously. They surround themselves with a team of people, including technical coaches (they are likely to have different coaches for different aspects), strength and conditioning coaches, a nutritionist, and a psychologist, among other staff members, and it is important that the team's members are all working together to aid the fighter and build mutual trust and rapport.

Consulting philosophy

I always find discussions around consulting philosophy interesting. I remember when I did my Master's degree we had to do various readings around the different philosophies, and it was almost a case of these are your options, now pick one. I feel that through the training route (certainly in the UK) you are basically required to justify your chosen philosophy, but I don't think it is quite as simple as that. Although a lot of my professional practice training was rooted in humanistic and gestalt principles, when I look back on my early consulting experiences, I would describe my philosophy as being very much cognitive-behavioral, and I think this would likely reflect the majority of neophyte practitioners since it enables a 'practitioner-led' approach (see Keegan, 2010 for an interesting discussion of teaching philosophies to neophyte practitioners). This approach is comforting when knowledge is limited and the need to be in control is highest. However, as I gained in experience and felt confident to relinquish control to the client, my original training in humanistic principles came much more to the fore, and now I describe my philosophy as an eclectic one, drawing upon a range of different approaches as I see fit. This is often dependent on things such as who the clients are, their age, their presenting issues, the nature of the work (e.g. time-bound or not) and the environment in which the work is taking place (e.g. privately or within a team or organization). Therefore, I think to encourage young (experience-wise not necessarily age-wise) practitioners to make a decision early on about their philosophy is unhelpful, since you almost need to bring the theory of the philosophy to life through experience to be in a position to establish what works best for you. My work within MMA has certainly been driven by an eclectic approach and, more specifically as Young (1992) described it, technical eclecticism – using one overarching theory but multiple techniques from a variety of frameworks. Humanistic philosophies drive a lot of my work, but I draw upon a range of frameworks and use a variety of techniques, especially from cognitive-behavioral therapy.

Effective strategies

Through reflecting on my experiences within MMA, I think there are five key areas that have been present in some form in most of my consulting experiences: (1) preparation (e.g. Cotterill, 2010; Gordon, 2012); (2) confidence (e.g. Biswas-Diener, Kashdan, & Minhas, 2011;

Sarkar & Fletcher, 2012; Vealey, 2001); (3) focus (e.g., Birrer & Morgan, 2010; Blanchfield, Hardy, De Morree, Staiano, & Marcora, 2014; Williams, Colley, Newell, Weibull, & Cumming, 2013); (4) identity (e.g. Brewer, Van Raalte, & Linder, 1993; Nasco & Webb, 2006); and (5) emotional control (e.g. Jones, 2003; Jones, Meijen, McCarthy, & Sheffield, 2009; Williams & Elliott, 1999). Each fighter is obviously unique, and the way in which these areas (if relevant) are addressed would differ between fighters and tailored to meet the individual's needs. Equally, in reality a lot of these areas are intertwined, but for the purpose of this chapter I am going to write about them in their own right and pick one or two strategies to explain in each area.

Preparation – preparing to perform

That doesn't just mean in competition as people might first think, but also preparing to perform in training, such as getting yourself ready to get the most out of your session. Getting things right in training is essential, and as the UK magazine title suggests, 'Train Hard Fight Easy'. Preparation is an extensive area, and a plethora of methods can be utilised. However, in my experience one thing I found was that whilst fighters take their preparation very seriously, especially when it comes to their technical and physical work, there wasn't always clarity over the exact purpose of a training session. Now it could be argued that this is implicit, since if they are doing a Brazilian Jiu Jitsu session, for example, then they are honing their skill in that area, but I would argue there needs to be a greater purpose than that to avoid the risk of simply going through the motions and to enhance the learning process. To assist with this, I came up with an acronym using the word 'purpose' to encourage fighters to use it to guide their training:

P – Plan: being clear on exactly what the plan is for a training session. This can be helped by answering two questions: (1) What am I trying to achieve, and (2) What is my measure of success?

UR – Utilise Resources: this is about encouraging fighters to use the resources they have around them to maximum effect (often in an initial session with them I will ask the question 'what resources do you currently have, that if used to their full potential could help enhance performance?'). Resources can include their own internal resources as well as external resources such as equipment, facilities and people.

P – Prepare: this might sound obvious, as I don't think I have met a fighter yet who doesn't physically warm up properly, but this isn't just about the physical element but also the mental side – ensuring that their mind is switched on, focused and in the appropriate mindset. For example, if they are doing a technical session where they are working on a specific skill, they should be in a mindset that will allow them to get the most out of that session. This might mean not being too hard on themselves if they make a mistake or allowing themselves to slow things down to get the movement pattern. It might also mean spending time doing some visualisation prior to the start of the session.

O – Optimal (arousal): by being clear on what the training session is about, it can guide where arousal levels for a session should be. For example, arousal levels going into a sparring session are likely to need to be higher than they are for doing a skill development session.

S – Strengths/Stretch: It is important that training sessions incorporate an element of both playing to strengths (so they can be maintained and strengthened) and also stretch areas – ensuring that sessions are challenging and hard, which fits with the notion of 'train hard fight easy'. I will often work with fighters to help them identify what are their areas of strength and stretch.

E – Evaluation: finally, it is important to get into the habit of evaluating each training session. This links back into the original questions of what am I trying to achieve and what is my measure of success. If you know these, then it's easy to evaluate against them at the end of the session. This is important for knowing the progress that is being made and building confidence as well as identifying continuous areas of development.

So as you've probably realised, within each of these areas lots of work can be done to help, for example, working with fighters on visualisation skills, working on identifying optimal arousal levels and how to increase or lower them as appropriate, working on learning to reflect (evaluative) appropriately and so forth. This simple acronym helps to provide an initial starting point from which work can be developed.

Another strategy that I have found to be very useful within the MMA work is "what-if" planning. This can be used to look at a whole variety of scenarios that could potentially occur, and I find breaking this down into four areas is helpful: (1) identify the what-if scenario; (2) determine the performance risk (low, medium, high); (3) identify what can be done to minimise the risk (of the 'what if' occurring); and (4) determine a strategy for what to do if it (the what if) occurs.

Confidence – the belief in oneself to be able to deliver a skill

Confidence is one of the greatest psychological demands on a fighter and arguably any athlete, but going into a fight confident and backing oneself is essential. Positive psychology (e.g. Biswas-Diener, Kashdan, & Minhas, 2011; Sarkar & Fletcher, 2012) really has a role to play within confidence, and historically I have spent a lot of time working with fighters to help them understand their strengths and enabling them to be clear on what strengths will assist them against certain opponents. This latter aspect is most effectively done in conjunction with a coach, where you are really just helping to facilitate the conversation. It should also be noted that being aware of strengths and actually using them are two different things; people often become complacent and neglect to use them at all. Going into battle, fighters don't want to be thinking about all the things they aren't so good at; they need to have absolute clarity over what they're bringing to the table, or indeed, the cage.

Confidence for me is also about mindset, and helping to promote a challenge mindset within fighters is a valuable piece of work. According to the theory of challenge and threat states in athletes (Jones, Meijen, McCarthy, & Sheffield, 2009), a challenge state, which is essentially an adaptive response to stress, is underpinned by a high level of self-efficacy, perceived control and a focus on approach goals. A challenge state also has its own pattern of cardiovascular activity, which enables efficient use of energy within the body; this is vital with the physical demands of fighting. It is also worthy to note that the difference between how athletes perceive an environment or task (e.g. challenge or threat) and how they perceive their ability to cope with that environment/task (i.e. their confidence) determines how well they are likely to adapt to that situation and thus achieve their goal(s) (Tenenbaum, Lane, Lidor, Razon, & Schinke, 2015). This area is therefore very closely linked with emotional control.

Focus – being able to maintain attention on the right things at the right time

I distinctly remember having a conversation with one of the fighters I was working with about how he felt he lost a fight due to getting too far ahead of himself. He remembers a particular point when he thought to himself, 'I've got this, I'm going to win'. Needless to say, that thought meant he had gotten too far ahead of himself, and as a result he wasn't focused on the moment, was caught off guard, and actually lost. Focus is a really important skill. Take your mind off what you're doing for a moment and it could all be over. Focus on the wrong thing at the wrong time and the opportunity could be lost. So there is work to be done on staying focused during the actual fight, but also prior to the fight, that moment when the fighter walks into the arena. Discussions aimed at creating awareness for a fighter of what types of things they need to be focused on at certain points during a fight, such as between rounds, floor work, or whilst standing up, can be a really helpful starting point for building strategies. Using self-talk, and in particular cue words, is a very effective way of maintaining focus. As with all these things, it is important to test this approach out in training prior to using it in competition. Ensuring they have a clear fight strategy can also help fighters to maintain focus, and facilitating conversations between fighters and their coaches regarding their communication between rounds is important since what they say in these moments can be very influential. Helping fighters to carefully choose the music they walk out to can also have a role to play since their heart rate is likely to sync to the rhythm of the music, and you want the music to help instill the right kind of focus.

A really effective strategy I have found is using music and visualisation together. The benefits of visualisation are well documented, and I recommend reading Williams, Colley, Newell, Weibull, and Cumming (2013) for a good guide on developing a visualisation script. Working with a fighter to establish a visualisation script for fight night, which the fighter then reads and records to his walk-out music, has been really effective for helping fighters to mentally prepare and maintain focus. The idea actually being that over time an association is built up between the music and the visualization so that the music on its own then elicits the effects of the visualisation. Some fighters I have worked with also used visualisation for working on specific skill development and honing particular moves, and coaches have even commented, anecdotally, that they have noticed the fighters' speed of learning increase as a result of this technique.

Identity – understanding who you are, in and out of the cage

Working with fighters on their sense of identity has been one of the most powerful and interesting aspects of my work. The majority of MMA fighters have a nickname, and I have found using this to build up a persona is really effective. It's about really enabling the fighter to understand the characteristics and attributes they draw upon in fight mode, and it links closely to the work on confidence and strengths building. As part of this, it is important to work on establishing what they're like when they're not in fight mode and characteristics and attributes they draw upon then. There are likely to be similarities between these two parts of themselves, so for example they might be determined within and outside of the cage, and in these instances it's about identifying exactly how that attribute helps them in the different environments. Building up this persona can also be an effective way of helping them to switch on and off, which can aid recovery. For example, when they are at home, they are not in fight mode, but at what point do they switch off from their fight persona? Is it immediately after they finish training, when they get in the car to drive home, or when they change their clothing? You can go into a lot of detail through exploring their identity properly, and this can also link closely into the visualisation script they build up. It is worth noting that this isn't about being two different people; it's about understanding which aspects of themselves they are drawing upon and when, then using those attributes to enhance performance.

Emotional control – channeling emotional responses in order to achieve optimal performance

MMA in many ways is all about emotion and a real purity of emotion. However, one of the biggest skills a fighter needs to develop is to learn to control that emotion and channel it in the right way. When working with fighters on this area, I tend to do an element of 'teaching' them about the way the brain operates under pressure – about the amygdala and the in–built fight–or–flight mechanism we all have and our need for survival. But fighting in many ways makes this difficult, because they are in "fight" mode, which isn't always optimal for elite per–formance, so it's a fine balance. As you probably know, our amygdala kicks us into a hijacked state when we feel threatened (physical or ego-driven), so we need to aim to reduce the likelihood of the amygdala kicking off. There is very limited research within MMA, but one group of authors (Vaccaro, Schrock, & McCabe, 2011) found that the most common fears of MMA fighters are injury and losing, and my experience would back these up. Both are essentially about loss, since the fear of injury isn't about getting hurt per se but about the risk to their career if they get injured, and having too many losses on their fight record isn't great for a fighter's career prospects. So work in this area is about helping fighters to understand their potential fears and how to reduce or eliminate them to stop the amygdala hijack from taking place.

Lots of the work already mentioned comes into this. For example, what–if planning can help to reduce fear, because if you have a plan in place for something, it is easier to rationalise it and also reduce the fear, since a lot of fear is driven by a sense of being out of control and the unknown. Visualisation is also really useful since it can again promote a sense of being in control and build confidence. Also working with fighters to help them understand how they interpret things that happen and how that influences their beliefs and behavior is effective. A simple example of this is a fighter feeling nervous. If they interpret this as a bad thing and an unhelpful feeling, then nerves are not conducive to performance. However, if they inter–pret a nervous feeling as their body's way of telling them they are ready to perform, then this can be conducive for performance. So helping fighters to create a sense of awareness around how they commonly interpret things and helping them to understand how they can view things in a more helpful way is time well spent. Also working on quick, simple, yet effective strategies for the one-minute rest between rounds plays a role, and engaging the coaches in this process too is important because, as mentioned earlier, they will be the ones talking to the fighters between rounds. Breathing techniques, cue words and imagery can all be useful strategies.

So many interrelated areas are important to consider when working with MMA fighters, and equally others areas haven't been addressed here, including mood management (especially relevant when cutting weight) and post-fight work incorporating effective reviewing of a fight and managing the flow from one fight to the next (usually a few months down the line).

Recommendations

As mentioned earlier, my work in MMA started as a result of a call I received from a fighter wanting to do some work. This is relatively uncommon, especially when you're starting out, since opportunities rarely land in your lap. Therefore, you have to be willing to be proactive and seek out opportunities. I think with the increasing understanding of the role psychology plays in performance, this is now becoming slightly easier, and within MMA there is certainly far more focus on the psychological side. This is evident even just from an increasing number of fight-specific magazine articles dedicated to the psychological side of fighting, and equally there are now more autobiographies out there from MMA fighters where the mental side of the sport is often highlighted.

That said, be aware that there is still a perception (certainly within the UK) to some extent that a psychologist is there to help athletes "fix problems". Whilst working with those athletes who might be struggling is naturally a part of the role, this really is just a part of the role. A lot of the time, a much larger aspect is working with athletes in order to enhance performance, such as athletes who are already doing well but are wanting to push their performance to the next level or enable themselves to perform at a certain level more consistently. Within the MMA world, this might include fighters who are taking on their first semi-pro fight or their first professional fight or fighters who have started their professional career successfully and want to be able to maintain those performance levels.

Our job therefore is to sell this notion – to educate and explain the performance enhancement benefits. I have never come across an athlete or coach who didn't believe that the psychological side of performance was significant, and when it comes to competition, highly significant. However, I have come across athletes and coaches who, despite this belief, don't invest in working on the mental aspect of their performance. In fairness, this hasn't been my personal experience with MMA; however, I imagine that it very well could be. Consequently, when putting yourself out there in a bid to gain work, you will experience knockbacks, but the challenge is to be more motivated as a result of this, not less. So avoid expecting athletes and coaches to 'get it', because I am telling you now, not all of them will. Yes, you get it, and it might be obvious to you, but it won't always be to them.

My advice therefore is to be really clear on what you can offer, what impact you believe you can have and how you will go about achieving this goal. This is particularly significant within the MMA world since all the fighters I have come across are very performance driven. Of course, all of this is a lot easier to establish with the more experience you get, but I still believe you can do this from day one. The 'how' part will vary among psychologists depending on their (emerging) philosophy and experience, but I think it is important to know there isn't always a right way to do things. Sure, there might be a recommended way, or ways that other people have found to work, but I'm a strong believer in finding out what works for you, and more importantly what works within the unique environment you're operating in (one MMA gym, for example, can differ from another). I think all too often we are afraid to try to do something a different way for fear of it not working out, but as the saying goes, 'nothing venture nothing gained'; at one time, the now-established ways of working were once untested.

As previously suggested, MMA fighters most likely operate out of an MMA gym, so the best option to gaining entry is to get in touch directly with a gym. A simple Google search will alert you to MMA gyms within your area, or take a look at fight promoter websites to see fighter profiles, where it will usually list what gym/club they belong to. A key thing to bear in mind is that sport is not a 9–5 job! Training and competitions often happen in the evenings and weekends, so you need to be prepared to workout outside of "normal" hours. Working with an individual fighter on a private basis is perhaps one of the easiest things to do from a logistical viewpoint since the relationship is just between you and them, you agree between you what you're going to work on and fit into each other's schedules as appropriate. You're not expected to report back to anyone else, you don't have other people's opinions to consider and it's entirely up to you how you operate. Contrastingly, when working with a number of fighters within the same gym, you might be expected to exchange feedback with a coach, to work on aspects that they feel are areas of concern for the fighter, or you might need to work on areas that fit within an overall strategy for performance and operate within certain time constraints. None of this is a problem and is probably the ideal way to work since a fighter will have a team of people around them, and working in conjunction with the wider team as opposed to in silo will be far more effective in the long run. However, it is important to bear in mind that when doing this, communication among all parties is absolutely crucial, and it is imperative that everyone is working towards the same goal and clear on what each other is doing.

So my advice for being effective when working within gyms includes being really clear from the start about the following:

Your remit (who you're working with, e.g. fighters and/or coaches; how much time you have; your payment)

How your work will be assessed (e.g. feedback from fighters; performance factors; coaches' feedback)

How you will deliver the work (e.g. one-to-one and/or group-based sessions; away from training and/or within training; your role, if any, at fights etc.)

Confidentiality (i.e. what information gets shared and with who) – As we are all aware, confidentiality is a key ethical consideration within psychology; however, for me personally, the more open the work is the better, but of course there can be things that fighters don't want coaches knowing. The reason I say the more open the better is because psychology isn't a stand-alone area of performance; it plays a role in every single aspect of a fighter's training and competition. Therefore, having your work reinforced by other coaches and practitioners can be really helpful, and having everyone on the same page ensures that all work is complementary and not opposing. But there is an element where things need to be confidential, so being clear with those employing you from the start is key. Also, agreeing with fighters how you will operate is important, and there are various options within this (e.g. operating where everything is confidential and if you wish to share anything with coaches, then you obtain explicit permission from the individual). Alternatively, you can have agreement where everything that is specifically performance related can be shared unless agreed otherwise but all non-performance-related aspects will be kept confidential. Whichever way you do it, I would recommend having written agreements in place.

To finish, it's worth noting that I have only ever worked with male MMA fighters. When I first started working in this field, I didn't come across many female MMA fighters (although I had worked with female kickboxers), and men dominated the MMA world. My experience is consistent with research from Masucci and Butryn (2015), but now there are far more female MMA fighters, perhaps since they were included in the UFC for the first time in 2013. I have never experienced any issues in the MMA environment due to being a female, and I think this comes down to areas I raised in the introduction around being a quick learner in new environments, being willing to get involved and experience what the environment is like (this can be achieved though observation and immersion) and through being honest and authentic in your approach. It is also very important that you learn to apply your knowledge in a way in which fighters can understand and relate. They won't be interested in what research might have been done or what a theory might say, but they will be interested in how you can add to their team to help enhance performance. Learning to apply your knowledge in a relevant, appropriate and useful manner is the most important skill for an applied psychologist. I strongly believe there are opportunities within the world of MMA, and increasingly so given the speed at which the sport is growing.

References

Andersen, M. (2000). Beginnings: Intake and the initiation of relationships. In M. Andersen (Ed.), *Doing sport psychology* (pp. 3–16). Champaign, IL: Human Kinetics.

Birrer, D., & Morgan, G. (2010). Psychological skills training as a way to enhance an athlete's performance in high-intensity sports. *Scandinavian Journal of Medicine and Science in Sports, 2*, 78–87.

Biswas-Diener, R., Kashdan, T. B., & Minhas, G. (2011). A dynamic approach to psychological strength development and intervention. *The Journal of Positive Psychology, 6*, 106–118.

Blanchfield, A. W., Hardy, J., De Morree, H. M., Staiano, W., & Marcora, S. M. (2014). Talking yourself out of exhaustion: The effects of self-talk in endurance performance. *Medicine & Science in Sports & Exercise, 46*, 998–1007.

Brewer, B. W., Van Raalte, J. L., & Linder, D. E. (1993). Athletic identity: Hercules' muscles or Achilles' heel? *International Journal of Sport Psychology, 24*, 237–254.

Cotterill, S. T. (2010). Pre-performance routines in sport: Current understanding and future directions. *International Review of Sport & Exercise Psychology, 3*, 132–115.

Fifer, A., Henschen, K., Gould, D., & Ravizza, K. (2008). What works when working with athletes. *The Sport Psychologist, 22*, 356–377.

Gordon, S. (2012). Strengths-based approaches to developing mental toughness: Team and individual. *International Coaching Psychology Review, 7*, 210–222.

Jones, M.V. (2003). Controlling emotions in sport. *The Sport Psychologist, 17*, 471–486.

Jones, M.V., Meijen, C., McCarthy, P. J., & Sheffield, D. (2009). A theory of challenge and threat states in athletes. *International Review of Sport and Exercise Psychology, 2*, 161–180.

Keegan, R. J. (2010). Teaching consulting philosophies to neophyte sport psychologists: Does it help and how can we do it? *Journal of Sport Psychology in Action, 1*, 42–52.

Masucci, M.A., & Butryn, T. M. (2015). Caged quandaries: Mixed martial arts and the politics of research. In R. J. Schinke & K. R. McGannon (Eds.), *The psychology of sub-culture in sport and physical activity* (pp. 168–181). New York: Routledge.

Nasco, S. A., & Webb, W. M. (2006). Towards an expanded measure of athletic identity: The inclusion of public and private dimensions. *Journal of Sport and Exercise Psychology, 28*, 434–453.

Ravizza, K. (1988). Gaining entry with athletic personnel for season-long consulting. *The Sport Psychologist, 2*, 243–254.

Sarkar, M., & Fletcher, D. (2012, October). Developing resilience: Lessons learned from Olympic champions. *The Wave, 36*–38.

Tenenbaum, G., Lane, A., Lidor, R., Razon, S., & Schinke, R. J. (2015). Adaptation: A two-perception probabilistic conceptual framework. *Journal of Clinical Sport Psychology, 9*, 1–23.

Vaccaro, C. A., Schrock, D. P., & McCabe, J. M. (2011). Managing emotional manhood: Fighting and fostering fear in mixed martial arts. *Social Psychology Quarterly, 74,* 414–437.

Vealey, R. S. (2001). Understanding and enhancing self-confidence in athletes. In R. N. Singer, H. A. Hausenblas & C. M. Janelle (Eds.), *Handbook of sport psychology* (pp. 550–565). New York: John Wiley & Sons.

Watson II, J. C., & Shannon, V. (2010). Individual and group observations: Purposes and processes. In S. J. Hanrahan & M. B. Andersen (Eds.), *Routledge handbook of applied sport psychology: A comprehensive guide for students and practitioners* (pp. 90–100). New York: Routledge.

Williams, A. M., & Elliott, D. (1999). Anxiety, expertise and visual search strategy in karate. *Journal of Sport and Exercise Psychology, 21,* 362–375.

Williams, S. E., Colley, S. J., Newell, E., Weibull, F., & Cumming, J. (2013). Seeing the difference: Developing effective imagery scripts for athletes. *Journal of Sport Psychology in Action, 4,* 109–121.

Young, M. E. (1992). *Counseling methods and techniques: An eclectic approach.* New York: Macmillan.

13

MENTAL TRAINING PROGRAM FOR A SUMO WRESTLER

Yoichi Kozuma

Sumo is an original Japanese style of wrestling with a very large fan base from the imperial family to the everyday person, all of whom consider sumo to be a national sport. It is also a sport that is steeped in the history and tradition of Japanese martial arts. According to historical records, it has been suggested that sumo started roughly 1,500 years ago as part of an ancient religious-based agricultural celebration, where villagers would gather at local shrines to either celebrate and pray to the heavens for a bountiful rice crop after planting or to thank the deities for blessing their village by providing a good harvest. Unlike the sport that we know today, sumo in ancient times was a community event where the winners of bouts were simply determined by brute force and sheer power over their opponents. Anyone could participate, and the winning prize for the participants would be a year's supply of rice to feed their families.

In Japanese history, there are two official chronicles of ancient Japan that mention sumo. Sumo has been documented in "The Records of Ancient Matters", known in Japanese as *Kojiki* (ca. 712), and "The Chronicles of Japan" or *Nihon Shoki* (ca. 720). Both of these chronicles are considered to be the oldest sacred sources for customs, ceremonies, consecration, and clairvoyance practices of ancient Japan from the early mythical origins to the seventh century, as well as historical accounts of the Imperial Court of those times. In the writings of *Nihon Shoki*, there is a description of a fatal match of power and strength between two sumo wrestlers named *Nomi No Sukune* and *Taima No Kehaya*, who wrestled in front of the Emperor at the Izumo Grand Shrine. It states that *Nomi No Sukune* killed *Taima No Kehaya* by kicking him to death during a sumo bout (Nitta, 2010). Since there is no historical evidence of this match, this account is considered to be a part of an oral tradition that the ancient chronicles are largely based upon; however, it should still be noted that this is an important historical account that recorded and documented the early days of sumo.

Sumo expanded from its beginnings as a religious celebration and appreciation by rice farmers into becoming an integral part of imperial events held at Shinto shrines for more than 300 years. Parallel to the growth in popularity of sumo to the common villagers, sumo also evolved into a way for Japanese warriors, or *samurai*, to practice martial arts and train for battle from the Kamakura Period (1147–1333) until the Sengoku Period, which is also known as the Warring States (1467–1615). Towards the end of the Sengoku Period, a famous Japanese warlord, or *daimyo*, named Oda Nobunaga (name styled in a Japanese manner with Oda as a family name) came into power. Oda Nobunaga overthrew the ruling feudal government at that time (1534–1582) and ended a long period of feudal wars by unifying half of the country under his rule. Although he is known as a ruthless military leader, it was also well known that he was a devoted fan of sumo and would hold sumo championships at his royal court starting around 1570 (Nitta, 2010). As a prize, he would hire the champion of the sumo tournaments to be one of his samurai retainers, a reward which was considered to be a great honor bestowed on any warrior. The popularity of these championship sumo tournaments continued a decade after his death by his heirs until 1592, when the new ruler needed his samurai warriors to go into combat in wars he started overseas with Korea and Ming China, as well as to fight battles with faction warlords who were against his rule (Nitta, 2010).

After nearly a century of warfare among the feudal lords, or *daimyos*, seeking to gain control of the nation, Japan was unified under a supreme military leader, or *shogun*, in 1603 (Nitta, 2010). During this era, known as the Edo Period (1603–1868), the foundation of sumo transformed from religious rituals or martial arts events into a more organized sport with professional sumo wrestlers. In the Edo Period, the shogun was the military de facto ruler of the entire country, with the Imperial Court tending to the administration duties of Japan (Kozuma, 2009). Since the ruling class of warlords was no longer at war with each other and the country was unified under a sustaining peaceful rule, the people were able to shift their priority from constantly trying to survive a life of impending death and starvation to a more stable life with leisure time for entertainment. During this time, three famous sumo wrestlers, who had gathered a devoted following of fans, appeared on the tournament circuit. Upon hearing of the popularity of these three sumo wrestlers, the shogun attended a sumo tournament with great interest. With the attention and approval from the ruling class, the popularity of sumo spread quickly throughout the newly unified nation of Japan. Sumo became a sport that anyone, regardless of social class, could enjoy, and its popularity still continues today.

What is sumo today?

Although outside of Japan sumo is viewed as a wrestling sport, to the Japanese, sumo is considered to be a form of *budo* or martial arts. When written in *kanji* (Chinese characters), *sumo* literally means to strike down another person; therefore, modern sumo should be classified as a competitive full-contact Japanese style of martial art wrestling. There are four grand tournaments held annually during the different seasons of the year, and each grand tournament lasts for 15 days. There is no weight class in sumo; therefore, all sumo wrestlers are matched with each other at least once during a tournament. To win a bout, a sumo wrestler must force his opponent to touch the ground with any part of his body or to be thrown out of the *dohyo*, the circular fighting ring. Two associations regulate the sport of sumo, one for the professional level and the other for the amateur level. The Japan Sumo Association is the governing organization for the professional sumo tournaments, and it hosts the four main grand tournaments throughout Japan as well as regional and international showcase matches every year, while the International Federation of Sumo organizes the amateur sumo wrestling events both in Japan and overseas (Nitta, 2010).

Although sumo is a modern sport now, the wrestlers live and train in centuries-old traditions and practices. Many of the ceremonies and rituals related to sumo are religious remnants carried over from the Shinto religion. The thatched roof that hovers above the fighting ring, the use of salt to purify the *dohyo* of evil spirits, the costume of the referees, and how the sumo wrestlers dress are all symbolic of Shintoism, an indigenous religion of Japan. Similar to other people living in religious communes, all sumo wrestlers are expected to eat, train, and live together while they are active professionally. In addition, just as in any commune, every aspect of the sumo wrestler's life – both in the fighting ring and during their off time – is controlled and dictated by the governing body of the sport.

Mental training for a sumo wrestler

Several years ago, the national public broadcasting corporation, called *Nihon Hoso Kyokai* (NHK), contacted me concerning a professional sumo wrestler. NHK told me that the professional sumo wrestler, who will be referred to as Sumo Wrestler K, was interested in learning more about mental training and would like to meet with me. At that time, Sumo Wrestler K was ranked as a *Sekiwake* (third highest position, with the highest position called *Yokozuna* or grand champion), and he had just lost his chance to be promoted to *Ozeki* (second highest rank under *Yokozuna*) for the second time. He was under a lot of pressure to be promoted because it was a time when foreign wrestlers dominated all of the high-ranking titles, including the reigning *Yokozuna* champion. The country wanted to see a Japanese *Ozeki* in its rankings and had pinned its national hope and pride on Sumo Wrestler K.

In order to achieve the rank of *Ozeki*, a sumo wrestler needs to win a minimum of 30 bouts over the three most recently held grand tournaments, winning at least 10 out of 15 bouts during a current grand sumo tournament to be considered for promotion. It must also be mentioned that the promotional criteria in sumo is often discretionary and not exact. Other than the necessary 30-plus win requirement, other circumstances, such as a recommendation from the executive members of the Japan Sumo Association, defeating the reigning champion, or winning the tournament, are also taken into consideration. Sumo Wrestler K was the top Japanese contender to be promoted; however, he was struggling to achieve enough wins to meet the minimum 30-win criteria. For two consecutive grand tournaments, he would easily attain the 10 wins, but when it was getting close to the end of the 15-day tournament, he would constantly start to lose to lower-ranking opponents. The next grand sumo tournament, which was three months away, was his last chance to improve his winning record to be promoted to *Ozeki*, or else his winning track record would have to be recalculated from the start again.

Sumo Wrestler K noticed that even during practice something was not quite right with his performances, and he felt that he was not on his game. He knew that he needed to do something, but he did not know how to proceed other than to train longer and harder. Since all of the broadcasting rights for sumo tournaments are controlled by NHK, the broadcasting company decided to make a documentary of Sumo Wrestler K's quest to achieve the *Ozeki* ranking. During filming one day, Sumo Wrestler K mentioned that he had heard recently something about mental toughness and the use of psychological skills for performance enhancement in other sports. He stated that he did not know much about mental training and wondered out loud if it could be applicable for him, but then quickly dismissed the notion since his sport after all is sumo. When the NHK documentary TV director heard about this, he asked Sumo Wrestler K if he was really interested in pursuing to learn more about mental training, because he knew someone he could introduce and mentioned my name.

The TV director knew of my work because previously I was in another NHK show called *Bakusho Mondayno Nippon no Kyouyou* (Japanese Liberal Arts and Science Education Presented by Bakusho Mondai). The premise of this weekly show is to introduce various research topics conducted by scientists and professors at Japanese universities in an informative and entertaining manner. A full episode was devoted to introduce my work with elite athletes and my mental training program (Ohta, Tanaka, & Kozuma, 2008). After watching a recording of that particular show, Sumo Wrestler K expressed his desire to meet with me to learn more about mental training. The TV director first contacted me to discuss the format of the documentary and wanted to know what type of consultation I could provide for Sumo Wrestler K. After listening to my explanation, the director decided that he would like to include a segment in the documentary of Sumo Wrestler K's introduction and application of mental training as he seeks for the title of *Ozeki*.

Before the meeting with Sumo Wrestler K

Due to NHK's exclusive broadcasting rights to air all of the professional sumo grand tournaments, the NHK TV director was able to share with me full daily recordings of Sumo Wrestler K's bouts from the previous 15-day grand tournament. I watched and analyzed every aspect of his 15 bouts. Key observations were made on his eyes, facial expressions, attitude, and body movements before, during, and after each of his bouts. Based on my analysis, a psychological technique pattern emerged with Sumo Wrestler K. It was clear that when he used the same pre-performance routine, he would win that particular bout; however, when he altered his routine in any way, he would lose to his opponent. My first recommendation in my notes for Sumo Wrestler K was to establish and improve his pre-performance routine.

Meeting the sumo wrestler

When Sumo Wrestler K first came to my sport psychology and mental training lab, he arrived with the TV director and camera crew. I introduced myself and explained that the first step would be to analyze his psychological aptitude through a Japanese standardized sport psychological test called DIPCA.3 (Tokunaga, 2001). The Diagnostic Inventory of Psychological Competitive Ability for Athletes (DIPCA.3) is used in Japan to evaluate an athlete's psychological aptitude of mental skills and mental toughness. There are 52 questions on the test, and based on the athlete's answers, the results show the athlete's mental toughness score as well as his or her weak and strong points of psychological aptitude for sports in 18 different factors. A list and brief explanation of the 18 factors for DIPCA.3 can be found in Table 13.1.

At first glance, the result for DIPCA.3 Factor 18 for Sumo Wrestler K showed that his mental toughness for competition was 185 out of a possible 240 points. This is considered to be at a high school athlete's level in Japan (see Figure 13.1). From my experience and based on studies using DIPCA. 3, professional athletes usually score higher than 210 points (Kozuma, 2002). The scoring is based on Tokunaga's study (2001), where he divided the DIPCA.3 scores by gender and categorized the scores into five levels from high to low. Tokunaga's study suggests that the low scores reflect athletes who are considered to be mentally weak for competitive sports and should focus more on their mental training, whereas the high scores denote that the athletes are mentally strong for competition. The mental toughness scores are

TABLE 13.1 Factors of DIPCA.3

Factor 1. Patience	Factor 7. Concentration and Focus
Factor 2. Fighting Spirit	Factor 8. Self-Confidence
Factor 3. Achievement Motivation	Factor 9. Decision Making
Factor 4. Motivation to Win	Factor 10. Prediction
Factor 5. Self-control	Factor 11. Judgment
Factor 6. Relaxation	Factor 12. Cooperation

Factor 13. Motivation for Competition = Sum of Factors 1–4
Factor 14. Psychological Stability and Concentration = Sum of Factors 5–7
Factor 15. Self-Confidence = Sum of Factors 8 & 9
Factor 16. Strategic Ability = Sum of Factors 10 & 11
Factor 17. Cooperation = Factor 12
Factor 18. Total Psychological Aptitude for Sports = Sum of Factors 13–17

Note: Lie scores serve as credibility index.

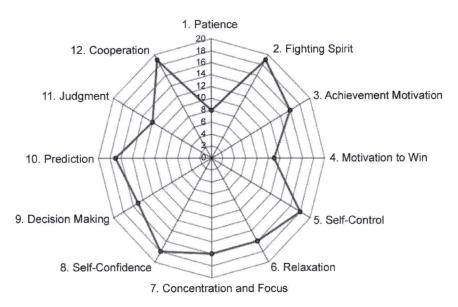

FIGURE 13.1 Overall DIPCA.3 results of Sumo Wrestler K.

available on DIPCA.3 for immediate feedback to the athletes after their final scores have been calculated. The five categories of the scores are listed in Table 13.2.

Further analysis of Sumo Wrestler K's DIPCA.3 scores also showed that he needed improvement in the areas of relaxation, self-control, patience, achievement motivation, decision-making, judgment, motivation to win, and concentration skills. Together we reviewed his DIPCA.3 results item by item, and I asked him if he had any explanations or comments in regards to the factor scores that he would like to add. He was not surprised at his results at all. He was more astonished by how accurately the results showed his current psychological aptitude. Using DIPCA.3 results as a baseline, I recommended a tailored mental training program

TABLE13.2 Five categories of DIPCA.3 scores by gender

	Very Low	*Low*	*Needs Improvement*	*High*	*Very High*
Male	Under 141	142–164	165–186	187–209	Over 210
Female	Under 131	132–154	155–178	179–202	Over 203

for Sumo Wrestler K to help enhance his mental toughness for his sumo performances. Sumo Wrestler K freely admitted that he needed help with his mental toughness for sumo. He readily accepted my recommendation and advice and was open and committed to learn new psychological skills as part of his training routine.

This was a highly unusual case for a professional sumo wrestler to be willing to receive consultation from a sport psychologist. The reason is because in the Japanese sumo tradition, their training approach has always been built on the foundation that sumo skills and maneuvers are passed down and taught through a hierarchy system from the older sumo wrestlers to the younger wrestlers. Their belief is that more demanding practices and training sessions will make the wrestlers stronger both mentally and physically. If a sumo wrestler is not winning his bouts, then he is simply not working and training hard enough. Since sumo's regimented training practices have a long history, they are considered to be inseparable from their sport, thus there is no room for any adaptation from the norm. The obligation for the Japanese practice traditions to be maintained is also supported by both professional and amateur sumo organizations, which have never considered the acceptance of Western ideas or training styles as part of their sport. It was only until recently that individual sumo wrestlers have slowly added weight training or have hired personal athletic trainers or training coaches by providing the extra funding themselves. To even consider applying psychological skills to sumo was a very brave and radical decision by Sumo Wrestler K.

Sumo Wrestler K's self-analysis

As part of my mental training program, in addition to the administration of DIPCA.3, I also give athletes a textbook with an accompanying mental training workbook to use (Kozuma, 2002). The workbook contains a questionnaire that measures athletes' knowledge of mental training and their awareness of their own psychological state of mind. Designed with yes/ no questions and short answers, the questionnaire allows the athletes to reflect on their current mental conditions in regards to their own sport. Examples of the short-answer questions include: How often can you achieve your best performance during competition? Do you have any anxiety before competition? Other sections in the questionnaire address the different types of pressure associated with sports, provide indications of how well athletes are balancing their mental/technical/physical training or practices, and compare their best and worst performances. For Sumo Wrestler K, the questionnaire enabled him to reflect on his professional sumo experience and assess the psychological approaches and strategies he uses for his bouts. After completing the questionnaire, we reviewed each of his replies to allow him to provide further explanation or comments in order to clarify his initial responses. When there was a discrepancy with his written responses and his oral explanation, I would point it out to him so that he could become more aware of his need to use mental training and to increase his motivation to include mental training as part of his physical training practice.

Pre-performance routine

Using the recordings of the past grand sumo tournaments, I selected several recording clips of his pre-performance routines to review with Sumo Wrestler K. I gave him a copy of the data that I had collected prior to meeting him, where I brought to his attention the differences I found between the pre-performance routines of his winning and losing bouts. I especially selected a match with *Ozeki* H, a higher-ranking sumo wrestler, who was considered to be one of his deciding bouts for his possible promotion to *Ozeki*. Before the bout, Sumo Wrestler K glared intensely at *Ozeki* H for a stare-down. This was an unusual pre-performance routine for him when compared with the 14 other bouts during that particular grand tournament. My comment on his pre-performance routine with *Ozeki* H was that it was the wrong routine for him because altering his actions caused him to breath differently, thereby disrupting the rhythm of movement that influences his muscles and body.

In sumo bouts, the first movement is called *tachiai*, an initial movement in the fighting ring when both sumo wrestlers' hands are on the ground and they are ready to charge towards each other. Since the winner of a bout is determined in one round that can last a few seconds to a few minutes, every split second counts during the *tachiai*; therefore, the quicker the sumo wrestler can charge at his opponent, the more advantage he will have to strategize his next move. For Sumo Wrestler K, his decision to make changes in his pre-performance routine impacted his normal breathing and body rhythm during the *tachiai*. As a result, the changes he made interrupted his concentration and created a negative distraction for him, thus slowing him down. When I mentioned this to him, he immediately understood and agreed with my analysis. I asked him why he decided to change his pre-performance routine to a stare-down for that particular opponent, and his reply was simply, "He annoys me." I further explained that showing his personal emotion towards an opponent before a bout will weaken his focus and will only generate negativity in his performances. My recommendation was that he should maintain the same pre-performance routine embedded with psychological skills for every single bout.

Introducing mental training

As stated previously, the first item on my mental training agenda is to give an introduction to the athletes on why mental training is essential in any sport by providing the athletes with a textbook and workbook (Kozuma, 2002). For Sumo Wrestler K, in addition to the mental training materials, I also modified my approach by providing information and explanation to him on why psychological skills are important specifically to sumo. In the interest of giving him a general overview of mental training, I showed him video recordings of my past consulting experiences with other athletes, as well as other mental training educational DVDs for athletes that I have released (Kozuma, 2008) to help educate Sumo Wrestler K. I emphasized that the objective of the mental training for him consists of seven basic psychological skills and techniques, namely goal setting, relaxation and psyching up, self-conditioning, visualization, concentration and focus, positive thinking, and psychological preparation for competition (Kozuma, 2003; Ravizza & Hanson, 1997). I stressed to him that in order for mental training to be effective, he would have to practice these skills every day. This gave Sumo Wrestler K a better understanding of the fundamental background of mental training, as well as a better perspective of what he was expected to do to fulfill his mental training program.

The seven psychological skills of mental training

1. Goal-setting program

I asked Sumo Wrestler K to write down his future goals in sumo and in his personal life. The goal-setting worksheet in the mental training workbook asks athletes to list their long-term and short-term dreams or goals for the next 50 years, 30 years, 10 years, 5 years, and 1 year from now, as well as for this season, this month, this week, and today. As he filled out the workbook, I noticed that he wrote about his life goals first and then his goals in sumo. It seemed that he was motivated about his future plans, especially the transitional career goals that he might have after he retires from professional sumo; however, he was not thinking that way at all. The answers to all of his goal-setting responses, both personal and professional, included only his current sumo career aspirations. He could not see beyond his current professional sumo life, nor could he see his future life after sumo.

In the DIPCA.3 results, one area that needed improvement for Sumo Wrestler K was patience, which is part of the motivation factor. At the time I met with Sumo Wrestler K, his sumo stable or group was caught in an illegal gambling scandal. The sumo master of the stable decided to increase the training and practice times in order to keep the sumo wrestlers busy and out of trouble. Sumo Wrestler K felt that he was being unfairly punished for the action of other wrestlers and was resentful of the extra training and practices the he was forced to do. My approach to increase his motivation and his dream of becoming a *Yokozuna*, or the highest-ranking sumo champion, was to guide him to think in details about how he is planning to achieve his goals. Having a detailed goal-setting plan mapped out not only for today, but for the future as well correlates with the quality of daily practices or training needed to achieve the goal. Writing down his goals helped Sumo Wrestler K change his attitude towards his daily training and helped him understand the meaning of his practices. Instead of regarding it as a punishment, he now realized that his extra mandatory practice time was an opportunity for him to move closer to his goal of becoming *Ozeki* and then *Yokozuna*.

2. Relaxation and psyching-up program

The impetus for Sumo Wrestler K to seek consultation from the field of sport psychology was due to his loss during the last tournament to another lower-ranking sumo wrestler, who he thought he could easily defeat. The loss of this bout was at a critical juncture in his sumo record career, because a win would have promoted him to the higher rank of *Ozeki*. Due to his low scores on the DIPCA.3 factors of relaxation and self-control, I introduced a relaxation and psyching-up program to him. This program utilizes a variety of relaxation and psyching-up techniques that I have created and developed for athletes in Japan (Kozuma, 1995). I have used my program for a multitude of athletes and teams with success, and it has been well received by both athletes and coaches. The relaxation and psyching-up program is a daily routine that incorporates relaxation music; smiling expressions; self-massage; breathing control from martial arts; stretching with breathing control; progressive relaxation techniques, first in a standing position and then in a supine position; simplified autogenic training; and meditation.

Sumo Wrestler K performed the progressive relaxation techniques, simplified autogenic training, and meditation for three minutes lying down. To return to a wakeful state and before standing up, he sits up and places his arms behind him to stretch and tilt his head back with his eyes closed to visualize his best performance for about 10 seconds. He will then open his eyes and get up to a standing position. With his eyes open this time, I asked him to visualize his best bout in slow motion and then increase the rate of his every move by recalling the bout at half (50%) of normal speed and then at normal speed. This part of visualization includes not only imagery but physical movements too; therefore, I had Sumo Wrestler K add motion to his visualizations of his winning bouts. After the relaxation and visualization exercises, the psyching-up component of the program takes about 10 seconds for a total of about 2 minutes to complete. The relaxation components take about 15 minutes; therefore, it only takes less than 20 minutes to complete the entire program.

When it was first introduced, Sumo Wrestler K really enjoyed the relaxation and psyching-up program and was excited to continue. You could easily see a change in his demeanor and the expression on his face. When he first arrived to our session, his face reflected a person who was worried or anxiety ridden. After learning and actually performing my relaxation and psyching-up program, his face brightened with a more positive outlook. He exclaimed, "This can really change how I feel. I will definitely come back to learn more."

3. Self-conditioning program

The self-conditioning program is a simplified version of the relaxation and psyching-up program with a slight change in the use of music. Both the relaxation and psyching-up music are utilized in the morning, but only the relaxation portion of the program and the accompanying music is used at night. My recommendation to Sumo Wrestler K was that he needed to practice the self-conditioning exercises every day in the morning as soon as he wakes up and at night before he goes to bed. In order to make it more effective, I allowed Sumo Wrestler K to choose his own music that he felt would be most beneficial and soothing to him. My objective for the self-conditioning program is for him to feel better when he wakes up and goes to sleep.

Each professional sumo wrestler is affiliated with an organization with training quarters known as a *heya* (or sumo stable in English), where he lives and trains. They are required to rise early in the morning to start their daily practice around 5 a.m. The sumo wrestlers train until mid-morning and then eat their first meal of the day together. Since they get up so early in the morning, they usually rest or take naps in the afternoon as soon as they have eaten. This type of eating pattern is a tradition for sumo wrestlers. Since there is no weight class in sumo, the larger wrestler will usually have an advantage over someone with less girth when they meet in the fighting ring. In order to increase their size, they eat only twice a day and then sleep right after their meals in order to gain weight. Since sumo wrestlers go to their practice immediately after waking up, I assigned Sumo Wrestler K to do the relaxation and psyching-up program twice a day. This way, instead of dragging himself with a negative attitude to his morning practice, with the relaxation and psyching-up program, he could have a positive start for this training day and increase the quality and meaning of his morning practices, as well as increase the quality of his sleep at night.

4. Visualization program

Sumo Wrestler K received a systematic visualization program as part of this mental training package, and I instructed him to conduct his visualization exercises immediately after the relaxation program. Visualization was a key component for him, because it is also an important technique used in martial arts. Traditionally, martial artists practice their skills through a prearranged organized movement practice called *kata*. The martial artists visualize an imaginary opponent's attack and execute physically the appropriate defensive responses or lethal offensive movements. Since in Japan sumo is considered as martial arts known as *budo*, or the way of the warrior, and as a martial artist myself, I knew that visualization would be a critical element of his mental training program (Kozuma, 2014). I informed Sumo Wrestler K that he should be able to imagine his best bout at any time and anywhere; however, in order to be able to do this, he must practice his visualization daily. I asked him to maintain a log of his sumo practices and bouts. The log was used as an instrument to keep a database of everything that he does for the mental training program. As Sumo Wrestler K filled out the log, I suggested that he should add movement to his visualization in a similar manner to *kata*. He took this advice to heart and was able to quickly implement movements into his visualization. Whether it was a winning or losing match, he would watch video recordings of his bouts on his mobile phone and would visualize with movements to recreate his winning performance or would change his maneuvers to re-strategize and re-visualize a lost bout into a winning performance. He practiced his visualizations every day and was able to imagine his best bouts during his training practices as well as at the tournament while he was waiting for his turn in the fighting ring.

5. Concentration/focus program

Sumo wrestling is a fast match, where winning bouts can be determined within a few second seconds. For this reason, the sumo wrestlers' concentration and focus are critical before the commencement of the *tachiai*. My main objective for Sumo Wrestler K was to target his concentration and focus during the time after he enters the *dohyo*, or fighting ring, and prior to the *tachiai*. Based on my analysis of his pre-performance routines, I strongly suggested that he establish a set pre-performance routine to use each time he is in the ring. Since he had a pre-performance routine that naturally evolved without any knowledge of sport psychology, we decided to add additional psychological techniques and skills to enhance his original routine. I was mindful to keep the parameter of the psychological skills and techniques in the new pre-performance routine to steps he could perform while he is in the *dohyo* without being penalized. Therefore, in addition to the traditional ceremonial rituals and procedures performed in the *dohyo* once the wrestlers enter the fighting ring, I also introduced breathing control, attitude and self-confidence techniques, a yawning technique to focus and refocus, a vocal shouting technique, a progressive relaxation technique, and a technique to establish and reestablish a focal point for concentration. I explained why each step of the new routine was crucial to help his concentration and focus and emphasized that going through the motions a couple of times was not enough. He needed to practice this new routine daily.

Since sumo is viewed as martial arts, training sessions are not considered to be enjoyable or easy. It is often a challenge to increase an athlete's concentration or focus at a competition site when the path to get there was nothing but hardship, loathing, and repugnance. In order to circumvent this traditional viewpoint, I used intrinsic motivation for Sumo Wrestler K by reminding him that his concentration and focus will be at their highest level when he is having fun and enjoying his upcoming bout or training practices. By having a positive attitude towards his sumo and all that it entails, it also increased his scores on the motivation and patience factors of his DIPCA.3 results.

6. Positive thinking program

When you watch Japanese athletes, you will notice that they are generally emotionless when they are winning or losing a game. This is because in Japanese *budo*, or in any sports for that matter, expressions of enjoyment or disappointment are not displayed in public. Expressions of one's personal feelings towards the outcome of a game are not socially acceptable, and this is especially true for martial artists, which also includes sumo. In sumo tradition, wrestlers must not show or express their emotions in public, even when they are not competing. Since this tradition is engrained into their training practices, competition, and daily lives for centuries, it was a challenge for Sumo Wrestler K to be able to perform any part of the mental training program in front of other people. He was afraid of how he would be perceived using a mental training program in such a strict, conservative domain. He was extremely worried how it would reflect on his standing as a professional sumo wrestler and was especially concerned about how the mass media would report on him integrating a nontraditional approach to sumo. For Sumo Wrestler K, being a public figure meant that his every movement is often scrutinized and immediately reported on television. To alleviate his concerns, I talked with him about how he could use positive thinking techniques as a foundation for positive self-talk and communication as well as a tool to build his self-confidence and attitude training. He could easily practice these techniques every day without garnering a lot of media attention. Since he felt that he should be more covert about his mental training in front of other people, I also suggested to Sumo Wrestler K to perform the mental training program in places where he felt most comfortable so that he would not feel self-conscious about it.

7. Psychological preparation for the tournament

Throughout my mental training sessions, Sumo Wrestler K received instructions and training on different types of psychological skills. However, he still needed guidance to see how these skills can be applicable for a sumo wrestler's situation. He understood that mental preparation and mental training were critical for his overall training practices as he headed for the next tournament, but he still needed daily support to reassure him that he was applying the techniques and skills appropriately. He felt he needed this reassurance so that he could stay focused on sumo and not be susceptible to distractions. Distractions can occur easily for sumo wrestlers due to the idle time they have prior to the actual bout. After their usual morning practice, the sumo wrestlers make their way to the tournament venue. Once at the arena, they have a warm-up session and then they dress in their respective colors for the tournament, where there is a hair stylist available for them to fix their hair. The way a sumo wrestler wears the traditional hairstyle is indicative of their rank in sumo, and they usually sit and chat with others while their hair is being done. Once they are dressed and their hair is complete, they are divided respectively as representatives of either the east or west stables, and they make their way to their designated hallways and wait for their names to be called. Some sumo wrestlers continue to warm-up or stretch in the hallway to prepare physically for the upcoming bout, but most of them loiter around until they hear their name. Once a sumo wrestler's name is called, he enters the arena and sits on the floor in the front row by the *dohyo*, along with several other wrestlers who are waiting for their bouts to start. Once the outcome of the current bout is determined, the winner of that particular bout serves a ladle of water to the next sumo wrestler, who enters the ring on the same side. After the soon-to-be-matched sumo wrestlers each take ceremonial sips of water, the two sumo wrestlers step into the ring on either the eastern or western sides of the *dohyo*. Once inside the fighting ring, more ceremonial rituals and movements need to be completed before the *tachiai* can start.

Through his daily mental training practices, Sumo Wrestler K was able to use his psychological skills as part of his warm-up routine while he was in the hallway waiting to be called. In addition, when he was sitting in the arena with the other sumo wrestlers and sumo fans waiting for the previous bout to finish, he was also able to perform his mental training skills to prepare for his turn in the *dohyo*. Every step along the way, from the time he left his stable for the tournament venue, his warm-up session, his anticipation for his name to be called in the hallway, his entrance into the arena, his time prior to officially entering the *dohyo*, and until the start of his actual *tachiai*, were all well practiced and well rehearsed. He was mentally ready.

Sumo tournament

After starting his mental training sessions with me, Sumo Wrestler K won his first seven out of 15 bouts straight in a row. He was doing great and was able to apply his psychological skills day after day. For additional support, we communicated three to five times daily during the tournament by telephone or email to answer any questions that he had or to simply give him advice. He was performing well, to the delight of his fans, and was often spotlighted in the media with the speculations that he would soon receive the *Ozeki* promotion. Then, just as before, he lost to a lower-ranking opponent.

In a television interview after his first loss, he lamented to the camera, "It is difficult to win at sumo." In our daily conversations, however, he told me that he knew that he did not lose due to any psychological reasons. He blamed the loss on his strategy of choice to use a certain maneuver to topple his opponent. It did not work, and his opponent was able to capitalize on the moment and shove Sumo Wrestler K out of the ring. We talked on the phone as he was leaving the venue. I suggested to Sumo Wrestler K that he should sing his favorite song in the car as he travels back to his training home, or *heya*. The singing suggestion was to help him to not dwell on his loss, but to refocus for the next day's match. The NHK documentary recorded him merrily singing in the car with his entourage as they traveled back to their training home. It was evident that he was trying very hard to apply mental training to see him through the tournament.

Sumo Wrestler K won his next two consecutive bouts before he lost again. Just as he performed in the last two grand tournaments, he lost to a lower-ranking sumo wrestler, thus once again jeopardizing his bid for promotion. He could no longer afford any losses, but as fate would have it, his most current loss occurred in the tournament schedule where all of his remaining opponents were at his level or ranked higher than him. His losing pattern was being repeated, and he was disappointed in himself again.

The remaining bouts in the tournament were against one *Sekiwake* wrestler (the same rank as Sumo Wrestler K), two *Ozeki* wrestlers, and a *Yokozuna*, the reigning champion and winner of the previous grand tournament. After Sumo Wrestler K's second loss, the *Yokozuna* was scheduled to be his next opponent the following day. The pressure for him to win was enormous. The entire nation was looking forward to the pairing of these wrestlers, and he knew that losing was not an option. He needed to defeat the *Yokozuna*.

The Japanese attached their hope on Sumo Wrestler K because at that time there were no Japanese *Yokozuna* or *Ozeki* ranked professional sumo wrestlers. Foreigners from Mongolia,

Bulgaria, and other countries commanded all of the higher sumo ranks, and out of all of the Japanese wrestlers, Sumo Wrestler K had the closest winning record to be considered for an *Ozeki* promotion. His problem was that when the possibility for a promotion was within his reach, he would falter and would start losing towards the end of each tournament, thus sabotaging his bid for *Ozeki*. His big boost for *Ozeki* consideration was when he fought with the *Yokozuna* at the previous grand tournament and actually won; however, after upsetting the *Yokozuna* and celebrating his victory over a reigning champion, he quickly lost to two lower-ranking opponents, thus falling short of the winning requirements needed. With the same *Yokozuna* as his next opponent at the current grand sumo tournament, it appeared that he could not break this pattern of losing at ill-appointed times in the tournament schedule. The sumo fans knew that his next match was the bout to watch, and he felt pressured by the mass media and by the public that he needed to defeat the *Yokozuna* again. He needed to win for Japan.

I analyzed his two losses and emailed him the reasons that might have contributed to the outcome of his bouts. My analysis revealed that his pre-performance routine was not the set routine that we had established prior to the tournament. He was making some changes unconsciously, because he was not even aware that he was doing the routine differently until I mentioned it. I reminded him to follow the established pre-performance routine that we had worked on and to also follow the steps in the mental training program just as he had been practicing with me. To prepare mentally for his fighting strategy, he continued to visualize his losses and wins on his own. The day before his big match, he also watched recordings of other sumo wrestlers who had defeated the *Yokozuna* before and merged their successful maneuvers with his own fighting strategy.

Based on the NHK TV documentary, on the day of the bout with the *Yokozuna*, he did his normal physical training practice with the rest of the wrestlers at his training home. Afterwards, while everyone was getting ready to leave for the competition site, he practiced alone by visualizing his winning bout with the *Yokozuna*. He also rehearsed his pre-performance routine, step by step, to simulate what he would do prior to the actual start of their *tachiai*. When he left the training home for the competition site, he was focused and had self-confidence that he would win.

When he arrived to the competition venue, he was calm. Prior to entering the arena and before he faced the sumo fans, he had performed all of the psychological skills that he had learned while he was waiting in the hallway for his name to be called. He had a positive outlook about his match and was mentally prepared when it was his turn to step into the fighting ring. Once he was in the ring, he did his pre-performance routine in the exact manner as he had practiced earlier in the morning. He was ready for his opponent, and he had no doubt in his mind that he would win.

Sumo Wrestler K defeated the reigning *Yokozuna*! He also collected an important scoring point to add to his overall record in the tournament, because he was able to win over the *Yokozuna*, thus further enhancing his possibility for promotion. After his big win, he defeated *Ozeki* H, the sumo wrestler he lost to during the last tournament when he decided to do a stare-down instead of his usual pre-performance routine. He won two consecutive bouts after his match with the *Yokozuna*, giving him a winning record of 12 out of 15 bouts and placing him second for the grand tournament. After the grand tournament, the officiating sumo committee decided to award Sumo Wrestler K with a promotion to the second highest rank of *Ozeki*. He was the first Japanese sumo wrestler to achieve the rank in five years.

Every step of his mental training practice was documented by the film crew and was broadcasted as a 30-minute episode on an NHK series that focuses on athletes, called "*Athlete no Tamashi*" or "The Soul of an Athlete" (2011). Banking on the wave of popularity of Sumo Wrestler K, the show aired immediately the day after the closing of the grand sumo tournament. Shortly after the grand tournament, when Sumo Wrestler K was officially promoted to *Ozeki*, segments of the show that highlighted his use of mental training were aired repeatedly on the news and on every sport-related TV show where he was a guest being interviewed about his promotion. It was also the first time that the entire process of how I tailor my mental training package to specific athletes or teams was filmed and shown to the general public. This exposure on television ignited a strong interest by other sumo wrestlers, as well as other teams, athletes, and coaches, to learn more about mental training. The positive portrayal in the media of the effectiveness of mental training also elevated the acceptance of Western sport training ideas and, most importantly, gave credibility of what sport psychology can offer to help support athletes.

Mental training beyond sumo

When Tokyo won its bid to host the Olympic Games in 2020, the city wanted to give the Japanese athletes every opportunity to improve their performance and increase their ability to win medals. Wanting to affirm the belief that the benefits of a home team advantage is significant, Tokyo increased its investment in sports by starting a project with three large universities, including the university where I teach, to develop and educate young athletes not only physically, but mentally as well, in preparation for the Tokyo Olympic Games. As I have started my work with these aspiring young athletes, they often mention that they saw the TV show about Sumo Wrestler K. Even though the NHK television show broadcasted only a fraction of the mental training techniques and the psychological support I provided to him, the popularity of the NHK television show about Sumo Wrestler K helped demystify sport psychology and mental training. It also helped shift the attitudes of those who are involved in sports toward more of an acceptance of the plausibility of merging Eastern and Western ideas within a Japanese sport tradition.

Japanese martial arts originated as a fighting skill for a person to survive a fatal situation. During the Edo period, when the nation was at peace, martial arts evolved away from the strict use in warfare into a way of life, especially for the samurai class. In order to protect these traditions, the Japanese do not view martial arts as a sport. It is a way of life for an individual and not a sport for entertainment. Since sumo is also considered as a form of martial arts, the traditionalists also wanted to protect sumo in order to keep it purely in the Japanese tradition. However, when winning becomes an issue, then it becomes necessary to seek out effective scientific training methods to enhance the athletes' performances from other sports as well as from abroad. This is where sport psychology and mental training can be used as a mixing agent to provide support to the Japanese athletes and teams (Kozuma, 2014).

Recommendations for applied practitioners

If an opportunity arises for other sport psychologists or certified consultants to work with sumo wrestlers or martial artists, it is important that one understands the traditional environment in which these athletes train. As in many sports, sumo wrestlers start to train at a very young age. The difference from many other sports is that sumo wrestlers enter a training home, or *heya*, in their teens. After graduating from junior high school, around the age of 15, aspiring sumo wrestlers are tested or invited to enter a *heya*. Their optimal formative years in sumo are groomed and taught only within the sumo world, often in isolation from family and friends, hence making sumo wrestlers' view of their sport very narrow, conservative, and traditional. With their governing bodies, organizations, and fans enforcing this traditional atmosphere, they have a tendency to become distrustful of anyone or anything that does not comply within their sumo world. With sumo wrestlers living and training in this type of environment, they are often not familiar with or exposed to other organized sports; therefore, having the knowledge of sport psychology is often not enough. Sports psychologists or certified consultants should also have experiences in coaching, teaching, and consulting with athletes in order to be effective (Kozuma, 2003, 2014). Having good communication skills is another factor that needs to be considered. Communication is dominated by superiors to subordinates, with only other young sumo wrestlers to commiserate with or to talk to about questions that they might have. Also, since they leave their families and friends to enter the *heya*, their social skills may be stymied, thus they may exhibit social ineptness by misinterpreting the social behavior of others or having difficulty expressing themselves to others, especially those outside of the sumo world. To gain their trust, it is important to have open communication with sumo wrestlers. Listen to their concerns and offer advice and suggestions that will work within the parameters of their tradition.

Thinking of Sumo Wrestler K as he stepped boldly into the *dohyo* to fight the reigning *Yokozuna*, I have come to realize that, for Japan, mental training has also come full circle. I was able to take Eastern ideas from martial arts, adapted and applied these ideas to Western sport psychology, and then reapplied them to Eastern sport situations. Based on my consulting work with many Japanese athletes and teams, this circular overlapping of Eastern martial arts techniques and Western sport psychology has not only been successful and suitable in my work, but is also becoming more acceptable in the Japanese culture (Kozuma, 2014). My recommendation for sport psychologists or certified consultants working in other cultures is to be cognizant that different sports may have different approaches to common aspects of their own ethnic culture, such as the relationship between coaches and athletes, ways of communicating, and rules that guide sport-specific interactions. Those who wish to work in Japan should know that to introduce modern psychological skills in training practices does not necessarily mean to Westernize their sport traditions. Blending new ideas from sport psychology to their tradition by adapting their traditional practices or techniques with psychological skills from abroad will make it easier to become more acceptable, thus more effective in providing support to Japanese athletes.

References

Kozuma, Y. (1995). *Asukara tsukaeru mentaru toreiningu kouchi yo [A mental training program for coaching]*. Tokyo, Japan: Baseball Magazine Publishers, Inc.

Kozuma, Y. (2002, 2014). *Imasugu tsukaeru mentaru toreiningu shenshu yo [A mental training program for athletes]*. Tokyo, Japan: Baseball Magazine Publishers, Inc.

Kozuma, Y. (2003, 2014). *Imasugu tsukaeru mentaru toreiningu kouchi yo [A mental training program for coaching]*. Tokyo, Japan: Baseball Magazine Publishers, Inc.

Kozuma, Y. (2008). *Chyugakusei no supotsu mentaru toreiningu [Sport mental training for junior high school students]* [DVD]. Tokyo, Japan: Gakken Publishers.

Kozuma, Y. (2009). Samurai and science: Sport psychology in Japan. In R. J. Schinke & S. J. Hanrahan (Eds.), *Cultural sport psychology* (pp. 205–217). New York: Human Kinetics.

Kozuma, Y. (2014). Psychological consulting with baseball players in Japan. In P. Terry, Z. Li-Wei, K. YoungHo, T. Morris, & S. J. Hanrahan (Eds.), *Secrets of Asian sport psychology* (pp. 56–68). Queensland, Australia: University of Southern Queensland.

Kozuma, Y. (2014). *Kakutougi no mentaru toreiningu [Mental training for martial arts].* Tokyo, Japan: Baseball Magazine Publishers, Inc.

Nakajima, T., (Writer) & Yoneyama, S. (Director). (2011, September 9). Kokoro wo kitaete tsuyoku nare: Kotoshogiku, Ozeki e no chosen [Television series episode]. In H. Takada & T. Mukai (Producers), *Athlete no Tamashi.* Tokyo, Japan: Nihon Hoso Kyokai.

Nitta, I. (2010). *Sumo no rekishi [History of sumo].* Tokyo, Japan: Kodansha Publishers.

Ohta, H., Tanaka, Y., & Kozuma, Y. (2008*). Bakusho mondai no nippon no kyouyou: Supo-kon nante iranai, supotsu shinrigaku [Japanese liberal arts and science education presented by Bakusho Mondai].* Tokyo, Japan: Kodansha Publishers.

Ravizza, K., & Hanson, T. (1997). *Heads-up baseball* (Y. Kozuma, K. Yoshida, H. Sekiya, K. Taguchi, T. Sakamoto, E. Watanabe, M. Ito, & N. Kida, Trans). Tokyo, Japan: Baseball Magazine Publishers. (Original work published 1995).

Tokunaga, M. (2001). *Besuto purei no mentaru toreiningu. [Best play for mental training].* Tokyo, Japan: Taishu-kan Shoten Inc.

SECTION III
Team sports

14

WORKING WITHIN POLO

A wonderland experience

Stiliani "Ani" Chroni

"Does your family play polo?" I recall feeling uneasy at hearing this question back in 1997 and mumbling an answer like "No, no, my family doesn't play and neither do I." I had been an insider in sport and understood how people were selected for coaching opportunities. Gaining the trust of a team or athletes can be challenging when a sport psychology culture does not exist. Since my background was not in polo, I knew that I would need to work twice as hard to pave a way into that field. My athletic and coaching background was in alpine skiing, which, similar to polo, is a male-dominated culture.

I grew up in a time and place where gender hierarchy, domination, discrimination, bullying, and harassment did not exist, neither academically nor in praxis. In the course of my ski life, through trial and error, I learned how to be less feminine around men (concerning behavior and dress code, which was my way of avoiding romantic mishaps), and I discovered how to collaborate with, disagree with, develop alongside, and receive support from men. This enabled me to find personal success, as well as deal with inappropriate jokes and rough sexist behaviors, while not jeopardizing my personal integrity. All of my experiences as an athlete and a coach provided me with a sense of confidence to venture into the world of polo and excel as a sport psychologist.

Student-athletes from The University of Virginia (UVA) polo team brought me into the world of polo and convinced me that I would be amazed by their sport. These young poloists (mainly men, but also one woman) impressed me with their commitment to advance their mental games in a sport psychology class. After spending some time around the UVA polo arena, one of the players asked me to do mental coaching work with him, as he perceived himself to be a weak link on the team. I completed more than 300 hours of supervised practicum with this player and also consulted with a few more polo players during my time on the UVA grounds.

Time flew by, and I found myself at the point when I needed to fully focus on my dissertation. My plan was to center my research on alpine skiers' competitiveness. I had studied Division I alpine skiers in the northeast United States for my Master's thesis, and I aspired to step up and study skiers at the international race circuit of central Europe for my dissertation. After what seemed like an overnight decision, I dropped the idea of interviewing skiers and decided to focus on professional polo players in Florida. My primary challenge was committing to trying something completely new, a population that no scholar had done research with before. To this day, academic research has not been conducted on polo, with the exception of a few publications that present medical cases of poloists' injuries.

Two of the UVA student-athletes opened the door to professional polo for me during the Florida high-goal season. This is played during the winter (i.e., a period of about four months during which tournaments of high-level polo are played in the US). One athlete had a brother playing professionally, and the other had a family friend in the sport. Both polo players agreed to be interviewed for my dissertation and, in turn, introduced me to other players. I spent the winter of 1997 in West Palm Beach collecting data and enjoying an incredible snowball effect that allowed me to meet great athletes and polo team organizations, as well as learn about high-goal polo.

During my time in Florida, one of the players I interviewed asked me to work with him to build his mental game. He had just been lowered from 8-goals to 7-goals (terms are explained below), and he was looking for a strategy that might raise his handicap. In one of his seminars, I recall Dr. Bob Rotella advising students to, "Get good at a sport and find a sport that can afford you; there are too many sport psychologists around tennis and gymnastics." So I found myself in the right place at the right time with the right education, and my trip to the wonderland of polo began.

Learning the sport and its culture

Polo is not a popular sport in terms of fans, media, and commercial support (Beal, 1993; Milburn, 1994; Price & Kauffman, 1989). It is characterized as an elitist and secluded sport, and it is expensive and demanding both physically and mentally. According to athletes and Milburn (1994), polo brings together many sports on one field. It is like playing several sports simultaneously: hockey, baseball, tennis, and soccer while riding a horse. At the start, I bought all the books I could find on polo. I also located some resources on equestrian skills and training horses, and subscribed to polo-related periodical publications, though not many existed back in the 1990s. Initially, these were sent to me by fax and later on by email, as use of the Internet matured. I was reading everything I could find on the sport. The best source of my polo education came from my time on the sidelines watching practices and games. I stood next to a groom or team manager, or a poloist's parent or wife, who would respond to my questions, no matter how childish they sounded. Besides watching polo live, I also watched/studied videotapes of games alone, or with a player or manager who would take me step by step through the game. For example, I learned to see the "line of the ball" and the "right of way" (when the ball is hit, it creates an invisible line that should not be crossed in a dangerous way; the player who hit the ball has the right of way, and others should not cross this imaginary line in front of that player to avoid a dangerous situation and penalty violation being called) or what happens during a "thrown in" and a "knock in" (when eight players fully mounted fight for one little whitish ball). One of the most difficult things for me was figuring out all the different penalty shots. Polo has multiple occasions for penalty shots depending on the severity of the violation, and I wanted to learn how to see these happening from the sidelines.

There was no other way for me to learn the sport, other than to study it 24/7. It was not my sport, but I was living, eating, and breathing polo. I even took a semester of Spanish language. Polo is a big sport in South America and especially in Argentina, so while most teams are bilingual during team meetings, almost all teams speak Spanish once on the polo field. I wanted to be able to understand some of what was said on the field. In addition, many of the players' grooms and organization managers were Spanish-speaking people.

Grooms and managers live in close relationship with the players. If they are employed long term by a poloist, they are well trusted by the player and take a lot of pride in working for him. Players discuss game performances, game strategies, teammates' performances, opposing teams' players and mounts, and their horse-strings with them; hence, they are important people in my work. I paid close attention to the care provided to the polo horses by the grooms. I learned to clean stalls and even tried to wrap horse leggings. I observed veterinarians working with players' horses. I learned a lot about the work that had to be done at a polo barn from 5 am until 5 pm – and I was never a horse person.

Polo 101: structure and language

To understand polo and be a good sport psychology practitioner in the sport, it's important to recognize the jargon, key elements, and demands that the sport and its structure places on players. Polo players are characterized by a "handicap" rating, which in everyday polo language is referred to as "goals". Handicaps range from 2-goals all the way up to the great 10-goals. Every year, recommendations from the club delegate are forwarded to the circuit handicap committee and then discussed, approved, or rejected at the national handicap committee meeting (this concerns US; other countries like Argentina and the UK hold their own handicap evaluations, thus a player may hold different ratings in different countries). The criteria used for these evaluations are general mastery of polo fundamentals (rules, playing, skills, position knowledge, teamwork), horsemanship, sense of strategy and conduct, as well as quality of horses [United States Polo Association (USPA), 2010] (there is one exception in this annual evaluation process, the so-called monster rule, which I describe later in this chapter). In addition, a player's winning record is talked about as a factor affecting one's handicap evaluation (though not included officially in the rating system). Player handicaps are important to the athlete. Teams are made up based on the sum of the players' handicap ratings. Tournaments are announced and played by teams of certain goal-sums (this way they balance the level of polo skills on a field). High-goal polo is played by teams with players whose handicap sum equals 22 or higher (usually tournaments of 22-, 26-, and 40-goal polo are organized). Medium-goal polo is played by teams composed of players who add up to less than 22-goals (usually 14- and 18-goal tournaments are organized). Medium-goal (and lower-goal) polo is played year round in many countries, while high-goal polo has different seasons around the world; Florida in the winter (USA), UK and France hold tournaments in late spring and summer, while Argentina has a fall season where the highest ever polo of 40-goal tournaments are played. Lastly, player earnings are also based on handicap ratings in conjunction with past winning records. Hence, players are greatly concerned about their handicap goals.

Polo teams consist of four men (three-men teams' play in arena polo, which is also the game played in the US universities/colleges). Three professional players and the amateur who sponsors the team – called the sponsor or patron – go onto the polo field. The patron is also rated by the handicap committee, and most often he/she is the player with the lowest handicap, and accordingly, possesses the weaker skills on the field. (More women appear to be involved as sponsors in polo than as professional players, which raises the question: What happens to all the women who play collegiate polo in the US after they graduate?). Polo teams may change their rosters as often as every three weeks, which is how long a tournament usually lasts. This means that there is not much time for building team cohesion, making the involvement of a sport psychology practitioner even more important. To this day, coaches are not often employed by polo teams; therefore, coaching responsibilities can rest on the shoulders of the highest rated player on the roster. In this case, the player is left to juggle two demanding and complicated roles, which include the care, preparation, organization, and strategy of the team, as well as his own and his horses' readiness for a game/tournament. Team managers, especially in high-goal teams, take on the organizational issues but delegate tasks like organizing practice or stick-and-ball sessions to the best player. From a sport psychology perspective, prioritizing and delegating tasks can be very useful skills for these players to develop if they haven't done so already.

Professional players play polo year round, and to do so they relocate themselves, their organizations (i.e., horses, grooms, barn set-up, etc.), and often their families from country to country in order to earn, but most importantly to challenge their level of play through good competition. Another truth in polo (most often experienced by medium- and low-goal players) is that players' contracts may die out at any time the on-field performance and game result was not the desirable one for the patron, the team manager, or the highest-rated teammate. Consequently, this increases the pressure for a win, thus separating the performance from the outcome, the controllable from the uncontrollable, the here and now from the past, and the under-par performance from the failure; these are all prospective areas a practitioner ought to explore to aid the players to keep performance in perspective.

Early challenges and how I managed

My ongoing involvement with polo and presence on polo fields, especially at the onset of my collaboration with poloists, helped me build confidence. Naturally, I was faced with a number of questions, which centered on three areas: my qualifications, the value of a mental coach, and whether a female practitioner was the right fit with male athletes. Through the years I built trust in my abilities as a mental coach for poloists, and today I can see things happening on the polo field, among teammates and within an organization; I can see hesitation, tension, reactions instead of responses, etc. Nonetheless, I still make it clear to players that polo was not my sport, and if at any time I need clarity, I don't hesitate to ask questions, rather than make false interpretations. What helped me overall throughout my career as a practitioner is that from the beginning I espoused the fact that I am an expert in sport psychology, while players are experts regarding themselves and the sport. If we put our knowledge and competences together, good things could come out of this partnership. This approach (i) lightened the pressure of my own expectations, (ii) gave us the room to make mistakes and grow from them, and (iii) and opened the door to capturing the trust of the players. Not being a polo insider, I was able to bring a fresh outlook into the working relationship that was free of the typical polo-insider biases, expectations, and preconceptions.

Trust in working relationships builds over time, and it has always taken some time for players to trust what I ask them to do, whether adding, changing, or deleting elements from their training regimes, and thinking and doing patterns. In the beginning, there were times that I felt hesitant to try some of the textbook techniques. These pros were older than I was, more experienced in polo, and expected solutions. Early on in my work, I remember being invited to a high-goal team practice and during a break having a player ask: "What do you see?" I can still close my eyes and see the sideline where I was standing when he approached with a steady gallop to ask the question. This was an important moment. I had to answer his question, and all I could think of was, "Okay, Bob Rotella is not here to help me out, I have no textbooks with me, so think, Ani!" I provided an answer and he "approved" of it, so that was a big relief and a first step forward in building trust with the player.

There was no literature on mental skills for polo, nor any practical experience I could borrow from other practitioners. That meant I had to improvise. I started by reading as many applied books and book chapters written on other sports, like golf, tennis, basketball, ice hockey, etc., and then transformed any ideas I liked to create a fit with polo speed, pressure, and anticipation. I also drew upon real-life ideas from the practical experiences depicted in the athlete and coach biographies as I was reading. Did I make mistakes? Yes, I did. Did I admit them to the players? Sure, I did, and then I tried alternative approaches. Did I make more mistakes than I have done on other occasions when working with new athletes? No, I do not think so. So throughout the years I kept studying, asking, and learning and gradually becoming more and more comfortable with polo. Whenever in doubt, I would brainstorm with colleagues and/or old supervisors of mine.

At the onset of my work in polo, I was a 27-year-old single woman entering a man's world. My relationship building process centered on the athlete but included winning the trust of the player's wife and providing the assurance that I was not a threat to their personal relationship. My presence created a new dynamic, presenting the need to spend time with the players before, after, and between games to discuss their work. Hence, I made a point of meeting a player's wife, girlfriend, or significant other from the beginning, to include her in part of our work where appropriate, and to work with her on ways she could best support her significant other in his pursuit of excellence in polo.

Improvising: an everyday deed for consulting with poloists

For the sport psychology practitioner, the elements presented in the *Polo 101* section above add to the physical, technical, tactical, equine, and equipment demands of the sport. While the fundamental mental skills for succeeding in polo appear to be similar to those reported in the sport psychology literature, the approach and use of techniques needs to be shaped to fit the sport, as well as the individual and the team. In one of the few books written about polo, Price and Kauffman (1989) wrote that in order "to win, an athlete must possess certain mental skills: concentration, positive thinking, the ability to control attitude and energy, the ability to manage pressure, continuous motivation, and visualization" (p. ix). From my time spent working closely with polo players and teams, I think a sport psychology consultant should focus on some core themes, including the following: player and sponsor motivation, player and team trust and confidence, player and team preparation routine, player engagement with the team, and pre-execution routines for the different penalty shots. Depending on the severity of the violation, a different penalty shot is awarded. Penalty shots differ in the distance they are hit from the goalpost (30, 40, or 60 yards) and whether the post will be defended by opponents or undefended. These facts signify a different approach for hitting the different penalties, for which a player should be prepared.

Sadly, there is no research on a sponsor's motivation to participate in polo and finance a team, but also play in it. Most sponsors I came in contact with clearly stated that they wanted to win – or "win at least one tournament", as they put it. They invested money in polo, spent time with the team, and expended the effort to play the best they can for their skill level. Professional poloists also want to win, and if they are not rated at 10-goals, they want to develop as players, to increase their handicap, job offers, and earnings. Therefore, the different levels of players, the different aspirations, the different reasons for being in the game, the different levels of commitment and determination need to be considered when working with a team.

In polo, teammates may play together just for one tournament, which as mentioned before is a span of about three weeks and begs the question of how much a practitioner can accomplish in three weeks when it comes to developing team cohesion, team goals, and the like. Too often teams literally get together, for the first time, only a few days before the tournament starts, and their different views, motives, approaches, and preconceived ways of doing things can have a negative impact on performance, especially if the players have not played together in the past. The differences tend to surface after the first game excitement, especially when there is a loss. Two losses in a row can lead to finger pointing, leaving it to the sponsor, the manager, and the highest-rated player to figure out what is not working. They look for what needs to be changed in their game, in the team horses, and even on the team roster. If there was no time before the tournament, it is then that team engagement/commitment and personal development through playing can be the focus of a sport psychology practitioner's work. Clarifying the reasons for engagement in polo and with the team and balancing the sponsor's goal to win at least a tournament or make it to all tournament finals with the players' game mindsets can help them overcome tension and shift focus to the controllable parts of on-field performance.

Medium-goal players are often asked and expected to do things beyond their skill level, and when they fail to execute on the field, the turmoil starts. Before a game, it is important for the high-goal player, who works on the team playing plan, to consider using his teammates for their strengths, rather than asking them to develop and/or overcome weaknesses during a game.

In working with polo players, some theoretical frameworks create an umbrella role in my approach to main performance themes, like handling pressure and believing in yourself. These come from Newburg, Kimiecik, Durand-Bush, and Doell's (2002) resonance model, which helps me work on player's engagement and commitment (see also, Newburg, 1993); Vealey, Hayashi, Garner-Holman, and Giacobbi's (1998) model of multiple sources of confidence, along with more recent publications on sources of confidence (e.g., Hanton, Mellalieu, & Hall, 2004; Hays, Maynard, Thomas, & Bawden, 2007), which helps me work on player and team confidence; Lazarus and Folkman's (1984) work on cognitive appraisal, which helps me work on pressure perceptions and interpretations, along with Kobasa and colleagues' work on cognitive hardiness (see 1979, 1982; and Maddi, 2002 for a recent review); and Rotella's (1994, 1995) writings and teaching about the two training and trusting mindsets that an athlete ought to possess, which keeps things in perspective (for a detailed discussion on this theoretical framework of mine, see Chroni, 2011). These days, when consulting with athletes who are struggling with pressure, I work with the possibilities offered by the Cognitive Activation Theory of Stress (Ursin & Eriksen, 2004, 2010), which connects one's stress experience with his/her coping and empowers the person and dealing with competitive pressure through learning from past experiences and individual interpretations.

In terms of specific psychological skills and techniques for poloists, I wrote in Chroni (2011, p. 65):

> I am cognizant of and trained on developing psychological skills through techniques, as these are presented in various sport psychology courses and handbooks. . . . I chose to use them when suitable, as means that will facilitate the person-athlete develop himself along with his/her training and trusting mindsets and not as the main course of my work. In line with that, it is important to mention that my consulting work follows the recently discussed holist approach to sport psychology (see Friesen & Orlick, 2010; Friesen & Orlick, 2011; Poczwardowski, Sherman, & Ravizza, 2004). If I had failed to see this poloist as a regular person; to recognize the man, the athlete, the husband, the father, the teammate, the hired-pro in him; if I had not spent enough time in tournaments and practices; it would have been difficult for our work to be effective and meaningful.

This statement holds true for all of my work, both in and out of polo. I see the person before the athlete. I see development before I see results, and I aim to help the athlete see it for him-/herself. A combination of the theoretical frameworks and my practical approach enables me to care for the person. In my practice, sport psychology is larger than mental skills training, and I always consider and explore players' fear(s) of failure, perfectionism, ways of relating to others, superstitions, mental toughness, values, and more. As Weir stated in his book, every sport teaches us something, and polo teaches players "pluck, endurance, submission to discipline, good temper, calmness, judgment, quickness of observation, self-control are all qualities as essential in a good polo player as in a good soldier" (2013, p. 268; original work published in 1901). Even if Weir, back in 1901 when his work was originally published, did not use sport psychology jargon, he touched on important features of a poloist's way of being and doing that a practitioner may need to work on. Once the groundwork is there, performance-wise a poloist can aim to be the best that he can be as he possesses the means to experience and cope with successes, obstacles, and setbacks. Whichever is experienced on any given day, he can view it as a point on his polo life-line, learn from it, and move on.

As I see things today, a poloist should aim high for himself, aim to become the strongest one among players in his handicap rating (an advantage for getting good and multiple job offers); the "monster rule" should challenge developing players and not frustrate or scare them away (according to this rule, an under-rated player's handicap may be increased during the playing year outside the annual committee evaluations). A polo player should learn to anticipate; as Pete Melros, the Argentine 10-goaler, said: "The most basic rule is to win the play before the ball comes to you" (as quoted in the USPA website); *and this can only happen if the poloist trains his mind as hard as he trains his horse and mallet skills.* A polo player should also learn that regardless of today's result, polo will be played again tomorrow; thus, he needs to move fast and light (not carrying leftovers from past performances) to the next play, next game, next tournament; he should reflect, choose what can be learned, leave the past where it belongs, and be in the here and now. To succeed, poloists need more than just mallet-ball skills and mounts; they need a strong mindset as a player and as a person. In all I have done to support poloists on their journeys towards higher goals, improvising to fit their needs and balancing life skills and mental skills were central, so that a poloist would be comfortable to live and play on and off the field.

Aspiring practitioners

To work effectively in polo, or in any sport, the first step is to learn about every aspect of the sport and to understand the roles, responsibilities, and main challenges that the athlete faces. Start by watching a live polo match to develop an appreciation for the game and then find a person who knows polo so you may watch games together and increase your understanding of the plays that evolve on a field and the rules and regulations in action. If you stay long enough in the sport, you will learn to see the players' combinations and relations on and off the field. You will also need to be culture-sensitive as polo is a multicultural sport with a strong South American element (see Schinke & Hanrahan, 2009 for readings on how to develop a cultural approach to applied sport psychology). The Argentine 10-goal player Juan Carlos Harriott was quoted to have said that "It takes hot blood and a cool head to play polo" (as quoted in the USPA website), which touches on the coexistence of the South American temperament and a mind that is focused and clear of emotional and other distractions when going onto the field of play.

Collegiate polo in the US can serve as a gate-opener both for applied practice and for research on polo. Do not expect to be invited to work with a 10-goaler right from the start, as 10-goalers have figured things out and know how to capitalize on the field, deal with pressure and setbacks, and do not require a lot of support from our end. Developing polo professionals could both benefit from sport psychology services and afford the service. Players who are handicapped at 5-, 6-, 7-goals are usually professionals who aspire to make a career in polo, and they are potentially interested in exploring methods to enhance their on-field performance. Making a career in polo does not always entail reaching the 10-goal handicap, which is difficult to achieve, demonstrated by the fact that only a few players are rated at 10-goals. However, playing for many years at the high-goal level and making a living out of polo has been achieved by a number of players worldwide.

I also urge anyone interested in polo to separate the professional polo players' life from the glamorous environment of polo games/tournaments and the world of some polo sponsors. Poloists are paid well to do their job, and they can afford a comfortable lifestyle if that is how they choose to live, but at the same time, they train in and play a costly sport. One thing people outside of polo often do not realize is how expensive the sport is and how difficult it is to advance one's handicap in order to be paid the big money.

In addition to developing their skills (e.g., mallet-ball skills, riding skills, team playing), players invest a lot of money, time, and effort into buying, making, and maintaining great horse strings. A string of horses refers to the group of horses that are prepared to play in a game or a tournament (possibly two tournaments in a row, then they need to rest). The number of horses in a string depends on the quality of the horses and how the player plays them; some players double their really good horses during games to get the maximum advantage from their mounts. Polo games have from 4 to 8 chukkers (i.e., periods of 7 minutes 30 seconds each). A professional poloist usually needs to have more than one string of horses, contingent on how much polo he plays. There are poloists who year-round own and care for 20 horses, 40 horses, or more. Horses, mares to be specific, are athletes themselves, who train, peak, and then need to be rested. They need highly skilled trainers, grooms, and veterinarians, all of whom add to the bill. Hence, each player who aspires to become a professional at some point establishes and maintains his own polo organization (e.g., barn, pastures, employees, vehicle for horses' transportation, etc.). Sponsors often lend or lease good horse(s) to players they hire in order to strengthen the team. To get hired with a contract that provides access to great mounts, one needs to be a strong player beforehand. Great polo horses can strengthen a player's game. Metaphorically speaking for the non-equestrian people, "equipment" can make a difference, but only when you have the skills to use it properly. For the poloist, a horse is his partner, who is greatly acknowledged in the game. In polo they award MVP twice: for the Most Valuable Player and for the Most Valuable Pony.

Today, professional polo players work harder than ever. When I started consulting in polo, they did not pay enough attention to their physical conditioning, yet things have changed. Personal trainers and yoga trainers are working with many poloists to build up their fitness level. To this day, I have not heard of other sport psychologists working with poloists, with the exception of a female psychologist who has worked with high-goal Argentine players in Buenos Aires. Poloists are out there, and the mental aspect of their game is one that can greatly benefit from our services. Despite the years I have worked with players and teams in the US and UK, I am far from being convinced that I have managed to change the polo culture to fully embrace sport psychology. By many individuals and organizations, I was considered to be a luxury expense. Getting my foot in the door was significant, and I encourage others to leverage the ongoing opportunities that exist to help more athletes in this amazing sport.

References

Beal, C. (1993). *Into polo*. Midland, TX: Prentis Publishing Company.

Chroni, S. (2011). A long-term consulting tale in professional polo. *Journal of Excellence, 15*, 60–75.

Friesen, A., & Orlick, T. (2010). A qualitative analysis of holistic sport psychology consultants' professional philosophies. *The Sport Psychologist, 24*, 227–244.

Friesen, A., & Orlick, T. (2011). Holistic sport psychology: Investigating the roles, operating standards, and intervention goals and strategies of holistic consultants. *Journal of Excellence, 14*, 18–42.

Hanton, S., Mellalieu, S. D., & Hall, R. (2004). Self-confidence and anxiety interpretation: A qualitative investigation. *Psychology of Sport and Exercise, 5*, 477–495.

Hays, K., Maynard, I., Thomas, O., & Bawden, M. (2007). Sources and types of confidence identified by world class sport performers. *Journal of Applied Sport Psychology, 19*, 434–456.

Kobasa, S. C. (1979). Stressful life events, personality and health: An inquiry into hardiness. *Journal of Personality and Social Psychology, 37*, 1–11.

Kobasa, S. C., & Maddi, S. R. (1982). Hardiness and health: A prospective study. *Journal of Personality and Social Psychology, 42*, 168–177.

Lazarus, R. S., & Folkman, S. (1984). *Stress, appraisal, and coping*. New York: Springer.

Maddi, S. R. (2002). The story of hardiness: Twenty years of theorizing, research and practice. *Consulting Psychology Journal, 54*, 173–185.

Milburn, F. (1994). *Polo: The emperor of games*. New York: Alfred A. Knopf, Inc.

Newburg, D. (1993). *The role of freedom in the performance of a professional musician and an Olympic swimmer*. Unpublished doctoral dissertation, University of Virginia, Charlottesville.

Newburg, D., Kimiecik, J., Durand-Bush, N., & Doell, K. (2002). The role of resonance in performance excellence and life engagement. *Journal of Applied Sport Psychology, 14*, 249–267.

Poczwardowski, A., Sherman, C. P., & Ravizza, K. (2004). Professional philosophy in the sport psychology service delivery: Building on theory and practice. *The Sport Psychologist, 18*, 445–463.

Price, S. D., & Kauffman, C. (1989). *The polo primer: A guide for players and spectators*. New York: Penguin Books.

Rotella, R. J. (1994, October). *Train and trust*. Audio taped lecture at the Introduction to Sport Psychology graduate course of the Department of Human Services, University of Virginia, Charlottesville.

Rotella, R. J. (1995). *Golf is not a game of perfect*. London: Simon & Schuster.

Schinke, R., & Hanrahan, S. J. (Eds.) (2009). *Cultural sport psychology*. Champaign, IL: Human Kinetics.

United States Polo Association. (2010). *The polo handicap*. Retrieved March 10, 2010 from http://www. uspolo.org/the_handicap.htm

Ursin, H., & Eriksen, H. R. (2004). The cognitive activation theory of stress. *Psychoneuroendocrinology, 29*, 567–592. doi:10.1016/S0306-4530(03)00091-X

Ursin, H., & Eriksen, H. R. (2010). Review: Cognitive Activation Theory of Stress (CATS). *Neuroscience and Biobehavioral Reviews, 34*, 877–881.

Vealey, R. S., Hayashi, S. W., Garner-Holman, M., & Giacobbi, P. (1998). Sources of sport confidence: Conceptualization and instrument development. *Journal of Sport & Exercise Psychology, 20*, 54–80.

Weir, R. (2013). *Riding*. London: Forgotten Books. (Original work published 1901)

Suggested readings and Internet links

Asociación Argentina de Polo. Accessed at http://aapolo.com/

Chroni, S. (2001). The process of competitiveness in polo: A way to enhance performance. *The Journal of Excellence, 4*, 60–75.

Chroni, S. (2014, June). What is competitiveness in polo and what being the best means to top polo players. *Hurlingham: Polo Magazine*, 26–27. Retrieved from http://www.hurlinghampolo.com/ backissues/summer_2014/#/26/zoomed

The Hurlingham Polo Association. Accessed at http://www.hpa-polo.co.uk/

United States Polo Association. Accessed at http://uspolo.org/

15

WORKING WITHIN THE NATIONAL HOCKEY LEAGUE

Paul Dennis

Personal/consulting background

My association with the Toronto Maple Leafs of the National Hockey League (NHL) began in 1986 as the head coach of the Toronto Marlboros of the Ontario Hockey League (OHL), a team that was owned by the Maple Leafs. The Marlboros were eventually sold to a group from Hamilton, Ontario, in 1989, at which time I joined the Maple Leafs coaching staff as their video coach. Having graduated with a Bachelor's degree in Physical and Health Education, as well as a Bachelor of Education and a Master of Arts in Sport Psychology, I was able to incorporate my professional training and coaching experience in assisting players, coaches, and management on the psychological components of optimal performance. Later I received my Doctorate in Sport Psychology from the University of Western Ontario, and as a result, my role expanded. In 1998, General Manager and Head Coach of the Toronto Maple Leafs, Pat Quinn, appointed me as the Player Development Coach for the organization. My primary duties were to assist all team personnel, including players, coaches, and support staff, in their understanding and acquisition of the mental skills required for optimal performance in sport. I also worked extensively with the scouting department by conducting interviews with draft-eligible players from North America and Europe.

The Toronto Maple Leafs are owned and operated by Maple Leafs Sports and Entertainment (MLSE). This private entity also owns the Toronto Marlies of the American Hockey League, the Toronto Raptors of the National Basketball Association, and Toronto FC, a member of Major League Soccer. I was fortunate to work with those teams throughout my 20-year career with the Toronto Maple Leafs. I also conducted workshops for the management group at MLSE on mental training for optimal gain in their respective areas of responsibility.

During my tenure with the Toronto Maple Leafs, several other opportunities were presented to me as a result of my affiliation within the professional sports industry. For example, Hockey Canada appointed me the mental skills coach for Canada's World Junior Hockey team, as well as Canada's National Sledge Hockey Team. I conducted internal reviews for Hockey Canada and designed the evaluation protocol on behalf of Hockey Canada for underage hockey players in Ontario who wish to apply for "Exceptional Status". Exceptional status, if granted, means the player would be eligible to play in the OHL as a 14-year-old. The rigorous interview procedure lead to players such as John Tavares (New York Islanders, NHL), Aaron Ekblad (Florida Panthers, NHL), and Connor McDavid (Erie Otters, OHL) being granted exceptional status. I was also appointed an advisor to the Canadian Hockey League Champions Program and a Special Advisor to the Board of Directors of the Greater Toronto Hockey League. After retiring from the Maple Leafs in 2009, I pursued my other passion, lecturing in Sport Psychology at Toronto's York University, a position I currently hold. In addition, I was also the High Performance Coach to York's varsity athletes and coaches in 2013.

It should be noted that prior to embarking on a career working with professional athletes and coaches, I was the head of the physical and health education department at Toronto's Father Henry Carr Secondary School. It was there I developed the passion for coaching, particularly ice hockey. The success I experienced in coaching one of Canada's elite high school hockey programs opened the door to more challenging ventures. Thus, had I not been involved in coaching, it is unlikely the opportunity to coach in the OHL would have presented itself. The experience gained coaching in the OHL, and the networking that ensued as a result, allowed me to interact with several people at the highest level of hockey in Canada and in the NHL, which led to a career in counseling elite performers on the importance of mental skills for optimal gain.

Sport context and sub-cultural understanding

The final scrimmage to determine the roster for Team Canada's entry into the 1991 Canada Cup tournament was held at Maple Leaf Gardens in Toronto. Upwards of 40 talented Canadian professional hockey players had been divided into two teams. Competition was fierce, and stars such as Steve Yzerman and Mark Messier were conspicuous by their absence. Yzerman because he left camp, and Messier because he hadn't arrived yet. Nevertheless, the presence of such icons as Wayne Gretzky, Al MacInnis, Scott Stevens, and future star Eric Lindros created a sense of optimism for Team Canada officials. As the video coach for Team Canada, I sat in the stands at the Gardens waiting for the scrimmage to begin. It was there I witnessed a unique phenomenon that can only be attributed to the charismatic physical and psychological skills of one of the world's greatest athletes. At that moment, I was able to gain tremendous insight into the sub-culture of elitism in sport by observing Wayne Gretzky.

Twenty minutes before the start of the scrimmage that would decide the final roster, Gretzky – arguably the greatest player to ever don a pair of hockey skates – came onto the ice by himself and began to stretch and skate slowly around the rink. Before the "Great One", as he was affectionately known, had completed one lap, three more of his teammates had arrived. All four players continued to skate counter-clockwise, engaging in idle chat as they stretched slowly and methodically. Within two minutes, the entire squad of Gretzky's brigade had reached the ice surface. While it was apparent that Gretzky's team was eager to warm up, their opponents had yet to set foot on Maple Leaf Gardens ice.

The preceding anecdotal testimony is an example of how one person's presence can influence others. Why were Gretzky's teammates so eager to join him on the ice well ahead of their scheduled scrimmage? Why were the opposing players still in the locker room? One may argue it was purely coincidental. I contend that the respect fellow teammates had for Gretzky's playing ability, his leadership qualities, and his psychological makeup inspired them to follow more closely in his path. In short, if the group notices the greatest player in the world is scurrying to leave for the ice surface early, then what better motivator can there be for a team?

Athletes that are like that truly have a different mindset, and I knew then that my goal in life would be to have all athletes who aspired for greatness try to adopt the mindset of Wayne Gretzky. Doing so would not guarantee that they would achieve similar results, but it guaranteed them a chance, and that is all one could ask for. Without defining what that optimal mindset was for elite players, those who aspired for greatness would not have much of a chance. What makes great athletes better than the rest? When one thinks of Gretzky and those of his ilk, what often comes to mind is their ability to think and to make the necessary decisions that give them the best chance to succeed, especially in pressure situations. But what allowed them to be in that position in the first place? A lot has to do with the passion they have for the game. The love of the game, the intrinsic motivation must be the emotional fuel that is used to propel them along the path to greatness.

We know that expert performers practice a great deal and that they are passionate about practicing; they don't view it as work (Ericsson, 2007). During my career with the Toronto Maple Leafs, I used to marvel at the practice habits of some of the greatest players to wear a Maple Leaf jersey – Mats Sundin, Doug Gilmour, and Wendel Clark in particular. There was no denying their commitment to practice hard. They devoted hours and hours to perfecting their skills. They would often be the first players on the ice and the last ones to leave.

They didn't limit themselves to improving their conditioning levels and puck-handling movements or shot selections. Although they were seasoned professionals, it was obvious that they weren't satisfied with their level of skill and what they had accomplished. They were students of the game. They would study their performances and look for ways to be better. During drills, they didn't go through the motions. They demanded perfection from themselves. They expected better results on the next drill compared to the one they had just finished. That's what separated them from the rest. They were just as passionate about practicing as they were about playing the game.

The best athletes had an unwavering belief in themselves, that they were capable of performing at the world-class level. They were extremely motivated to accomplish the challenging goals they had established – that is, to win a Stanley Cup. To accomplish this challenging goal, the best players had mastered the quality of perseverance in the face of adversity, frustration, and failures. The reason for that is they think optimistically. By doing so, it increases the likelihood that their expectations will be met. They don't pout when things don't go their way. They don't allow the situation to dictate how they'll respond; rather, they are in control of the way they approach every challenging situation they face.

They inspire others because they never give up. They have a unique way of persevering and staying the course regardless of how difficult the task might be. This is because the mindset they have adopted is one of hope and optimism. Some athletes who don't believe in themselves often give up in the face of adversity, and they refuse to try hard. These types of athletes are convinced that increased effort is futile. They will never realize their potential because they are easily discouraged.

Overall, the best players have the ability to withstand adversity and not give up when things don't go their way. In other words, they have outstanding coping skills, which allow them to stay focused on the task and manage their thoughts and emotions effectively. They are optimistic in their outlook and believe that they are in control of the way they respond to every situation they encounter. They are highly motivated with a high degree of self-efficacy.

They understand the importance of team cohesion. These qualities are the foundation of a strong mindset. They are patterns of thinking that could be learned through counseling techniques, and they became the primary focus for me to impress upon players and coaches throughout my career.

Initial challenges and consulting philosophy

During my tenure with the Toronto Maple Leafs, I met with several hockey players to discuss the role the mind played in performance situations. Hockey players, like many athletes, have been conditioned to focus primarily on physical skills and conditioning. Those are crucial components of performance, but psychological issues often have a significant influence on how an athlete executes. For example, during challenging times, players often told me that, "I've lost my confidence", "I'm having trouble focusing", or "I'm not as motivated as I once was". In order for me to assist them, it was important to stay current in the literature and apply the knowledge gleaned to give them the best possible advice pertaining to their needs. To that end, I subscribed to outstanding journals, such as *The Sport Psychologist*, the *Journal of Clinical Sport Psychology*, and the *Psychology of Sport and Exercise Journal*. I'm also a member of the American Psychological Association and the Association for Psychological Science. Another hands-on advantage for me was working with some of hockey's superstars, such as Mats Sundin, Joe Nieuwendyk, Eddie Belfour, Doug Gilmour, Curtis Joseph, Wendel Clark, and others. They all had unique mindsets of their own, and they had experienced numerous ups and downs in their careers. I was able to incorporate some of their strategies into my consultations with other players while working toward building a mindset to help them in their pursuit of hockey excellence. Finally, one of the most influential men in my life was former Maple Leaf team captain George Armstrong. He played for 20 seasons in the NHL, all with the Maple Leafs. He won four Stanley Cups, and he was the last captain to carry the Stanley Cup off the ice for Toronto in 1967. Based upon his experience, I sought his advice. He told me that it's important for an NHL player to "always prepare for the moment, don't wait for the moment to prepare". Thus, I thought it was essential to emphasize mental preparation so that athletes would remain cognizant that each and every day, they were preparing for the opportunity to compete and win in the NHL.

When players feel they have lost confidence and they are not playing as well as they should be, they want and need to know why. If they asked the coach, sometimes the response would be "work harder in practice" or "you have to get stronger". Neither may be accurate. Performance is not limited to physical skills, nor is conditioning the answer to all athletes' confidence problems. Coaches and athletes need to be more open-minded about the role the mind plays either in games or practice sessions.

Adopting the proper mindset meant that the athlete focuses on things that he controls. It would be convenient if confidence was enduring, but it's not. Confidence will waver from time to time. What has to be unwavering is the belief the athlete has to be persistent in his attempt to regain confidence. The challenge was to have the athlete trust that what you were telling him would be to his benefit. In his mind, he might be saying, "Why should I listen to you? How many games did you play in the NHL?" I knew this was an obstacle that had to be met head-on.

In order to win the confidence of those I worked with, my philosophy for counseling had to be predicated on trust. In order to gain the trust of players and coaches, they had to believe that I was competent in my field. Having a doctorate was certainly advantageous, but it was not enough for them to embrace me. My coaching experience at the OHL and NHL levels, combined with my professional qualifications, were the contributing factors for them to trust me. They also needed to know that I had integrity and that I would never disclose confidential information they shared with me to anyone else. There was still a stigma attached to players who required a counseling session with a mental skills coach – that is, he must have a weak mindset. Thus, my counseling sessions with individual athletes remained in strict confidence. Finally, I was able to earn the trust of the athletes I worked with if they knew that I cared for their well-being, and I did not view them as an asset, but rather as an integral part of the Toronto Maple Leafs family. My philosophy certainly complemented the General Manager and Head Coach's philosophy as well. On the first day of training camp, Pat Quinn told our players that there are three things you must hold sacred in order for you to be a contributing member of the Toronto Maple Leafs. First, he said, is your family. Second, your religion, whatever that may be. And third are your teammates. If any of these three is out of sync, you will have trouble playing for this organization.

Another significant challenge in my position while working with young professionals was teaching them the importance of body language. Several players viewed themselves as victims when things didn't go their way. If they were limited in their ice time, for example, or they were "healthy scratches" from games, several of them did not handle those situations well. They often pouted and behaved very immaturely. I broached the subject by telling them that body language and how they chose to portray themselves could often make the difference between whether they have a promising career or a short one. It can be the difference between having the chance to succeed or giving your opponent more motivation to beat you.

What messages do athletes send with their body language? For example, a discouraged hockey player might skate slowly to the bench with his eyes fixated on the ice, with his shoulders rounded and stick dragging behind him in one hand. If so, the message that resonates for all to see is that this player is feeling sorry for himself. In this instance, the opponent will sense vulnerability and will become more energized as a result. In short, poor body language provides opponents with a significant psychological advantage. More importantly, if our head coach observes poor body language in the form of sitting quietly on the bench with head down and not supporting teammates, then he might interpret that the player has 'quitter-type tendencies'. The coach will not have the confidence to continue to play this type of athlete. In addition, those negative emotions that are causing the player to portray poor body language are contagious. His teammates could easily become discouraged and adopt similar poor body language. One possible explanation for poor body language is because, as performance deteriorates or mistakes occur more frequently, some players become locked onto the negative emotions they are feeling. Consequently, they are more likely to get into a downward spiral, and poor body language results. Players must have the ability to refocus and come back strong. This is accomplished by controlling the controllables, which includes how they choose to portray themselves to others. As challenging as it might be, they must do everything within their power to remain focused and upbeat. Even if players feel discouraged, they can maintain a sense of optimism and determination through positive body language, which includes holding the head high and having a "more determined than ever" facial expression. In other words, adopting an open posture leads to a more physical presence, which allows players to refocus on the task at hand.

Refocusing can be accomplished by restructuring thoughts, which means shifting focus from what is wrong to what is right about one's performance. Mentally tough players use adversity to their advantage by remaining optimistic in their outlook. Mistakes are inevitable, and what is most important is how players respond to the mistake. It's essential for the players to remember that if an opponent can sense fear from one's poor body language, they will have a superior advantage. Engaging in negative thinking will influence body language and give the impression that one is giving up. There will be times when players lack confidence and the ability to remain focused and upbeat, but at the very least, they can fake it by adopting positive body language. When a player can successfully demonstrate proper body language, he has essentially introduced a somatic intervention which transfers to more affirmative thinking, such as restoring or furthering one's belief in himself.

One of the most significant challenges was to try to impress upon athletes and coaches the power of their own thoughts in contributing to outstanding performances. There were times when a less-confident athlete would obsess about what could go wrong, and he would vividly picture a previously disastrous outcome. An athlete lacking confidence is more likely to have more negative than positive thoughts. When that occurs, trying to suppress the thought will not be productive. The harder he tries to make the thought disappear, the more likely it is that he will retain it and feel uneasy while doing so. Since the conscious mind cannot think of two things simultaneously, the best way to deal with this situation is to recall a previous example from a game that gave him great pleasure as an athlete. It could be his best performance of all time. By focusing on positive experiences from the past, this means he cannot be worrying about a time when he underachieved. That helps to build confidence and put him in a better frame of mind.

Even though they are professionals, some athletes can generate considerable worry in their mind and become anxious and emotionally charged before or during the game. For example, a player who experiences self-doubt often becomes obsessed with making mistakes, or not playing well, or losing. The self-doubt becomes the catalyst for experiencing an overaroused state, which includes increases in heart rate, breathing, and muscle tension. If players don't know how to cope – that is, they can't calm themselves down – they'll find their thoughts and emotions spiraling out of control. In these situations, players look for guidance from the coach on what to do. I've observed far too often members of the Leafs coaching staff unwittingly bring more tension to an already tense situation, and therefore, they are unable to assist the athlete. The following counseling techniques were recommended to help players navigate their emotions during games or practices.

First, I recommended the importance of identifying the cause of their discomfort. Many athletes under duress may not talk openly about what's bothering them. During my discussions with players, I would ask them to list as many reasons as possible to help explain the cause of the stress they were experiencing. Rarely were these explanations related to skill, ability, and conditioning. In fact, they were almost exclusively psychological. Some of the common stressors that led to their self-doubt included harsh coaching, losing, negative attacks from the media, and injuries. Many were very sensitive to fear of failure and negative social evaluation from their coaches, teammates, fans, and opponents. Those who feared failure did not respond well to coaches who were overly critical. They needed the opportunity to discuss their feelings openly. I was often the source for them to discuss the stress they were experiencing. In these instances, I would point out that some of their teammates were just as nervous and feared failure in the same way, but they interpreted the situation as an opportunity and a challenge to be better, not as a threat. That often led to a more calming influence for the fearful athletes.

Second, I encouraged them to shift their focus from what's wrong to what's right. There are many positives when playing hockey. The positives must be highlighted. When a player was struggling, I had him recreate an event in his mind where he would see himself scoring, making a great play, or taking a hit to make a personal sacrifice for the benefit of the team. This will be discussed in more detail in the next section of "employing effective strategies". In addition, I suggested that he accept the fact that success is not restricted to winning or losing a game. A successful outcome could be defined in terms of the amount of self-improvement he gained, the degree of effort and persistence he put forth, and the amount of enjoyment he derived from playing to the best of his ability. Losing should be viewed as a temporary setback and a challenge to try harder the next time. In other words, playing in the NHL is a process orientation. I often asked our players which is more rewarding, the journey or the outcome? Many would say the journey (i.e., the process), because they learn so much about themselves, and it's something that they have complete control over, such as the passion for competing, unyielding work ethic, and resilience. I endorsed the notion that by adopting this mindset, then the numeric values associated with outcome were more likely to be achieved, rather than if they focused on those elusive numbers and outcomes exclusively.

Employing effective strategies

One of the many rewarding tasks assigned to me during my tenure with the Maple Leafs was to coordinate team-building events. Team-building events were designed to bring coaches, athletes, and support staff together to discuss specific goals and the methods by which those goals would be achieved (Yukelson, 1997). Members of the Toronto Maple Leafs came from several different countries, including Russia, Sweden, Finland, the Czech Republic, Slovakia, Canada, and the United States. It was a priority to emphasize the importance of team cohesion. The term *team cohesion* has been defined as "a dynamic process which is reflected in the tendency for a group to stick together and remain united in the pursuit of its instrumental objectives and/or for the satisfaction of member affective needs" (Carron, Brawley, & Widmeyer, 1998, p. 213). One year I conducted a "values team-building" session for the Maple Leafs. Values are beliefs that influence behavior and serve as guidelines to evaluate behavior (Crace & Hardy, 1997). Moreover, as suggested by Estabrooks and Dennis (2003), discussions of how team success will be determined as related to team values would be beneficial. Thus, a modified version of the Crace and Hardy intervention model was introduced to the Toronto Maple Leafs at the beginning of the 2005–2006 season. Although the authors recommend that the players and coaches be introduced to the principles behind team-building interventions, it was felt that professional hockey players already had a clear understanding of what constitutes a functional team environment.

Thus, the session began with players divided into four groups of six, each table with a group leader who was one of the team's captains. I asked the leaders to discuss in their groups the important beliefs that would help guide their behavior and motivation for the upcoming season. After a 20-minute discussion, the group leaders reported three or four of their group's most important beliefs. A general discussion ensued, and the players collectively rank-ordered the beliefs.

Resulting team values summary, 2005–2006 season

The players presented 10 beliefs to the coaching staff. They were transformed into a plaque, and each player took ownership by signing his name to it. The plaque was mounted in the dressing room as a reminder of what the group valued as a team. Throughout the season, head coach Pat Quinn often referred to one of the values as a theme to begin his team meetings in preparation for an upcoming game. In addition, if the team was underachieving, he would target one of the belief statements. For example, if there was a lackluster effort after a period, Quinn would refer to "loyalty", which the players had defined as not cheating themselves or their teammates from giving their best effort. Coach Quinn implied that they were letting each other down and not adhering to their own values. Such tactics would help motivate the players into giving a more concerted effort to achieve their goals. A summary of the 10 beliefs is as follows:

1   Team Toughness: Mentally and physically, never quit. Stick up for one another.
2   Team Speed: We must all take short shifts so we can wear down our opponents by the third period. We'll be able to win the close games if we can do this.
3   Team Defense: We can score, but in the past we've hung the goalies "out-to-dry". We need a commitment to play solid defense.
4   Work Ethic: On and off the ice, strive towards your goal. Push yourself to be better.
5   Accountability: Being truthful and up front to your teammates. Don't make excuses. It has to be 24 players held accountable by each other and the coaches.
6   Respect: Respect must be earned. Respect each other's roles and what different players bring to the table, for example, goal scoring, checking, penalty killing.
7   Positive Attitude: We need to be more positive. No complaining about line combinations, defense partner, and so on.
8   Loyalty: Don't cheat yourself or your teammates from your best effort. If you play 5 minutes or 20 minutes, work hard whenever you get the chance.
9   Leadership: There are 24 leaders in this dressing room, no passengers.
10   Commitment: Make the commitment to team concepts, systems, and off-ice conditioning.

From an individual perspective, the most effective strategy employed with players consisted of watching video combined with imagery. Martin, Moritz, and Hall (1999) proposed that if athletes want to improve their confidence, then Motivation General Mastery (MG-M) imagery should be used. To that end, I had a film library of highlight packages for each member of the Toronto Maple Leafs. When one of the players had lost confidence in his game, then the two of us would meet privately and implement a strategy that would give him greater hope and optimism. For example, former Toronto Maple Leafs player Steve Thomas spoke publicly on Hockey Night in Canada and in the Toronto press about the work we accomplished together. Essentially, when Steve felt he lost his scoring touch, and as a consequence, his confidence, together we would watch approximately 90 seconds of his highlight tape 15 minutes prior to the warm-up of his next game. The highlight tape consisted of him scoring tremendous goals – goals that were very opportunistic. It showed him celebrating with his teammates to the thunderous ovation from the home crowd. In addition, there were images on the tape of Steve being introduced to the Maple Leafs fans as one of the game's "three stars". After he watched this tape, I would turn off the lights in the video room and instruct him to recreate as vividly as possible in his mind the thoughts, feelings, and attitude associated with what he just witnessed on the television monitor. I asked him to use all of his senses – sight, sound, smell, touch, and kinesthetic – while reliving those moments. I further instructed him to remember the feeling he had after those games in which he was a standout, and how he interacted with his teammates, coaches, and even his wife and two children following the game. At the very least, he experienced a spritz of adrenaline that made him not only ready to compete for the next game, but it also boosted his confidence because the evidence he was observing on the monitor, and reliving in his mind, was real. It was something that he had already accomplished.

During my first road trip as the head coach of the Toronto Marlboros of the OHL, the General Manager Frank Bonello turned to me at the front of the bus as we pulled into Kingston, Ontario, and said, "Tell the players to turn off their headsets. They shouldn't be listening to music prior to the game, they should be getting ready". It was our first manager-coach disagreement. I said, "Frank, they are preparing. The music increases their arousal levels and that's what they need. I'm not going to tell them to turn it off".

Arousal refers to an athlete's physiological state and ranges from deep sleep to extreme excitation. The power of music can motivate athletes to superior performance by regulating arousal levels (Karageorghis & Terry, 2011). When an athlete listens to fast, upbeat music, physiological processes such as heart rate and respiration increase. For most hockey players, having increased arousal levels prior to a game is essential. In addition to increased arousal, music also promotes thoughts that could inspire a greater work ethic. With the Toronto Maple Leafs, I constantly observed how players prepared for games. Music was always popular, but not all players have the same music tastes. Some relaxed to certain tunes, whereas others used songs to get them charged up. Veteran players often prepared the playlists prior to games. One veteran always played the same annoying love ballads by a group called Air Supply (e.g., "I'm all out of love" and "Every woman in the world to me"). It was a clever strategy in my view. Under normal circumstances, listening to love songs would act as a sedative and reduce arousal levels. In this instance, the Leafs players preparing for the game couldn't stand those songs, and they yelled and threw hockey tape at the player who chose those songs, who also sang along with Air Supply. I think it was the aggressive reaction of all the players toward the teammate that got everyone psyched up to play. It was a risky but effective strategy because the music had the opposite effect. Instead of reducing arousal levels, as most soft songs do, the team became extremely agitated and energized because of their disdain for love songs. Overall, we found the effects of music to be very powerful. Players were able to increase their arousal level before games with playlists that featured upbeat, lively music. I did have to spend some time with Maple Leaf coaches who were "old school" and did not appreciate or understand the role that music played in helping to regulate one's arousal levels.

Recommendations for aspiring practitioners

Since there will be multiple challenges presented to practitioners, the ability to deal with these challenges is manageable when the sport psychology practitioner has specialized in the particular sport. Having expert knowledge of one's sport is an important step in building trust with the individual athlete and/or organization with whom the practitioner works. Although I did not compete at the professional level, I was fortunate to coach at a very high level of competition, (e.g., Ontario Hockey League, Canadian Interuniversity Sport, and the National

Hockey League), and as a result, the management team as well as the athletes associated with the Toronto Maple Leafs organization readily accepted me.

National Football League Hall of Fame coach Bill Walsh wanted athletes and support staff in his organization, the San Francisco 49ers, to have high degrees of emotional intelligence because they would be enthusiastic, inquisitive, and would thrive on work (Rapaport, 1993). As practitioners, we are committed to enhancing the performance of others, which requires a certain degree of emotional intelligence. In order to assist the clients that we are fortunate to work with, it is imperative to have a sense of empathy, one of the characteristics of emotional intelligence. It has been suggested that empathy is the foundation for positive relationships and the ability and motivation to recognize and respond to other people's fears (Neale, Spencer-Arnell, & Wilson, 2009). Having the ability to empathize with our clients is not the same as sympathizing. To understand their challenges and to be able to put them in a position to succeed requires a combination of empathy and the knowledge base to choose the best intervention to assist them. In one instance, I had to deal with a Maple Leafs player who was devastated when he learned he was a healthy scratch prior to a game. I allowed him to vent, to get everything off his chest. He was very critical of the head coach, and his anger was palpable. I could easily feel his pain. Once he had calmed down and had nothing left to say, I said to him, "Let's assume that everything you're saying is correct. The coach is treating you harshly and not giving you a chance. Now, what are you prepared to do about it?" I put the ball back in his court. I allowed him to play the role of a victim for a short period of time, then I had him restructure his thoughts to be more proactive, more mentally tough, and to find a solution on his own. It worked very well. His mindset changed, and he began to discuss what he had to do in order to change the coach's perception of him.

Finally, a phrase coaches often use with athletes is "less is more". In other words, don't try to do too much. When the opportunity presents itself to work with athletes or sports organizations, practitioners might be wise to follow the same advice. First-time practitioners often may have the best of intentions by prescribing multiple strategies for athletes to incorporate into their daily routines. The possibility of overprescribing strategies may confuse the athletes to the point that they become so obsessed with the intervention that they lose focus on the task at hand. Assisting athletes or coaches with their mental skills takes time. There are no quick fixes, even though the client or coach may believe there are. I frequently reminded coaches and athletes that in order to appreciate the destination, such as winning a Stanley Cup, one must become totally immersed in the journey itself. The journey is all revealing. It reveals whether each athlete and coach associated with the team has the grit to endure during challenging times. Duckworth and Gross (2014) suggested that grit requires an individual to maintain allegiance to his/her ultimate goal despite profound disappointments and setbacks. There will be disappointments and setbacks for the practitioner as well. So not only do practitioners have to provide expertise for the athletes they work with, but they need to have a clear understanding of their own grittiness and their own strengths and weaknesses. In other words, practitioners may have to work on their own mental skills, as well as their clients'.

References

Carron, A. V., Brawley, L. R., & Widmeyer, W. N. (1998). The measurement of cohesiveness in sport groups. In J. L. Duda (Ed.), *Advancements in sport and exercise psychology measurement* (pp. 213–226). Morgantown, WV: Fitness Information Technology.

Crace, R. K., & Hardy, C. J. (1997). Individual values and the team building process. *Journal of Applied Sport Psychology, 9*, 41–60.

Duckworth, A., & Gross, J. J. (2014). Self-control and grit: Related but separable determinants of success. *Current Directions in Psychological Science, 23*, 319–325.

Ericsson, A. (2007). Deliberate practice and the modifiability of body and mind: Toward a science of the structure and acquisition of expert and elite performance. *International Journal of Sport Psychology, 38*, 4–34.

Estabrooks, P. A., & Dennis, P. (2003). The principles of team building and their application to sport teams. In R. Lidor & K. Henschen (Eds.), *Psychology of team sports* (pp. 173–174). Morgantown, WV: Fitness Information Technology.

Karageorghis, C. I., & Terry, P. C. (2011). *Inside sport psychology*. Champaign, IL: Human Kinetics Publishers.

Martin, K. A., Moritz, S. E., & Hall, C. R. (1999). Imagery use in sport: A literature review and applied model. *The Sport Psychologist, 13*, 245–268.

Neale, S., Spencer-Arnell, L., & Wilson, L. (2009). *Emotional intelligence coaching: Improving performance for leaders, coaches and the individual*. London, UK: Kogan Page.

Rapaport, R. (1993, January). To build a winning team: An interview with head coach Bill Walsh. *Harvard Business Review*, 110–119.

Yukelson, D. (1997). Principles of effective team building interventions in sport: A direct services approach at Penn State University. *Journal of Applied Sport Psychology, 9*, 73.

16

WORKING WITHIN PROFESSIONAL FOOTBALL

Mark S. Nesti

The work described here is based primarily on my experiences of delivering sport psychology support inside a number of professional soccer clubs over a 10-year period. At each English Premier League club where I worked, my role consisted of providing psychological support to players and staff at first team levels and carrying out a small amount of work with youth players who were transitioning into the professional ranks. This required a commitment of between three to five days a week at each club. I had managed to gain entry into this traditionally very closed and inaccessible environment because of a number of interrelated biographical factors. The most important of these factors was that, in each case, the manager (head coach) possessed a very positive view about the value of sport psychology. Given the important role of the head coach within an elite professional soccer club, it is essential that this individual is seen to strongly support the sport psychologists and the role they adopt with the staff and players. My own background and contextual knowledge has also been vital to being able to work successfully in elite professional soccer. Having played the game semi-professionally and tutored many soccer coaches on sport psychology courses, I had a good understanding about the unique culture of the sport at professional levels and the specific performance demands. In addition to these experiences, I spent several years in various management and leadership roles in private and public-sector industries outside of sport. It was within these organizations that I developed a greater understanding and appreciation of the importance of organizational psychology and culture in building individual excellence and team success. In relation to being able to carry out one-to-one sessions with more than 200 first team staff and soccer players from the English Premier League, I benefitted considerably from the opportunity to study existential phenomenological psychology during my graduate work in sport psychology at the University of Edmonton in the 1980s. Existential phenomenological psychology gave me a more grounded and 'hard-edged' perspective that added to the knowledge and skills I had developed through earlier studies of humanistic counselling theory and organismic approaches to cognitive psychology (Ronkainen & Nesti, 2015).

Culture

Premiership soccer is a fast-paced, unstable, and intense environment. Short-termism is the order of the day. With each match, clubs have an opportunity to secure vital points in their efforts to avoid relegation, win titles, or secure qualification for European competitions. The perceptions around sport psychology in this culture can range from acceptance that it must deliver results very quickly if it is to be seen as worthwhile, to the more infrequently encountered view that long-term development of players and teams is something worth waiting for. I was fortunate in that most of the time I worked in clubs where there existed a high level of acceptance that the benefits from psychological interventions would be more likely to emerge in the longer term.

As an applied practitioner, my understanding about the importance of culture to the work of a sport psychologist has increased over time. Prior to my applied engagement in professional soccer, I had always expected that knowing the game, and its ways of working from the inside, would be important. What I did not fully appreciate was that being able to analyse this particular culture, and operate alongside its idiosyncratic qualities, would be essential in allowing me to survive in this sport at the highest professional levels.

Although the sport psychology literature often refers to the role of a sport psychologist as a performance-focused mental skills practitioner, the reality is that much of what is carried out in practice often relates to far broader issues around culture and organizational processes. In order to be able to work effectively in the culture of elite level professional soccer, it is crucial that sport psychologists have an appreciation of the very complex and political contextual factors that exist in this world, and accept that a key part of their job will be to work on broader organizational issues to assist individual and group performance.

However, culture refers to much more than organisational processes, operational mechanisms, and daily practices. It includes all of these factors and others that are harder to identify clearly, but which nevertheless have a significant impact on the working environment. Viewed from this perspective, culture refers more precisely to traditions, unwritten rules, precedents, values, and patterns of belief. An organisation's culture is determined more by the ideals that govern it, the vision it pursues, and values it adheres to. Usually, many cultural markers are unseen, perceived, and felt, rather than visible and explicit. And while it may be correct to point out that professional sport culture differs from amateur sports, in my experience elite level soccer culture has a number of unique features that must be borne in mind by sport psychologists to carry out their role effectively. I would also argue that English Premier League soccer has a culture quite different to other elite level competitions. Given the huge financial involvement, media interest, and profile of this sport, this culture can be described as one where ultimately results are everything. Therefore, the culture of Premier League soccer clubs tends to be one of volatility and rapid decision making, with a ruthless focus on achieving success. It is often a very abrasive, harsh, self-centered, and individualistic environment. The financial resources of clubs also mean that they are increasingly well-organised, systematic, and technically advanced organizations. In other words, the culture of many elite professional soccer clubs is one where great effort is directed at producing and maintaining a calm and focused performance environment within a turbulent situation.

This type of environment could be described as a sub-culture, in that although much of what exists is similar to other professional sports cultures, several unique elements will be encountered in professional soccer. Recent work by Schinke and McGannon (2015) highlights how important it is that sport psychologists take time to understand a particular subculture and adjust their practice to meet the needs of those working in these settings. In professional soccer, sport psychology must therefore adapt to be seen as a valuable addition to the reality faced by the club where the focus is on immediate success, which will (hopefully) be followed by even greater long-term achievement in the seasons ahead. Within these organizations, managers, senior coaches, and staff are cognizant of the fact that clubs who 'know who they are' frequently are the best at being able to plot a course of survival, or maintain high levels of success over the long term. Therefore, when sport psychologists are appointed, they must acquire a deep knowledge of the organization and appreciate how they can influence the identity of the club and its culture. During my early experiences working inside elite professional soccer clubs, I made many mistakes because of a failure to fully understand the culture. For example, I assumed that there would be excellent levels of communication between coaching staff and other specialists employed by the club. The reality was more nuanced. I found that there was deep distrust between some departments and roles, including those who worked most closely together. This was difficult to detect at first because of the considerable amount of informal communication and banter (Nesti, 2010) among these individuals. I mistook this to mean that an open and transparent culture existed; I had to learn quickly that this was not the case, and make efforts to adjust my own style of communication to meet this reality.

Challenges to confidentiality and building trust

Several authors (e.g., Eubank, Nesti, & Cruickshank, 2014; Relvas, Littlewood, Nesti, Gilbourne, & Richardson, 2010) have recently claimed that sports psychologists will be largely ineffective in delivering their work in professional soccer clubs where they fail to understand the culture and types of stressors they are operating within. Empirical research (Fletcher & Wagstaff, 2009) has identified a number of important organisational stressors that sports performers, coaches, and others must cope with in order to achieve their aims. These include communication failures, role conflict and ambiguity, a lack of clarity about roles, and work overload. The challenges that sports psychologists face when operating in Premiership soccer clubs involve offering their service within an environment where there are other distracting influences, such as media interest, the activities of agents, and contract negotiations. Other sources of organisational stress may include rapid changes in playing and coaching personnel, interdepartmental infighting, interference from club owners in team affairs, and unrealistic demands on family life. Premier League clubs frequently have players from more than 20 different nationalities on their roster; this diversity means that sport psychologists will find themselves working in a multicultural environment, where players have different religious beliefs, cultural practices, and attitudes towards sport psychology. Within such a fast-paced, ruthless, and 'win at all costs' environment, sports psychologists who fail to read the cultural matrix in order to offer something that is viewed positively by players and staff will have a very uncomfortable experience, and eventually, will be likely to have their contract terminated. This is because in elite professional soccer, at least in the UK, the employment security of most staff is very poor. If the head coach or other senior member of staff believes that someone is not able to positively influence the success of the team, or worse, is seen as having a negative influence on events, he will be removed from his post. The justification offered by those in professional soccer for this harsh approach is that failure to achieve results on the pitch will quickly lead to unemployment for the majority of the first team staff. This is borne out by the fact that currently in the English Premier League, for example, the head coach and their staff team, on average, survive for about 17 months in their jobs.

Another important challenge confronting sport psychologists is how they manage to operate within a culture without becoming assimilated by the culture. It is necessary for sport psychologists to be part of the culture, but apart from it, at least to some extent. This will allow them the space needed to provide an informed but critical voice; this is crucial because of the role demands around culture change and confidential support to players and staff. An important idea in relation to the challenge of maintaining some professional distance is the notion of congruence between professional practice and philosophy (i.e., values and beliefs) (Lindsay, Breckon, Thomas, & Maynard, 2007). For example, congruence can be applied to work between the individual player and sport psychologist, or this concept can be extended to the relationship between club identity and culture. Sport psychologists will need to become familiar with the current identity of the club to ensure congruence between the team identity and that of the club. Alongside this, they must look beyond the club to the history, values, and traditions that make up the culture of the city, town, or region where the club is based. For example, cultural connections between clubs and their respective supporters often represent incredibly powerful bonds based on religious, ethnic, political, and historical ties. A close level of congruence between the team, club, and local identity is absolutely essential. The relationship between these three elements is fundamental, and indeed can even be considered the most important factor in the club's success and continued existence.

Beyond issues around congruence, other more practical challenges need to be faced. Recruitment of coaches and other support staff, and the identification of specialist roles in areas like sports science and performance analysis, has typically evolved in quite a haphazard way. There is also a tendency for knowledge about jobs and roles to be kept informally by the individuals rather than being recorded in written form and in formal documentation. Although this approach has certain advantages, such as ensuring that bureaucracy and managerialism are kept at bay, such an ad-hoc and loose arrangement often means that there is little in-depth or accurate understanding among staff of each other's roles and professional responsibilities. This can lead to problems where, for example, failure to appreciate the full scope and range of a colleague's role may lead to conflict and result in staff undermining each other's work. This behaviour could have a negative effect on professional relationships and even adversely affect the view that players might have about the value of different roles within the club and the individuals that perform these roles.

Sport psychologists should expect to be involved in this type of work because this clearly impacts performance of the staff, players, team, and the club. The growth in staff numbers in professional soccer clubs means it is now common for most clubs to have a sports science and medical staff team amounting to 15 to 20 or more individuals. The number of full-time coaches can range from six or seven people working with the first team, and sometimes up to 10 staff supporting Academy (youth) level operations. Taken as a whole between first team and Academy levels, especially at more established Premier League clubs, there may be 40 to 50 or more staff operating in full-time and part-time roles across all of these functions. Given this challenge, sport psychologists will be called upon to function more like an organisational psychologist or human resource manager (Nesti, 2010). Amongst other tasks, this will involve them in designing and implementing a system of professional and personal support for the back-room staff. This could involve writing job descriptions, establishing appraisal mechanisms, running staff away days, offering continuing professional development sessions, and generally supporting the personal development and training opportunities of all staff. To conclude, sports psychologists may be rather surprised to find that alongside an expectation that they will work closely with players to enhance their psychological skills and qualities, they may be identified as the most appropriate person to take on the task of organisational psychologist, *whether or not they feel qualified to carry out this role!*

I believe that to carry out this type of work, specific skills and personal qualities are necessary. One of the challenges in this regard is because of the education and training most sport psychologists have received. Although some sports psychologists have had previous experience of delivering this type of organisational psychology support, and may even possess qualifications that will assist them in carrying out these duties, this is not the norm. As I have pointed out (Nesti, 2004), the tendency of most university-based sport psychology programmes is to concentrate on mental skills training and literature that focuses on quantitative group-based research designs investigating a range of emotions. This is poor preparation for sport psychologists who may find themselves delivering an organisational psychology role.

At the elite level in professional soccer, especially beyond youth sport levels, it is usual to find that most of the players already possess excellent mental skills. As has been reported by researchers investigating a number of other sports (Fifer, Henschen, Gould, & Ravizza, 2008), high-level performers have usually acquired excellent skills in relation to concentration, maintaining confidence, the use of imagery, and goal setting. This has taken place after guidance from coaches and on occasion from sports psychologists; often it has been learned by the individuals as they have progressed through the competitive sport environment. It could mean that sport psychologists who can only deliver mental skills training will be unable to get jobs in elite professional soccer. In addition, Nesti and Littlewood (2011) have pointed out that sport psychologists hoping to work with first team professional soccer players must be proficient in the use of counselling-based approaches. This is because, as they argue, at this level most of the work focuses on the development of self-awareness, self-knowledge, and other personal qualities, rather than learning mental skills, and often includes work on dealing with broader life issues. In this way, they propose that sport psychologists should offer a performance-focused and caring approach – one aimed at helping the player or member of staff to improve performance, but not at the expense of their humanity and sound ethics. To do this work effectively, sport psychologists must possess a range of counselling skills and the key personal qualities of empathy, presence, and authenticity (Nesti, 2004).

Using a person–centred psychological approach to counselling practice has been discussed in Buber's (1970) work. His book was described as one of the most profound and important books of the last century, at least for those involved in psychotherapy, education, and psychology. Buber's notion of an *I thou* dialogue, which describes when two individuals meet in a moment of 'pure' communication, is something that I have found very helpful in my work with elite professional soccer players. Buber's work emphasises that the task facing sport psychologists is in many ways similar to others who assist people to become more authentic, or fully themselves. The important links between pursuing greater authenticity and sport performance and personal fulfillment have been discussed by Corlett (1996) and Ronkainen and Nesti (2015). Dialogue with professional players around this concept using ordinary speech and everyday language is possible, because these individuals are often very clear about what they stand for and who they are. They understand the importance of striving to become more authentic, because they know from past successes that their best achievements have come when they have taken responsibility for themselves, instead of following others, or blaming events beyond their control. Working with a Premiership player on the notion of authenticity is not about establishing a prescriptive plan or identifying a neat and tidy strategy for action. Instead, it involves dialogue about an important psychological quality that, although it may never be fully attained, is nevertheless found in all elite level performers, and which must be pursued by the players in their own unique way.

Trust

One of the most important elements that impacts on the likely success of the sport psychologist in this culture is that of trust. The trust between the manager and the sports psychologist is of great importance. Without this being securely in place, players, coaches, and even other support staff may find themselves doubting the value of having a sports psychologist within the team. During periods of success and achievement it is easy to ignore or forget about the importance of trust. However, when the inevitable crises appear, all work at the club will be scrutinised and assessed closely. During these moments, the level of trust that is in place between the psychologist, staff, and players will be evident.

The focus of teams going through difficult times should be on factors in their control and ensuring that both immediate and longer-term goals and tasks are given due consideration. There is little doubt that the best sports organisations and top businesses manage to maintain this type of dual focus during their successful periods, and more importantly, when experiencing more challenging times. Sport psychologists may find that they receive less support to carry out confidential one-to-one work with players during the inevitable tough phases. Such situations, whilst understandable, reveal that it is common to find that the counselling work carried out by the sports psychologists is only fully acceptable in the good times. This may lead them to question how fully committed the manager, key staff, and players are to their work. Sometimes the players will remain keen to meet with the sport psychologists during challenging moments, even if the manager does not want this to take place. With long-term involvement and a greater understanding about the value of one-to-one work, the sport psychologists should be able to overcome these problems, and continue to offer support to the players in good times and bad. This is about trust; the level of trust that the staff and players have in the value of the work provided by the sport psychologists, and ultimately, it is about the trust they have in them as a person.

Professional soccer players and youth players hoping to make the grade at professional clubs (Gilbourne & Richardson, 2006) will inevitably encounter many of the following experiences over their careers: being dropped from the starting lineup or first team squad; suffering injury and loss of form; being sent out on loan or sold to another club; and being praised one week and vilified the next by the media, supporters, and other stakeholders. These experiences place great demands on the mental skills and psychological qualities of players. They also remind individuals that gaining someone's trust in them can sometimes be a long and tortuous process. Trust is a very commonly used term in professional football. It extends to trust between players on the field of play, to the trust that a manager has in his/her staff and players, and trust players have in their support staff, including the sport psychologist.

For players to be able to develop trust in themselves, which allows them to take on the many exciting and tough challenges in professional soccer, is of major importance. Research to date has offered much on motivation, confidence, and other psychological skills in elite level sport (Fifer, Henschen, Gould, & Ravizza, 2008). Surprisingly, there are very few references to trust in the sport psychology literature. Future studies should turn their attention to examining why trust is mentioned so readily in professional sport including soccer, what this refers to, and how it can be developed.

The identity of sport psychologists in professional soccer is vital to how their work will be received and the levels of trust from staff and players. If sport psychologists are working full time within a club, there will be a different set of opportunities and challenges to face. It may be harder for the sport psychologists to convince players that their work with them will be completely confidential. On the other hand, it may be easier to build trust and to develop closer working relationships with both players and staff that can assist their work. The identity that I have usually been able to adopt has been congruent with my understanding of the role of sport psychologists in professional soccer. By operating part time but from within the club, usually on three to five days a week, I have been able to operate as an outsider who is on the inside. This allows the psychologist to enter into the day-to-day world of players and staff, whilst maintaining a necessary distance to be able to gain the trust of players around issues like confidentiality and integrity.

The identity of sport psychologists in this type of environment is not something that can be lived only when on duty. In many ways, this is quite similar to those professions, such as medicine, teaching, and the clergy (Gamble, Hill, & Parker, 2013), where there is a need to embody and be personally convincing in a vocation. It is no exaggeration to claim that beyond technical skill, theoretical knowledge, and personal qualities, the professional whose work is a vocation is always on duty. In one sense, it is possible to say that for these individuals and sport psychologists, 'who we are is what we do!' In other words, our values and professional ethics must be part of who we are, integral to how we see ourselves, and in that sense, part of the deepest core of our self. This type of demanding identity will ensure that the often-experienced skepticism and negative perceptions around psychology and sports psychology can be ameliorated by the credibility of the *person* of the sport psychologist. This is the cornerstone of personal and professional trust that is so essential to the work of sport psychologists in elite professional soccer.

According to many staff and players in professional soccer, trust in sport psychologists is dependent on finding someone who is an authentic individual and who happens to have the skills, competencies, and knowledge of sport psychology. In this sense, the wish is not for a sport psychologist *per se*, but for a person of integrity, who knows him- or herself (i.e., has a high degree of self-knowledge), and who clearly has knowledge and skills around psychological factors relating to performance sport *that they as players and staff do not possess*. This final point is extremely important. The identity of the sport psychologists working in this demanding level of sport must be about both aspects of what it is to be a professional. They should have a personal identity and set of values of the professional individual pursuing a vocation. They must also be highly knowledgeable about the discipline of psychology and be able, when called upon, to provide staff and players with a richer, more in-depth, and ultimately more useful answer to a particular situation, event, or problem.

Confidentiality

From a professional practice perspective, trust has been a key applied value in my work in professional soccer. Gaining the trust of the manager, players, and senior staff in the role of a sport psychologist involves a number of factors: (a) being able to meet the needs of those you are working with; (b) becoming part of the team; (c) being able to explain your role accurately to different audiences or clients; (d) displaying integrity; (e) being able to pursue clear goals; (f) demonstrating an in-depth understanding of the culture and its practices; and finally, (g) being able to maintain complete confidentiality at all times. All of these factors are of crucial importance, and sports psychologists will constantly work to achieve these during their time with a club or consultancy. However, confidentiality differs from other qualities in the list in that this must be met fully by the sports psychologists from their first moment at the club.

In relation to one-to-one work, most of my counselling-based sessions have taken place in private rooms at the training ground, where confidentiality was easier to guarantee. However, some of the most useful encounters have occurred in very different types of locations. For example, dialogue with players has occurred in the changing room, on the training pitch, in the dining room, and even in the showers. As has been previously noted by Ravizza (2002), this makes the work of sports psychologists very different when compared to the normal working practices of most other professional psychologists. The data from these more unplanned, spontaneous, and sometimes fleeting sessions may be every bit as important as that emerging from more organised and scheduled meetings.

A Premiership soccer club usually contains a large squad of motivated and high-achieving players. These individuals are used to playing regularly, or at least being part of the squad for games. During a season there can be conflict and bad feeling among players, and the manager or their senior staff, as a result of not being selected for the team. It is important to remember that a prolonged absence from match play can impact negatively on a player's fitness levels and undermine confidence, self-belief, and motivation. This can result in a frustrated and despondent individual, who may not train as well as he could. Such a situation could lead to the player having a negative attitude towards his work. This could impact on the player's attitude around the training ground and can heighten tensions between players and between the player and the senior staff and manager.

The fluctuating nature of form, confidence, and results will almost always mean that there will be significant changes to the playing squad and starting lineup over a season. This can happen very rapidly where players are suspended, injured, or dropped because of a tactical necessity to set the team up in a different way. In these situations, sport psychologists must closely examine their professional practice, values, and ethical codes of conduct. Questions around who is the client may be particularly pertinent at this point. Confidentiality during these delicate situations is clearly of the utmost importance to the effectiveness of the work and the continuation of the sports psychologists in their job.

Operating in a fully confidential way is very difficult in the culture of professional soccer. Apart from confidential practice being essential to carrying out the role, additionally there are ethical matters to consider. It is clear from ethical codes of practice promulgated by various sport psychology and psychology professional bodies that sport psychologists owe a duty of care to carry out their work in a consistent and professional way. Where they have been appointed by a Premiership club or professional soccer team, they must do all that they can reasonably do to fulfill their obligations around confidentiality. This means that confidentiality must be protected at all times for the individual player. Their main client is the player or member of staff, and not the team or the club. To fail to carry this out properly could lead to unethical and unprofessional behaviour on the part of the psychologists and could destroy the trust that is so essential to doing work with players in such a publicly sensitised environment as elite professional soccer.

Consultancy philosophy

The most important theoretical and philosophical grounding for my applied work in profes-sional soccer is derived from existential psychology. Existential philosophy, phenomenology, and existential psychology emphasize the importance of personal meaning in relation to the development of an individual's identity (Ronkainen, Tikkanen, Littlewood, & Nesti, 2014). Existential psychology was the first approach in psychology to propose that the question of identity was the most important issue confronting individuals and communities (Nesti, 2004). The existential approach, unlike most others in psychology, tends to view identity as something that involves the individual, his/her cognitions, emotions, and social processes, environment, and culture. Two very important concepts derived from existential philosophy – phenomenology and existential psychology – have been useful in providing a theoretical underpinning for my work. The first of these relates to the idea of authenticity. At its most basic level, authenticity describes the importance of being oneself. The existential view argues that, in order to achieve this as an individual, team, or club, self-knowledge is essential. In order to give all of oneself, it is necessary to 'know who you are and what you stand for' (i.e., your own identity). Authenticity is extremely important in high-achieving performance environments, and it has been discussed extensively by Corlett (1996) in relation to sport philosophy and psychology.

Second, a 'sense of self' should be viewed as the core of someone's identity, and this should encompass a particular set of qualities. These should be based on high levels of self-awareness (Ravizza, 2002) and self-knowledge (Corlett, 1996). Existential notions about identity suggest that to function optimally in highly demanding performance environments requires individu-als and organisations to know themselves in–depth, act according to this view of themselves more often than not, and display a synthesis between flexible, open, and dynamic qualities, alongside a set of more fixed and long-standing values.

The types of issues frequently confronting professional soccer players are listed below. Authenticity, self-awareness, and self-knowledge are the essential skills and qualities that players must develop to deal positively with these anxiety-inducing experiences. Common experiences include de-selection from the starting lineup, falling out with the manager or coaching staff, problems around motivation, financial matters, going on loan, competitive anxiety, existential anxiety (May, 1977), dealing with expectations, and knowing roles and responsibilities on the field of play. These issues and a number of other challenges are faced by professional soccer players on a daily, weekly, and seasonal basis.

In trying to capture the details of one-to-one dialogue with players (and staff on occasion), I often ask the player for their reflections on what we had covered at our last session. To help this process, I usually provide them with a copy of a brief report that was sent after our meet-ing. In my experience, some players read this material carefully, whilst others seem satisfied not to engage in reflections based on written accounts. Over the years I have carefully tailored the language, format, and length of my reports to meet the players' needs to ensure that they benefit from this piece of work. There is a great variety of responses to the written word, and some players have informed me that they would prefer to have more brief notes provided after meetings, to remind them of what has been discussed. Other players have reacted positively to 1,500-word reports, which they not infrequently share with significant others, such as wives, family, and agents. The sport psychologists also benefit in that the reports provide a detailed account of what was discussed with the player, and the reports can be used to check progress.

Work with players

Identity and authenticity are best addressed through sport psychologists working on a one-to-one basis with first team players and staff. This involves a form of sport psychology counselling concerned with helping individuals to improve performance and enhance their sense of well-being. This approach (Nesti, 2010) is based on a holistic perspective, which views performance as being strongly connected to every aspect of an individual's life. As has already been mentioned, this perspective is guided by existential and humanistic psychology principles, and it emphasizes that success and achievements will only be attained where there is an acceptance of important cultural features of the environment. A player who fails to appreciate the needs of, or meet the demands of, the host culture may create considerable tension with other teammates, staff, and supporters. However, this must not be encouraged in the player at the expense of pursuing greater authenticity.

The example provided below describes how these issues were handled with a Premiership player in a club the first author worked at over a number of years. The player had been recruited from a top-level club in another country, and he had been signed for a considerable transfer fee. The overarching aim of the work was to help the player improve his understanding of the expectations that supporters and the local media would have about his on- and off-field behavior, the way the game should be played, and the type of character and personality that was viewed positively in this culture. The role of the sport psychologist in this context was to act as an intermediary to help the player adapt to meet the team identity and the demands of the local culture. In order to achieve this goal, the process was actively and visibly supported by the manager. This was crucial in helping the player to appreciate that this was a central and important issue that was being approached seriously.

A series of compulsory and structured meetings between the sports psychologist and player focused on explaining the detailed history of the club, the current identity of the team, and the performance philosophy of the manager and his coaching and support staff. These confidential sessions provided an opportunity for the player to ask detailed and candid questions about the style of play, team identity, and expectations of the staff and supporters. It also provided a safe space where the player could describe his professional and personal identity and begin to examine the level of adaptation that would be necessary to succeed in the new environment. This intervention was conducted over five sessions to help the player move closer to meeting the identity of the team and the club, without abandoning his own self-identity and efforts to become more authentic. The sessions focused on historical and current material (e.g., reading and film footage), values and traditions of the club on the one hand, and those of the broader local culture on the other. This information was extended to provide an account of the demographics of the area, wealth, occupational and industrial heritage, health, educational attainment, and how the city was generally perceived elsewhere in the country. The sport psychologist ensured that this work was conducted in a way that was relevant and meaningful to the individual player, and that technical language and psychological concepts were reduced to a minimum.

During sessions with the player, attention was directed at finding out why he had chosen this club and how it fitted into his professional and personal development. Elite level professional players often face a number of choices about which clubs they join to further their careers, but the reasons behind their decisions usually remain confidential. Dialogue took place about how he had faced difficult challenges at earlier stages of his career, and time was spent clarifying how these experiences could help him in the current situation. There were many moments when the player talked about the anxiety he was feeling about facing a new performance challenge, and how he felt isolated and uncomfortable in the new surroundings. Throughout the encounters, focus was on accepting that difficult experiences should be embraced and not allowed to undermine the player's aim to be more fully himself (i.e., authentic). Although goal setting and imagery were used to enhance confidence for specific match-related tasks, most of our dialogue was about understanding the local, national, and club cultures, and finding ways in his own words, 'to stay true to myself, and show who they have really bought, but respect where I have joined!' This work helped the player to successfully adapt and adjust to meet the cultural requirements of his new club and their identity, while continuing to develop psychologically, and in the words of the manager, be able, 'to show us the real you, the one we were happy to buy for a club record fee, because when we see the real you, this is when you are your best!'

Recommendations

The topic of identity (Balague, 1999) and authenticity in Premiership soccer clubs, and their relationship to culture, has a considerable impact on the day-to-day practices of my work as a sport psychologist working within the game. Unfortunately, within the discipline of sport psychology, there remains very few references to these concepts and their influence on applied practice. In this chapter, I aimed to briefly examine this topic in the hope that these terms will become more familiar in applied sport psychology. In some ways, this point relates to the suggestions put forward by a number of experienced practitioners (Corlett, 1996; Nesti, 2010; Ravizza, 2002), who argue that the training and education of sport psychologists is often lacking in knowledge around philosophy, anthropology, cultural studies, and sport-social psychology. In other words, sport psychology has often adopted a narrow, individualistic, performance-focused agenda when in reality very little can be achieved without an awareness of the culture and environmental factors that operate on individuals and the team.

It is hoped that future researchers will adopt broader theoretical perspectives, such as those contained in existential and humanistic psychology and philosophy, to allow them to consider topics like identity, values, and culture across different sports. In terms of professional soccer and understanding the experience of delivering sport psychology in this sport, it is essential that the discipline assists newly qualified individuals and students to widen their reading. In particular, there is a need for more awareness about the importance of organizational psychology and a greater level of engagement with personal approaches to counselling that view performance enhancement and care for the athlete as symbiotic.

To gain entry into this type of work, I feel it is important that sport psychologists consider if they have the requisite skills, knowledge, and personal qualities. In my experience, many newly qualified and less experienced practitioners underestimate how important their values and personality are to being able to survive and be effective in professional soccer clubs. To assist this point, I would like to see professional practice supervisors help their supervisees engage in opportunities aimed at personal development. In pursuing this, words like *courage*, *integrity*, *trust*, *humility*, *authenticity*, and *passion* should become sought-after qualities of someone's character. I would add that maybe some individuals are unsuited to working in such abrasive and volatile cultures as professional soccer, and that in recognising and accepting this fact, many sport psychologists should avoid these environments in favor of sport cultures in which they will be more effective.

Finally, at conference presentations in Europe and North America, it is common to hear the most experienced and skilled sport psychology practitioners talking about the need to view the athlete they are working with as a person first and a sports performer second. If this means anything, it must be that in working with an athlete, the sport psychologist must listen to everything that the client considers to be important to his/her success. In my experience with high-level professional soccer players, very rarely does this mean that discussions focus exclusively on developing better mental preparation routines, self-talk strategies, or relaxation techniques. Much more time is devoted to listening to players discussing their understanding of who they are, how people see them, and how they sustain themselves as a person who is required to repeatedly deliver exceptional performances, week after week, over many seasons.

In terms of recommendations for sport psychologists who are hoping to gain entry into the world of professional soccer, there are four that I would suggest are of greatest importance. First, it is essential that sport psychologists have a good understanding of the culture of professional soccer, possess some knowledge about the game, and have a passion for the sport. At this level of soccer, the coaching and other support staff are often highly motivated about their work and see it as the most important thing in their lives. Although it may seem unfair, in my experience sport psychologists will only be able to build strong relationships with others and generate interest in their work at the club if they can demonstrate a similar level of commitment.

Second, sport psychologists must have knowledge and skills that can add something different from what already exists at the club. This is not as easy as it sounds, because at this level of sport, most coaches and other staff have acquired a very good understanding about psychological factors through their own experiences as performers and supporting players. Although this knowledge is rarely based on research and theory, it can still be at an advanced level and relate closely to the specific demands of the sport.

Third, in such an abrasive and fast-paced culture, sport psychologists must be very resilient. A strong sense of self based on a high degree of self-awareness and self-knowledge is vital to being able to survive and thrive in the unique sub-culture of professional soccer.

Finally, in order to work effectively at first team levels, it is essential that the head coach and director of performance (where there is one) visibly and consistently support the work of the sport psychologists. This is more likely to happen if the head coach is convinced that the sport psychologists will assist performance of individuals and the team. The way in which this is achieved will reflect the practice philosophy of the sport psychologists. I believe the best approach that is the most effective, ethically sound, and professional is to offer support aimed at improving the personal well-being *and* performance success of all staff and players at the club.

References

Balague, G. (1999). Understanding identity, value, and meaning when working with elite athletes. *The Sport Psychologist, 13*, 89–98.

Buber, M. (1970). *I and thou* (W. Kaufmann, trans.). New York: Scribner.

Corlett, J. (1996). Sophistry, Socrates and sport psychology. *The Sport Psychologist, 10*, 84–94.

Eubank, M., Nesti, M., & Cruickshank, A. (2014). Understanding high performance sport environments: Impact for the professional training and supervision of sport psychologists. *Sport and Exercise Review, 10*, 30–36.

Fifer, A., Henschen, K., Gould, D., & Ravizza, K. (2008). What works when working with athletes. *The Sport Psychologist, 22*, 356–377.

Fletcher, D., & Wagstaff, C. R. D. (2009). Organizational psychology in elite sport: Its emergence, application and future. *Psychology of Sport and Exercise, 10*, 427–434.

Gamble, R., Hill, D. M., & Parker, A. (2013). Revs and psychos: Role, impact and interaction of sport chaplains and sport psychologists within English premiership soccer. *Journal of Applied Sport Psychology, 25*, 249–264.

Gilbourne, D., & Richardson, D. (2006). Tales from the field: Personal reflections on the provision of psychological support in professional soccer. *Psychology of Sport and Exercise, 7*, 335–337.

Lindsay, P., Breckon, J. D., Thomas, D., & Maynard, I. (2007). In pursuit of congruence: A personal reflection on methods and philosophy in applied practice. *The Sport Psychologist, 21*, 335–352.

May, R. (1977). *The meaning of anxiety*. New York: Ronald Press.

Nesti, M. (2004). *Existential psychology and sport: Theory and application*. London: Routledge.

Nesti, M. (2010). *Psychology in football: Working with elite and professional players*. London: Routledge.

Nesti, M., & Littlewood, M. (2011). Making your way in the game: Boundary situations in England's professional football world. In D. Gilbourne & M. Andersen (Eds.), *Critical essays in applied sport psychology* (pp. 233–250). Champaign, IL: Human Kinetics.

Ravizza, K. H. (2002). A philosophical construct: A framework for performance enhancement. *International Journal of Sport Psychology, 33*, 4–18.

Relvas, H., Littlewood, M., Nesti, M., Gilbourne, D., & Richardson, D. (2010). Organisational structures and working practices in elite European professional football clubs: Understanding the relationship between youth and professional domains. *European Sport Management Quarterly, 10*, 165–187.

Ronkainen, N. J., & Nesti, M. S. (2015). An existential approach for sport psychology theory and applied practice. *International Journal of Sport and Exercise Psychology*. Advance online publication. doi: 10.1080/1612197X.2015.1055288

Ronkainen, N. J., Tikkanen, O., Littlewood, M., & Nesti, M. S. (2014). An existential perspective on meaning, spirituality and authenticity in athletic careers. *Qualitative Research in Sport, Exercise and Health, 7*, 253–270.

Schinke, R. J., & McGannon, K. R. (2015). Cultural sport psychology and intersecting identities: An introduction in the special edition. *Psychology of Sport and Exercise, 17*, 45–47.

17

WORKING WITHIN PROFESSIONAL RUGBY UNION

Stephen D. Mellalieu

Overview

Rugby union is a sport that is more than 150 years old. It is one of the most popular contact team sports in the world, played at the professional, amateur, and junior levels by both males and females in nearly 200 countries across the Northern and Southern Hemispheres (www. worldrugby.org). The Rugby World Cup, a quadrennial international rugby union competition, attracts a global TV audience of more than 5 billion viewers, with the New Zealand All Blacks being the current holders of the trophy at the time of this writing. The sport also has a rich tradition of promoting strong cultural and societal values, including teamwork, discipline, respect, enjoyment, and sportsmanship.

Despite the presence of coaches or trainers and medical staff in the sport since the mid- to late 1960s, a major change in the science of rugby union came with the introduction of professionalism in 1995 (until then the game had been played under a strictly amateur ethos). Increased resources were invested into the preparation of teams, resulting in the growth of sports science and medicine support services. The growth in support staff in the sport has also created a rise in the provision of psychological support to various teams and governing bodies. Today, although not commonplace, most professional and elite international teams will have accessed, or had exposure to, some form of sport psychology consultant (SPC) or associated mental skills support services. For example, the New Zealand All Blacks, the most successful international team of all time (76.43% win percentage), have employed the services of Gilbert Enoka as their resident SPC for more than a decade.

In line with the overall aim of this text, my goal in this chapter is to describe my experiences of working within professional rugby union. I firmly subscribe to the view that in order to provide a context to your professional philosophy, it is very important to acknowledge your personal background (cf. Poczwardowski, Sherman, & Ravizza, 2004). Initially, I discuss my upbringing and how this brought me to working in the professional game. I then touch on the sport context and how the various sub-cultural understandings were gained. Following this, I discuss a part of the sport psychology vocation that is often overlooked in the professional practice literature, namely, the initial challenges to gaining access and trust with a client or organization and how these are achieved (cf. Andersen, 2000). Using Poczwardowski, Sherman, and Henschen's (1998) framework for planning and implementing psychological services, I then discuss my consulting philosophy developed for the environment and include examples of strategies that I have personally found effective when working in a professional rugby context. Finally, I conclude the chapter with some recommendations for both neophyte and experienced practitioners intending to work in rugby union regarding how to gain access and practice effectively within the sport.

Author background and how this brought me to rugby union

Rugby union is the national sport of Wales and is considered a large part of our national culture. For a small country of 3 million people, we have a proud history of producing successful teams, being consistently in the top eight of the world rugby rankings and having won the annual premier northern hemisphere competition, the European Rugby 6 Nations tournament, on 38 occasions out of the 120 years it has been held. Such is the passion for the sport, that when the team plays a test match, it is a significant cultural event, and the entire nation stops to watch. Consequently, being born and brought up in Wales, I didn't have much choice of a sport to follow, or to become involved in, other than rugby union. I started playing the game from a young age (5 years old) and was very privileged to gain junior international representative honors for Wales at Under 15s, 18s, 19s and 21 levels. At this stage of my life, like many aspiring young performers in the specializing phase of their careers, I aspired to represent Wales at full senior international level and was prepared to do everything possible in my powers to realize that dream. This included my choice of degree course (Sports Science) and university (Loughborough, which is renowned for its sporting excellence) for college study in order to learn as much about the science of sporting performance as possible.

As with many young athletes, the college years proved the realization that the time and effort invested were not producing the desired outcome, and the dream began to fade and then change, from one of representing my country at the national sport level to one of wanting to coach or provide strength and conditioning support to players and teams at the highest level in the game. My revamped career aspirations and the insightful content and excellent teaching I received in my degree course then persuaded me to continue my study and pursue a Master's program in sports science. The seeds of my interest and an eventual career in sport psychology began, like for so many of us, with the people who first introduced the topic to our attention. I was very fortunate to have Professor Graham Jones as one of my lecturers at university, someone who was highly regarded in the field, not only in terms of his applied consultancy with Olympic teams and athletes, but also for his extensive knowledge and publication background in stress and performance in sport (see e.g., Jones, 1995). One of his former graduate students, Dr. Austin Swain, was also a sport psychology lecturer at the department and was the Director of Rugby of the college team, but also crucially was working at the time as the sport psychologist to the England Rugby Union team. Austin would regular share his experiences with us of his work and practice with the team, most notably his work with the team in the build up to, and following, the 1995 Rugby World Cup in South Africa, in which England reached the semi-finals. Fate had it that Austin was also my personal tutor for my degree course and research project supervisor (for which I looked at the topic of anxiety and performance in rugby union). Austin's work, and multi-roles as researcher, teacher, and practitioner, were the realization for me that I could pursue a career in sport psychology, and eventually aspire to work in this profession in the sport that was very close to my heart.

After my Master's course, I studied for a doctorate in psychology, specializing in stress and performance in rugby, while qualifying as a chartered sport psychologist at the same time. Again I was very fortunate to have two PhD supervisors (and training mentors) in Dr. Steve Bull and Dr. Chris Shambrook, who although they did not have rugby playing experience or consulting backgrounds in the sport, were both highly experienced sport psychology practitioners in Olympic and professional sports. I was therefore again exposed to the potential for working with elite athletes in the profession, further enhancing my efficacy for this career. At this time, I was still able to combine playing rugby with my academic studies. I always wanted to apply my training and experiences in sport, particularly rugby, to work in the game. Initially, in my neophyte years, more opportunities came to work with athletes from other disciplines and national and professional sports organizations, although I still kept coaching roles with various rugby teams, notably with the college rugby team at the university where I was lecturing.

Through my coaching role with the university, I began to liaise with the academies of the local regional professional rugby teams, partly because our own university team always contained a number of players from the academies, but also as one of my administrative roles at the university was elite athlete support liaison officer, whereby I regularly provided support and advice to individuals pursuing their dual athlete-student career pathways (cf. Wylleman & Lavallee, 2004). One common challenge was helping the players to manage their playing load and availability to the various teams they were involved with, requiring ongoing dialogue with the academy managers of the local regional professional rugby teams. From this relationship with the academy managers, and once they became aware of my daytime job, I was invited to deliver sport psychology education workshops and one-to-one consultations with the academy squad from one of the professional regional teams. After a period of time providing support services to the academy and building relationships with the athletes, support staff, and coaches, I was then invited to begin working with the senior professional team of the organization.

How the sport context and sub-cultural understanding of the organization were gained

In terms of understanding rugby union and its context and sub-culture, for me personally, this was acquired from my prolonged engagement within the sport. At the time I began working with the professional team, I had been involved in the sport in some form as a player or coach for some 20 years, so I was acutely embedded in the culture of the sport. While these experiences provided me with a level of insight into the workings of the sport, I feel my perspective or awareness of this social milieu only became fully realized when I undertook my professional training and supervision as an SPC. Hours of engaging in reflective practice upon my initial work with clients from a range of sports helped raise my self-awareness regarding my background and my experiences within my own sport and sharpened my perspective on understanding the dynamics of a sport or organization that I was providing support to (cf. Anderson, Knowles, & Gilbourne, 2004; Gilbourne & Richardson, 2006).

Allied to this lived experience of the sport, I also had a long-standing academic interest in the social psychology of teams and groups. The origins of this interest can be traced back to my undergraduate days and the discovery in the university library of Donelson R. Forsyth's (1990) text on group dynamics, which exposed me to a number of concepts that resonated strongly with me in relation to my experiences in rugby. Thereafter, I sought to digest as much literature as possible around team and group dynamics in order to understand what made rugby teams function and how this knowledge could be used by psychologists to work to enhance a team's performance. Indeed, one of the by-products of this process was that several classes in my early years of lecturing were focused around the psychology of teams.

My subsequent efforts as a neophyte SPC practitioner working in team sports were focused on understanding and enhancing the specific dynamics of the team itself, drawing upon then-new frameworks such as Carron and Hausenblas's (1998) conceptual framework for the study of sport teams. However, as my experiences and understanding of working with sports and sports organizations grew, I became increasingly interested and focused on the psychology of the organizational environment within which teams were based. Specifically, I was interested in the roles of the individuals and leaders in this organization that were responsible for the creation and regulation of such high-performance environments and the ensuing culture they perpetuated. This has subsequently influenced any consultancy work I undertake with sports organizations in terms of seeking to ascertain a level of contextual intelligence or understanding of how a sport organization operates (Brown, Gould, & Foster, 2005).

Initial challenges to access and trust with the organization and how they were overcome

One of the key cultural factors inherent within the sport of rugby is the notion of physicality and the demonstration of aggression (due to the contact-based nature of the game). This attitude has traditionally manifested itself in an 'act tough' and 'no pain no gain' culture, whereby players (particularly in the male version of the game) are encouraged to show no emotions and 'man up' in the face of any adversities experienced, such as injury, de-selection, and defeat (cf. Tibbert, Andersen, & Morris, 2015). This particular culture is reinforced by the fact that strength and conditioning (S&C) is very much at the forefront of any training and preparation teams engage in. So much so that in professional teams the S&C coach is typically responsible for the planning and organization of the practice schedules, with head coaches planning their sessions around these physical preparation and conditioning routines, in order that the load players are exposed to and subsequent recovery time they receive is monitored and managed appropriately. In many teams, therefore, the 'Conditioner is King'! This strength and physical focus culture has meant the sport traditionally has not had exposure to or engaged with some of the factors related to the mental side of the game and those commonly associated with SPC practice (helping individuals manage stress, anxiety, emotion, etc.).

In addition to the predominance of a physical focus in the sport, sport psychology does not have a long history or cultural tradition within the game. Whilst technical skill coaches, medical and conditioning staff are positions indigenously associated with a professional rugby union team, very few teams have, or have had, a full-time SPC on their payroll. In the past this has contributed to common (mis)perceptions of sport psychology and associated professionals who seek or have sought to work in the sport. Labels such as 'shrink', 'head doctor', and 'quack' have all been given to SPCs working in the sport in the past. In my experience, these labels are further reinforced by a lack of formal consideration of sport psychology and mental skills in many of the National Governing Body coach education certificates and courses within the game. While some coach education training programs do allocate time and attention to psychological factors related to sport performance and coaching, this tends to center around appreciation of mental skills training for players. Little consideration has been given to understanding the different ways in which SPCs practice (i.e., consulting philosophies) and can be effective in helping not only individual athletes and teams but also their coaches and support staff and the clubs themselves at an overall organizational level.

Taken collectively, these cultural practices inherent in the sport have contributed to a lack of understanding surrounding what SPCs are, how they function, and how they can help well-being and performance within a team. This has typically resulted in what has been termed a 'cognitive bias' or 'negative halo effect' (Linder, Brewer, Van Raalte, & De Lange, 1991) against any SPCs who attempt to work in the sport. At best, SPCs working in the sport are still typically seen as the person who is there to 'sort players' heads out' or be the person to pick up the pieces when a player's 'head has gone' due to injury, poor performance, de-selection, or some other challenging aspect of their job. This is very much in keeping with the stereotypical 'shrink' as opposed to 'stretch' skill set that SPCs can bring to a team or organization, whereby an SPC is seen as someone who is there to pick up the pieces and problem solve as opposed to promoting overall learning, growth, and enhance performance.

The perceptions of SPCs and some of the cultural practices described are not an uncommon barrier facing many SPCs entering a new sport environment for the first time, particularly those in male contact-based team sports (cf. Gilbourne & Richardson, 2006). I was very conscious of this challenge when I was initially asked to begin my work within the professional side of the sport. In order to overcome this potential challenge, I felt the role or approach that I initially needed to take working with the organization was to be viewed (labeled) as one of a mental skills/performance enhancement coach, as opposed to a psychologist or counselor. In all my subsequent dealings with the members of the organization, wherever possible, when asked what I did or what my role was, I tried to give this consistent message. One way this was achieved was by comparing my role with that of the other members of staff in the organization that people were familiar with. I often used the following explanation:

> Well, you (the player) have a coach to work on physical (S&C) development, a coach to work on your technical skills such as passing, tackling, etc., a nutritionist to help you with what you eat; my role is to work on your mental skills, such as helping you to be mentally switched on as best you can for training and matches, helping you to stay as focused as you can be during games.

A key element in this initial attempt to gain trust was a focus on the rhetoric I used on being solely performance focused in my work, thereby relating all my work to helping players develop their practical skills to enhance their on-field performance, as opposed to any off-field (i.e., shrink) work. Again, this approach was very much based on avoiding or counteracting the negative halo effect surrounding the term psychologist and its associated negative connotations with dealing with players' off-field problems.

A further challenge for SPCs to gain access and trust working within a sport such as rugby union, aside from the perceptions and inherent cultural practices, is one that faces any new member of a professional sports organization, or indeed any new employee in the workplace. That is how they become integrated with the rest of the employees (i.e., players and staff) in order to perform one's role and function effectively. Ravizza (1988) noted in his commentary on how to gain entry to be an effective SPC that it is important to build trust and credibility not only with players but also with the support staff, coaches, and management. As sport psychology is not 'part of furniture' traditionally in rugby union, then it is likely the rest of the staff will not all know what an SPC does and subsequently accept them and their workings from day one. Unlike a new S&C coach or staff member, an SPC is unable to gain relatively immediate impact or credibility by, for example, visibly delivering coaching/conditioning sessions or conducting assessment of the team/players with testing equipment, with relatively immediate feedback to all parties concerned.

The key feature for me, therefore, in developing the beginnings with a team or organization is to have a determined strategy or way of working (modus operandi) for that initial phase of work with the team. For me, when I work within the sport for the first time, in the initial phases I focus on trying to understand the environment as much as possible and build working alliances and relationships with individuals (Tod & Andersen, 2012) through immersion in the sport and its culture (cf. Bull, 1995). In adopting this approach, it should be acknowledged that there is a large element of feeling like the 'invisible man' (or woman) sitting and watching training sessions. This practice can often feel counter-intuitive, in that as an SPC you will naturally see areas or immediate problems where you think you can be effective, and therefore a strong desire may exist to intervene or provide advice in these contexts. For me, however, if the quality of the working alliances and relationships with the various individuals within a team or group are not established yet, then it may be unwise to engage in direct intervention work, as this may threaten the SPC's development of trust, initial credibility, and long-term acceptance into the group.

A further strategy to work towards integration by seeking to understand the cultural environment of the team is to identify the key gatekeepers who provide access to the various subgroups within the team or organization. In many instances, this may be one of the coaches – often one or two will be initially more aware of SPC practice and therefore more receptive to an SPC's efforts. In other teams, it may be a member of the medical staff, such as the physiotherapist (athletic trainer). In any group of coaches and support staff in a professional team there will naturally be those who have more empathy towards SPCs and acknowledgement of the value they can bring to that organization. Often it is those individuals who are sensitive to the various demands the players experience, and whom in their roles required support or advice in terms of how to manage or deal with these challenges.

For me, my playing and coaching background has also enabled me to have a degree of credibility with a number of members of the organization, some of whom were gatekeepers to accessing the inner workings of the team and the players. As rugby union is a cultural-based sport where players will have grown up representing their local club, and hence their local community, there is a strong sense of pride and history, and also lots to talk about in terms of teams, matches, tournaments, and players played with and against. This background in the sport was therefore very helpful in the 'getting to know each other' period, in which I was attempting to immerse myself in the culture and building working alliances and relationships with the group. I cannot understate the extent to which being able to engage in initial conversation about 'do you know this player or this club or this individual' helped to gain trust and break down potential psychological barriers.

Consulting philosophy developed for context

As discussed in the previous section, based upon my experience of playing, coaching, and studying rugby union, my modus operandi or approach to working in the sport has very much been one of having full (as opposed to zero) knowledge of the game. I have therefore sought to locate myself firmly as another expert member of the support team, or if you like an insider, as opposed to someone from outside of the sport with no understanding or experience of the game itself. In this respect my philosophy is driven by the need to integrate psychological services into the existing high-performance environment as part of a multi-disciplinary team (MDT) systems-based approach (Reid, Stewart, & Thorne, 2004). This is based on the SPC being viewed, and operating as, a member of the support staff with equal status and recognition to other members, such as the medical, analysis, and S&C practitioners.

Within this service framework, when I began working with the organization I sought to adopt a traditional cognitive-behavioral philosophy working within an MDT environment with individual clients. As highlighted in the previous section, this initial position was very much performance-focused and underpinned by educational-based mental skills training. However, like most SPCs working with a single client group over a period of time, my consulting philosophy has evolved as I have grown to understand and become immersed in the culture and the organization. For example, based on the challenges some of the neophyte players face in their first or second year on the professional roster of the squad across their sporting, social, educational, and personal domains, I have adopted a holistic lifespan development approach (Wylleman & Lavallee, 2004). As I have developed prolonged working relationships and alliances over time, this lifespan development perspective has become pertinent to supporting those individuals (including staff) further along their professional careers, in terms of contract termination (being released), moving to another team, and/or preparing for retirement or transition from the sport.

The development of working relationships and therapeutic alliances over sustained periods of time has also allowed me to engage more frequently with supporting non-performance-related sub-clinical matters experienced. Here I have sought to initiate my counseling training skills and competencies, taking a humanistic approach to helping individuals help themselves in the broader context of their lives beyond sport (cf. Poczwardowski, Sherman, & Ravizza, 2004). This prolonged engagement over time with the client group has also meant that my philosophy has evolved beyond merely working with the individual as the client, and now incorporates providing solutions and support for the team and the organization itself. In this respect, I would now consider my current role having greater breadth than that of a traditional SPC, to one that seeks to promote learning, development, and well-being throughout the organization.

Effective strategies for working in professional rugby union

My day-to-day practice in the sport is in keeping with my context-specific consulting philosophy of fully integrating or immersing myself within the organization. Specifically, where possible the medium through which I seek to deliver my support is practical and rugby-based. This begins with ensuring I have a level of visibility and presence during the working day. I try to be present at the training venue before, during, and after sessions, attend all team briefings and staff meetings, and have a presence at the players' team recreational area. Such a 'hi–vis' approach ensures I am able to engage in conversations with players in and around their environment and daily routines, so that discussion is easily facilitated (cf. McCann, 2000). The players have full and busy daily training schedules, so being able to prompt them into reviewing or following up on interventions delivered is key. In this respect, a lot of these initial conversations and subsequent interventions are brief contact-based in nature (Giges & Petitpas, 2000). These initial contacts then provide the opportunity to follow up the conversations with more formal scheduled and structured sessions at times that are mutually convenient to the athlete or staff member and the SPC. Most importantly, the ability to deploy brief-contact interventions also allows any pressing matters to be managed at the time in situ.

The 'hi–vis' immersion approach to consulting also allows for ongoing observation of the professional sporting environment and the day-to-day social interactions between individuals and groups, both in and away from the training, practice, and competition environments. Having the capacity to observe individuals in their natural environment is an invaluable source of evidence for an SPC in numerous ways, such as getting to understand individual personality and behavioral tendencies, social networks, interpersonal skills, and how players perform in competition and training in their sport. All of these strategies allow SPCs to garner further evidence with which to build robust personality profiles of their clients in their natural environments to validate and/or unpack the various challenges that the individuals and the organization experience.

A further example of what I feel is an effective strategy consulting in a professional rugby union environment is seeking to keep my consultations very much rugby (and therefore performance) focused. This is particularly pertinent in the context of initial dealings with clients with whom I have not developed, or had time to develop, a strong working alliance or relationship. When discussing performance-related matters, I usually look to begin by sitting down with players and reviewing their training/competition performances on video footage. Again, this approach is based on understanding the natural environment the players know and are most comfortable with (i.e., athletes are most at ease discussing their performance). Watching and reviewing video footage is a culturally inherent part of the professional sport, so I see this as the starting point for initial discussion and ask the players to go through and verbalize their performance/training footage to me. This then allows exploration of the reasons behind the performances issues, from where I then seek to examine the psychological process or contributions to these performances in more detail. This sport- – to-psychology approach for me is not only effective in building trust and a working therapeutic alliance with the client but also allows for effective diagnosis and subsequent resolution of client-related issues.

The second element of this performance-related approach is the implementation of practical sessions with athletes. This is where I go onto the playing field, training ground, or in the gym and undertake individual sessions with the players. Again, the premise behind this strategy is seeking to build effective relationships with athletes in their natural environments where they are most comfortable. Here, I may only be merely physically assisting clients with their practice routines or drills, such as holding a contact pad or catching, collecting, and returning the balls to the throwers or kickers practicing their respective throwing into the lineout or place kicking at goal. However, this strategy provides the context with the players to discuss elements of their performance of that skill or elements of their overall game/training performances, thereby once again seeking to integrate the mental with technical, tactical, and physical elements of their performance.

In both these on- and off-field contexts, I seek to use the language and terminology that is common in rugby union culture. The language is firmly intended to be non-threatening and non-stigmatic without any psychology-related connotations or overtones. For example, a meeting with a player is a 'catch-up' as opposed to a 'consultation', 'session', or even 'therapy'. With players the focus is very much on not only reviewing performance, but also to evaluate 'learning' and 'take-home' messages from the catch-ups. A common term I use with the players at the end of our session is to identify their 'work-ons', areas of an aspect of the mental side of their game that they need to target for practice and improvement. This term is already widely accepted and used by players (and coaching staff), in relation to technical and physical elements of performance preparation.

An additional aspect of my SPC role is in providing support to injured athletes. Like with most professional sports, long-term injury is an inevitable part of an athlete's job, presenting numerous psychological challenges to all parties concerned, and rugby union is no exception. Statistically, it is likely that at any one time during a season nearly one-third of the players on a professional team's roster will be injured (Brooks, Fuller, Kemp, & Reddin, 2005). The return to play (RTP) group of athletes under the supervision of the medical staff is therefore an important element of the organization where the skills of an SPC can utilized. For example, at the initial onset and diagnosis of a long-term injury, I work in conjunction with the medical staff to assess the mental well-being of the injured players in terms of how they are coping emotionally with the trauma, and then seek to provide social support and crisis intervention counseling. Once an athlete is post-operation, I seek to help the player to deal with the frustrations of being injured and not being able to train or 'go to work', any anxieties about missing out on competitions, matches, and selections, and general concerns about being able to return to full levels of performance and continue to have a professional sporting career. Example interventions at this stage center around crisis intervention counseling, rational emotive therapy to put the injury into context in their own lives and the wider world, allied with short- and medium-term process goal setting to sustain motivation through the early phases of rehabilitation, and building resiliency to deal with any setbacks that inevitably occur on the route to fitness. As athletes near the RTP stage, strategies become targeted to enhancing physical and mental reintegration back into the performance environment. From an SPC perspective, my efforts are focused on helping the players to develop robust self-efficacy perceptions regarding their ability to engage in various aspects of training and performance they will encounter, and to enable them to 'hit the ground running' to being a full professional again. Strategies include use of video modeling (self and peer) of key performance behaviors and actions, and cognitive-general imagery for re-learning of team plays/strategies. At all stages of this process, it is very much a systems approach whereby I work with the various medical and S&C team members dealing with a particular player. Sometimes interventions are delivered directly by myself, other times indirectly, supporting the medical team in their own interventions with the players. This process of deciding to work directly or indirectly with the client is one that, as discussed earlier, is very much contingent on understanding the quality of the therapeutic alliance developed with each individual and assessing who in terms of the support staff is best suited to deliver the relevant support.

As well as providing support to the players, one of the other elements of my time spent within the organization is working directly with the coaching and support staff. One of my main activities is to help act as a sounding board to the individuals to listen to the numerous issues they encounter in their roles and seek to facilitate discussion to work toward developing strategies to remedy or improve issues. These issues mainly revolve around the challenges support staff have with players with respect to underperformance in training and competition and/or exhibiting behavior in training and competition that is incongruent with expectations and norms. Here I try to adopt a solution-focused therapy approach (Høigaard & Johansen, 2004) that is goal-directed in its essence. I seek to help guide the individual to develop strategies for dealing with the matters/individuals concerned as opposed to merely providing advice or answers. Often it is a case of working with the staff member to identify and understand the behavioral characteristics, motives, or intentions or the player or individual concerned, and develop interventions that assist or resolve the matter.

A final role I undertake with coaches and support staff is working to enhance the specific and overall learning of the players by considering the structure and content of the practice, preparation, and review schedules implemented in their training programs. Here I feel my skill set from both my education and academic backgrounds is particularly useful. Specifically, I work with the support staff to look at how we can maximize the learning and development that players take from each training session. This may range from maximizing learning from a technical rugby skills session, to enhancing the quality of an S&C weights-based session, to enhancing the ability of the players to engage in reflection on their own training and competition performances. This facet of my role often overlaps with supporting the coaches in dealing with the frustrations of players underperforming or not responding to coaching interventions. We seek to develop a combination of learning strategies for individual players and enhance the learning environment in which they operate.

Recommendations for working effectively with athletes and sport organizations

To conclude, here are some key considerations I would offer for aspiring practitioners regarding how to gain access and work effectively with athletes, teams, and when appropriate, sport organizations, in a professional team sport such as rugby union:

1   At the initiation and beginning stage of the development of the support provision, be aware of the boundaries that exist to developing working alliances for the provision of effective psychological support in professional team sports. These may include cultural factors and practices unique to that sport or organization and a lack of education/information about sport psychology practice and what an SPC is and can do for an individual, team, or sporting organization (Pain & Harwood, 2004).

2   Familiarize yourself with the unique culture of the environment you are entering. What are the historical traditions, cultures, and values within the sport? What group dynamics currently exist overall within the organization and locally within the squad or team? What is the natural environment within which the members of the organization are most comfortable? Seek to understand the language, both formal and informal, employed within the unique culture of that organization or team and the subsequent discourse and rhetoric in the way it is communicated among its members.

3   When shaping your service delivery philosophy with the team/organization, it is critical that you know yourself in terms of your competencies and boundaries. Work on your self-awareness of understanding your competencies both as a practitioner and as a human being, when shaping your personal service philosophy for that particular team or

organization. For me with the current client my knowledge and skills in the sport lead me to adopt an immersion approach in the culture to best meet the needs of the client and my own skill set. Bear in mind that a different context and a different set of skills and competencies may warrant a different approach.

4   When you begin working with the team or organization, remember you are essentially a new member on the team roster or payroll, and you should account for this accordingly. Seek to build effective working relationships across the team/organization. Effective working alliances in professional team sports such as rugby union come from immersing oneself into the organization by being a fully integrated member of the support staff. This takes the investment of both time and effort and mirrors the commitment invested by the athletes (and support staff) in the pursuit of excellence.

5   In keeping with an MDT approach to building effective working alliances, it is important to consider that the training of mental skills and the provision of psychological support in professional sport do not exist in a vacuum. The delivery of effective interventions strategies by the SPC should adopt approaches that seek to consider the multifaceted elements that underpin the successful physical health and well-being of professional athletes and support staff. SPCs should seek to understand and utilize the best medium (e.g., direct/indirect) through which to build effective relationships with individuals and subsequently develop and deliver psychological-based solutions within the organization. In particular, be aware of the constraints relating to the temporal, spatial, and delivery issues of your practice (i.e., where? when? and how?).

6   Understand that the nature of the service delivery you undertake with your client is transactional and requires an ongoing evaluation of the organizational culture within which the support service is provided. Be prepared to adapt or change the support you provide as the nature of your relationship with and within the team or sport evolves. The pursuit of excellence in team performance is constantly evolving for all of those individuals involved in professional sport, so why shouldn't your approach also evolve? Here, the ability to engage in effective reflective practice is essential. Seek to adopt a mindfulness approach to reflection in action. Try to ensure that you keep considering and locating yourself and your actions in the culture of the environment of the team or the sport, and seek to maintain a reflexive view as much as possible regarding your SPC practice once immersed in that culture.

References

Andersen, M. B. (2000). Beginnings: Intakes and the initiation of relationships. In M. B. Andersen (Ed.), *Doing sport psychology: Process and practice* (pp. 3–16). Champaign, IL: Human Kinetics.

Anderson, A., Knowles, Z., & Gilbourne, D. (2004). Reflective practice for sports psychologists: Concepts, models, practical implications, and thoughts on dissemination. *The Sports Psychologist, 18,* 188–203.

Brooks, J. H., Fuller, C. W., Kemp, S. P. T., & Reddin, D. B. (2005). Epidemiology of injuries in English professional rugby union: Part 1 match injuries. *British Journal of Sports Medicine, 39*(10), 757–766.

Brown, C., Gould, D., & Foster, S. (2005). A framework for developing contextual intelligence (CI). *The Sport Psychologist, 19,* 51–62.

Bull, S. J. (1995). Reflections on a 5-year consultancy program with the England women's cricket team. *The Sport Psychologist, 9,* 148–163.

Carron, A. V., & Hausenblas, H. (1998). *Group dynamics in sport* (2nd ed.). Morgantown, WV: Fitness Information Technology.

Forsyth, D. R. (1990). *Group dynamics* (2nd ed.). Pacific Grove, CA: Brooks/Cole Publishing.

Giges, B., & Petitpas, A. (2000). Brief contact interventions in sport psychology. *The Sport Psychologist, 14*(2), 176–187.

Gilbourne, D., & Richardson, D. (2006). Tales from the field: personal reflections on the provision of psychological support in professional soccer. *Psychology of Sport and Exercise, 7,* 325–337.

Høigaard, R., & Johansen, B. T. (2004). The solution-focused approach in sport psychology. *The Sport Psychologist, 18*(2), 218–228.

Jones, G. (1995). More than just a game: Research developments and issues in competitive anxiety in sport. *British Journal of Psychology, 86,* 449–478.

Linder, D. E., Brewer, B. W., Van Raalte, J. L., & De Lange, N. (1991). A negative halo for athletes who consult sport psychologists: Replication and extension. *Journal of Sport and Exercise Psychology, 13,* 133–148.

McCann, S. C. (2000). Doing sport psychology at the really big show. In M. B. Andersen (Ed.), *Doing sport psychology: Process and practice* (pp. 209–222). Champaign, IL: Human Kinetics.

Pain, M., & Harwood, C. (2004). Knowledge and perceptions of sport psychology within English soccer. *Journal of Sports Sciences, 22,* 813–826.

Poczwardowski, A., Sherman, C. P., & Henschen, K. P. (1998). A sport psychology service delivery heuristic: Building on theory and practice. *The Sport Psychologist, 12,* 191–207.

Poczwardowski, A., Sherman, C. P., & Ravizza, K. (2004). Professional philosophy in the sport psychology service delivery: Building on theory and practice. *The Sport Psychologist, 18,* 445–463.

Ravizza, K. (1988). Gaining entry with athletic personnel for season long consulting. *The Sport Psychologist, 2,* 243–242.

Reid, C., Stewart, E., & Thorne, G. (2004). Multidisciplinary sport science teams in elite sport: Comprehensive servicing or conflict and confusion? *The Sport Psychologist, 18,* 204–217.

Tibbert, S. J., Andersen, M. B., & Morris, T. (2015). What a difference a "Mentally Toughening" year makes: The acculturation of a rookie. *Psychology of Sport and Exercise, 17,* 68–78.

Tod, D., & Andersen, M. B. (2012). Practitioner-client relationships in applied sport psychology practice. In S. Hanton & S. D. Mellalieu (Eds.), *Professional practice in sport psychology: A review* (pp. 273–306). London: Routledge.

Wylleman, P., & Lavallee, D. (2004). A developmental perspective on transitions faced by athletes. In M. Weiss (Ed.), *Developmental sport and exercise psychology: A lifespan perspective* (pp. 507–527). Morgantown, WV: Fitness Information Technology.

18

WORKING WITHIN ELITE PROFESSIONAL CRICKET

The role of a sport psychology consultant

Stewart T. Cotterill

Personal/consulting background

I have been practicing as a sport and performance psychologist since completing my formal university education in the early 2000s, and over that time I have been fortunate to gain experience in a wide range of sports and other performance contexts, such as business, the performing arts, and medicine. My interest in sport psychology though predates my "formal" sport psychology education. During my adolescent years, I was a talented track and field athlete, with good potential for success in both pole vault and 400-meter events. If I am honest, I was good but just not committed enough. I simply did not have the 'leave no stone unturned' mentality that is required to be a success. So, as a university undergraduate student, the opportunity to try to understand why I was not motivated enough in more detail was very appealing. I had enjoyed studying sport and geography (UK A-levels) while at school, so in the absence of a better idea, I decided to pick both subjects and do a joint degree in Physical Education, Sport Science, and Geography at Loughborough University. I must admit though, in the first year of the degree programme, I almost opted for sport sociology rather than sport psychology (an advantage of a sport science degree that covers all aspects of the subject to allow students to make an informed choice). I was also fortunate in my time at Loughborough to be taught by leading sport and exercise psychology academics, including Austin Swain, Graham Jones, a novice (at the time) Chris Harwood, and Stuart Biddle. After finishing my degree, I took a couple of gap years working in Europe and then returned to complete a Master's degree in Sport and Exercise Psychology. At the time, I also thought I needed a PhD to really be an effective sport psychologist practitioner, so I registered for a PhD part-time at the University of Edinburgh focused on pre–performance routines in sport. What emerged from my route into the profession was a passion for consultancy, applied research, and teaching – all of which have formed a core part of my career ever since to a greater or lesser extent. I took my first teaching position at Bournemouth University, and at the same time completed my British Association of Sport and Exercise Sciences (BASES) supervised experience and achieved accreditation to be able to practice. Subsequently, I have also become a British Psychological Society (BPS) chartered psychologist and a Health and

Care Professionals Council (HCPC) registered sport and exercise psychologist. The HCPC regulates professions on behalf of the UK government and began regulating psychology in 2010. In my applied work, I started small, working with sports scholarship athletes and teams at Bournemouth University. This opportunity to gain experience as a "psychologist" was crucial. It is now a point I always make to aspiring sport psychologists, whether students or the candidates I supervise through to full qualification. The important thing is to gain experience as a psychologist. There is always a tendency to want to spend time with elite performers and teams. Unfortunately, when you are not qualified, your ability to engage in any real psychology work with these groups is limited. Working at an amateur and more participatory level affords you the opportunity to hone your psychology and psychologist skills, so when you do get the opportunity to work at a more elite and professional level, you have complete confidence in your abilities. Also, through doing this, you have worked out what your approach is and the techniques you predominantly seek to apply.

One of the sports I worked with at Bournemouth University was the cricket team. I also gained some experience shadowing a colleague who was working with a professional cricket academy. The next step in the journey, as is so often the case in sport psychology, involved me being in the right place at the right time. I had recently moved to the West of England to work at the University of Gloucestershire, and Somerset County Cricket Club was looking for a psychologist to work with its academy. Luckily (for me), the Academy Director asked the region's Lifestyle Advisor for a recommendation. The Lifestyle Advisor was based on the South Coast of England and asked the colleague I had shadowed previously for a recommendation. Knowing I had just moved to that region, he recommended me. As with so many opportunities in sport psychology in the UK, it was a case of being in the right place at the right time and having the right people recommend you. This is still pretty much the case working as a sport psychologist in professional sport in the UK. I have recently conducted research interviewing sport psychologists working in professional cricket, and the responses were pretty consistent. Generally speaking, the cricket clubs don't really know what being "qualified" is, so they don't ask; they simply go on recommendation instead from people whose opinions they trust.

Contextual and sub-cultural understanding

Ahead of my time working for the England and Wales Cricket Board (ECB) on the England Performance Programme (EPP), I had already gained significant experience in the sport of cricket. My Dad was a talented cricketer when I was growing up (playing and captaining well into his 50s), and as a result I had grown up playing and watching the game. As previously highlighted, I had also gained experience working with cricket players at Bournemouth University and had gained employment at Somerset County Cricket Club working with the Academy team. Based on my work with the Academy, I was recommended to do some work with the professional (senior) squad at the club. This involved a lot of time watching cricket, which in turn allowed me a lot of time to sit and talk about the game and to develop an understanding of the culture within the club. Building upon this experience, after two years working with the professional squad, I applied for, and was successful in, being employed as the Performance Psychologist working for the ECB on the EPP. Interestingly, while I interviewed well, it was only the recommendation from the captain and head coach at the County Club where I was working that really swayed the decision in my favour. This was another case of recommendation rather than professional qualification. This position at the ECB enabled me to significantly enhance my understanding of the game. I was lucky that on the EPP, all of the other support roles (strength and conditioning, physiotherapy, nutrition, lifestyle advice, and discipline-specific coaching) were provided by the 'national leads' in their relevant areas of expertise. This enabled me to access cutting-edge expertise within the sport.

In terms of developing context and cultural understanding, I think it is important to be an expert in your domain, which helps to engender respect with colleagues. I also think the previous advice I was given when training as a sport psychologist about getting coaching qualifications in a sport is a little wide of the mark. I think it is an advantage to know less about the sport, because this then gives you a mandate to spend lots of time asking questions, especially the really dumb ones! The other significant advantage of this approach is that it enables you to engage in significant dialogue with individual performers or coaches in a nonthreatening way by talking about their sport rather than themselves. This helps to build rapport with the client(s) to then go on to do "real" work in the future.

It is probably important, at this point, to say a little about the demands of cricket. Cricket is an interesting sport in that it is both a team and an individual sport. While operating as a team sport, it is composed of very discrete passages of play, which involves a player (the bowler) bowling the ball at another player (the batsman). At the same time, the batsman is also taking on the rest of the opposition team in the field (Thelwell, Weston, & Greenlees, 2007). These batting and bowling skills can also be referred to as "closed skills" due to the distinct beginning and end to each passage of play. Both batting and bowling require the execution of a complex sequence of actions. Müller, Abernethy, and Farrow (2006) suggested that cricket batting in particular is a very difficult skill, with minimum error tolerance and severe time constraints. They further suggested that batting takes place at the functional limits of the human visuo-motor system. As a result, the ability to prepare for optimal performance is crucial.

The format of the game itself can be very varied. There are currently 20-overs per team (3–4 hours), 50-overs per team (7–8 hours), and 4- or 5-day formats of the game (both teams bat and bowl twice each). In the context of cricket, an 'over' represents a series of six balls 'bowled' at the batsmen by one specific 'bowler'. At the end of this series of balls, there is a slight delay in play and then another player begins another series of six balls. These different formats of the game, in turn, can present varied psychological challenges. At the international level, the sport is characterised by nations touring other countries in a reciprocal relationship. These tours can lead to players, coaches, and support staff being away from home for anything from a few weeks to many months.

The culture within these centrally administered programmes is an interesting one. Players are selected as part of an annual process. As a result, players tend to come and go. Some players are selected once and never again, while other players can spend a number of years on the programme. This has significant implications for the incremental development of the players. My job as a consultant in these cases is to help the players to progress and improve. Due to the nature of the environment, this often requires the simultaneous development of both a long-term and short-term strategy, depending upon whether the player ultimately stays with the programme. While I personally have experience with playing cricket, this is not at a high level. As such, I would reflect that my involvement in the cricket sub-culture was performance focused. Finally, the nature of these sorts of programmes involve players staying in hotel accommodation for extended periods of time away from their normal support structures and social activities. As a result, replacement activities such as playing video games (often one player brings a projector with another bringing the games console), playing golf, watching movies, and drinking are common.

Challenges to trust and access

When I started working with the EPP, I was fortunate to be progressing from working with players in the same sport and at a similar level. This prior experience in the sport afforded me some initial acceptance. Also, the fact that the professional team I had been working with were coming off of arguably their most successful season in their history also helped regarding my reputation by association. The design of the programme also worked in my favour. The competitive season for professional cricket in the UK is April through September. During this time, the EPP staff worked behind the scenes on identifying the most talented professional players nationally. This process started with a long list and was whittled down to a final list of around 16 players by September. The winter programme then began in October and ran through March. Also, the ECB adopted a policy to focus on the most talented younger (18–23 years old) players rather than the "next best" group. This meant that the norm was for "new" players to be selected for the programme, which meant that to these players I was just the sport psychologist on the programme, rather than a new starter. If anything, the biggest challenge was the coaching staff, who were all ex-professional players and experts in their own domain (batting, bowling, fielding, wicket-keeping). Due to the nature of the environment, and my involvement in it, it was crucial that I got buy-in from the coaches. This was important as I was only employed for a number of days a year with the ECB, so I was never around all of the time. It was a challenge going into an established environment where all of the other coaches and support staff saw each other regularly. While we had reasonably regular planning meetings for our work on the programme, these were often monthly outside of the winter programme. All of the other staff were full-time employees of the ECB and were all permanently based in the same building at the National Cricket Performance Centre (NCPC). This meant that I was literally out of the loop a lot of the time. This provided a challenge in developing the close working relationships that were required to be an effective practitioner. This meant that any intervention plans would need to be embraced by the coaches, who were with the players through all of the training and competition phases in the programme, if the plans were going to be successful. Across the coaches and support staff, there were individuals who I connected with early on, with others taking longer to lay the foundations for an effective working relationship. I was preceded in this position by another sport psychologist. As such, the majority of the coaches had prior experience working with a sport psychologist. However, at the time, the number of days the consultant had working with the programme was significantly less. This resulted in an approach where the psychologist really worked with the coaches and not the players. With an increase in sport psychology consultant time, the performance director had wanted greater interaction between the players and the sport psychology consultant. This shift was initially difficult for one of the established coaches to accept. There was also another coach who was relatively new into the role who had not really used sport psychology consultants before, which also presented a challenge.

Consulting philosophy

Throughout my initial education as a sport psychologist, I was treated to a constant diet of four main approaches to working as an applied consultant: cognitive, behavioural, humanistic, and psychodynamic. At the same time, I was taught that in sport psychology the most common approach was cognitive-behavioural, and pretty much instructed that this was the way it should be and how I should work. However, the more I have learnt over the years, particularly since working as a practitioner, the more I have found that this really does not tell the whole story. Indeed, the longer I practice, the more I feel that consultancy models of practice are not as well defined as the literature would have us believe. Admittedly, I would agree that the predominant approach in the domain of sport and exercise psychology is still cognitive-behavioural in its ethos, but times are changing. In part, the lack of clarity that exists reflects the unique nature of sport psychologists and the work that they do. In "purer" forms of therapy and counselling, practitioners are defined by their approach rather than the domain. For example, a cognitive-behavioural therapy (CBT) practitioner deals with a range of issues using a CBT approach, whereas in sport we are more defined by our domain (sport) rather than our approach.

I also find it interesting that I was taught about the psychodynamic approach in a way that suggests that it is one mode of practice, but on closer inspection the range of registered therapies under this umbrella is surprising. In the UK there are more than 400 different variations of psychotherapy that are approved for public consumption. So maybe it is less about which therapeutic approach you advocate and more about how you use it.

A single psychological issue such as depression could be "fixed" from a number of different perspectives, each of which might be as impactful as another. This then raises the question: "Is it the specific approach or the ability of the consultant?" In sport we are starting to see a generation of applied practitioners who are not so bogged down in this CBT history, who are willing to employ a wide range of approaches and techniques to elicit the required behavioural, emotional, and cognitive changes. Increasingly, I am seeing more existentialists, psychodynamicists, and positive psychologists in applied practice. There are also consultants who embed Eastern philosophies, meditation, and mindfulness comfortably into their practice.

Also, unlike other domains of psychology, I don't think that these approaches are as exclusive in sport; increasingly, there is evidence that consultants are combining aspects of different approaches to develop their own models of practice. This is similar to the approach adopted in psychotherapy, where practitioners have developed their own versions of existing practices that take into account their own beliefs, strengths, and skills.

In terms of my own practicing philosophy, I would describe myself as a positive, cognitive humanist. Positive in the sense that I firmly believe in the central tenet of positive psychology to focus on optimal human functioning, aiming to discover and promote the factors that allow individuals and groups/teams to thrive (Seligman & Csikszentmihalyi, 2000). Second, I am cognitive because I seek to influence cognitions and beliefs (Beck, 2005). Finally, I am humanist because I fundamentally believe that each person is unique, and the best insight into the problem – and ultimately the solution – is the client (Rogers, 2003).

Building upon this philosophical foundation, my applied work specifically focuses on three main areas: performance awareness, strengths focus, and effective decision-making. These three core areas are built upon a foundation of general mental health. So, my work with clients (initial needs analysis and interventions) all emerge from these core areas and a foundation of robust mental health.

> *Performance awareness* – Clients understand their personality/character and also understand their "secure basics"; they are aware of their own limiters and enhancers, understand their performance abilities, and appreciates their risk-taking tendencies.

Strengths focus – Clients understand their personal strengths (realised and unrealised strengths, learned behaviours, and weaknesses) and sport-specific strengths (batter, bowler, fielder, etc.).

Decision-making – Clients have good perception/anticipation skills, have a clear understanding of personal decision-making processes, and can readjust when the environment changes.

Client initial needs analysis

With all of the players I have worked with on the EPP, I have adopted the same three-step needs analysis process. The first step is to undertake a personality assessment with the players (Myer-Briggs Type Indicator, MBTi; see Myers & Kirby, 1994). The second step focuses on collecting contextual information from relevant parties (coaches and support staff currently working with the players at their club). The third step focuses on a one-to-one discussion with the players. This discussion explores a number of different aspects of the players and their game, including general background, history in the sport, cricket strengths, general strengths, "mental game" abilities (e.g., decision-making, concentration, emotional control, motivation, confidence, and resilience), and other mental health and lifestyle issues (e.g., perfectionism, self-efficacy, stress and anxiety, and coping with touring).

The MBTi tool is used as part of the analysis for two specific reasons: (1) it forms a core component of my practice, and (2) it is already extensively used in professional cricket circles in the UK, and as a result has currency and familiarity within the sport. My preference for using the MBTi instrument stems from its usefulness in developing a deeper understanding of the clients, their preferences, and as a result the most effective methods to employ when communicating and working with them. The MBTi approach was developed by Myers and Briggs (see Myers & Kirby, 1994) and is built upon Jung's theory of psychological types (Jung, 1971). The tool categorises individuals as one of 16 different personality types, which are each composed of four preferences that emerge out of four specific dichotomies (Extraversion-Introversion, Sensing-Intuition, Thinking-Feeling, Judging-Perceiving). The approach suggests that the personality type that you are determines the way you interact with the world around you. The MBTi tool has been in development and refined since the early 1940s. The current version (M) is composed of 93 items that require responses in a forced-choice format. MBTi type has been applied in a wide range of contexts and specifically in developing people's understanding of their decision-making, emotional intelligence, communication, conflict resolution, and stress, amongst other areas.

An individual's MBTi type is determined via a three-step process. The first step involves the individual completing a version of the MBTi questionnaire. This provides a score for the individual on each of the eight preferences. As a result, the questionnaire suggests a type for the participant and a strength score (how strong the indication is in each of the four contrasting pairs). The second step involves the individual, working with a qualified MBTi practitioner, choosing which type he or she thinks best fits. This works on the notion that the individual is the expert in himself or herself, and as such is best placed to decide. The MBTi practitioner's job is to help the individual to reflect and to also present examples to clarify understanding for what the preferences in each dichotomy mean. At the end of this process, once the individual has articulated his or her preference, the results from the questionnaire are presented. At this point, and the third and final stage, the individual reviews both the questionnaire result and his or her personal preference, and ultimately decides what his or her overall preference is.

The strengths focus of the initial needs analysis is based upon the work of Alex Linley (see Govindji & Linley, 2007) and is focused on both personal strengths (realised and unrealised strengths, learned behaviours, and weaknesses) and cricketing strengths (batter, bowler, fielder, etc.).

The discussions about the mental game abilities of the player were underpinned by a pre-existing approach within the performance domain of cricket that focused on the following six key areas of mental game performance:

Decision-making – Will deliver a big performance when it counts, thinks clearly under pressure, makes correct decisions, and executes the relevant plans.

Concentration – Knows when and how to switch on and off, also knows what is relevant and important, so can focus on the right things.

Emotional control – Able to manage both positive and negative emotions, can leave emotional events behind, and can achieve a good emotional state.

Motivation – Wants to be the best and will do everything required to achieve it, always gives 100% in training, and leaves no stone unturned in the pursuit of excellence.

Confidence – Confident in the ability to perform in any situation and against any opposition. Just knows they will succeed.

Resilience – Takes setbacks in their stride, and it just makes them more determined.

Players and their coaches rated the player on each of these six areas on a scale of 1–10. This served as a starting point for a developmental discussion about each area.

Recurring strategies – two examples

While a wide range of specific issues have emerged in my time working on the EPP, two that I have focused on are the refinement and enhancement of player pre-performance routines (PPRs) and the enhancement of decision-making ability.

Pre-performance routines

In the sport of cricket, preparation to perform has been highlighted as being crucial to performance. The great Australian Batter Justin Langer summed this up, highlighting that "the key to concentration is filling your mind with what you need to do to ensure a successful action, for me to bat there must be nothing but the ball on my mind, this occupies my thoughts before every shot" (2008, p. 40). There is now extensive literature advocating the importance of developing and deploying effective PPRs for discrete skill execution. In looking to develop and enhance the pre-performance used in cricket, the definition offered by Moran (1996) is a very useful starting point. Moran defined PPRs as "a sequence of task-relevant thoughts and actions which an athlete engages in systematically prior to his or her performance of a specific sports skill" (p. 177). This definition of pre-performance routines highlights two very clear and equally important components: task-relevant thoughts and task-relevant actions. Any intervention that seeks to maximise the effectiveness of the developed routines should seek to address both of these two important components.

In working with the players on the EPP, I adopted a five-step approach (Cotterill, 2011) to the development and enhancement of player PPRs. These five steps were: (1) assessing current practice, (2) clarifying behaviour meaning, (3) developing a focus and function for each behavioural component, (4) routine construction and agreement, and (5) practice.

The first step of assessing current practice seeks to determine the existing pre-performance practice for each of the professional players. This was achieved by both observing and videoing the players while in "nets" practice to develop a clear understanding of what they currently do.

The second step that focused on clarifying behaviour meaning involved talking to the players about their existing routines and showing the players exemplar footage of their behavioural routines. This approach was used to develop an understanding of why the players engaged in the relevant pre-performance behaviours and whether they were functional.

The third step focused on developing a focus and function for each behavioural component. This step sought to identify each discrete behavioural component of the routines and to develop an agreed-upon function. This step involved the players executing their existing behaviours in a practice environment, then after each ball was bowled or faced, discussing with the consultant what each of the behaviours meant and what functions the player felt that it served. Players were also encouraged to discuss any existing psychological strategies that they employed in conjunction with the highlighted behaviours.

In order to reinforce these highlighted functions, the players and I then developed a specific mental component to accompany the well-developed behavioural components. This fourth step sought to explore what the players were seeking to achieve in the preparation period (e.g., relaxing, focusing, setting stance, engaging in imagery). Once the meaning of the behaviour was highlighted, a relevant trigger/cue word was negotiated that fitted with the meaning and time period associated with that behaviour.

Once the routines had been developed, the fifth and final step required integrating each routine into regular practice. The first part of this process involved vocalising the thoughts that had been developed to go with the relevant behaviour. This approach sought to fulfil two specific requirements. First, for the players to "learn" the mental components of the routines; and second, to create an association between the behaviour and the cue words. Once this had been practiced, the next step was to remove the think-aloud aspect, recognising that trying to verbalise the thoughts was cognitively more demanding and disruptive.

Decision-making

Cricket is a game where decision-making is of paramount importance. For each discrete passage of play (ball that is bowled), the batter needs to make a decision about the shot that is going to be played, the bowler needs to make a decision about the type of ball that is going to be bowled, the wicket keeper needs to decide where to stand, and the captain needs to make decisions regarding the positions of the fielders. As a result, effective decision-making is a crucial component of performance and one of the key factors that distinguishes expert compared to novice players.

My work over a number of years in professional cricket led to the development of an applied framework of decision-making development in cricket (see Cotterill, 2014). This framework highlighted three specific points of intervention, all of which were used during my work with individual players on the EPP. The first point of intervention relates to the factors that impact on the individual and the context in which the decisions are made, and is referred to as the "conscious cognitive" stage. These factors have the potential to indirectly impact upon the decisions that batters and bowlers make during a game of cricket, including past experience, the context of the game, the tactics the team is employing at that point in the game, the skill level of the individual player, the individual's predispositions to act in a certain way, and the cricketing strengths the player possesses. Interventions at this point seek to focus on developing/maximising the positive impact of the influencing factors (experience, context, tactics, skills level, tendencies/predispositions, strengths).

With 'past experience' highlighted as a key factor influencing decision-making, accumulating greater experience should be a key focus of any development programme. This is both in terms of making decisions but also in terms of executing the required skills. It is essential though that both of these aspects of effective decision-making are practiced in realistic performance environments.

The context relates to the specific characteristics of the situation or the game. Is the game a "must win"? It also relates to the environmental factors, such as the weather and the opposition that the team is facing.

The 'tactics' aspect focuses on developing the player's (and team's) understanding of what is required in different formats of the game. The required approach for a T20 game will be different from that in a 50-over or four-/five-day game. Players need to practice the ability to be able to play in these different "styles" in the differing contexts.

Put simply, players should deploy the skills that are more well learnt, so as a result skill level is important. It is better to have only two different types of shots and to execute them flawlessly than to have the ability to play a number of different shots but without a good success rate. Ecological validity is important, and the environment for skill execution needs to be as realistic as possible.

It is also a truism that players should play their natural game built upon their personal tendencies and predispositions. The existing natural game can be modified a little, but trying to play in an "un-natural" way is not going to be successful. Playing in this way will feel less comfortable, and the decision-making will become less fluent and more laboured (taking longer and as a result decreasing the available movement time). So, players who are naturally cautious should play cautiously.

Playing to existing 'strengths' is a positive tactic. However, this is only really possible if the individual player is aware of what those strengths are. As a result, the player needs to work closely with the coach and possibly sport psychologist to develop a clear understanding of what the existing strengths are and how to most effectively deploy the strengths to maximise performance.

The second point of intervention (perception-action coupling) relates to the point at which the player selects one course of action over another. Cricket players have to develop effective perceptual skills to "pick up" important sensory information in a very short space of time. It is possible for players to train the visual attention system to pick up on specific cues through a process called perceptual attunement. In essence, players need to be exposed to realistic decision-making scenarios but left to develop individual perceptual skills, and not to be guided by what the coach or other players deem to be important. Training should then increase the pattern recognition skills for individual players. Additionally, this approach to decision-making training may help players to develop both the procedural and declarative knowledge required for effective problem solving in situations and scenarios that have not been previously encountered. Perception-based video training is another technique that can be utilised at this stage. While not as good as the real thing (facing the opposition), it does enable players to develop a perceptual awareness of the opposition in terms of their batting/bowling and to begin to develop appropriate responses. Accumulating experience of the visual cues presented by an opponent is the most effective way to get better at predicting their behaviour.

A second approach that I have successfully adopted at this stage is the use of "battle zone" training (Vickery, Dascombe, & Duffield, 2014). Small-sided games have been suggested as a way to develop decision-making, technical ability, and metabolic conditioning. In cricket this can be achieved by setting up challenges between the batter and bowler. These "games" have specific rules regarding what they are trying to achieve. So, the bowler will get a point if the batter misses the ball or plays the ball into the wrong areas. The batter gets a point if the bowler bowls in the wrong area and for all of the "runs" he or she scores. The size of the playing area will determine the number of fielders who are used. So, if the performance game takes place on a full cricket pitch, you use the full complement of fielders. If the performance game takes place in an indoor space, you reduce the number of fielders accordingly to ensure the relevant intensity as required. This deployment of decision-making skills in a pressured environment also helps in the transfer of technical skills from the practice to the performance environment.

The third and final point of intervention (abort and reset) relates to the need to sometimes respond to a rapidly changing performance environment. The "deception" aspect of cricket becomes more important at higher levels. Indeed, at the elite level, batters and bowlers are engaged in a battle to conceal their true intentions until the last minute. For players to effectively develop these skills, they need to engage in practice that reflects these environmental demands. To develop this ability in batters, the bowlers (the opposition) in that particular session need to be given explicit instructions to try to deceive that batter and to seek to vary the deliveries bowled accordingly. Practical sessions seeking to achieve this outcome would focus on techniques for the bowler to conceal the ball (e.g., with the other hand running in), or to seek to vary the pace of the ball at the point of release. This could also be achieved by manipulating the demands on the batter, such as moving the bowling crease closer to the batter, further reducing the available time and focusing the player to identify earlier perceptual cues. The cognitive demands on the players can also be manipulated by varying the goals/targets outlined for the scenario work. To develop this ability in the bowler, the batter in a specific session should be instructed to vary the approach adopted, trying new things, stepping down the pitch, and stepping across the stumps to force the bowler to react at the last minute. The batter may "set up" in a different place from normal, changing the positional relationship between the batter, the bowler, and the wicket. Also, the batter could engage in pre-planned movements prior to the ball being bowled, such as changing his or her grip (such as changing from left-handed to right-handed) or stepping closer to the bowler (down the pitch) as the bowler is running in to bowl. It is also important to remember that while replicating the physical environment is the ideal, much can be achieved if the focus is on, as much as possible, replicating the psychological demands of cricket.

One way in which these aims can be achieved relates to prior knowledge. A scenario can be set up where one group is given a specific brief regarding what is required. So, if this was a group of bowlers, it might be relating to bowling the ball on a specific line at a specific length. Once this information is conveyed to the bowlers, the coach can them tell the batting group what the focus of the session is for the bowlers. This in turn enables the batters to predict and pre-empt the bowler's movements. The knock-on effort for the bowler will be to vary the one factor they can within the constraints of the task – that is, the speed of the delivery. Similarly for the batters, the focus of the session might be looking to score runs in a specific location. Again, with the bowlers knowing this and restricting these options, the batters will need to modify their decision-making and shot selection accordingly.

Recommendations for aspiring practitioners

The world of applied sport psychology practice is still very much about recommendation and reputation. In my 8-plus years working in professional cricket, I have only seen two positions advertised, and those were both with the ECB. The norm is for consultants to be recruited following recommendation. There is though an issue with this approach regarding whether the consultants hired are appropriately qualified. Also, the focus on bringing in consultants rather than employing practitioners is problematic. Through the process of formally employing someone, the professional clubs would need to articulate the job description and what the role requires. When consultants are brought in for a number of days, they are often asked to "do" sport psychology, but there is no real recognition of what that might look like, what it might involve, and crucially what success might look like. As a result, when gaining access, it is crucial that aspiring consultants negotiate real clarity regarding their role and against what performance indicators they will ultimately be assessed.

Recognising that entry is ultimately usually based upon recommendation, it is crucial for aspiring practitioners to actively seek to network. It is one of those things that is often mentioned, but it is true. You need decision-makers and consultants to know who you are and what you do. You also need to be strategic and first think about what you want to do (the sport, level, etc.), and then seek out individuals who operate in those domains or in the relevant geographical area.

In order to work effectively in any domain, you need to gain experience. This doesn't necessarily need to be in the particular sport, but it helps. The first step is to be an expert in psychology. To achieve this, you need to take time to hone your skills and to develop your confidence in your ability to undertake the needs analysis, provide an assessment, and apply relevant interventions. In the first instance, getting experience at a lower level of performance is the pragmatic way to approach this, mainly because you will get the opportunity to do much more. Then, when you get the opportunity to work at a higher level, you are confident in your ability and in the role of an experienced psychologist. Ultimately, this is what the client is looking for.

The second main aspect to working effectively is to know your approach. There has been too much made of the eclectic approach in sport psychology. This idea that you can pick and choose your approach to the situation is flawed. The advantage that a cognitive therapist or psychotherapist has is complete clarity in the way they are going to approach the issue. As a sport psychologist, my professional training left me woefully underprepared in this regard. It took me around 5 years after becoming accredited to really focus my approach. I look back to my early years as a consultant and see much that I would have done differently and ultimately better if I had developed the clarity I have now. Having a clear understanding of your philosophical approach enables you to develop clarity regarding your process. This also gives you confidence because you know "your way" and the way you will go about things with new clients. This ultimately helps you to be much clearer regarding what you are going to do, but also crucially being able to communicate the plan to your clients.

When working for sporting organisations, it is important to understand what they stand for. What are their strategic targets? How are they measuring success? What are they ultimately trying to achieve? Knowing this information can help you to ensure you are also meeting their needs, as well as those of the individual performers you work with. Second, you need to quickly understand, and begin to use, the context-specific language that has developed. You have a relatively short window of opportunity when you first start working in the sport/ context to ask "stupid" questions. My advice here would be to find out about everything you can, then embed this language into your interactions with the clients and organisation. Finally, be an expert in sport psychology. Remember, that is why you are there. Also, remember the qualifications you have been awarded and the experience you have gained. The client wants you to be an expert in psychology. We know that everyone thinks he or she is an expert when it comes to the psychology of sport, but you need to demonstrate in what you do and how you do it that you are "the" expert. Also, be sure to challenge any unrealistic expectations or falsehoods in the environment. When it comes to the psychology of sport and performance, ensure that everyone ultimately sees the environment, the issues, and ultimately, the solutions, from your perspective.

References

Beck, A. T. (2005). The current state of cognitive therapy. *Archives of General Psychiatry, 62*, 953–959.

Cotterill, S. T. (2011). Experiences of developing pre-performance routines with elite cricket players. *Journal of Sport Psychology in Action, 2*, 81–91. doi:10.1080/21520704.2011.584245

Cotterill, S. T. (2014). Developing decision-making for performance: A framework to guide applied practice in cricket. *Journal of Sport Psychology in Action, 5*, 1–14.

Govindji, R., & Linley, P. A. (2007). Strengths use, self-confidence and well-being: Implications for strengths coaching and coaching psychologists. *International Coaching Psychology Review, 2*, 143–153.

Jung, C. G. (1971). *Psychological types*. Princeton, NJ: Princeton University Press. (Original work published 1923)

Langer, J. (2008). *Seeing the sunrise: Crows nest*. NSW: Allen & Unwin.

Moran, A. (1996). *The psychology of concentration in sports performers: A cognitive analysis*. Hove: Psychology Press.

Müller, S., Abernethy, B., & Farrow, D. (2006). How do world-class cricket batsmen anticipate a bowler's intention? *The Quarterly Journal of Experimental Psychology, 59*, 2162–2186.

Myers, K. D., & Kirby, L. D. (1994). *Introduction to type dynamics and development: Exploring the next level of type*. Mountain View, CA: CPP, Inc.

Rogers, C. R. (2003). *Client-centered therapy: Its current practice, implications and theory*. London, UK: Constable & Robinson, Ltd.

Seligman, M. E. P., & Csikszentmihalyi, M. (2000). Positive psychology: An introduction. *American Psychologist, 55*, 5–14.

Thelwell, R. C., Weston, N. J. V., & Greenlees, I. A. (2007). Batting on a sticky wicket: Identifying sources of stress and associated coping responses for professional cricket batsmen. *Psychology of Sport and Exercise, 8*, 219–232.

Vickery, W., Dascombe, B., & Duffield, R. (2014). Physiological movement and technical demands of centre-wicket battlezone, traditional net based training and one-day cricket matches: A comparative study of sub-elite cricket players. *Journal of Sport Sciences, 32*(8), 722–737.

19

WORKING WITHIN PROFESSIONAL BASEBALL

Reflections and recommendations on the practice of sport and performance psychology

Charles A. Maher

I did not become involved in sport and performance psychology in professional sports armed with a strategic plan. Quite simply, I evolved into the area over the course of time, based on opportunities that presented themselves to me and based on my assessment of the needs of athletes, coaches, general managers, and others. I have been a licensed psychologist for a number of years, beginning in 1978. Since 1988, I have practiced sport and performance psychology with many professional sports franchises, not only in Major League Baseball – which is the focus of this chapter – but also with NFL football, NBA basketball, NHL hockey, boxing, and tennis. In addition, I have used sport and performance psychology principles and procedures in working at the collegiate level with football teams, with men's and women's basketball, as well as in the performing arts and business organizations worldwide. My professional practice in sport and performance psychology has grown immensely over the years. I have been very enthused about this practice and where it is headed, both in professional baseball and beyond. Most importantly, I have been able to sustain myself in this wide-ranging kind of practice, year after year, without interruption.

This chapter is centered on my work in professional baseball only. As such, the purpose of the chapter is to (1) describe my background and entry into sport and performance psychology practice in professional baseball; (2) discuss how I developed an understanding of and appreciation for the culture, norms, values, traditions, and expectations which are part and parcel of professional baseball and its operations; (3) consider how I established myself in professional baseball operations; (4) delineate the systems framework which I have used to guide my work with professional baseball players, coaches, support staffs, and executives; (5) provide a few examples of the programs, products, services, and systems that have structured my practice in professional baseball settings; and (6) offer recommendations for early career practitioners who aspire to work in professional baseball.

Relevant professional and personal context

My professional career has been as an educator, psychologist, and administrator; its path has been long, circuitous, challenging, and satisfying. I started out my career as a teacher of special education, physical education, and guidance and counseling in public and private schools, including particular work with behaviorally disordered and emotionally disturbed adolescents. I went on to become a school psychologist, director of special services, and an assistant superintendent of schools in a public school system. During the early years of my career, I also coached basketball and baseball at the high school and college levels. All of these early-on professional experiences provided me with tremendous backgrounds in understanding the needs and concerns of students and staff members and in appreciating the relevance and importance of working "on the line" with real problems and issues. Furthermore, these professional and personal experiences allowed me to learn how to think about, design, implement, and evaluate programs and services to enhance behavior and performance in a range of settings and with diverse target populations.

Following my work in the schools and related agencies, I then progressed to become a tenured faculty member – Full Professor at Rutgers University – being based in the Graduate School of Applied and Professional Psychology. I was a member of the core faculty in that unit and at that institution for 33 years, instructing and supervising doctoral students in school, clinical, and organizational psychology. I also was Chair of the Department of Applied Psychology. During my tenure at Rutgers, I designed and implemented a Concentration in Sport Psychology for our doctoral students and for post-doctoral licensed psychologists who wanted to concentrate part of their doctoral studies and post-doc training in the sport psychology field. The Sport Psychology Concentration was very successful; it was in operation from 2002 until it ceased operations in 2011, when I chose to go to Professor Emeritus status.

I first became involved in sport psychology with professional baseball in 1988, when a pitching coach with the Chicago White Sox asked if I could assist their organization in the area of goal setting and in developing a program that focused on the mental side of the game. Since I had played and coached baseball at both the high school and college levels and since my research work always had been focused on individual, group, and organizational performance, I agreed to work with the White Sox. Thus, from 1988 until 1994, I worked with the players, coaches, and staff of the Chicago White Sox baseball organization. I became progressively involved in the design and implementation of a sport psychology program with that professional baseball organization, which I believe was the first one of its kind in professional baseball. The sport psychology program focused on helping players set attainable goals, educating them about how to develop and improve their mental skills, and providing psychological assessment services to the scouting department.

In 1995, I was recruited by the Cleveland Indians baseball organization to formulate and install a *system* for the delivery of sport psychology services. This service delivery system grew over the years to encompass many programs and services. Moreover, this sport psychology services delivery system focused on the mental and emotional development of players, coaches, and staff members not only as performers but also as people. It also included a psychological assessment component for the provision of assessment services to the scouting and player development departments. In turn, over the years, my role with the Cleveland Indians baseball organization has expanded from being not only a sport and performance psychologist, which I still am, but also to include directing the Indians' department of personal and organizational performance, which encompasses performance services to both baseball operations and business operations.

Currently, in addition to me, we have three highly qualified and skilled performance coaches who provide applied sport psychology and mental skills services to Cleveland Indians players and staff at all levels of the organization, from rookie ball up to and including the major league level. Additionally, I am President of the Professional Baseball Performance Psychology Group, which consists of the individuals who provide mental skills and related services in 23 of the 30 professional baseball organizations.

Understanding and appreciating the baseball culture

Since I had played and coached baseball at the high school and collegiate levels, I had a good understanding of the baseball culture. However, it was not until I began working at the professional level in baseball that I came to understand and appreciate over the course of time the distinct and unique professional baseball culture. Such understanding and appreciation has come about only through being embedded with players, staffs, and teams in their work, year in and year out. It did not come from theories, books, or conferences, although some systemic material has been influential to me in my work (Locke & Latham, 2002; Salmon, Stanton, Gibbons, Jenkins, & Walker, 2012).

I have come to understand and appreciate some very important and specific professional and personal viewpoints about the culture of professional baseball, and especially how it operates. Thus, the following viewpoints are worth noting, especially for practitioners who want to break into professional baseball. In addition, these viewpoints should be taken into serious account for experienced practitioners as well, who also have interests in becoming involved in professional practice in professional baseball:

1   *Professional baseball is a business; make no mistake about that contention.* In this regard, the basic task for ownership is to generate a profit, a return on its investment in players, staff, and facilities. While this may seem cold and crass to some in sport and performance psychology domains, the fact is that baseball as a profession, just like any other profession, must be approached in a business-like manner. Everything in professional baseball is linked to this reality. Without this understanding and an appreciation of blending business with professional practice, it is highly likely that a sport psychology practitioner will not be satisfied with working in professional baseball.

2   *Players and baseball operations staff (e.g., managers, coaches, athletic trainers, front office personnel) are professionals; typically, they have a precise and routinized way that they approach their jobs and an informal way of relating to one another.* They work closely and admire individuals who want to be part of things that are larger than themselves as individuals. For the most part, players and baseball operations staff are mature adults; they are not high school or college students, many of whom are self-centered and naïve to professional tasks and processes. Professional baseball people have failed more often than not and, thus, they want to learn from failure and develop. They have families, commitments, and expectations for success. Their livelihoods depend not only on their success but also on the success of teammates and the organization as a whole.

3   *Professional baseball is very well structured at individual, team, and larger systemic levels.* Professional baseball is organized by a front office (management), a player development system (minor league teams), and a major league club. Professional baseball teams are then supported by medical services and psychology services including sport psychology services. Even though it is a business, professional baseball has a very strong educational and instructional foundation. This foundation exists because in order to succeed, players need

to learn how to play the game physically, mentally, and fundamentally, as well as to learn to listen and to make adjustments to their games (Maher, 2011). Especially at the minor league levels, but also at the major league level, professional baseball staff must be very good educators, instructors, and guidance counselors.

4 *Unlike years gone past, professional baseball now is a year-round commitment on the part of the player.* With a six-month schedule of games just about every day, players and staff need to benefit from learning to balance baseball, which is their profession, with the other important aspects of their lives. Here, being willing to clarify values is an important personal undertaking on the part of the player and staff. In the professional baseball culture, the saying often is heard: baseball is what you do but it is not who you are (Maher, 2011).

5 *Since playing professional baseball can be described as being a "grind", due to its day-to-day activities, having a growth mindset typically is useful for success* (Dweck, 2008). In this regard, most players at the professional level, especially at the major league level, are able to focus on the process of playing the game and taking charge of the process, rather than overly identifying with results and personal outcomes (Maher, 2011).

6 *Preparation and routines are part and parcel of professional baseball.* Without purposeful and customized routines, players and staff would be at risk for leaving too much to chance. Getting ready for a game and having an effective routine between pitches also is an integral part of the professional baseball culture (Weiner, 2009). This is necessary since performing well can be enhanced with systematic approaches to being ready to compete.

7 *The notion of mindfulness – mind in the moment, without judgment – is becoming increasingly a part of the professional baseball cultural landscape.* It is an area where sport and performance psychologists can make a valuable contribution and take a leadership role, if they proceed in a systematic, context-focused, and evidence-based manner (Dimidjian & Segal, 2015; Kabat-Zin, 1990).

Becoming a part of the operational routine of professional baseball

In order to become an integral part of the operations of the professional baseball franchise, I have done and accomplished many things that I have reason to believe have been responsible for sustaining my professional practice and my credibility with players and staff for almost 30 years. In a progressive, step-by-step manner, I want to convey the following thoughts and actions that have helped me to be an integral part of professional baseball:

1 **Being humble**. I recognized, early on, that I needed to be humble in who I was and what I brought to bear in my work in professional baseball. Without doubt, baseball is a game of failure for players and field staff, as well as managers and coaches. In this sense, all of these individuals will fail more than they succeed, over the long course of a season and even during their careers. Most baseball professionals understand this reality and embrace the notion of continuous improvement, and I needed to do the same. Without humility of who you are and what you can contribute, and what can actually be controlled, you will not be perceived as part of the professional baseball family.

2 **Being around**. I had to get to know the range of people with whom I would be working – players, managers, coaches, athletic trainers, strength coaches, and front office

executives, among others. To accomplish this, I had to be around them as much as possible so that I could listen to them, discuss things with them, and get to know them. More specifically, I had to be at off-season workouts, cage work, bullpen sessions, batting practice, clubhouse, games, travel, etc. The things I could discuss with players and staff by being around included how they saw the game, what they believed and considered to be important, who was part of their family, and other things. My philosophical approach and research predilections could wait until I developed rapport and trust, which could only be solidified by being around.

3   **Assessing needs**. Once I was perceived as being around, as someone who was interested in them, trustworthy, and being someone who would listen to them, I then was accepted into the baseball family. Then I could really proceed to the next step and seek to begin to understand what the needs of players and staff were, not only as performers but also as people. I could now conduct needs assessment activities geared to answer the following kinds of questions that would assist me in supporting their mental and emotional development and performance: (a) How can I prepare so that I am ready to perform (as a player or coach), day in and day out? (b) How can I stay engaged in the game, pitch to pitch, and make adjustments? and (c) How can I use feedback about my performance and myself, in order to get better, on and off the baseball field?

4   **Understanding relevant context**. In relation to needs assessment, I had to place the needs of players and staff into a relevant context. In this regard, professional baseball is a multicultural game. Players and staff come from many cultures and ethnicities beyond the United States, including, in particular, Latin America and the Pacific Rim. Relatedly, professional baseball occurs in real time and real space, with diverse and involved constituencies, both on and off the field. The task of making sense of baseball is not an experiment or a clinical trial; the environment is not error variance in the world of professional baseball (Weiner, 2009). Once I was able to understand the relevant context of professional baseball, I then was able to make very specific sense of how to custom design programs and services to various populations of players and staff (Kaufman, 2000).

5   **Recognizing contributions**. Baseball is a game that encompasses the contributions of many professionals, on and off the field. This includes players, coaches, athletic trainers, strength and conditioning staff, scouts, and front office executives, among others. In this regard, it was very important to me to recognize these people, for their contributions, rather than erroneously and egotistically and trying to take credit that performance was of my primary doing, something that I could not prove. This kind of collaborative recognition showed players and staff that I knew the value of their work. In turn, such a professional stance allowed me to be perceived by these people as being a member of the larger "baseball team". My acceptance into the larger sphere of professional baseball operations was enhanced in this way.

6   **Delivering on requests**. In order to assist players, coaches, and others with their performance and professional development, it was crucial for me to deliver on my professional involvement and collaboration with them. To deliver on these requests, I needed to have a professional approach and process that I could rely on and be consistent with its use. This approach and process included the following: (a) clarifying the needs and concerns of the individuals whom I was going to assist; (b) assessing their performance and personal needs, as indicated by my contacts with them; (c) understanding the relevant contexts;

(d) based on needs assessment results and the context, involve them in the design and implementation of a program; and (e) monitor their progress and make adjustments as necessary. This kind of professional and collaborative approach enabled me to structure my work in a practical and useful manner and in a way that was respected by most others in the game. More specifically, the approach helped me to gain credibility with my clients, since what I was doing was out in the open, transparent, and familiar to them in their educational and instructional work with players.

7 **Building positive expectations**. In order to succeed in the world of professional baseball, it was important for me to be confident not only in myself, but also in what I knew and how I could relate to the range of possible clients. In essence, I had to not assume anything but, rather, build positive expectations about myself and my work. To do this, I had to manifest and engage myself with players, staff, and others in the following ways: (a) be prepared – know the needs of my clients; (b) work with them to find methods and procedures that would be effective in their contexts; (c) bring a positive mindset and approach in working with them; (d) be confident that we would be able to implement a plan and program and make adjustments in it no matter what the results; and (e) execute and evaluate.

8 **Being a good listener and learner**. Throughout my work in professional baseball, but especially at the beginning of my career, I recognized quickly the need to listen to my clients about what they needed and to use that information to proceed in my professional approach with them. Relatedly, and most importantly, I wanted to learn everything that I could about the game, its culture, and operations, on and off the baseball diamond. I still am listening and learning about professional baseball, and I am excited about what I am learning and its continued development.

Systems framework for sport and performance psychology in professional baseball

The basic way that has guided my professional practice in sport and performance psychology over the years has been the use of a systems framework, which I created so as to fit into professional baseball (as well as other sports). More specifically, I have developed my systems framework and improved on it over the years based on my review and evaluation of my work with it, along with taking into consideration aspects of general systems theory as well as program planning and evaluation methods (Kaufman, 2000; Maher, 2012; Miller, 1978). The use of a systems framework has been very important to me in my work in professional baseball, especially since this sport addresses many levels of an organization, as well as individuals and groups. In essence, the systems framework which I rely on consists of three separate, yet interrelated levels of service delivery. These are as follows:

1 **Individual level**. This level is about direct service to the individual player and consulting service to an individual coach or other staff member with respect to the mental and emotional development and performance of a player.

2 **Team level**. This level is about service to entire teams and teams within teams (e.g., pitchers, position players) in areas such as communication, interacting productively, and mutual accountability.

3   **Organizational level.** This level is about service to baseball front office executives, with particular respect to development and analysis of policies, programs, and systems that have to do with mental and emotional development, team development, and organizational development.

Following is an overview of how I have been guided in my practice at each of these three levels in professional baseball.

Individual level

At this level of the systems framework, the focus of my work has been in four separate, yet interrelated dimensions, both by me as well as in consultation with an individual coach. The first dimension is that of the player as a *person*. With respect to this dimension, I have focused my work on assisting individual players to learn about themselves, especially in terms of how they understand their values, personality, and vision for baseball success. For instance, with players at all levels of professional baseball, but especially those at the Rookie Ball, A, and AA levels, it is important to help them to clarify their values – that is, the things which provide them with meaning in their life, beyond the game of baseball. Values clarification is helpful to both minor and major league players in learning how to balance the demands of playing baseball (their profession and its day-to-day grind) with the rest of their lives (the meaning of their lives). Players at all levels of professional baseball have reported that learning more about themselves as people has been central to their development as performers.

The second dimension at the individual level of the systems framework is that of the player as a "*coper*". My work at this level has included workshops and one-on-one sessions, aimed at guiding and instructing players about how to cope effectively with people, places, and things that can put them at personal risk. This kind of personal guidance also includes consideration of matters having to do with drugs of abuse and performance-enhancing substances and helping players to establish positive support systems (people, places, things). The process of playing professional baseball occurs in a high-risk environment; players travel excessively and are on the road away from friends and family for a considerable amount of time. No matter what the level of play – minor or major leagues – players are faced with opportunities to use drugs and to engage in other activities that can very quickly derail their careers. Learning how to be a good "coper" serves to enhance their personal development and performance.

The player as a *teammate* is the third dimension of the individual level of the systems framework. My activities at this level have primarily been one-on-one meetings with each player. These sessions are intended to assist the individual players so that they can accept their roles, responsibilities, and relationships as part of a professional baseball team and organization. For example, a pitcher who has been in professional baseball for several years may have been in the role of a starter through college and up to the AAA level of professional play. However, the player development staff now have projected this individual in a relief pitcher role. In this context, the pitcher needs to accept that new role, along with the responsibilities of being in the bullpen during games.

The player as a *performer* is the fourth dimension at the individual level of the systems framework. In terms of this dimension, and primarily through workshops, group meetings, and individual performance sessions, players have been instructed and guided in becoming skilled at the following: (a) how to prepare for game competition, especially through the use of productive routines, such as developing a five-day routine between starts for a starting pitcher; (b) how to compete, pitch to pitch, maintaining a mind in the moment focus and presence, such as when a batter needs to put the ball on play and move the runners during a crucial time period in the later inning with men on base; and (c) how to make sense of their individual game performance results and to make adjustments to how they play the game, such as when their game performance did not go as expected and the player needs to focus on his behaviors and what he can do to improve, rather than such things as statistical outcomes.

Team level

At this level of the systems framework in professional baseball, the focus of my work has been as a consultant to team managers and coaches in the following ways.

In the area of *team input*, my work primarily has been centered on helping the team manager and coaches to understand and make sense of their team, especially during spring training and at the beginning of the season. This kind of team-level assistance has involved gathering information to describe the overall makeup of the team, particularly with respect to the team's relevant demographic characteristics (e.g., number of Latin American and other players on the roster); mental skills levels (e.g., based on our mental skills rating system); fundamental skills (e.g., strong points and limitations of their approach to hitting using coach rating scaled); and years of playing experience at both the minor league and major league levels.

With respect to *team process*, my work has centered around assisting the manager and coaches in becoming specifically informed, via feedback, about how the team is engaged in the process of playing the game by (a) assessing the manner in which players and staff prepare for games (e.g., quality of work in the batting cages and on-field drill work before the game); (b) documenting collective routines of players, including both position players and pitchers, and how consistent those routines have been as the season progresses; and (c) providing feedback to the manager and coaches about the team's cohesion and leadership, along with the degree to which they appear to have been focused on the process of playing the game and not on results and statistics (e.g., using a naturalistic observation protocol).

In terms of the *team outcomes* area, my work has been concerned with assisting the manager and coaches to pinpoint valid and reliable performance data (e.g., number of first pitch strikes delivered; on-base percentage of position players) and to use that data when considering adjustments with players or groups of players, such as in the positioning of infielders on defense.

Organizational level

At this level of the systems framework, my focus has been on assisting baseball front-office executives, such as general managers, player development directors, and scouting directors, in the following ways.

At the organizational level, I have served as a technical and process assessment consultant to the director of scouting. In this capacity, I have helped the director and scouting staff in developing methods, procedures, and databases that have to do with the mental and emotional development of amateur draft prospects. The resulting information then is placed into a draft prospect profile, which depicts the mental and emotional strengths and limitations of each player (draft prospect) who is being considered to be drafted by the organization.

In addition, I have collaborated with the director of player development in designing and implementing systems for individual player development plans for minor league as well as for major league players at all levels of the organization. In this regard, each player development plan includes the following components: (a) skills assessment in the area of hitting, fielding, pitching, and other domains; (b) developmental goals that if attained will help the players be better performers; (c) activities and methods that the players can implement in order to make progress toward and attain their goals; and (d) progress evaluation criteria and timelines.

I have also served as an executive coach to the general manager and other executives with respect to their mental and emotional growth and development. The focus of my work here has been on helping these individuals, given their roles, to learn to be effective at managing time, information, and relationships with their supervisees.

Finally, at the organizational level of the systems framework, I have also been involved in other systems design and program development activities, based on need and organizational context, such as helping the player development director to install continuing education programs and guiding the general manager in identifying appropriate candidates for front-office positions.

Examples of professional practice

Within the context of the systems framework for practice in professional baseball that I have described in the previous section of this chapter, I have been actively involved with many programs and other products during the past 30 years. Here are just a few summarized examples:

At the individual level of service delivery

At this level, a common service has been the assessment of the mental and emotional development of the individual player. The intention of this service is to use a range of methods, including personality questionnaires, mental skills checklists, and behavioral observations. I reviewed the resulting information with player development staff. In addition, feedback is provided to each player by means of an individual meeting. Players and staff at all levels of the organization from rookie ball up and including the major league level have found this to be a valuable service. Another service at this level has been teaching the individual players how they can clarify their values (e.g., what is most important to their lives beyond baseball), as well as to maintain a journal of their experiences (e.g., their game performances and reactions to those experiences) and how these experiences have affected their values. In addition, I have used a consulting approach with team managers and coaches in helping them to identify what are the core mental and emotional reasons why players may be inconsistent in their performance, such as those time periods when a position player is having inconsistent at bats and poor plate discipline. Another example is that of teaching the players how to use deep breathing and centering techniques so they can maintain their composure during challenging game situations, such as for a pitcher when there are two men on base and no outs in the last inning.

At the team level of service delivery

One kind of service at this level is that of developing a team performance profile, divided into pitchers and position players. Based on previous player assessments and rating scales used by me, along with those completed by the team manager and respective coaches, the kind of profile has delineated the mental and emotional strong points (e.g., focus, confidence) of the players in an aggregate form, as well as areas where improvement is needed, such as composure. Another team level service has consisted of holding weekly mental skills meetings with players and their coaches to discuss relevant areas such as self-confidence, maintaining effective levels of emotional intensity, and keeping their minds in the moment during game competition. Yet an additional team level service example is that of providing verbal feedback to managers and coaches about how they interact with and communicate with players during pre-game work and during games, based on my observations from the field and the dugout. A final team level service example is that of conducting coach development seminars during the off season and as part of spring training, where they learn such things as how to manage their emotions, deal with conflict, and fine tune their career path and aspirations.

At the organizational level of service delivery

At the organizational level of service delivery, one basic example is that of designing and implementing leadership retreats for general managers, assistant general managers, and player development directors. As part of these retreats, the agenda typically has dealt with a range of matters having to do with organizational development, such as how and when to provide feedback to team managers and coaches and also how to establish and maintain productive relationships with ownership. Another organizational level service example has been offering coach development seminars and workshops on topics such as professional self-management, dealing with emotions during game competition, and charting a career path. A third example at this level has been that of designing a process for involving player development managers and coaches in the assessment and mapping of the organizational culture of baseball operations through the use of a customized baseball culture survey. A final example at the organizational level has been evaluating the worth and merit of off-season mental and emotional development programs for players using a program evaluation plan specifically constructed for that purpose.

Recommendations for early career professionals

For those practitioners who are at the early stages of their careers in sport and performance psychology and who think that they would like to work in professional baseball, I have generated a range of recommendations in this section. First, before you do anything else, conduct an accurate and honest self-assessment in terms of what are your strong points and limitations. This self-assessment should focus on yourself as a practitioner and then and only then as a person. In so doing, challenge yourself as to why you would like to work in professional baseball, especially if you have a deep interest or passion for the game. Then, based on your self-assessment, formulate for yourself a baseball-related professional development plan. As part of the plan, identify what you need to learn more about and what you need to become more skilled at so that you can present yourself as a viable candidate to work in professional baseball. Next, seek to gain employed professional experience in working as a sport psychologist in team sports, especially baseball if at all possible. This experience may be at the high school or college level and may occur under the supervision of an experienced sport psychologist. Relatedly, once you have gained professional experience working in baseball at the high school and/or college levels, formulate and follow through with a systematic approach to a position search in professional baseball in the following manner: (a) send out a resume to the general manager of a team that you may want to work for, along with a cover letter as to why you would like to work as a mental skills coach in professional baseball. In the cover letter, emphasize the benefits that you can bring to the organization, its players, and staff; (b) develop a "capability portfolio", which would include copies of the programs and services that you have provided to baseball players, coaches, and teams. If you are invited to be interviewed for a position, have that portfolio with you. Furthermore, recognize that baseball professionals, such as coaches and players, are collaborators and like to work together as a team. In this regard, you will need to leave your ego and theories at the door and be willing to be a team player if you would like to work in professional baseball; (c) be willing to put in long hours seven days a week, especially during the season. Being around the clubhouse, training room, and field will be expected of you; and (d) learn to focus your attention and work on the needs of players, staff, and executives and listen to what they have to say that they would like help with and to learn more about. In this regard, be conservative in what you say and do.

References

Dimidjian, S., & Segal, Z. V. (2015). Prospects for a clinical science of mindfulness–based intervention. *American Psychologist, 70*, 593–620.

Dweck, C. S. (2008). *Mindset: The new psychology of success*. New York: Ballantine Books.

Kabat-Zin, J. (1990). *Full catastrophe living: Using the wisdom of your body and mind to face stress, pain, and illness*. New York: Bantam Books.

Kaufman, R. (2000). *Mega planning: Practical tools for organizational success*. Thousand Oaks, CA: Sage.

Locke, E., & Latham, G. (2002). Building a practically useful theory of goal setting and task motivation. *American Psychologist, 57*, 705–717.

Maher, C. A. (2011). *The complete mental game of baseball: Taking charge of the process, on and off the field*. Bloomington, IN: Authorhouse.

Maher, C. A. (2012). *Planning and evaluating human services programs: A Resource guide for practitioners*. Bloomington, IN: Authorhouse.

Miller, G. A. (1978). *Living systems*. New York: Macmillan.

Salmon, P. M., Stanton, N. A., Gibbons, A. C., Jenkins, D. P., & Walker, G. H. (2012). *Human factors methods and sport science: A practical guide*. Boca Raton, FL: CRC Press.

Weiner, B. J. (2009). A theory of organizational readiness for change. *Implementation Science, 4*, 44–67.

Aesthetics and the performing arts

20

FROM THE SPORT WORLD TO THE BIG TOP

Jean Francois Ménard's journey with Cirque du Soleil

Leslee A. Fisher and Jean Francois Ménard

Jean Francois Ménard (JF) has worked with Cirque du Soleil from 2008–2012 as a full-time performance psychology specialist and since 2013 as an independent contractor. In March 2013, he built his own consulting and public speaking business (Kambio Performance, Montreal, Canada; see website in the reference section of this chapter). In November 2014, I (Leslee) had the pleasure of experiencing a 6-hour workshop related to performance psychology consulting and public speaking given by JF Ménard at the University of Tennessee. While describing the nuts-and-bolts of how he works with high-level performers, JF gave UT workshop participants insight into the activities he uses in his practice, the basic principles he works from, the mental skills he deems crucial to performance, his business plan, and two impromptu sessions with participants. In person, he is engaging, connecting, energetic, and challenges his audience to be the best version of themselves possible through the use of storytelling, exercises, metaphors, video clips, and humor (Ménard, 2014b). I then had the opportunity to collaborate with JF on this chapter, in which we explain his background and the experiences which lead him to becoming an engaging and sought-after performance psychology consultant and public speaker.

In this chapter, we begin by highlighting JF's sporting and academic backgrounds and how they relate to performance psychology. In particular, taking a sport psychology class with Dr. Terry Orlick at the University of Ottawa in Canada opened JF's eyes to the possibilities of blending his previous sport and personal skills in performance psychology consultation. Then, we share some strategies he uses to gain a contextual understanding at Cirque du Soleil, explain some challenges he has faced, and mention some key elements that shape his consulting philosophy. Based on JF's experiences, we follow up with recommendations for aspiring practitioners in the field of performance psychology. Finally, we conclude the chapter with a quick overview of JF's performance psychology business. From this point forward, and after a brief introduction of each section, you will hear JF's consulting philosophy presented in his own words and shaped by my (Leslee) intention to pull out the most crucial points.

Sport history and background related to performance consulting

In this section, JF explains how his personal psychology of performance, as well as his previous experiences in sport, have helped shape who he is as a consultant. For example, JF learned a great deal in his youth sport experiences about how his "perfectionist" and negative attitude inhibited him from becoming the best performer that he could be.

High expectations of self and close attention to detail

I was obsessed with sport, both as a fan as well as an athlete, for as long as I can remember. Born in Green Valley, Ontario, Canada – a small rural town with 200 inhabitants – I was a straight-A student-athlete who always worked hard to achieve, both on and off the playing field. I had high expectations of myself and was a huge perfectionist. I also paid close attention to detail, particularly about the sport "superstars" I watched on TV. I memorized the numbers they wore on their jerseys, their stats, their habits, and information about their personal lives. I was always fascinated by what made "the best" the best in their field, and I was definitely attracted to those who had "success" because I wanted to become an expert in some field as well. Even close family and friends were convinced that I was going to excel at something later on in my life because of this attitude.

Competing in a variety of sports

In addition to playing competitive hockey, I competed in softball and squash until my mid-twenties. I was captain of many teams I played for, allowing me to gain crucial sport leadership experience. Also – just for fun – I competed in several other sports, such as volleyball, badminton, golf, and soccer. Competing in a variety of sports turned out to be a blessing in disguise for my consulting practice; I find that I pull from those experiences now to understand the sport "lingo" and the reality that athletes face from many different sports. I also purposefully played both individual and team sports, as well as different positions while playing team sports (e.g., defenseman in hockey, shortstop in softball, forward in soccer, etc.); I believed that they made me grow in different ways, such as learning how to play a role, being a teammate, and taking responsibility. I truly believe that sport is the best education for the workplace later on in life because of learning teamwork, sharpening concentration skills, bouncing back from setbacks, dealing with stress, working towards goals, and understanding organizational skills.

From pessimist to optimist

I now consider myself a very positive and optimistic person. However, I used to have a negative attitude during competition, a fact that most people who meet me find hard to believe. When I was younger, I did not know how to handle defeat. I acted like a "sore loser" and I was very good at finding excuses for my poor performance. However, when I began listening to my mentors (e.g., great coaches, my parents, and influential school teachers), I became a much better and mentally stronger athlete because they educated me about the power of having a positive and constructive mindset. Another important factor for me was noticing the student-athletes around me whom I admired and wanted to emulate. For example, there was one guy who had less talent but more success than I did, and the only difference that

I noticed was his positive attitude. So, I started mimicking his way of being and found success when I did.

By overcoming my negativity – and seeing the results in my performance – I now understand the value and advantage of having a positive and constructive mindset. Having gone through this process personally has allowed me to teach performers this lesson, as well as understand and pinpoint negativity and pessimism in the clients I work with.

Lifelong learner

After my high school experience, I enrolled in the undergraduate Kinesiology Program at the University of Ottawa in Canada. This opportunity gave me a greater understanding of the human body and how it can function optimally. I registered in courses in physiology, nutrition, sport administration, biomechanics, anatomy, sport psychology, and training methods. I believe that having taken these courses gives me a great advantage in understanding what an athlete needs to perform optimally, both physically and mentally. For example, I understand exactly what athletes mean when they talk about what they need to eat, how they need to feel physically, how they need to move better, and how they are dealing with injuries.

In addition, of utmost importance was the sport psychology class I took with Dr. Terry Orlick, a pioneer in sport psychology consultation. Terry and I connected immediately, and Terry told me that I would be a great sport psychology consultant one day *if* I decided to take that route. This relationship developed through Terry's class and his belief in me really opened my eyes to the sport performance domain and made me want to know even more about it. I felt as though I had the heart for helping others, as well as the specific skills of being a good listener and understanding others quickly. Terry's kind words served as a pivotal moment in my career.

So, I continued in the Ottawa Master's degree program in sport psychology. Not only was I honoured to spend time with some of the best sport psychology consultants in the world (e.g., Dr. Terry Orlick and Dr. Penny Werthner), but the program was also intervention-based with a heavy course load and a 400-hour practical and hands-on internship. During the Master's degree internship, I purposefully chose to work with a wide variety of clients in seven different sport contexts and in two different languages, French and English. I worked with children and adults, males and females, and international and local-level athletes. I feel that working with such a diverse population in two different languages and the constant challenges this presented was the best preparation and investment for my future performance consulting career.

I continued in the Ottawa PhD program with Dr. Pierre Trudel, known for his research in sport coaching and sport intervention methods. A research project I undertook focused on helping coaches better understand how they could use both formal and informal learning structures to become more knowledgeable, creative, and competent in their work. More specifically, I wanted to create and validate a new intervention strategy that could be used to help coaches in their development. I argued that this intervention strategy would be unique because it was based on research from both sport psychology and sport pedagogy; I wanted to make coaches better "learners" as opposed to just better "educator/teachers". By virtue of reading the literature and preparing my doctoral dissertation proposal, I hoped that this research project had a huge potential to help coaches become aware of their learning processes. And, I also hoped that this, in turn, would allow coaches to become more knowledgeable, productive, and creative in their respective coaching practice.

Now that I am out of an academic setting, I continue to value the importance of ongoing learning. I push myself to read one self-development book per week and engage in challenging discussions regularly with the best performers and sport psychology consultants in the world. For example, I recently took a trip to Southern California to spend time with performance psychology guru Ken Ravizza, who is arguably one of the best consultants in our field. My personal motto about ongoing learning and personal development is made up of two parts: "Learn from everyone and follow no one" and "If you want to be the best, hang around the best!"

Making and maintaining connections

It is said that the average person knows approximately 300 other people very well. So, when I attend conferences and seminars, I push myself to meet at least five new people a day, and try to find a way to leave a good impression, making sure they remember me in some way. By doing this, I open myself up to a potential of 1,500 new connections for future opportunities (5 new people × 300 of their connections = 1,500)! This strategy has paid great dividends over my career, to this day.

In fact, I highly value regularly attending conferences and meeting people, partly because I am "addicted to learning" and partly because I believe that attending conferences helps performance consultants both make and maintain contacts in the field. For example, in 2007, I attended a coaching conference in Beijing, China and was sitting beside a man named André Fournier. Fournier worked at a high-performance center in Montreal. Fournier was talking to a group of Chinese men sitting near him about Cirque du Soleil coming to China. Even though I was not involved in the conversation, I asked Fournier why he was talking about Cirque du Soleil, and Fournier stated that his friend was a vice president in the company. So, I stayed in contact with Fournier over the following month and "bugged" him about organizing a meeting between himself and a decision-maker like Fournier's friend at Cirque. I was looking to make contacts in one of the best performance companies in the world. It was a long shot; however, I figured I had nothing to lose . . . and everything to gain. I was persistent over those four weeks because I wanted to make sure that this opportunity would materialize. Fournier then gave me an opportunity to do a visit of Cirque headquarters, and, once I had my foot in the door, I asked about whether any performance consultants were working with the acrobats. As it turned out, there was; I got the consultant's contact information who was working there already and stayed in touch with this person about employment opportunities. When an opportunity arose to interview for a performance psychology consulting position, I did and was fortunate enough to be chosen to do all three interviews for the job. Therefore, I left my doctoral program after only one year because Cirque du Soleil offered me a position as a performance psychology consultant.

I believe that this achievement was a direct result of my perseverance. I believe that you just never know what is possible until you go for something. Besides, the worst thing that can happen is getting "no" as an answer or getting shut down, and "no" never killed anyone!

Leaps of faith

I knew very little about Cirque du Soleil (a company defined by some as *the* best entertainment company in the world). In fact, I had never even seen a show. I also had no artistic experience or experience working with people on stage. I was only 25 years old at the time, as "green" as one can be coming straight out of one year of a doctoral program. It was truly because of my persistence and positive attitude that I was selected for the position. At that moment, I realized that credentials and experience are important but do not mean everything; a willingness to leap, learn, and adapt can bring one opportunities that might never have been imagined by oneself or others.

Gaining contextual understanding at Cirque du Soleil

In this section, JF explains how he – as a full-time employee – had to teach himself about the corporate structure and politics of such a large and global business as Cirque du Soleil. He also gathered a tremendous amount of information about the company by watching videos of each of the 21 shows (the number of shows occurring during the beginning of his employment), doing research on circus history and circus performers, and cultivating relationships with Cirque employees.

Observation and just "being there"

Since I did not have any experience whatsoever working with a circus, I believed that it was very important to understand the subculture as quickly as possible. A Cirque du Soleil colleague mentioned that it usually takes about one year to get used to one's working environment, to understand its patterns, values, and politics, its "do's and don'ts." I spent a lot of time observing the artists in the training studios, watching how both the artists as well as the coaches worked. I took a lot of notes and asked a lot of questions based upon these observations. Being in the environment served as the best way for me to gain entry and make myself available for quick discussions with the artists and coaches. In fact, many of my consultation sessions were done in the training studios before, during, and after training sessions. I believe that my regular presence showed performers that I cared; the artists appeared to love it when I observed their training sessions. As a result, the consultation sessions were much more productive.

Understanding the business side of performance

One of the biggest challenges I faced was making the transition from the sporting world to the circus world. It became very clear that sport was not circus and circus was not sport. At the time I was hired, Cirque du Soleil was a 5,000-employee company, and to this day, it is a large, successful business, and an artistic world managed by many former circus performers. Like any big company, it can feel very bureaucratic, with a strong hierarchical structure.

Being "green," at first, I was working hard to figure out how to be part of a working team in a global company where the focus was not on "winning" but on how "the show must go on." I also discovered that I needed to be careful about my communication patterns within the company, as in who I spoke to or what I spoke about. I was not used to corporate "cliques" and focusing on who had power over whom. I came in extremely eager to learn and to make changes. However, I quickly realized that not everyone was open to that; certain employees who had been a part of the company for a long time loved the way things were and worked with strongly engrained habits. That was a valuable lesson for me in terms of approaching performers gently to show them what I had to offer.

Understanding Cirque du Soleil's programming and history

To become even better acquainted with the company, I watched videos of all 21 shows existing at that time. I also watched documentaries about the company and read documents, books, and surfed websites and blogs to understand the history and values of Cirque du Soleil. I understood that investing time at the front end in understanding the company and its shows was a positive investment for my future work with the performers. I also spent a lot of time learning about the history behind different circus acts in general (e.g., clowns, acrobats, high-wire artists, musicians, jugglers, etc.); each component of Cirque has its own learning and training methods in addition to unique histories.

Cultivating relationships

Next, I began to organize one to two meetings/lunch dates a week with former artists, artistic coaches, acrobatic coaches, different directors, administrators, and some of my closest working colleagues to gain some personal information and knowledge about Cirque and the different performance roles. This is because I realized that there was only so much that I could learn on my own. In these meetings, I made a deliberate effort to have an open mind and to adapt to the special sub-context I was facing every day. I also spoke both English and French, which was helpful because the working language with the employees was French, whereas it was English with the artists. In fact, a large proportion of artists are from Russian-speaking countries, such as Russia, Ukraine, Belarus, and Kazakhstan, so I pursued Russian language courses to develop basic communication skills in these languages. I learned how to say "hello," "goodbye," "thank you," and "good morning" in 10 other languages. The artists appreciated this gesture tremendously, especially because it showed that I had paid close attention to the country and town that each came from, other countries in their region, their sporting backgrounds, the way they had been coached, and their level of expertise. I felt that by cultivating these relationships, I could build trust with the artists; this worked, as it led to increased confidence in me and what I had to offer.

Helping with non-sport skills

I quickly realized that my task as a performance psychology consultant was not only about teaching performance and mental skills to performers; it was also about teaching them professional work-related skills. For example, I have helped Cirque employees represent Cirque worldwide, respect colleagues, be on time, understand the job they have to do, and manage their travel schedule. In addition, I have helped the artists develop a strong work ethic, become good work colleagues and autonomous learners, and have a willingness to adapt to changes. From my own experience, I also knew that transferring from a sport environment to a circus environment was challenging for performers due to the major differences between the two performance realms. To that end, I had the artists reflect on which skills were transferrable from sport to circus and which ones needed to be learned and prioritized. These discussions occurred via group brainstorming exercises that I set up, and they were always interesting because the artists came from a variety of different levels of experience and had very diverse sport backgrounds.

Challenges to overcome related to working with Cirque du Soleil

In this section, JF fleshes out the challenges he faced in his initial work with Cirque performers. These included, for example, adjusting to the mental and physical demands related to being the best entertainment company in the world, managing expectations about performance consultants, and cultivating cultural competence.

Adjusting to high mental and physical demands

In addition to underestimating the importance of power dynamics in a global company, I also misjudged the high mental and physical expectations that the company had of its employees. Cirque du Soleil demands a lot from its employees because they want to be the best entertainment company in the world and remain there in the future. This was very intimidating for me in the beginning; I was working with the "best" and the company was expecting nothing but the "best" out of me. Being young and in great physical shape (by working hard at it!), I first believed that I had all the energy I needed to manage challenging projects in this high-pressure situation. However, I quickly found out that my position was extremely demanding. I was working long hours at Cirque du Soleil, thinking too much about taking care of others versus myself, and, as a result, I was coming home at night exhausted. It became extremely important for me to make energy management a priority so that I did not burn myself out. As a result, I made sure to be physically fit so that I could deal with the stress and the high demands of this context. I also used many relaxation techniques, such as yoga and mindful breathing, to cope with stress at work. I truly believe that being in great mental and physical shape is what allowed me to do well in my daily tasks. I also became really good at taking efficient pauses during the workday. For example, at Cirque headquarters, I had a hiding spot I used (e.g., an isolated toilet in the last floor of the building) where no one could find me; it became my regular relaxation/reflection laboratory. No one knew about this place (until now!). I would shut my phone off for 10 minutes and allow myself a short amount of time to relax and recharge.

Managing expectations about consultants

I also quickly realized that performance psychology was not common in the circus world, even though I felt that it was much needed. Gaining respect from employees and getting them to understand what I could offer was not always an easy task. I believe that this occurred for two reasons: (a) sport psychology did not appear to be an option in many performers' countries, either in their sport clubs or in their training facilities – in fact, a good number of performers (e.g., acrobats, clowns, jugglers, and high-wire acrobats) initially viewed me as a clinical psychology professional, which they interpreted to mean that they would only see me if they had severe mental problems; and (b) Cirque was also known for hiring "the best in the world" in terms of artists, coaches, choreographers, directors, makeup artists, costume designers, and dance teachers. I came to understand that this meant the possibility of big egos and many people who thought they already knew everything they needed to know. Finding my own voice in this environment while trying to gain respect was not an easy task. As previously mentioned, I built trust and confidence through focusing on doing great work, having weekly meetings with company employees, seeking information from everyone interacting with the performers, being open to learning from the artists about their required mental and physical skills (e.g., many had been world champions in their respective sports), and working to satisfy both the artists' and the company's needs.

Cultivating cultural competence

Beyond the language barrier, working with performers from different nations was a great challenge. As mentioned previously, I took Russian language courses and learned how to say common phrases in many other languages. I am convinced that learning to speak other languages was one of my greatest investments because the artists appreciated that I took the time to get to know them, their countries, and their language. This, in turn, created trust between us.

Working with interpreters in both individual as well as group work was also a challenge. For example, a one-on-one consultation was not so much a one-on-one session, but a one-on-one-on-one session, meaning that everything that I said went through someone else before it got to the actual performer. That meant that I had to have confidence that the message was translated correctly in both directions. I also had to trust that the interpreters kept confidential what was being said. In addition, doing group work was just as complicated. For example, if I had a group of 20 artists who spoke four different languages, that meant there were interpreters for four different languages translating at the same time. The amount of noise generated in the room because of this was not something that I anticipated. I also had to learn how to speak more slowly to give the interpreters time to translate. This took a lot of getting used to in the beginning.

Becoming an exemplar "employee"

My position with Cirque was also my first "real" job. That meant that my identity went very quickly from "student" to "employee"; this transition entailed many adaptations. For example, I had to relocate to a new city – from Ottawa to Montreal – where I did not know many people. I also began working from 8:30 a.m. until 5 p.m. every day, filling out a timesheet, writing reports for my bosses, and having regular weekly meetings with different work teams. It was a challenge to get used to this new routine. However, to prove that I was a valuable employee, I became deliberately more polite and respectful, showing others that I had a great willingness to learn and adapt, and made sure that I kept an open mind. I also paid close attention to those company colleagues who were "successful" and their personality traits (as a direct result from my previous pre-college experience watching "successful" athletes), learned how to best communicate with each person I interacted with, and attempted to gain the respect of my colleagues. I organized many social events and other team-building outings; this was also a direct outgrowth of what I learned during my hockey team captain experience – that social outings and team-building stimulated team chemistry.

Practicing what I preached

Another way I coped with all the challenges that I faced was through practicing what I preached, especially in terms of my own positive self-talk. For example, I continuously reminded myself that I was good with handling challenges and that I actually felt very comfortable reaching out and asking colleagues for help when I did not have all the answers. I also envisioned setbacks and mistakes as ways to learn and grow instead of seeing them as my having a lack of understanding. I also regularly reflected on my excellent sport psychology training and mentorship during graduate studies at the University of Ottawa. I focused on how I could do great work at Cirque because they hired me, and that must have meant that I had both current and potential consulting skill. In addition, each time I walked into the Cirque headquarters building, I would tell myself, "I am extremely privileged to work here." I would do this because I noticed that many of my colleagues often forgot how fortunate they were to work for the best entertainment company in the world; I did not want to fall into that trap. Something else I would say to myself while sitting at my desk was, "There are a bunch of sport psych consultants who would love to have their butts in this chair right now!"

Consulting philosophy

In this section, JF describes what goes into his consulting philosophy. He believes, for example, that developing close relationships is the number-one priority when working with performers from any performance domain.

Developing close relationships

First and foremost, it was always a priority for me to develop and maintain a close relationship with the artists and performers I worked with. Many of them came from continents far away from Canada, so they were away from home, family, and friends. Without crossing professional boundaries, I believe that it is important to serve as someone who cares about performers and wants to help them become the best that they can possibly be. I try to do this by focusing on their passion, staying true to themselves, respecting their values, and making sure that they are happy throughout the training process.

Another strong value of mine relates to being in the field often with performers, meaning that at Cirque, I was constantly in the training and acting studios. I also believed that I was there to do what was best for the artists and not necessarily the company; while I respected the company's rules and regulations, I tried to treat the artists as people/individuals and not as employees.

Doing both individual and group work

During a typical week, I conducted both individual and group sessions. At Cirque du Soleil, the individual needs were different from artist to artist, so it was crucial to meet with each one regularly to make sure that s/he was on the right track. In addition, only a limited amount of time during the artists' busy schedules was devoted to performance psychology; therefore, I had to make sure that I used it wisely. Group work was very beneficial in terms of artists getting to know each other, developing chemistry, and creating bonds. In fact, group sessions were the only times during the week where artists could be together as a group with their own interpreters. This became a very important moment for them during the week: it was the only time that they could talk with other performers directly in their own languages. These group discussions were, in fact, critical to their development as performers. I had a lot of fun facilitating these discussions, trying to get the very best out of every artist on the team. These "bonding times" also served as a great investment for future working relationships between artists.

Multidisciplinarity

My working philosophy also includes a multidisciplinary approach. In the case of Cirque, this meant that myself and other professionals, such as the physiotherapists, nutritionist, other coaches, and administrators, worked as a team and in the same direction. This ensured that every artist got what s/he needed in order to perform well. I also made it a priority to keep this professional "team" informed through quick team emails, desk discussions, talks with coaches in training studios, etc. I felt that it was my responsibility to make sure that every other team member had the "current" update on every artist. There were also monthly evaluations with the artists where the professional team would sit down for 30 minutes and discuss each artist's progression in the training program. At these meetings, three types of feedback were given: (a) acrobatic, (b) artistic, and (c) performance psychology/professional skills. My responsibility was to evaluate the performance psychology and professional skills of each artist; I was also the last person to speak, and that meant that I wrapped up the overall evaluation.

Confidentiality

Respecting confidentiality was extremely important to me, and the artists really appreciated it when I kept confidential what they shared during our private meetings. In fact, it was my ethical responsibility. It was an honour to know that artists felt comfortable sharing personal issues with me, as well as seeing me as someone they could trust. Often, it appeared that I was one of the few people in their lives whom they felt comfortable talking with about their fears, failures, or any other personal issues.

Teaching life skills as well as performance psychology skills

I also realized early on that performance consulting goes far beyond teaching mental skills into the area of the overall development of the performers. In fact, I spent a large portion of my time with Cirque performers helping them understand what it meant to reach their full human potential. This includes developing a personal understanding of commitment, confidence, goal-setting, work integrity, etc. Coming from a variety of cultural backgrounds, these terms meant different things to different performers. Therefore, it is important to find out from individual performers what they believe are the most underdeveloped qualities in themselves.

Becoming "comfortable with the uncomfortable"

I also spent a lot of time explaining and demonstrating how to be "comfortable with the uncomfortable." For example, Cirque artists are expected to learn new roles, perform on demand up to 400 times a year, as well as take calculated risks. This means helping artists step out of their own comfort zones, but not too far away so that they feel overwhelmed or that they cannot learn new skills. In addition, most artists at Cirque came from a sport background; this made the artistic training difficult for many of them. They were, therefore, experts in acrobatic training but beginners in artistic training. Learning how to tolerate being a beginner and regularly making mistakes as well as not "being great" at something are tough feats to handle for skilled performers. I tried to work with each performer to reframe learning and making mistakes as positive versus negative experiences.

Some effective performance psychology strategies

Next, JF discusses how he uses stories, metaphors, and visual illustrations to teach performers about sport psychology concepts without using sport psychology jargon. He also employs activities such as "sensalization" exercises instead of the "traditional" imagery.

Stories

In my work at Cirque – and in my own business – I use a tremendous amount of stories to explain performance strategies and mental skills. This is particularly useful in helping performers to understand a concept – by using illustrations – particularly when working with performers who speak different languages. For example, I often relayed stories from past Cirque artists and performers about how they prepared for shows while touring. Or, I would describe how previous artists adapted when something went wrong on stage. Stories served as a powerful way to help performers see how other successful performers had dealt with diversity. I also shared with the artists personal stories that came from Cirque fan emails from around the world. Many of these emails explained how some of the shows changed people's lives. These personal, heartfelt stories demonstrated how much the artists had the power to positively influence spectators every night on stage, something they would sometimes forget.

Metaphors and analogies

I also like using metaphors and analogies on a regular basis to explain important concepts. For example, I use a picture of a bamboo tree to explain the importance of being flexible and adapting without breaking. I also use a staircase analogy to explain to performers the step/progression process required to go through their training programs. Metaphors are a great way to understand performance psychology concepts without using performance psychology lingo that many performers have never been exposed to. I also use educational videos from YouTube that contain metaphors to reinforce performance psychology concepts. I truly believe that pictures are worth a thousand words.

Team-building

Many training programs at Cirque are short in duration, so it is crucial to get the artists to bond as quickly as possible. For example, one particular icebreaker and team-building activity that I used required toilet paper. I had the artists start by peeling off a long length of toilet paper and hanging onto it. Then, for every square of paper, each artist had to share something about him/herself with the group. Artists would talk about their families, hobbies, past accomplishments, favorite foods, favorite music, etc. This activity was great at getting the group to bond together quickly.

Recuperation sessions

Recuperation sessions were also part of the artists' weekly training schedules. They included breathing techniques and relaxation exercises, such as deep breathing, progressive muscle relaxation, meditation, t'ai chi, and yoga. These served to reinforce the notion that while artists were expected to work very hard during the week, just as important was time to recharge. These techniques were also useful when the artists were on tour and needed to recuperate and recharge between shows.

Sensalization exercises

I use the word "sensalization" to refer to what most practitioners would call imagery or visualization. I believe that it is important to label these types of activities "sensalization" because imagery is supposed to be a *sensation* exercise and not a *visual* exercise. I spent a good amount of time teaching Cirque artists this technique because they did not have much training time together when they were performing 400 shows per year. So, these sensalization techniques compensated for the lack of training and allowed for optimal preparation for each show.

Self-confidence strategies

In my Cirque group work, I also had performers do some brainstorming activities with big white sheets of paper and colorful markers. I had them focus, for example, on defining self-confidence and coming up with strategies to build and maintain self-confidence. I would purposefully pair artists from different countries together to get them used to working with people who did not speak their own language. I also did this because I saw how much valuable information they had to share with each other; they were the best in the world, and both myself and the other performers learned a lot from being exposed to what they shared and had experienced.

A focus on "excellence" versus "perfection"

I speak with almost everyone I work with about the difference between being "perfect" and being "excellent." Most performers are perfectionists, especially those who have competed in judged sports in their lives. In fact, in my work at Cirque, this was a key conversation that I had with performers. Perfectionism was some performers' biggest enemy to their progression; however, once they understood the concept of being "excellent" as opposed to being "perfect" (e.g., working with mistakes, allowing oneself to feel uncomfortable regularly, putting one's focus on the little achievements instead of big ones, etc.), their progress skyrocketed! So, I had performers focus on being *excellent* every night.

Counterintuitively, for Cirque artists, this meant *not* giving everything they had to their performance every night (e.g., 100%). Rather, it meant giving 85% every night while being excellent. Because of performing 400 shows a year, giving 85% 400 times per year was more realistic than giving 100% every night. Strategically, the best method to get them to buy into this belief was to encourage the artists to give 100% of their 85%!

Recommendations for aspiring practitioners in performance psychology

In this section, JF describes additional recommendations for aspiring practitioners, given the multiple lessons he has learned at Cirque and since developing his own private consulting business. These include suggestions such as having a personal connection with each client, a continued love of learning, and becoming culturally competent.

Having a personal connection with each client

While maintaining professional boundaries, I believe that those aspiring to do this type of work should never underestimate the power of having a personal connection with each client. Treating the client as a person first and as a performer second is really important; this is because sport is not who one is, but what one does. I firmly believe in the power of showing openness, being friendly, and having a caring attitude. In fact, I take the first 5–10 minutes of any individual session to ask each client how s/he is doing; this sets the tone for the remainder of the session and also the developing professional relationship. In this way, I demonstrate that performers are people who just want to be treated normally. I also never use the word "my" client because I feel that I do not "own" people.

Immediately focus on the positive

At the beginning of each session, I ask clients to rate themselves on a scale from 1 to 100 in regards to their current state. Their self-evaluations serve as a good ice-breaker for the session. For example, if a client answers "85," I will ask, "Tell me more about this 85%." In this way, I can pick up on whether the client is using a pessimistic or optimistic style, and then teach him/her to focus on the positive only. This strategy is also very practical; I can learn immediately what current state the client is in.

Demonstrate that you want to learn

I believe that it is critical to be a lifelong learner. This entails networking with other professionals and asking them performance-related questions, even if they appear "dumb" or out of touch. This also involves reading self-development books, attending conferences and seminars, watching TED talks, surfing websites and blogs, and watching inspirational videos as a way to learn. I believe that there is no excuse for *not* educating oneself.

Demonstrate that you "know your stuff"

Since my work at Cirque and in my own practice involves working with some of the best athletes and performers in the world, I have to be the best performance psychology consultant that I can be, or else I will not survive in the elite performance world. This demands a lot of effort and work on my part to be knowledgeable and creative (e.g., see above under learning). And, I work very hard to demonstrate and offer this knowledge and creativity to clients regarding my take on performance skills and strategies.

Learn about the cultural context as quickly as possible

Working with Cirque du Soleil, I realized that it was extremely important to learn the basics and essentials of the subcultural context one is working in as quickly as possible. However, it is also important not to learn everything. By this, I mean that sometimes knowing too much about the politics of the sport or about the subcontext you are working in can work against you in terms of forming potential biases (e.g., by listening to gossip from other coaches or performers) instead of listening to clients directly.

Get involved with the other professionals working around the athlete as much as you can

It is important to connect with other professionals who will be spending time with the performers you are working with. Working as a team using a multidisciplinary approach is more powerful than trying to work by yourself. In addition, I often ask other professionals, such as coaches, strength and conditioning practitioners, and nutritionists, about their perceptions of performance psychology. In this way, I can point out many commonalities to performance psychology that these professionals are using, even though they may not call what they are doing "performance psychology" (e.g., strength and conditioning coaches telling athletes to focus on their breathing to control a movement; technical coaches telling athletes to use a few key words to remember the technical skill during performance). Building relationships with other professionals that performers are working with, as well as dispelling myths about performance psychology, should be part of one's job as a consultant.

Don't prepare too much for individual sessions and group workshops

I have a 50/50 rule in terms of preparing for my sessions – I prepare 50% and then leave the other 50% for adaptation. A well-respected Cirque clown taught me this – that improvisation is what distinguishes great entertainers from mediocre ones. Since you never know what the people in front of you want – and you must be *present* and *listen* carefully to pick up on that – being adaptable through being present and listening is a powerful tool. I believe that consulting is not about YOU (the performance psychology consultant) – it is all about the client. The same goes for my group seminars; if my presentation plan was 100% set in stone, then the content would be based on what I – the consultant – think is important, not on what the clients in front of me necessarily want. As it turns out, this type of improvisation is usually what the clients I work with say they love the best about our time together as well.

The 4 Hs

I swear by the 4 Hs to ensure optimal functioning:

> *Healthy* – there is no way you can be at your best if you are not in tip-top physical and mental shape.
> *Humble* – you never become successful on your own. Also, success is not so much what you accomplish but rather who you really are.

Hungry – you need to constantly stimulate your creativity, train your brain, create a habit of wanting more, and become addicted to learning.

Happy – too many people need success to become happy; I believe, however, that you should be happy regularly and then success will arrive on its own.

Give yourself goals/challenges

I challenge myself often, such as putting myself through tough physical trainings to be extremely fit, reading about a book per week to keep learning, and trying new sports and hobbies to push myself outside of my comfort zone. This allows me to stay sharp and also to feel what it is like for my clients as they try to achieve their goals outside of their own comfort zones.

Do not work too much

In our busy world, I discovered that it is really easy to burn yourself out. Therefore, recovery is the key ingredient to ensuring proper energy for one's job, just like it is for the elite performers we work with.

Use preparation rituals for yourself

Before consultation sessions and presentations, I use deep breathing, key words, and activation exercises to get myself ready for my professional responsibilities. I have found that these rituals have a calming and focusing effect on my mental state prior to walking into a consulting session or presentation.

Finding humour and other ways to "click" quickly with clients

Another secret weapon I use is humour. It has an immediate connection effect! I also try to find something in common or a personal connection (e.g., hobby, similar acquaintances, etc.) with each client. These strategies help to get clients hooked early on in our consulting relationship.

Do follow-ups, but not too many

I believe that you need to be strategic about how many times you see and speak to a performer, and that this is related to timing. For example, I often surprise clients with fun messages when I think the time is right. I am also a firm believer in training athletes to become independent; I know I am doing my job correctly when the client only needs support every few weeks or so. If the client is always asking to talk to or see you, then s/he may be dependent on you. I believe in making my clients self-determined.

Focus on doing great work

Last, but not least, I believe that the bottom line is: Do the best work that YOU can do. Focus on the client and make sure to eliminate distractions. Great work is the best marketing that there is.

Epilogue: Kambio Performance

My rich experience at Cirque du Soleil led me to create my own business, Kambio Performance (www.kambioperformance.com) in 2013. Kambio Performance specializes in mental performance services to help athletes, performers, and business leaders reach their full potential. The name "Cambio" (the "C" is replaced by a "K") is a word of Spanish origin that means "change." My fundamental belief is that the willingness to CHANGE is the initial factor that enables a person to EVOLVE towards reaching performance EXCELLENCE. The company offers practical and innovative tools, through consulting and public speaking, which foster positive behavioural changes that lead to optimal performance. Due to my previous experiences and expertise, I am fortunate to have become one of the most active performance psychology consultants in Canada, working with some of the best Canadian Olympic athletes, as well as performers in over 15 different performance fields (e.g., musicians, surgeons, businessmen, nurses, students, coaches, Cirque du Soleil artists, etc.). I also speak regularly to companies and corporations about performance excellence. Over the years, I have also had the honour of speaking to students and professors within some of the best university sport psychology programs in the world. I also have fun serving as a sport psychology commentator for the French Canadian TV sports channel RDS (the French Canadian version of ESPN).

References

Ménard, J. F. (2014a). *Kambio performance*. Retrieved from www.kambioperformance.com
Ménard, J. F. (2014b, November). *Performance psychology workshop*. Knoxville, TN: The Black Cultural Center, The University of Tennessee.

21

PERFORMANCE PSYCHOLOGY IN BALLET AND MODERN DANCE

Sharon A. Chirban and Miriam R. Rowan

Authors' backgrounds

The authors of this chapter arrive at their individual understanding of performance psychology for dancers from two remarkable vantage points. Miriam Rowan is a doctoral candidate of the PGSP-Stanford PsyD Consortium in Palo Alto, California, where she has honed expertise in clinical psychology. Rowan is also firmly rooted in the world of classical ballet with an extensive career as a ballet dancer. She trained at the School of American Ballet in New York City, before continuing professionally for seven years, six with the San Francisco Ballet. Miriam's knowledge of sport and performance psychology has origins in her application of various mental approaches, including mindfulness, throughout her development as a dancer, and her reflections on the seemingly inherent developmental challenges of training. Challenges she observed included bullying in dance schools, poor self-esteem and harsh evaluations of one's body image among classmates, exposure to high levels of public scrutiny, and lack of alternative skill sets for post-dance career stability. She noticed some dancers seemed to benefit from strong-mindedness. Her interest grew into a major career change, and her present research activities include cognitive and mindfulness approaches to treatment of social anxiety and the treatment and prevention of eating disorders in athletes.

Dr. Sharon Chirban, a clinically trained psychologist, re-specialized in sport psychology after being in private practice for five years. Since 2000 she has worked with dancers, performers, and athletes, and in her clinical private practice she specializes in athletes/dancers with eating disorders. Dr. Chirban entered into sport and performance psychology through her involvement in youth sports with her three children. When they were young and entering competitive sports, she began to appreciate the psychological demands of early specialization, the intensity and focus of individual sports (figure skating, ice hockey, and gymnastics), and the concomitant effects of high-commitment child athletes on family life and sport/life balance. At times Dr. Chirban felt "kids needed to be saved from parents" who over-identified with their children's achievements. She came to learn that there was a term in the sport psychology literature – "achievement by proxy" – for this issue. Jellinek, Tofler, Knapp, and Drell (1999) described parental over-engagement in gymnasts. This dynamic is not unique to gymnastic parents, but they described the dynamic that occurs when parents' own sense of self becomes defined by their children's achievements (e.g., stage mom; hockey dad claiming his 4-year-old is NHL-bound). Parents may exploit their children's talent, placing them at some physical and mental risk while being impervious to their children's relationship to their activity. Chirban worked with athletes who prayed for an injury so they could stop their high-level sport when coaches and parents could not hear their loss of interest in their activity. At times parents fall prey to rationalizations: "they made a commitment," "it will strengthen his college application if he stays with one activity for a long time," "it could help pay for college."

In partnership with sports medicine physicians, Chirban also worked with hundreds of injured athletes facing losses related to injuries that took them off their training track or caused early termination from their sport. Chirban frequently sees athletes struggling with injuries that are traumatic (hypothetical email excerpt from an 8-year-old's mother):

> *I am a family physician, with a normally happy, sports stress resistant son who I believe is having PTSD bumps in the road while trying to return to basketball tournament play after a "horrific" (in the words of a witness) arm fracture on Nov 3rd. I was not there but several witnesses said his arm dangled backwards when he got up from the basketball floor by himself. The opposing coach nearly vomited.*

Athletes' injuries can also be frustrating and sometimes demoralizing, such as the case of one athlete's fourth ACL tear in her Division I college career; the career triathlete unable to meet his previous 5-minute running pace following surgery for a torn hip labrum; and the vast and varied athletes struggling with devastating symptoms of Post-Concussive Syndrome.

Dr. Chirban refers to herself as a "comeback specialist." She addresses the unique challenges athletes/performers face as they attempt to return to former levels of play/performance when recovering from an injury or returning after significant time away from their performance domain. The "sport ethic" (Hughes & Coakley, 2001), a dominant set of norms that athletes/performers use to define what it means to be an athlete/performer and to successfully claim the identity as an athlete/performer, often impacts both the cause and treatment of injured players. Research indicates that four norms make up the sport ethic, whereby an athlete (1) makes sacrifices for "the game"; (2) strives for distinction; (3) accepts risks and plays through pain; and (4) accepts no limits in the pursuit of possibilities (Hughes & Coakley, 2001).

"Dancer" in this context is easily interchangeable with "athlete," as such norms are seen among dancers. For example, reflecting on conversations with former dancers, Miriam notes frequent personal sacrifices made by some dancers for their careers and/or dance companies. Indeed, dancers strive for distinction and aspire to the highest ranks. Working through pain is a professional given. Stories about pressure to carry through a performance season with a sprained ankle or bulging disc abound. Self-imposed pressures exist to avoid losing established parts, missing out on future casting, or "falling out of favor" with or "being forgotten" by artistic directors or choreographers. Pressure to return to work quickly may also be the result of external social pressure, as is the oft-asked question, "when will you be back?" A dancer may develop a fear that his company artistic director and/or fellow dancers will inaccurately attribute his slow recovery from injury to poor motivation or malingering. Reasons for a rushed return may also include wanting to reconnect with one's peers, financial pressures/incentives of freelance work, and not wanting to miss out on "once in a lifetime" company tours.

The trials and tribulations facing athletes/performers coming back to sport and perfor-mance are often fueled by the sport ethic. "Over-conformity" to this code occurs when performers experience sport/performance as so exhilarating that they continue participat-ing despite injury; they view such a commitment will increase the likelihood of recruitment and sponsorship; and when exceeding normative boundaries infuses excitement into athletes' lives, facilitating greater commitment and passion to one's sport and increasing bonds between fellow athletes. Performers often problematically approach recovery from their non-injured training mindset. These issues often confound the process of a good comeback. As part of pro-viding comprehensive care to athletes, Dr. Chirban joined the staff of The Division of Sports Medicine at Boston Children's Hospital. The Division has had a long-time relationship with the Boston Ballet, providing on-site medical care to dancers and off-site care for emotional and performance-related support. Dancers have been a regular part of her sports medicine clinic and her private practice.

So what do we know about dancers?

Chirban gave a talk entitled "Rest and Recovery During Intense Performance" at the begin-ning of the *Nutcracker* season at the Boston Ballet in October 2013. Her opening slide was "What do race car drivers and ballerinas have in common?" She then proceeded to show a video clip of a Formula One compilation video with excerpts from racing moments highlight-ing 50 years of Formula One racing. It is easy to point out the differences within these two per-formance domains, but dancers immediately identified with the drivers in many ways. The list of similarities that the company arrived at included: equipment, costume, shoes, mental attitude, intensity, focus, fans, audience pressure, endurance event, reliable support system, and flow. The dancing of the *Nutcracker* is the endurance event of ballet. In Boston, it means being prepared physically and emotionally for 48 performances in three and a half weeks. The stress, strain, and exhilaration of this event depend on the unique qualities of the dancers, their age, as well as their years of experience tackling this marathon. It means being prepared for more than one role while being cast in different roles for different performances often occurring on the same day. Newer professional dancers are often overwhelmed by the task of being stage ready for so many performances in multiple roles, while still "proving themselves" in their company. More experienced dancers have to fight the boredom factor, keeping this ballet fresh – finding new ways to do the same role with the same exuberance and enthusiasm that each audience expects.

Another similarity between drivers and dancers that Chirban pointed out was MET (the metabolic equivalent of task), which is the physiological measure expressing the energy cost of physical activities. MET is defined as the ratio of metabolic rate during a specific physical activity to a reference metabolic rate (Jetté, Sidney, & Blümchen, 1990). Performers across domains have to deal with the psychological cost and the physical cost of the demands of their performance activity. Self-management around rest and recovery for dancers is an acquired skill with lots of experimenting with what works for each individual. To avoid burnout (aka under-recovery), dancers are encouraged to increase recovery activities during intense periods of performance. Recovery activities are very deliberate and mindful ways to ensure that there is adequate rest – physically and emotionally. Defining adequate recovery is highly personal – a trip to the mall may be recovery for one person and a restorative yoga class may be recovery for another. Hanging out with non-dance friends is refreshing for some but exhaustive and draining for others.

The dancers also identified with the intensity and focus of the drivers. There is an immediate recognition of what it feels like to narrow focus, be in a meditative state of preparation, with each tying of a shoelace seemingly done with the greatest of intention and focus. In both worlds, entering a *flow state* (that state of complete absorption with energized focus, full involvement in the activity) is necessary for optimal performance. The "do or die" reality in these domains is in fact different. A dancer may risk a fall, misstep, or a performance failure, but "life" is not on the line in the way that racing at top speed puts the driver at risk. If, however, you have ever met a dancer prone to perfectionism, the situational stress of failing often *is* experienced as if human life is on the line.

As a way of introducing dancer context, we presented similarities between dancers and other athlete/performers. From this point on in this chapter, we are going to focus on the dancer, with attention to ballet and modern dancers, extending the understanding to readers of the unique context of these performers/clients.

The dance world: performance context of dancers

Daily dance classes are at the foundation of modern and classical dance performance. In a survey by Weiss, Shah, and Burchette (2008), modern dancers reported spending an average of 8.3 hours per week in class, with the upward range of 14.3 hours per week. To our knowledge, ballet dancers would likely meet at least a comparable time investment per week. Classes take place in a studio space. *Barres*, handrails used by dancers for balance support during in-class warm-up exercises, commonly line three walls and large mirrors line the front of the room, although for various artistically based purposes, mirrors may infrequently be covered or taken down. Classes for aspiring dancers typically occur in the afternoons and evenings following academic work, although in some performing-arts schools they occur at other times in the day. Classes in this training context are the primary means of training and may include technique, variations/repertory, pointe, or partnering classes. For professional dancers, *company class* most often occurs first thing in the morning and serves the purpose of warming dancers up for a full day of rehearsals and/or performances.

Among professional dancers (modern and ballet), there appears to be various understandings of the purposes of company class, which may include a place to warm up, a venue for casting, and an opportunity to improve one's technique. Company class is best considered to serve some combination of all three of these purposes. Classes, including those in modern and ballet schools and companies, begin with smaller, slower, and more stationary movements and build gradually in physical intensity and scale of movement, often ending with large jumps.

Some modern classes begin in the center of the room or with floor work, whereas ballet classes traditionally begin at the barre. *Combinations* are the strings of movements set to music that make up a class. Combinations are typically choreographed by the presiding instructor and most often taught immediately prior to their execution by dancers taking the class, although in some classes there is set warm-up choreography that need not be explained each class. As later discussed, combinations represent a first opportunity for the development of keen attention and short-term auditory and visual-spatial memory, which is required on an even larger scale in rehearsals when longer and increasingly unique bits of choreography are taught. Although class is not the performance per se, there is a belief among some in the dance world that classes should be approached as performances in and of themselves. This is in part because maintaining the same conditions when practicing is understood to yield the most reliable results in performance. This belief may, however, cause stress for a dancer when the expectation of a "full-out" performance-level execution in rehearsal conflicts with a dancer's physical and/or mental limitations (e.g., natural physical aging, injuries, burnout) or the dancer feels "over rehearsed."

Following classes, rehearsals build to the performance and follow classes in the workday. A rehearsal flow begins with the dancer's task of learning pre-determined steps communicated directly by a member of the artistic staff (teacher, coach, or in the ballet, a *ballet master* or *ballet mistress*), a guest *répéteur*, or veteran dancers, and sometimes with the assistance of past performance videos. Rehearsals for a new piece of choreography may deviate from this path. Rehearsals for new works require the dancer to carefully interpret communications of the choreographer and his/her desired vision and be at ease through a sometimes tedious process of learning, discarding, and revising steps from the first rehearsal through the performance date.

As the performance date approaches, the dancer's task in later rehearsals is that of "cleaning" the steps. This non-exhaustively includes refining musical interpretations, the execution of steps, and spacing of dancers on the stage. Rehearsals draw greatly on a dancer's auditory and visual-spatial short-term and long-term memory, sustained attention, cognitive flexibility, and tolerance for ambiguity. Dancers often find classes and rehearsals inspiring and rewarding, but they also represent a tedious process, which serves the end goal of a well-executed performance.

Performances are the raison d'être for most dancers. Performances also require their own preparation. Dancers have several backstage preparations prior to stepping onto the stage (e.g., costume changes, makeup application, warm-up, preparation of pointe shoes for ballet women). Mental preparations are also an integral part of the performance process. Every dancer must find his/her own way to manage the stress of the unpredictable (e.g., a pointe shoe being too soft, the music starting too soon, a group of dancers being too far downstage, an in-performance slip or injury) and maintain focus and equanimity in front of large audiences. Under this pressure, dancers must also find a way to balance predictably executing the well-rehearsed steps with the essential qualities of spontaneity and emotional expression required to truly capture the audience.

In the midst of this culturally distinct class, rehearsal, and performance regimen, there are rank, status, and gender differences in dancer performance pressures and experiences. For example, dancers in *apprentice* positions, who are typically younger, lower paid, and cast less frequently than established company members, may view company class as an opportunity to be seen and chosen for new roles by artistic staff. These apprentices experience a much greater pressure to perform well in company classes than does a dancer at the top of the company hierarchy. In a similar vein, a male ballet dancer may in some cases have less concern than a female dancer with regards to expendability and losing assigned parts. This gender difference reflects the continued prized status of many male dancers within the dance world due to the infrequency with which boys in the United States are put into dance relative to need. It also reflects the high level of competition among women in a context where there are infinite numbers of aspiring female dancers. Such gender differences may facilitate poorer self-esteem and higher levels of stress among female dancers, and perhaps an equally detrimental lack of motivation for some, yet certainly not all, men. This phenomenon, however, may not similarly apply to modern dancers.

Despite discrepancies between subgroups of dancers, for the sake of this chapter much of the elite modern and classical dancer experience can be described generally. Dance, after all, represents a highly distinct culture that may be conceptualized as currently removed from much of mainstream US culture. For example, among dancers of both genders, an impressive focus on dance at an early age has been anecdotally observed to prevent dancers from participating in typical and necessary developmental experiences (described in great detail in a later section). Many dancers don't enter romantic relationships until their twenties. Among some dancers, there may also be a mistrust of outsiders (non-dancers), due to lack of experience with other populations, leading to isolation. Specialization in this case may paradoxically prevent dancers from gaining exposure that would otherwise inform their work and serve competitive advantage.

The isolation of specialized dancers from mainstream culture may play a role in their reticence to seek mental health care services. In Dr. Chirban's experience, performers frequently have a preference for the rare provider such as herself, who possesses extensive clinical and consulting experiences within the dance context. Dr. Chirban earned her knowledge of the dance population through careful listening to the dancers who were referred to her, access to other professionals well established in the dance medicine community, and exposure to dance through her children as they explored ballet, jazz, and modern dance as expressions of their own. In the sports performance and performance psychology world, credibility as a provider can be gained either way. Performers sometimes have an even more specific preference – the provider with the same background sometimes makes intuitive sense as there is shared language and knowledge that is immediate. John Lam, a principal with the Boston Ballet, spoke at the Boston Children's Hospital 2014 Dance Medicine Conference. He shared his experience of two serious injuries and their impact on his emotional state and his career. For reasons related to insurance, he sought out the help of a sports psychologist well known in the Boston area, not affiliated with the Ballet – with about as much experience as any of the senior people in the performance psychology field. Yet, John talked about the psychologist's limited understanding of his specific injury (Achilles tendon tear) and the context of his job (professional dancer) as a personal frustration when working with this sports psychologist. He felt he had to explain too much to catch the professional up with where he was. Lam was an excellent candidate to work with a psychologist either with a dance background or who knew his world and his injuries intimately. This time-saving knowledge on the part of the clinician is particularly crucial to dancers, who are so often involved in a busy performance season. Similarly, dancers may be involved in intensive physical therapy or catching up on missed choreography, in addition to their typical schedule in the beginning stages of recovery, and the extra time and money involved in furnishing a therapist with subculture-specific details can become more burdensome than beneficial for the dancer. This may even act as a deterrent to seeking treatment.

The desire for a dance-informed clinician is not universal amongst dancers. Some performers prefer a provider who is one step removed but very familiar with the performance context with lots of experience with athlete/performers in the same performance domain. The advantage of having been an athlete or performer in the same domain is that it allows for a high degree of shared knowledge; however, a clinician's high personal familiarity with the subculture presents possible risks with regards to identification, and there may be a need for continued role clarification. It does get reported on occasion that the provider who had been a competitive tennis player or figure skater, when working with an athlete in the same domain, sometimes steps outside of the mental skills box into athletic coaching. Athletes report discomfort with this kind of boundary confusion. The performance psychologist working with a performer outside of his/her domain of expertise has the burden of a careful and sensitive acquisition of knowledge of the client's performance domain, whereas the psychologist with a high-level performance background must stay mindful of the limits of identification with the client.

Performance domain

Mental preparations and processes are integral to the dance performance process. Successful performance is aided by a dancer's ability to regularly uphold one's own quality of art, tolerate unpredictability, maintain equanimity, and balance many contrasting performance art demands.

Although dance may be considered akin to the aesthetic sports of gymnastics, rhythmic gymnastics, and figure skating, the product of dance is much more than body aesthetics, mechanics, physics, and timing. With the exception of dance competitions like the USA International Ballet Competition (USA IBC), dance is not formally judged (e.g., points are not given for number of pirouettes), but high-quality performance is crystal clear to the trained eye. Dancers' performance success hangs on their level of sensitivity, self-awareness, and ability to maintain the quality of their own performance. This involves attending to and reflecting upon one's own adherence to all factors of a strong performance, including body aesthetics, musical timing, athleticism, and connection with the audience, among others. Some dancers are easily able to effectively and productively self-critique, whereas others have difficulty with this task. The necessary process of self-critique is ubiquitous among art forms but is ripe for maladaptive cognitive distortions. Some dancers may experience anxiety or upset when looking at the realities of their own dancing. This may lead some to avoid self-critique altogether and others to appraise their dancing catastrophically or personally. A consequence of maladaptive negative cognitions is decreased performance. Psychologists working with dancers may find cognitive restructuring techniques helpful in uncovering negative patterns of avoidance or defeating self-appraisals, which may hinder performance. Some dancers may view harsh self-critique as essential to good work and may even be initially threatened by a therapist's encouragement of new and more healthy cognitive processes.

Beyond adequate self-evaluation skills, every dancer must develop a set of coping skills for managing the stress of the unpredictable. There are elements of unpredictability in individual performances and in the overall career path due to factors such as the field's competitive and physically intensive nature. Although dancers often rehearse in a controlled environment, surprises are inevitable in the context of live performance. A dancer slips. Pointe shoes come untied. The conductor cues the music too soon. Clinicians working with dancers on performance-related issues may find it useful to focus on developing equanimity through such techniques as a mindfulness practice. Dancers who are coached to practice acceptance of the uncontrollable may become more resilient in the face of unexpected performance mishaps. With experience, many dancers are able to learn important improvisational skills to cushion the consequences of unpredictable events in performance.

Highly experienced dancers are finely placed within a mindset that balances near mechanical execution of well-rehearsed steps with essential qualities of spontaneity and emotional expression required to truly capture the audience. This is essentially the achievement of a flow state (e.g., Nakamura & Csikszentmihalyi, 2001), where emotions and spontaneity are not blocked by routine but synthesized with expertise and technique into a high-level performance. Interestingly, self-consciousness may hinder such a flow state in performance (e.g., Nakamura & Csikszentmihalyi, 2001). Clinicians may assist dancers in understanding when their performance may benefit from a certain "letting go" of self-awareness. Particularly self-conscious dancers may be well assisted by clinician efforts to increase confidence in their intuitive sense.

Dancer characteristics

As is clear from aforementioned discussions, the pressures on a dancer are exceptional. Dancers must achieve and maintain the beauty of a fashion model, charisma and emotional depth of an actor, athletic abilities of an Olympian, as well as extensive musical understanding. For female ballet dancers, there is the added dimension of performance *en pointe*. Given the many ways it behooves a dancer to aspire, dancers develop a highly specific and specialized mind. It is important to acknowledge here that myths abound with regards to an ideal temperament, character, or personality profile of a successful dancer. Some dancers cite humility as a key to success, while others cite entitlement. Yet anecdotally it seems that no one distinct temperament "makes it" over another. A highly emotionally sensitive dancer may be thought by some to have difficulty managing competition, but she may perform unwaveringly well in the context of specific supportive factors (e.g., superior athleticism, high levels of ambition, social savvy, family supports). When subscribed to by teachers and/or artistic staff, however, colloquial beliefs such as this one can dictate which students are groomed for a professional dance career and which ones are not. Clinicians should be advised to carefully attend to and address unchecked beliefs of teachers, coaches, and/or artistic staff that may be projected upon a dancer, coloring his context, and shaping beliefs about himself and his career trajectory. Despite this, clinicians may experience many unique, and often beneficial, mental qualities when working with dancers, non-exhaustively including mental flexibility, fearlessness, grit, resilience, and refined sensitivity to detail and aesthetics.

Mental sharpness, flexibility, and fearlessness are assets in dance. As one of Rowan's dancer colleagues puts it:

> you've got to be willing to put yourself out there and try just about anything . . . resistance to change and being slow to learn are killers . . . choreographers know who is mentally with them, but even more than that are all the ballet masters who know you can dance a different part or with a new partner every night . . . they'll put in a good word for you

Dancers may also experience the demands of being switched back and forth between roles of team player (in the corps de ballet) and individual performer (solo or principal dancer). A dancer who is new to professional life may be required to "do their time" in smaller roles or the corps de ballet. She may develop keen special awareness and an understanding of how to move with others. She may learn to dance in tandem with others and blend in rather than stand out. As she grows in her career, perhaps she will get opportunities for solo roles on top of existing duties. A solo role would require her to flexibly access skills as a stand-out, individual performer. The demands of switching between these two discrepant skill sets may develop exceptional mental abilities, but for some dancers these demands can increase mental stress and injury. New stage opportunities are exciting, but straddling two very different styles of dance and an increased workload adds new pressures. Clinicians may help dancers foster the ability to check in with their level of stress and provide them with interpersonal skills to successfully communicate their boundaries with artistic staff while maintaining emerging opportunities.

Dance requires an internal sensitivity to bodily states and emotions. Keen sensitivity may facilitate a dancer's expression of emotion in performance or attention to pain leading to successful interventions at the early stages of injury. A modern dancer may particularly benefit from high levels of emotional expressiveness. Conversely, anecdotal evidence suggests that in the context of a rigorous schedule and a competitive dance company, this same sensitivity may hasten burnout and perhaps onset of mental illness. Dancers with an emotionally sensitive makeup may benefit from support and validation in a therapeutic context.

Dance education breeds intense discipline and time-urgent goal-directedness in many dancers. This mentality is well illustrated by the following quote by revered ballet choreographer and founding artistic director of the New York City Ballet, George Balanchine: "Why are you holding back? What are you saving for – for another time? There are no other times." Intensity of drive is admirable and mostly desired, but there are side effects of this mentality. Injuries, for example, are inevitable in this line of work, and dancers are sometimes known to hide, dance on, and return prematurely after injuries. At times, dancers may be motivated to conceal and/or dance on an injury due to an upcoming casting opportunity that they do not want to miss. This motivation to hide an injury at the risk of developing chronic physical ailments speaks to the reality of fleeting opportunities for career mobility via soloist and principal casting.

Resilience is an advantageous quality when facing the many inherent obstacles and setbacks of a dance career. A dancer who is able to mentally overcome a disappointing year of poor casting may more likely transition into a better next year than a dancer who is despondent to the point of quitting. Further, dancers who have overcome difficult times build new strengths and perspectives, which will facilitate endurance in the face of future challenges. Clinicians may work to facilitate young dancers' adoption of optimistic explanatory styles in the face of early career disappointments.

Dancers who are able to exercise a healthy detachment from the disappointing career events may do better than those who tend to believe setbacks are a result of their inherent flaws. For example, at times a dancer may interpret artistic choices personally, leading to cognitions such as: "I'm not good enough" or "she [the director] doesn't like me." Dancers possessing such thoughts often struggle with self-doubts that go beyond the realm of dance performance. These thoughts may also lead to self-defeat (aka self-fulfilling prophesies). In retrospect, one retired dancer advises, "It's sooo not personal . . . I always felt like 'I am the product,' so it was so easy to internalize and take criticism personally. As a teacher now, I see kids struggle with x, y, and z (turnout, jumping, turns) and it doesn't change their value or how I view them as a person." Clinicians can help young dancer-clients notice such personalization and learn to consider the many other factors contributing to minor career obstacles.

Dance style and personality

If we ask you to close your eyes and picture a ballerina, a quick and easy image comes to mind. If we say Baryshnikov, the image of a male ballet dancer is easily conjured up in your mind. With your eyes closed, if we asked you to think of one word commonly associated with ballet, what word comes to mind? Perfectionism. It is the ubiquitous trait of ballet dancers, teachers, and artistic directors. A modern dancer is not so hard to visualize either. On television, "Dancing With the Stars" has put a face on many dance forms and made all forms of dance into family-time TV. If you think modern dancer, what word comes to mind? Expressive. Modern dance encourages dancers to use their emotions and moods to design their own steps and routines. It is not unusual for dancers to invent new steps for their routines, instead of following a structured code of technique, as in ballet.

Across dance genres there are differences in personality. Fink and Woschnjak (2011) noted varying ways that different dance forms (including ballet, modern/contemporary, and jazz/musical) tap into dancer creativity. A modern dance career demands the use of improvisational skills that pull for enhanced verbal and figural creativity, as measured by a psychometric test of creativity, compared to ballet dancers. On psychometric tests of psychoticism and openness to new experiences, modern dancers scored higher than ballet dancers, whereas ballet dancers scored higher on tests of conscientiousness.

For female dancers, a continuum of (body and movement) aesthetics from ballet to modern dance arguably ranges from light and airy to powerful and weighted. A similar continuum may exist for men, but at a smaller range, with a general expectation across dance forms that male dancers appear strong. A dancer's aesthetic may change dependent on the nature and style of choreography they dance, as well as artistic directors' preferences. Ballet dancers are frequently asked to dance shoeless and with a lower center of gravity, and among female modern dancers (but not among males) ballet training is most often the gateway into modern dance (Weiss, Shah, & Burchette, 2008).

Despite the crossover between classical ballet and modern dance today, there are lasting differences in dancers who are bred from these traditions. Such aforementioned aesthetic differences shape dancer personalities. Notably, personalities of classical ballet dancers are often shaped by the dance domain's demand for perfection. The quest for flawlessness is at the very core of ballet. In dance, the matrix of perfectionism is both influenced by the demands of the dance aesthetic and the personality style of the dancer characterized by imposing high standards on oneself combined with the tendency to engage in overly and unrealistic critical evaluations of one's achievements (Flett & Hewitt, 2002). Stoeber and Otto (2006) differentiated between healthy and unhealthy, and non-perfectionism. Healthy perfectionism is conceived as individuals with high levels of personal standards and low levels of evaluation concerns. Unhealthy perfectionism is high in both.

Dancer identity

Ask most dancers about themselves, and early in the conversation you will likely hear the phrase, "I am a dancer." This statement reflects the strong connection between an individual who dances and his or her occupation as a dancer. Given the early age at which professional and pre-professional classical ballet dancers embark on the career path and the lack of early exploration of other areas of their identity due to intensive focus on dance training, at times a ballet dancer's identity, with her hyper-focus on the body and its movements, may entirely eclipse the self. As Wainwright, Williams, and Turner (2005) stated, "the vocational calling to dance is so overwhelming that their balletic body is their identity" (p. 49). Further, in light of the subjective nature of dance and the inherent dependence on the preferences of artistic authorities with regards to jobs and casting, dancers may develop aspirations that are externally set by their dance community and authority figures. This may be particularly pronounced for dancers, and in particular women, who have experienced the (all too common) infantilizing communications made by dance instructors and artistic staff. They may be unable to access their sense of self and personal values beyond a dance identity in the development of their goals, and their value as human beings may be contingent on the approval of others.

In fact, van Staden, Myburgh, and Poggenpoel (2009) noted "a tendency of classical dance to stimulate the setting of externalized goals that may lead to self-destructive behaviors such as eating disorders, depression, maladaptive perfectionism, and problems with career transitions" (p. 20). These researchers recommended that psychologists focus their work with dancers on interventions facilitating a "sense of empowerment, self-development, and self-actualization as individuals and as artistic performers" (p. 20). The development of healthy self-esteem may often occur by way of social experiences in adolescence. Dance requires a transcendent something, and such ambiguous measures of evaluation lead to a high level of subjectivity in the evaluation of each dancer. There are advantages to such subjectivity, which at times opens opportunities for and appreciation of idiosyncrasies in performance. At the same time, this subjective nature may present a somewhat unpredictable career path. Even those dancers in the upper echelons sometimes experience a sense of unpredictability.

We have discussed the subjectivity of dancer evaluation and the consequence of dancers attending heavily to (including making self-evaluations based on) implicit and explicit feedback from those wielding the most influence over their careers. Indeed, subjective evaluation may lead to self-esteem contingent upon social approval and efforts to meet externally set standards and expectations (Grossbard, Lee, Neighbors, & Larimer, 2009). The strongest performances are those where the dancer is able to attend to the moment rather than remaining preoccupied with fearing and managing potential evaluation by others. This task requires the dancer to "fully and conditionally accept himself whether or not he behaved intelligently, correctly, or competently and whether or not other people approve, respect or love him" (Ellis, 1977, p. 101). The strength of this contingent self-esteem characteristic of some dancers must be considered in the context of development, and specifically the social learning occurring in the context of professional dance training during the teen years. The environment of their teen years includes hours each day in a dance studio with their classmates and teachers.

The dancer's body

Dancers are at three times the risk of developing an eating disorder than are non-dancers (Arcelus, Witcomb, & Mitchell, 2014), and dancer eating disorders appear to be particularly tied to professional pressures to remain thin (Holderness, Brooks-Gunn, & Warren, 1994). Although eating disorders are known even among laypeople to be prevalent among ballet dancers, modern dancers are not often thought of as possessing disordered eating behaviors. In dance, the aesthetic tradition varies by dance style. In modern and jazz, dancers are on average somewhat underweight but not markedly so. Ballet, however, demands a prepubescent body shape. Dancers strive to maintain a weight around 15% below ideal body weight. For many, this meets one aspect of the criteria for anorexia. In a study done by Burckhardt, Wynn, Krieg, Bagutti, and Faouzi (2011) of 127 female dancers who had started dancing at around 5.8 years of age and were now a mean age of 16.7, only 42.5% of dancers were found to have normal body mass index (BMI), and 15.7% had a severe degree of thinness. On average, menarche was late in this sample, and food intake from all food groups except animal proteins was below the recommendations for a normally active population, where food intake was twice the recommended amount. Bone mineral density (BMD) was low and associated with nutritional factors. Dairy products had a positive correlation and non-dairy proteins had a negative correlation with BMD. There was a positive correlation between BMD and years since menarche.

The culture surrounding female dancers (e.g., rewards for thin appearance, revealing uniforms, low weight facilitating easy lifting by male dance partners) may implicitly and explicitly encourage disordered behaviors. In a study of professional dancers, 83% had a lifetime history of Anorexia Nervosa and Bulimia Nervosa. An eating disorder is a clinical mental disorder defined by the *Diagnostic and Statistical Manual* (DSM-5) and characterized by overvaluation of weight and shape, abnormal eating behaviors, an irrational fear of gaining weight, and false beliefs about eating, weight, and shape. Disordered eating, most common among high-performing dancers, includes various abnormal eating behaviors including restrictive eating, fasting, frequently skipped meals, diet pills, laxatives, diuretics, enemas, overeating, binging, and purging. Clinicians encountering such eating-disordered presentations in dancers may find it useful to address dancers' overvaluation of weight and shape through emphasis on the body as a strong and functional tool to be used in the service of artistic expression rather than as the end goal.

As a final note in this section, dance is considered among the lean aesthetic sports within eating disorder literature, alongside such sports as ice skating and gymnastics. For this reason, we draw your attention to literature on eating disorders among ice skaters and gymnasts as a resource where the limited research on eating disorders in dance leaves off (e.g., Thompson & Sherman, 2011, pp. 38–40).

Distinct developmental trajectory

In order to understand the identity development of a dancer, it is helpful to look closely at a dancer's experience during adolescence. Typical (non-dancer) adolescent years are characterized by several formative transitions and developmental tasks, including puberty, individuation from parents, increased independence, self-reliance, and exploration of romantic relationships, among others. Success in adulthood is often contingent upon the extent to which such developmental tasks are completed. In the context of rigorous dance training en route to a professional career, adolescent dancers may gain experiences beyond their years while missing others. For example, many dancers leave home in their early teens to train at elite dance academies. They gain early maturity and professionalism while on the job market prior to high school graduation. At the same time, dancers' high level of early specialization means many have often chosen a career prior to adequate identity exploration. Career life often takes priority over personal and family matters. Dancers have cited making many personal sacrifices, including missing out on dating in high school and college, high school prom, and family Christmas for *Nutcracker* performances, among others. We recall one ballet dancer recounting, "I felt socially behind for awhile . . . and friendships were hard with 'normal' people who didn't understand dance and dancer friends who were your competition. I felt isolated and to this day I would not consider myself to have a best friend from childhood because of this." Clinicians may encourage dancers to find ways to maintain a sense of social connectedness outside of dance to limit the extent of these personal sacrifices while ensuring continued commitment to their craft.

Marcia (1966), in her theory on adolescent development, describes a pattern of "identity foreclosure," whereby the adolescent makes a commitment to a particular identity without initial identity exploration; this foreclosure may be especially common among some ballet dancers. A dancer may be fearful to deviate from his fixed course. He may not experience adaptive risk taking, trying new things, or developing a keen sense of personal values and interests. This developmental pattern may be particularly constraining for the dancer facing career-/identity-threatening events, such as career transition.

Injuries may shake a dancer's core identity and result in temporary or permanent loss of a job, friendships, and/or familiar dance community. As Wainwright, Williams, and Turner (2005) put it, "Critical injuries threaten to terminate a dancer's career and so endanger their embodied sense of self" (p. 49). Injuries may also lead a dancer into depression (Greben, 1992). Conversely, injuries may present a young adult dancer with opportunities to explore other areas of his or her identity. While on leave, dancers may have time away from their tight-knit dance community. Space may open for the development of new friendships or interests.

Lifecycle of a dancer

Class is where the dancer spends her entire career learning and developing her craft. Most elite dancers start young in an initial *Exploration Phase*. The child is encouraged by parents and teachers to have fun, learn new skills, and form relationships with peers. Once talent and passion are recognized, there is the *Investment Phase*. Early specialization has been part of the history of dance, since it takes many years to train a dancer's body, and focus in the *Investment Phase* is on achieving technical mastery. The number of classes taken increases, and families search for the best "fit" school or studio where long-term systematic talent development may occur.

Following the *Investment Phase*, the *Elite Performance Excellence Phase* is entered into when students are promoted to the pre-professional level. Training takes up many hours per day, and the goal is to turn training and technical skills into personalized performance excellence. An *Excellence Maintenance Phase* follows, whereby a professional dancer focuses on maintaining the excellence he or she has achieved. Even within this phase, dancers continue to compete for leading roles. This developmental trajectory begins early for ballet dancers and slightly later for modern dancers.

In class, the demands on the dancer are physical, emotional, and neurocognitive: "Movement produces (kinesthetic) information which can make a substantial contribution to observational learning of a motor skill; specifically, in learning movement quality" (Gray, Neisser, Shapiro, & Kouns, 1991 p. 134). Attention, short-term working memory, and processing speed are required for remembering combinations in class. For example, I (Chirban) met a pre-professional dancer who needed help with audition anxiety. She was 19 years old and had adequate technique to audition for professional companies within the US, but she "failed" in her auditions and didn't know why. When we deconstructed her specific fears, it became clear that her difficulties with learning combinations within the time frame required to compete in a successful audition was a result of a learning disability. Neuroanatomical limitations made it such that her brain was preventing her from executing what her body could otherwise do. Unlike in academic environments, "special accommodations" for performers with slower processing speed or other cognitive challenges are unheard of, and dancers with mild learning disabilities may fall through the cracks. For this particular dancer, we developed strategies for memorizing and compensating for her relative disability to improve her competence in auditioning. As her competence and mastery of combinations increased, her confidence swelled in the background. With the newly applied skills, she got her first job!

Classes, rehearsals, and auditions all draw on attention, short-term memory, and processing speed. For rehearsals, however, long-term memory is particularly important, as choreography must be stored and recalled both the next day and a month later. With experience, dancers learn ways to encode information using various strategies, including mental visualization, repetition, and writing down steps.

Career transitions

Despite a distinct developmental trajectory and identity, dancers are taught to gracefully transition from step to step. This, however, does not always generalize to life transitions faced upon retirement. Career transition may be particularly trying in light of the early age dancers begin their career and the tight-knit community in which dancers exist. The impacts are often largest for dancers with the longest careers. This subset of dancers have often achieved high positions (i.e., soloist, principal), and having dedicated 25-plus years of their life to the craft, they are now in their mid-30s to 40s. They are highly specialized and lack other marketable skills and confidence needed for success in a career beyond dance (Greben, 1992). This transition is especially trying for dancers who did not earn a comfortable company salary or worked mostly freelance jobs with an irregular flow of income and often no other benefits (Greben, 1992).

Further, dancers are accustomed to a career that provides artistic, personal, social, and spiritual expression. For example, dancers are accustomed to living and working in a small community of people with similar interests. Although dance companies are highly competitive, they are described by some as a family. Upon transition, "a dancer might need to stop expecting a new line of work to match the deep fulfillment of professional dance" (Aguirre, *New York Times*, 2007). Dancers have described retirement as "a death" or "a divorce." Grief work around the loss may be particularly useful in the initial stages of retirement. Clinicians may also explore with clients the many areas dance had previously occupied in their lives and discuss ways in which clients may find their needs fulfilled in other ways. For example, cultivating a new creative hobby, form of exercise, or friend to satisfy certain needs that are no longer met by dance.

Due to the close-knit quality of co-worker relationships within dance companies, we anecdotally find that dancers often carry on romantic relationships with co-workers. This differs from work cultures in other fields, which often prohibit intra-company dating. It is worth noting that those dancers who have non-dancer significant others may brave the transition with increased ease and success compared to those in romantic relationships with other dancers. It may be that dancers with non-dancer romantic partners are afforded vicarious learning experiences via one's non-dancer partner. This advantage may also be related to increased financial stability due to the fact that the non-dancer member of the household is not also undergoing career transition. Further, unlike the romantic partner who is also a dancer, the non-dancer partner is likely not tied to his or her own dancer identity and dance family.

Recommendations for practitioners interested in dance work

So what are the takeaways from our discussion for those consultants who work with dancers or would like to develop this expertise? Note your own biases when working with dancers. Popular media depictions of dancers (e.g., recent movies like *Black Swan* and TV shows like

Dance Moms) are not accurate depictions of clients' experiences. One way to gather accurate representations of dancer experience and dance culture is to watch dance live. Dancers are often incredibly passionate about what they do. As a clinician, it is important to have some respect and understanding for the appeal of the art form prior to working with dancers and be able to demonstrate that appreciation for their work/identity. It may also be helpful to observe a dance class and/or dance performance prior to working with dancers. Dancers will be wary of working with someone who they feel holds negative biases about the art form or is simply uninformed. Whatever you do, do not refer to dance as a "sport"! Although dance is an athletic endeavor, it is foremost a performance art. More palatable language might refer to dancers as "athletes," "artists," and "dancers" and dance as an "art form" or a "performance art."

Dancers are highly skilled nonverbal communicators, but given the nature of their work, their verbal abilities may be less developed. Clinicians may assist dancers in learning verbal communications skills (e.g., assertiveness skills) that may empower them to navigate their career (e.g., articulate interests and career goals to artistic directors). Dancers may depend on and be especially sensitive to feedback from others. Given this, clinicians may feel pulled to provide such in their consulting. Weigh the benefit/risk when providing direction, as dancers tend to be rewarded for their compliance. Consider the biological impacts acting on the dancer's psychological state (eating disorders, long-term stress, overexercise, and injuries). Being familiar with dance language, actual risk factors, and common dance injuries increases the clinician's credibility as a competent provider. Language is often the key element in crossing the performance divide.

Clinicians can keep in mind that dancers may need help when increasing their social support outside of their workplace. Dancers often face challenges when trying to bridge gaps between professional and personal circles. The unique lifestyle and demands around a performance schedule is not always easily understood by school friends, non-ballet work friends, family, and significant others. Clinicians need to be careful not to sensationalize your dancer clients or express over-eagerness about their career and identity as a dancer. If you do so, it may be difficult for dancers to have needed space to express their doubts, complaints, and frustrations with the career.

It can be very helpful to build relationships with other professionals that dancers have relationships with (physical therapists, primary care physicians, sports medicine physicians, etc.). This network can help support the dancer and help coordinate care when injuries, illness, or emotional challenges arise. Collaboration provides the richest platform for supporting and working with dancers. The work a consultant does with dancers will provide richness, depth, and complexity to a consulting practice. Being part of the dancer's world enables identification with the performer and the performance domain. We have been inspired to *pas de deux* (French for "the step of two"), because the work of a consultant is very much a dance step shared by the dancer who walks in the consulting door.

References

Aguirre, A. (2007, October 27). Tentative steps into a life after dance. *New York Times*. Retrieved March 5, 2015 from http://www.nytimes.com/2007/10/21/arts/dance/21agui.html?pagewanted=all

Arcelus, J., Witcomb, G. L., & Mitchell, A. (2014). Prevalence of eating disorders amongst dancers: A systemic review and meta-analysis. *European Eating Disorders Review, 22*(2), 92–101.

Burckhardt, P., Wynn, E., Krieg, M., Bagutti, C., & Faouzi, M. (2011). The effect of nutrition, puberty and dancing on bone density in adolescent ballet dancers. *Journal of Dance Medicine and Science, 15*(2), 51–60.

Fink, A., & Woschnjak, S. (2011). Creativity and personality in professional dancers. *Personality and Individual Differences, 51*(6), 754–758.

Flett, G. L., & Hewitt, P. L. (Eds.). (2002). *Perfectionism and maladjustment: An overview of theoretical, definitional, and treatment issues.* Washington, DC: American Psychological Association.

Gray, J. T., Neisser, U., Shapiro, B. A., & Kouns, S. (1991). Observational learning of ballet sequences: The role of kinematic information. *Ecological Psychology, 3*, 121–134.

Greben, S. E. (1992). Dealing with the stresses of aging in dancers. *Medical Problems of Perform Artists, 7*(4), 127–131.

Grossbard, J. R., Lee, C. M., Neighbors, C., & Larimer, M. E. (2009). Body image concerns and contingent self-esteem in male and female college students. *Sex Roles, 60*(3–4), 198–207.

Holderness, C. C., Brooks-Gunn, J., & Warren, M. P. (1994). Eating disorders and substance use: a dancing vs a nondancing population. *Medicine & Science in Sports & Exercise, 26*, 297–302.

Hughes, R., & Coakley, J., (2001). Positive deviance among athletes: The implications of over-conformity to the sport ethic. In A. Yiannakis & M. J. Melnick (Eds.), *Contemporary issues in sociology of sport* (pp. 361–373). Champaign, IL: Human Kinetics.

Jellinek, M. S., Tofler, I. R., Knapp, P. K., & Drell, M. J. (1999). The "achievement by proxy" spectrum: recognition and clinical response to pressured and high-achieving children and adolescents. *Journal of the American Academy of Child & Adolescent Psychiatry, 38*, 213–216.

Jetté, M., Sidney, K., & Blümchen, G. (1990). Metabolic equivalents (METS) in exercise testing, exercise prescription, and evaluation of functional capacity. *Journal of Clinical Cardiology, 8*, 555–565.

Marcia, J. E. (1966). Development and validation of ego-identity status. *Journal of Personality and Social Psychology, 3*, 551.

Nakamura, J., & Csikszentmihalyi, M. (2001). Catalytic creativity: The case of Linus Pauling. *American Psychologist, 56*, 337–341.

Stoeber, J., & Otto, K. (2006). Positive conceptions of perfectionism: Approaches, evidence, challenges. *Personality and Social Psychology Review, 10*, 295–319.

Thompson, R. A., & Sherman, R. T. (2011). *Eating disorders in sport.* New York: Routledge.

van Staden, A., Myburgh, C. P., & Poggenpoel, M. (2009). A psycho–educational model to enhance the self-development and mental health of classical dancers. *Journal of Dance Medicine & Science, 13*(1), 20–28.

Wainwright, S. P., Williams, C., & Turner, B. S. (2005). Fractured identities: Injury and the balletic body. *Health, 9*(1), 49–66.

Weiss, D. S., Shah, S., & Burchette, R. J. (2008). A profile of the demographics and training characteristics of professional modern dancers. *Journal of Dance Medicine & Science, 12*(2), 41–46.

22

MY JOURNEY INTO SPORTS PSYCHOLOGY

Strategies, challenges, and case studies

Lois Butcher-Poffley

The author's background and how this brought her to the performance context

I did not get into sport psychology in the traditional way. I was not an athlete. I was a dancer, a singer, and a pianist. Born and raised in New York City, I have been involved in dance, music, and theater since I was a child, starting formal dance training at age 5. My teachers were former Radio City Rockettes, Broadway gypsies, and faculty from the Joffrey and the Harkness Schools of Ballet. By the time I was 18, I had appeared in numerous musicals, was taking upwards of 10 dance classes per week, and was a teaching assistant at my local studio. In high school, I discovered my voice, and after getting a few vocal roles and becoming a soloist in my high school chorus, I enrolled in a conservatory. This added more classes to my schedule outside of school and, somehow, in the midst of all this (and much to my voice teacher's displeasure), I managed to spend considerable time performing with a cover band. My performing career continued through college and beyond. I loved what I did. I loved being in the studio as much as being on stage. As a performer, I felt the highs of tremendous accomplishment and the lows of knowing I was nowhere near good enough. There is great vulnerability standing in front of an audience, wearing your heart on your sleeve, hoping people like you. And when a critic or panelist reviews your work, it can shoot you to the moon or cut through your soul. From my perspective, the arts are very personal.

I got involved in sport psychology when I was working as a dance coach for a local gymnastics club. I struggled with getting the girls to transfer their dance skills from the studio to the floor exercise mat and the beam. I was a psychology major with an education minor. I instinctively knew I needed something. I talked with Carole Ogelsby at Temple University and discovered I needed to approach my gymnasts with a different mindset, and sport psychology became my new life. While I now do considerable work with athletes, my world is still very much grounded in music and dance. Most of my athletes are in artistic sports (gymnastics and figure skating predominantly), and I spend considerable time working on artistic issues with them. When I look at my work with performing artists, it has occurred to me that musicians, especially, are my convenience population. I have access because of proximity. Since so many know me, they trust me enough to get into a conversation. Once we get talking, they discover I know how to help, and we end up working together, however briefly.

How the sport context and sub-cultural understanding were gained

It makes sense that sport psychology and its toolbox of techniques would be an important resource for anyone in dance, music, and theater. The performing arts are, in many ways, similar to sports (MacNamara, Holmes, & Collins, 2006). Even before I knew about sport psychology, I always knew dancers and musicians were athletes because I was one. While we cannot make exact comparisons, we can certainly agree that the arts world parallels the athletic world: intense physical training (lessons and coaching), auditions (tryouts), the rehearsal process (practice), and the intensity of the performance itself (game time) require incredible physical stamina, concentration, and coordination. Dance teachers and vocal coaches have similar roles to sport coaches. Like athletes, artists get into early specialization, beginning training as young as 3 to 5 years of age. We get overuse injuries, burnout, and abruptly end careers because of catastrophic injury. And, like many of those athletes who specialized early and decided to change sports later on, many conservatory students drift away from the classical world and land in jazz and pop because of the emphasis on skill, rather than emotion (Kirshnit, 2005; MacNamara, Holmes, & Collins, 2006; Nagel, 2009).

Like sports, you are always being judged in the arts, but in my experience, there is a difference in the way judgment is delivered. In sports you often have objective statistics to inform you of the quality of performance. The arts have no stats. They are subjective. When your teacher says: "Give me *more*," you have no quantifiable measure to go by. Your interpretation and emotions are part of your art. But if one thinks a movement is artistic, beautiful, and enough, another may find it flawed, ugly, and lacking.

You cannot quantify your appearance, but you can be judged on it. Most of my life was spent in dance class, where you are confronted with walls of unforgiving, full-length mirrors. You wear a leotard and tights that fit like a second skin showing every lump, bump, and fold. You are focused on making every movement, every gesture, every bodyline just right. Then, the subjectivity hits you like a slap. I had a teacher stand behind me, grab a fold of skin on my waist, and announce: "You have too much fat . . . right here!" I wanted the floor to open up and swallow me.

Then, there are auditions, which can be brutal. I've been there, and I have been on both sides as performer and panelist. Your turn comes up, they look you over, and you are immediately dismissed. You have not uttered a sound, sung a note, or danced a step. Why? Wrong type. Perhaps you get to do something. The panel still may say nothing. If your performance is critiqued, it is rare to find the panel supportive and helpful, such as offering instructional feedback and giving the performer hope for the future. Some experts feel it is their personal mission to shred the performance, delivering feedback with considerable derision or sarcasm (Bunting, 2007; Nagel, 2009). I have seen many performers reduced to tears. As a dancer, I remember an audition where a choreographer shouted at us: "Cows! You sound like a thundering herd!"; "Land softly! What are you? Elephants?"; "Sounds like *someone* needs to lose some *weight*!"

Auditions are also a must if one wishes to further musical education and get into a conservatory. Conservatories are the gold standard for the performing arts. They are historic, based on European models, and for the most part, they concentrate on purely classical training (Bottstein, 2000; Kingsbury, 1988). The students do not have it easy. The work is hard, intense, and demanding. I was a conservatory student, and I have worked with former conservatory students. In this setting, the emphasis is on the technical rather than the interpretive, and technique rules over emotion to the point where it may appear antithetical to the need for artistry (Bottstein, 2000; Kirshnit, 2005). Teachers and performance coaches may tell you conflicting things. For example, one singer I worked with told me her teacher said all the technique she learned before was wrong, and she needed to "be torn down and re-built." Meanwhile, her vocal coach at the same conservatory told her the exact opposite. It was hard for the singer to decide which instructional messages were worth keeping. Some students' beliefs about their playing/singing are impacted dramatically. Some lose their power over their own performance, as this singer did. Another singer I worked with graduated from a renowned conservatory and felt unable to go on to a solo career. This singer's belief in her talent was diminished, and a gorgeous voice had lost its power. The performer was encouraged to find a new teacher in a new place and start from scratch. In this case, it worked. The new teacher understood the singer's voice. It was my job to help exorcise the negative messages and coaching received before. Over several sessions, we successfully re-framed what had been heard in conservatory. For the grand finale, the singer wrote it all down, put it in a box, and burned it in a fireplace. A new belief in being an artist took root, and now the singer is working with a new teacher and getting plans for a solo career back on track.

Initial challenges to access and trust and how these were overcome

I have always been part of the music environment, speaking that language, and being the performer. Access was never an issue because performing artists are my convenience population. The musicians and singers I work with are either friends of friends, people I know from "being in the business," individuals I meet while at concerts, or they hear about me via word-of-mouth, or the Certified Consultants of the Association for Applied Sport Psychology (CC-AASP) web page (if it was suggested they seek out a sport psychologist). For me, gaining access to this population has not been a challenge. Trust was never at issue either, because I am/was one of them; and it certainly helps that because of my background, I am not influenced by reputations or stereotypes. A lot of what I do is brief and informal because it suits the musician's comfort level and schedule. For example, making a formal appointment rarely fits into a rock musician's day. Many times, appointments are spontaneous because of performance or touring schedules. I will get a text, then rush off to meet the musician at a coffee shop because that's where he/she is.

The consulting philosophy developed for the context

I found that working with rock musicians especially requires a somewhat laid-back approach. As a performer, I understand the lifestyle. I have lived and worked with professional musicians (my daughter, for example, is a working musician, as well as a professional dancer), and this is a population whose schedules can go from completely empty to extraordinarily chaotic in a very short period of time. They work freelance, and their changeable schedules often reflect a shaky personal economy as well, which can generate considerable anxiety.

This is a population under pressure, and making and keeping a performance enhancement appointment, for example, is low on their priority list (Brzezinski, personal communication, November 12, 2014). Between performance anxieties, the last-minute addition or cancellation of a gig, a bad review, or potential money crisis, I spend considerable time deconstructing projected catastrophe(s). I encourage them to be in the moment (a definite mindfulness orientation), while inserting cognitive re-framing, and encouraging them to let go of what they cannot control. We talk about what they are doing, thinking, and feeling when things are going well. Then we look at how we can make going well a constant. In my experience, and working with the artists I have access to, I have found there are vast differences in their training at formal music schools. This is based on the type of musician the school wishes to produce, classical or otherwise (Bunting, 2007). Obviously, there are many different types of musicians in the world from many different schools and backgrounds. For example, artists coming from conservatory training are very structured and conscious of correct technique (Bunting, 2007; Kingsbury, 1988); artists who come from programs that focus on modern styles of music were most likely encouraged to improvise. And artists who gravitate towards certain genres will be more likely to use improvisation, regardless of training.

I cannot say I have one single philosophy or methodology when it comes to this work. I fly by the seat of my pants most of the time, creating interventions to suit what is going on right in that moment. I think the most important thing I do is to make myself available. After that, I do my best to be a good listener, be kind, keep the artists present and focused, and be patient with their egos. I make sure they know that when in session they can say *anything* because it is a no-judgment zone. This is an important consideration, especially when working with someone who is "a big name." It is also important to understand the type of musician. The following cases come from the world of popular music. This means we must keep in mind several distinct differences from classical music. Giddings (2008) summed this up nicely: (1) popular music is more creative because being in a rock band can require any given member to be composer, lyricist, or arranger; (2) popular music depends on the ear and is improvisation based; (3) popular music is memory based; (4) it is versatile; (5) it has an aural tradition; and (6) it is not always written down. The one similarity according to Giddings: rock bands are a form of chamber ensemble.

Examples of effective strategies when working with performers in the context

It should be noted that the individuals described in the following cases were very matter of fact in their problem-solving approaches. These musicians were not candidates for some of the traditional performance enhancement techniques like meditation, progressive relaxation, biofeedback, or diaphragmatic breathing. We also did not have the time, place, or equipment to get into some of them. Both musicians were pragmatic. They recognized a problem. They wanted a solution that would fix it quickly, efficiently, and simply. The case studies to follow use pseudonyms, and details have been masked to protect their identities.

Case 1 – Jam Band Guy

Meeting Jam Band Guy (JBG) was spontaneous, serendipitous (for me), and a matter of convenience (for JBG). I was at an event where I was able to get into a conversation with the members of a (well-known) jam band after they performed. We hit it off, and during conversation it came out that I was a sport psychology/performance enhancement consultant. This set off a barrage of questions about sport psychology and the techniques used to help improve performance. This led to the big question: could I help him?

JBG presented some interesting challenges, and his issue was a tough one. He was a member of a well-known jam band that was originally formed by his college friends. They are frequently on tour and, at the time, had an album on the charts. He had music training, plays keyboards, and sings. As the first one up during the jam, he was feeling stuck, and felt he lacked the imagination and creativity needed to get the jam off to a flying start. We discussed his feelings about "jamming solo"★ and what he could do to get past the performance anxiety it generated. Due to touring, we had only one in-person session and two via the internet.

To understand JBG's challenges, one must understand the unique nature of the jam band genre. The jam band's expertise lies in their ability to improvise ("jam") for lengthy periods of time, often extending one 3- to 5-minute tune to 25-plus minutes. It is about being able to internalize the genre-specific rules while making things up as you go along, and being able to sustain for as long as your solo takes. It is spontaneous, exploratory, and very risky for the musician as it tests creativity, stamina, and musicianship. Improvisation has its roots in jazz. Biasutti and Frezza (2009) described improv as "a multidimensional concept including technical, expressive, and social elements . . . a process characterized by the use of pre-existing musical formulas and patterns (use of repertoire), which combine with other more creative fragments" (p. 240). In my musical life, the most easily recognized jam bands are The Grateful Dead, Little Feat, The Allman Brothers Band, and Jefferson Airplane. More recently, I would add Dave Matthews Band, Phish, Blues Traveler, and the Zac Brown Band to the list. Jam bands are now their own subculture, and they attract a large, devoted, multigenerational audience (Haid, 2008).

The demands of the jam, especially for the keyboard player, are complex. In any rock jam, the keys player goes first (DeCordova, personal communication, December 20, 2014). Essentially, the song is played through once, then each musician takes a turn, performing his/her best licks (those musical phrases stored in memory), picking up cues from the other musicians, or cues from the song itself, working with the chord progressions and the original form of the song (Levitin, 2006). The musician seems to possess a "sixth sense," letting the music dictate where things should go while working within the constraints of the harmony, melody, rhythm, and style of the song.

In the rock world, jamming requires physical technique, a solid understanding of the music, spontaneity, creativity and originality, and stamina since the musicians continue playing backup as each band member takes his/her turn. It is nothing like the recording studio, where multiple takes come together to produce a perfect product. In a jam, Jourdain (1997) says: "musicians work through a hierarchy of ready-made movements. Thousands of patterns of scales and arpeggios and chord progressions are deeply channeled in their nervous systems. These motions constitute a sort of muscular intelligence that is essential to improvisation" (p. 176). JBG plays an electronic keyboard, which takes this channeling to a different level.

★ Jamming Solo – Jam Band Guy was referring to the traditional order of the rock jam: keyboards always go first followed by guitar, then horns (if any), then bass, then drums. Drums are always at the end. Each instrument's segment can last up to 10 minutes (DeCordova, personal communication, December 20, 2014).

JBG uses his muscular intelligence to play the technical side of the music, but he also adds electronic embellishments to enhance the creative, emotive side of the music. That requires additional movement, with split-second decision making for changing or enhancing tonal qualities.

There is little or no instruction on improvisation for musicians, regardless of genre. Coyle (2006) compared it to "playing well with others," not unlike what we were taught as children. Coyle says you have to know how to approach the other musicians in the jam. If you're jamming, you need to play rather than perform. You look and listen for a space to join in, because successful improv/jamming is as much about paying attention to what's going on as it is about playing. It's also critically important to check your ego at the door, relax, and get into the groove. In other words, it's all about the fun.

"Improvisation is often compared to talking or having a conversation. In order to have a coherent interchange, the speakers need to be somewhat fluent in the same language" (American String Teachers Association, 2002, p. 53). Like a conversation, jams often cover a range of emotions. The player may change key from major (happy) to minor (sad) and back again, or increase tempo (happy) or decrease it (sad) to convey what he/she wants to say. Syncopation, variations on melody, volume changes, rhythmic changes, vibrato, consonance/dissonance, and articulation changes (e.g., legato, staccato) all add interest to the improvisation (Biasutti & Frezza, 2009; McPherson, Lopez-Gonzalez, Ranken, & Limb, 2014).

According to Jourdain (1997), we all improvise constantly, and we use words instead of tones. We also follow certain rules. For example, we rarely halt a conversation for a lengthy time to formulate our next sentence, and we often say to ourselves, "why didn't I think to say that?" after a conversation has ended. As Jourdain put it, "Verbal eloquence is hard to come by. Most of us have trouble enough ad-libbing coherent sentences, much less polished paragraphs. Musical eloquence is every bit as challenging" (p. 174).

JBG is a talented, skillful, trained keyboardist, and he describes his issues with jamming as "jam block." He doesn't feel he has the creativity to break out and let loose, so he freezes. He feels lost outside the formal structure of the song, and he is dependent on the structure of the written music (sheet music) during performance (Zimmerman & Boyle, 2002). Typically, he keeps his jams as short as possible, and they are usually much shorter than those of his bandmates. This is not conducive to a successful jam. In a jam, the band members must do three things: act solo, interact as band members, and co-act all at the same time. According to Pargman (2006), to co-act means to "perform individually, but at the same time as others" (p. 154). JBG also mentioned that he "can't get into the zone like the rest of the guys" when jamming. What he didn't realize is that exceptional performance doesn't necessarily require being in the zone (Klickstein, 2009). Every well-rehearsed piece becomes unique in live performance; and every jam, whether it has been specifically inserted into a song or is a spontaneous burst of music in someone's living room, is unique as well. JBG needed to trust what he knew from the technical side. He needed to get away from the crutch of his sheet music. He needed to trust that he was thoroughly prepared because he memorized, practiced, and rehearsed; but he needed to trust his creativity just as much.

Clearly, as a member of a well-known band, there were certain expectations and pressures from the public, the industry, and his bandmates. He set high expectations for himself, too, and this is why I chose to address JBG's issue as a form of performance anxiety. I purposely stayed away from the misnomer of stage fright, because he was not afraid of the stage, and as a performer myself, I understand how the connotations can generate negative feelings and associations. JBG's anxiety was generated by the potential for making mistakes and fear of not being as technically proficient as his bandmates in creating a complex, interesting segment (Nagel, 1993, 2004). He had all the skills necessary to be more assertive on stage, and be successful in the jam, but because of his technical training, he was relying on his sheet music. He needed to make things as automatic as possible, but he also needed to go beyond the song, putting in interpretation and expression with skill to make it meaningful (Brugues, 2011; Nagel, 1993).

After listening to his descriptions of his own jams, I realized he did not much like what he was playing. To me, a successful intervention would get him to like what he played. We knew JBG could follow the form of the jam, and if we could get the piece to mean something on an emotional level, he could create a musical memory. A musical memory would make the jam that much easier to remember (Bruser, 1997). He would be able to pick up on cues, fillers, and licks from his bandmates and use some of his go-to musical patterns for additional flair. We needed to decrease the discrepancy between his expectations and what he was actually doing (Pargman, 2006).

Imagery was not a good option for JBG. Jamming changes every time, so we would not have a consistent, repeatable performance with the same notes, licks, and fillers every time. Instead, we decided to structure the solo. The literature has shown that continued practice of skills generates more precise, automatic performance and increased flexibility in adapting to changes in task demands (Gorrie, 2009; Green, 2003; Lotze, Scheler, Tan, Braun, & Birnbaum, 2003; Pargman, 2006). We also know that practice and preparation are keys to good performance (Brugues, 2011; Green, 2003), but improv cannot be practiced like other forms of music; logically, there have to be ways to get better at it. So I decided to make it a simple shift from following orders (e.g., following sheet music) to making choices about the qualities of the song (Buonviri, 2013). We put the focus on one musical attribute at a time (e.g., rhythm, dynamics, articulation, and tone quality), while the holding the others constant.

While this seems counterintuitive to what a jam is all about, I felt planning the solo would give JBG an idea of what he wanted it to look like. We called it "making a sketch." The sketch would provide a counterattack to his negative thought processes and give him the structure he needed to feel safe. JBG had the basic skills, so he was assigned four tasks: (1) learn to play the piece by ear; (2) sing the melody to himself over and over; (3) listen to previous recordings of the improvised piece to understand the harmonic progressions and frequently used motifs; and (4) play with it. This allowed him to practice in a very personal way. It was something that was very familiar and a large part of his musical training. Practice made him feel more prepared because he was over-learning and over-rehearsing (Brugues, 2011; Schuter-Dyson & Gabriel, 1981). According to Biasutti and Frezza (2009), all of this practice is one way of developing the skills necessary to improvise, and because he is a low risk taker, using what's already in his repertoire would make it easier for him to get more comfortable with improvising. We decided to have JBG copy the behavior of the others in the band as well, because modeling would also be helpful (Pargman, 2006).

The results were interesting. In his e-mails, he told me his jamming improved. He began playing his part of the jam longer, and reviews noted the improvements in his playing. In his second e-mail, he told me he started performing in a side project with another nationally known singer (one of the original jam band members); and while jamming is not required in the side project, he breaks out every so often, which has helped his performance anxiety.

Case 2 – Rock Drummer Guy

I had a very short time to work with this client, as he was off to Europe five days after the initial contact. Rock Drummer Guy (RDG) is older (late 40s), with a successful background as a player in a well-known rock band 25 years ago. That band produced only one album, but it made the charts. They toured nationally and internationally as both an opening act and the main act, and they played some of the biggest music venues in the world. Their music videos were shown on MTV. They were famous. They were high profile; they had celebrity; but that was a long time ago. It was hard to know what to expect, because RDG did not really know what his problem was. During this initial contact, he said he didn't feel quite so successful at present. He described feeling like a "has-been," and expressed feeling "out of it" because his bandmates were more musically educated than he was.

RDG is currently performing with a European band that is very popular outside of the US. The band frequently tours across Europe and has continuous bookings in their home country. Because of their popularity, the band consistently plays big arena shows, and they are making a lot of money. We had five days, and then he was off on a six-week tour of Eastern Europe and Russia. Given the short notice and the need for quick interventions, the first session required rapid information gathering, immediate analysis, diagnosis, and the creativity to come up with something he could do right away as a preliminary intervention. The goals were basic: identify his perception of the problem, find out what his music background actually consisted of, find out what makes him feel "less than," and see if there is a difference in how he feels playing on stage vs. solo practice vs. band practice. We decided to meet in a neutral location (coffee shop), and I made the decision to eliminate the typical time constraint of the 50-minute session. We would see where things went without worrying about time.

I had prior acquaintance with RDG, and he knew I was a music person. I felt the easiest approach was to get into the discussion of what he knew from the academic side (technique, theory, harmony). At his lead, we started with a discussion of his knowledge of sound, acoustics, and sound technology (amps, best bass/treble balance, use of in-ears etc.). This is very detailed and intricate, highly dependent on weather (dampness is not friendly toward sound gear or instruments), size of venue, available set-ups, and equipment quality. There is an entire science of musical acoustics, but RDG did not acquire his knowledge in the classroom. He acquired his knowledge practically, in small clubs, state-of-the-art rehearsal studios, arenas, stadiums, and theaters. His practical education was as valuable as any gained in the classroom, if not more. His experience, combined with his musical instinct, enabled him to fine-tune the band's equipment to mesh almost seamlessly with the existing equipment in any venue. This is an art in itself. It turns out he had far more education than he realized.

I steered the conversation in the direction of his drumming skills and found RDG is a self-taught drummer. He cannot read music, nor can he read percussion notation. He feels inadequate compared to his bandmates, since all of them had years of music lessons. Two of them went to formal music school and studied theory and harmony, and they play more than one instrument. I asked why this is bothering him now, especially after his previous success. He said he feels lost when they are discussing things in "music language," for example, modulation from major to minor keys, harmonics, and time signatures. He wants to learn "music language" so he can "keep up with the discussion." On stage, RDG can certainly keep up as a player. It made sense that his feelings had more to do with what goes on off-stage, on the tour bus, and in the rehearsal studio. He also felt this lack of formal music education limited his contribution in writing and developing new songs and arrangements. Even though he is a notable player, and has had considerable success, he was struggling with self-efficacy. This was not surprising. Poor working conditions (many venues are not terribly clean or well maintained), job instability ("you're only as good as your last gig"), and performance anxiety (see Nagel, 2004) contributed to neuroticism in rock musicians, and also found, but not surprisingly, it might actually be necessary for good performance (Gillespie & Myors, 2000).

In a roundabout way, I asked about his drumming skills and who were his biggest influences. His affect improved as soon as he started talking about his heroes. He started to open up more, he drummed on the table, and he began to show me what he could do as quietly as possible given where we were sitting. He imitated and demonstrated, getting so involved he seemed to go off into some other dimension. However, when we started talking about his career again, things changed. This is a musician with considerable success under his belt, but I quickly discovered that reinforcing his career highs was not the way to go when probing for information. In fact, he did not particularly want to talk about his career at all. Gorrie (2009) writes about how successful performers rarely feel the need to talk about how good they are. Even if they have a bad day or a bad show, they don't talk much about it. In Gorrie's experience, less successful performers constantly beat themselves up when they don't do well, but they do it through exploiting the faults of others. RDG didn't feel the need to talk about his success. RDG didn't blame anyone for where he was or what he was doing. In fact, this part of the discussion simply got him annoyed.

According to what RDG revealed in our discussion: (1) His age is getting in the way. Most of his bandmates are at least 10-plus years younger than he is, and as RDG puts it: "my ego is taking a beating"; (2) He frequently feels like a "has-been" compared to his bandmates. Even though the front person is as old as RDG, he still feels like the old man who has lost his edge; (3) He is still struggling to adjust from the MTV "glory days" to the present. He justifies the present with remarks like "at least I'm making good money"; (4) He believes "this old dog cannot learn new tricks," yet he has learned everything possible about the latest sound technology and has kept his drumming skills fresh and current; and (5) RDG still gets "good-looking, younger chicks," which is apparently a source of great pride. I only mention this because his face was noticeably brighter when he brought it up.

So if he did not want to take theory and harmony classes, yet he was happy with his drumming skills, felt like a "has-been," but was successful and making money, what did he want from the session? We finally got to the heart of the matter when we began discussing what was important to him about his drumming, and where he sees himself in 10 years. "I want to know I'm still good. I want to know I made it. I want to know it ain't over till it's over."

This led to a discussion of Ringo Starr of The Beatles. I told him that after playing in a skiffle band, Ringo's stepfather bought him a drum kit, and the rest is history. He did not have formal drum lessons. He was a part of (arguably) the most successful rock band in history, and Ringo, at age 74, is still playing (www.drumlessons.com/drummers/ringo-starr). We also talked about John Bonham of Led Zeppelin, another major rock drummer (#2 on the *Rolling Stone* magazine top 100 list) who never had formal drum lessons (www.drumlessons.com/drummers/john-bonham). A bit of information I wish I had known at the time, but didn't find out until much later, was that drum legend Buddy Rich and Genesis drummer Phil Collins never had formal training either (DeCordova, personal communication, December 20, 2014). This would have added more power to the discussion, but at least I have it in my back pocket for any future consultations with Rock Drummer Guy.

RDG made it clear that being a drummer is all he wants. He loves it and wants to keep playing without giving himself a time limit or retirement date. I managed to get him to look at his considerable previous accomplishments by asking about the famous people he worked with (a good predictor of success for the future) and the major concerts and festivals he played. This became a lengthy, impressive list. When I asked how he got the jobs, he was quite modest and self-effacing. He told me he did not know, and that the jobs just happened. I followed up with the one question I feel is more important than any other: "Did you have fun back then?" He said he did then added "but it's different now." I asked why it wasn't fun anymore. What he was worried about?

I knew this would take us back to music theory, but he didn't want to discuss the obvious solutions (e.g., taking theory classes, learning the conventional and/or traditional mechanics of music). It became evident that we needed to find a way to improve his feelings of self-efficacy and get him out of comparing his current band with the one from his past. We needed a present-centered focus because he was very aware he couldn't go backwards. We had to focus on what he could work on in the here and now, and then set up his future. I encouraged him to put his present focus on what he does right as a musician and what was good right now (he's working, touring, etc.). Then we took the next step and discussed what he has to look forward to in the next 30 days (short-term goal), and the final step, what he wants to do down the road (long-term goal).

Pargman (2006) talks about rational thinking and the self-evaluative nature of performers. Performers tend to make attributions about performance outcomes and causes. I convinced him to make a list of his skills – a list that literally covered everything he did as a member of every band he's ever been a part of. The skills list and the informal list of his accomplishments became a rational thinking exercise that used empirical evidence to help him review his extensive, impressive resume. He was able to see the extent of his drumming skill set and how much he knew as a musician without formal training (quite a bit, as it turned out). It provided insight into his talents as a sound man and pointed out how well he was regarded by his bandmates. I have used this exercise with athletes in the past, and while it took longer than usual with RDG, the payoff was that it showed him he still had a lot to offer.

The next step was regaining confidence. As RDG put it, "It's one thing to see all this on paper, it's a whole other thing to feel it." The entertainment industry is high stress, and for rock musicians the constant touring, the isolation and separation from their usual social support system, and the inconsistent paydays can drain the life out of the performer (Gillespie & Myors, 2000). Despite the relative stability of his current situation, RDG still feels he is on shaky ground. Unsurprisingly, thanks to the inconsistencies and extremes of the music industry, rock musicians score high on anxiety, yet they are highly creative. Creativity may be a release from musician anxiety, a direct result of maintaining the high standards, high achievement, and high pressure necessary to stay in the industry (Gillespie & Myors, 2000), but this pressure to maintain can also contribute to loss of confidence, substance use, and depression (Hernandez, Russo, & Schneider, 2009). Bruser (1997) says "no matter how confident we are, we feel vulnerable in the vast world of music and musicians" (p. 8). It is a formidable undertaking to play an instrument, combining mind, memory, emotion, creativity, and, especially in the case of the rock drummer, considerable athleticism (Jourdain, 1997). I feel it is also an incredible act of bravery to put yourself on a stage in front of thousands of people and play your heart out.

It was important to get RDG to attribute his success to his innate talent (Hernandez, Russo, & Schneider, 2009). We used a combination of imagery and acting. Our mantra became "Fake it till you make it." I instructed him to fake it by straightening up his posture, smiling, being a bit more playful in rehearsal and on stage, and told him to remember the famous musicians he's played with. It was important to stress being in the here and now, and that the fake it part would become a habit (Gorrie, 2009). We talked about him imagining himself playing exactly the way he wanted, in the arena, having a great time, having the guys follow him because, after all, he was the heartbeat of the whole show and, most importantly, letting himself feel the rush of the performance.

Our second meeting was four days later, and it was clear his feelings of being a "has-been" had lessened after employing the faking it strategy and imaging successful performance. He mentioned that during rehearsal one of the guitarists asked for his input regarding a bridge between two songs in a medley. He felt he taught the guitarist a few things ("We went back and forth, and he followed me, but then the kid *really* did not know *I* could follow *his* lead like that! We wrote a whole *new section*!"). He contributed. He felt necessary. The improvement in his affect was definitely visible.

After this revelation, my big question to RDG was, "What will you take on tour?" He did not get the question, so after some clarification that I was not referring to clothes and toiletries, he started to talk about equipment. That led to a renewed discussion of his concerns about his playing, but this time it was more about maintaining his new level of confidence. My response: "Leave that baggage behind – it's 25 bucks a bag, anyway!" That got a laugh and an important acknowledgement. He decided to use this as his mantra for this short tour. We talked about purchasing a new portable drum pad to use at home and on the tour bus. He had not invested in a new one in years, so I encouraged him to buy himself a little present. I also suggested electronic sticks ("You mean like the 80's?"). This generated a good-natured cost-benefit analysis of the item, and I suggested he use them to play along with his favorite music on his iPod. I also encouraged him to use the iPod to listen to his band's recordings to see what he could enhance. I purposely chose the word "enhance" over the word "change." To me, using the word "change" implied what came before was not good enough, and this was not the case. Clearly, his band was good enough or he would not have had such success. To me, *enhance* suggested he could add to what already worked. I suggested he look at "putting another layer on" what he already had.

At present RDG is still working with the same band outside the US. He spends more time overseas than here, and he now owns a house there. He seems to have a steady girlfriend, and after seeing his social media postings, things seem to be stable. We have not consulted since, and that is not a surprise. In fact, I would have to say this is very typical of the working musician lifestyle and mindset.

Recommendations for aspiring practitioners regarding how to gain access and then work effectively with the performer

If one wants to work with musicians, I certainly cannot guarantee easy access. I have been very lucky because I have been a part of that world. My experience is unique, one of pure chance, and happened thanks to my background in music, dance, and theater. I suppose one could contact local music or dance schools, or if the individual has some background in the performing arts, contact conservatories, but these are relatively closed environments. And for those who want to dive into a School of Rock, I am pretty comfortable saying you may have a problem getting in the door unless you know somebody. I do not want to be the voice of negativity, nor do I want to discourage anyone, but I cannot say gaining entry into the arts world is easy. Like high-level athletes, successful musicians are often suspicious of folks who hang around them or try to offer them some type of service. There is also an additional layer of technical expertise needed. Successful musicians, singers, and dancers have a level of knowledge that encompasses their individual art and the emergence between their art and the mechanics of sound, lighting, and production values. Artists must cross genres, as well. For example, dancers and classical singers are also actors since many pieces demand they perform a specific role in the overall production or portray a certain character. These artists need to know how to work with an orchestra and conductor, and they need to understand the language of stage directions. Consultants interested in working with this population need to have the experience and knowledge that gives them the necessary credibility. The consultant needs to be flexible with erratic schedules, and the consultant needs patience – lots and lots of patience.

References

Biasutti, M., & Frezza, L. (2009). Dimensions of music improvisation. *Creativity Research Journal, 21,* 232–242.

Bottstein, L. (2000). The training of musicians. *The Musical Quarterly, 84,* 327–332.

Brugues, A. O. (2011). Music performance anxiety – Part 2: A review of treatment options. *Medical Problems of Performing Artists, 26,* 164–171.

Bruser, M. (1997). *The art of practicing: A guide to making music from the heart.* New York: Three Rivers Press.

Bunting, P. (2007). A tale of three cities. *The Strad, 118,* 44–48.

Buonviri, N. (2013). Idea bank: I can't do that! Improvisation for classically trained musicians. *Music Educators Journal, 99,* 23–25.

Coyle, S. (2006). Here's how: Play well with others. *Acoustic Guitar, 17,* 38, 41.

Giddings, S. (2008). Popular music education: A different type of musicianship. *Musicien Educateur au Canada, 49,* 31–35.

Gillespie, W., & Myors, B. (2000). Personality of rock musicians. *Psychology of Music, 28,* 154–165.

Gorrie, J. (2009). *Performing in the zone.* Retrieved from www.thezonebook.com

Green, B. (2003). *The mastery of music.* New York, NY: Broadway Books.

Haid, M. (2008). Jeff Sipe: The art of the jam. *Modern Drummer, 32,* 96–10, 105.

Hernandez, D., Russo, S. A., & Schneider, B. A. (2009). The psychological profile of a rock band: Using intellectual and personality measures with musicians. *Medical Problems of Performing Artists, 24,* 71–80.

Jourdain, R. (1997). *Music, the brain and ecstasy: How music captures our imagination.* New York: Harper Collins.

Kingsbury, H. (1988). *Music, talent and performance: A conservatory cultural system.* Philadelphia, PA: Temple University Press.

Kirshnit, F. (2005). The problem with conservatories. *The New York Sun.* Retrieved from http://www.nysun.com/arts/problem-with-conservatories/198-46/

Klickstein, G. (2009). *The musician's way: A guide to practice, performance, and wellness.* New York: Oxford University Press.

Levitin, D. (2006). *This is your brain on music: The science of a human obsession.* New York: Penguin.

Lotze, M., Scheler, G., Tan, H-R. M., Braun, C., & Birnbaumer, N. (2003). The musical brain: Functional imaging of amateurs and professionals during performance and imagery. *NeuroImage, 20,* 1817–1829.

MacNamara, A., Holmes, P., & Collins, D. (2006). The pathway to excellence: The role of psychological characteristics in negotiating the challenges of musical development. *British Journal of Music Education, 23*(3), 285–302.

McPherson, M. J., Lopez-Gonzalez, M., Ranken, S. K., & Limb, C. J. (2014). The role of emotion in musical improvisation: An analysis of structural features. *PLoS ONE, 9,* e105144.

Nagel, J. J. (1993). Stage fright in musicians: A psychodynamic perspective. *Bulletin of the Menninger Clinic, 57,* 492–503.

Nagel, J. J. (2004). Performance anxiety theory and treatment: One size does not fit all. *Medical Problems of Performing Artists, 19,* 39–43.

Nagel, J. J. (2009). How to destroy creativity in music students: The need for emotional and psychological support services in music schools. *Medical Problems of Performing Artists, 24,* 15–17.

Pargman, D. (2006). *Managing performance stress: Models and methods.* New York: Routledge.

Ringo Starr (n.d.). DrumLessons.com. Retrieved from http://www.drumlessons.com/drummers/ringo-starr

Schuter-Dyson, R., & Gabriel, C. (1981). *The psychology of musical ability* (2nd ed.). New York, NY: Methuen, Inc.

Zimmerman, M. P., & Boyle, J. D. (2002). Aural perception and musical development. In M. R. Campbell (Ed.), *On musicality and milestones: Selected writings of Marilyn Pfederer Zimmerman with contributions from the profession* (pp. 177). Champaign, IL: School of Music, University of Illinois at Urbana-Champaign.

23

SYNTHESIS AND REFLECTIONS ON PROFESSIONAL SPORT CONSULTING

Dieter Hackfort and Robert J. Schinke

Fundamental commonalities, symmetries and variations in conceptual, methodological, and practical approaches

After reading all of the above chapters, the reader will detect that several consistent themes resurface across the expert practitioners. These symmetries are briefly identified in this section, with each explaining how one might develop longevity within one's chosen context. The characteristics include the following: cultural competence, knowledge underpinnings, the capacity to work within a team/organizational context, and an understanding that performances in professional contexts are embedded within a business model, that sport psychology consultants must be highly inquisitive, and that there must be a continuous thirst for knowledge based on emerging techniques and approaches. The majority of the authors highlighted *cultural competence* explicitly or at least implicitly. This competence might be gained from an earlier contextual knowledge of having been an athlete or coach within the context, or by being an astute observer and an inquisitive person. Either way, understanding one's context is a necessity. *Knowledge underpinnings* in terms of specialist knowledge seem to include conceptual approaches and methodological or technical training in such skills as cognitive-behavioural approaches, social cognition, and mental skills techniques. Several of the authors (e.g. Symes or Harwood) referred to a frame, which might be regarded as humanistic. A humanistic view of humankind necessarily is inducing or associated with the attitude that one ought to accept the client as a cooperative partner in the endeavour of performance enhancement, as opposed to treating the athlete as a person to be treated as a patient. Further features of this view are honesty (faking is no option) and empathy are essential, as are trust and confidentiality. The *capacity to work as part of an integrated support team embedded in an organizational context*, alongside sport scientists, coaches, management, and even agents is emphasized to be necessary regardless of whether the performer is in a team or individual pursuit. It is argued (see Hackfort in chapter ten) that peak performance in elite/professional sport always requires teamwork. Furthermore, performances within professional contexts tend to always be *founded on a business model*, where there are consumers and where the performer is hired to provide a service denoted as entertainment. The nature of professional sport in terms of context and content (kind of work) also necessitates that the *practitioner remain inquisitive* in terms of the most recent knowledge. Many of the authors spoke about the importance of ordering academic journals and reading fervently from the beginning to the end of their careers. Granted, there are also unique aspects to each context, but the broader characteristics just identified are common themes across the authors, symmetries they (and we) encourage you to consider as you seek to engage in or sustain a career working in professional sport.

Contextual or sub-cultural circumstances in working with professional performers

The specific person–task–environment constellation – that is, the action situation (see Hackfort, 2006) built up by the professional athlete/performer, the task at hand, and the socio-economic conditions – has to be considered as it represents the basic reference system for any engagement, approach, and intervention by a sport/performance psychologist (see also Nitsch & Hackfort, 2016). The professional performer is fully committed to her/his craft, as there is often no safety net other than to perform at a very high level, worthy of a sustained audience of consumers. The practitioners who work with these full-time performers have chosen to practice with full-time performers. With that commitment, sport/performance psychologists venture into contexts where they must belong and then contribute to making a difference for the better. Sport psychologists must also retain and deepen their positions, not only for their own sake, but also for the sake of the people who will follow in their footsteps. Far too often, these editors (Rob and Dieter) have heard stories and witnessed practitioners of our craft who migrate from context to context, never staying long enough with any performer or team to be considered other than a superficial additive. The people we find interesting are those who develop roots in organizations, where they become valued for the work they do. These professionals might live under the radar or above it depending on the performance context and the demands associated with their roles, but they stay and expand the breadth of their services beyond what might be traditional mental training or clinical services, into offerings that are contextually driven and culturally infused. These long-standing consultants become versed in such aspects as appropriate proxemics, level of language, context-specific terminology, and the style of life associated with being a member of (and in) the context. Contextually knowledgeable practitioners, then, are not only educated in their scientific discipline, they are also experts in their understanding of the environment where the athlete and sport organization coexist.

Specific demands, special competencies, and particularities in attitude and ethical orientation

The person working in professional contexts requires a breadth of skills, beyond the capacity to become rooted within the context. Among these, the practitioner needs to be trustworthy in the eyes of the performer and also the company/organization the performer is employed by. To work within a professional context requires the ability to understand that there are several layers of clients, in relation to a single contract. There is the performer, and there is also the coaching staff, the management, ownership, agents, media, and fan groups. The astute and capable psychologist/mental coach needs to interface with many of these people. Understanding channels of communication, relationships, and interpersonal dynamics is a skill set that is often not taught but yet a requirement.

Then there is the quality of being without ego when working with high-profile performers. A renowned practitioner once told one of us that he likes to "work in the shadows". Though working in the shadows might be what is needed (maybe sometimes or often), even more important is the willingness to work in and out of the shadows as needed, not for one's own benefit and to be regaled. Instead, the job is to fill holes within one's purview as these are called for, and not because these garner any form of recognition. Recognition often comes when we least expect it, and this is often not in a public forum, and if it is, most certainly not for personal gain. One of the most meaningful compliments bestowed on a practitioner is a renewed contract, and more so, an expanded purview.

Authors in this book have emphasized that there is the need to remain current in the knowledge base of one's profession. This latter quality suggests a strong motivation to enhance knowledge, openness for new information, and commitment. The practitioner is then pushed to always bring new insights, approaches, and refined skills that have been tested by researchers, so as to ensure that the performer and organization continue to develop in relation to professional, psychological competencies. Organizations such as the International Society of Sport Psychology (ISSP), the European Federation of Sport Psychology (FEPSAC), and the Association for Applied Sport Psychology (AASP) place value in scientist–practitioner models, where theory and application inform each other, leading to precise, testable, and viable practice. We hope that the next generations of practitioners (this is what we will consider especially to be the readership of this book given their disciplinary diversity) who read this book will share with us in the desire to hone one's practice.

In this context, it is also important to mention that it is not uncommon for sport/performance psychologists to be anchored in a single theoretical approach that was not developed in or for sport or sport-specific usage. Within elite or high-performance areas, there is often uniqueness derived from only one person and one example, embedded in a single context that is not replicated elsewhere. In consequence, it is necessary to reflect on individual cases and consider anecdotal experiences, as much as theory or practice from outside of the current circumstance or demand. It is often simply not possible to refer to what is marked to be "evidence based". Many reports on a sport psychology engagement in professional sports start with an anecdotal and individual case description focusing on a problem, which is identified to be mental, induced by or attributed to a mental malfunction or lack of knowledge, emotional stability, or resilience. Subsequently, concepts for intervention are considered which are appraised to be especially designed and appropriate to overcome the specific challenge. Alternately, concepts might be adopted, which are used in general by this consultant and which he or she takes up to derive a solid understanding, systematic classification, and a more structured encounter. Regardless of the approach chosen, the top priority is to co-develop one or several solutions and then offer these to the client or organization so that the best alternative is chosen. Underlying the quest and implementation of solutions is the primary intent to support development within the performer and the organization.

For an appropriate understanding of this domain, it is essential to know that performers and coaches in professional sports and other high-performance areas are (a) extraordinary people at least with regard to the special performance area and (b) experts in this domain with special experiences and competencies. This means that concepts and evidences derived from studies with regular people by using standard methodologies are sometimes insufficient or perhaps misleading in relation to very specific contexts and extraordinary people (for example, see chapter 10, about achievement motivation). Furthermore, performers are experts in their performance domain, and even though they might not have a formal education in psychology, what they have acquired is special, subjective, or individual concepts suited to who they are and where and how they perform, which is necessary to learn and to know for the design of effective strategies and to take up a reasonable starting point (see Hackfort, 2001). The sport/performance psychologist can identify critical explanations, attributions, orientations, and discuss alternative perspectives and possibly a better-suited understanding and approach. The goal might be to convince the athlete/performer to consider a more efficient or refined strategy. Hence, it is a providential method to (a) learn about the sport and the special features of the sport in highly demanding circumstances (sport specialist knowledge discovery); (b) to signalize that the athlete or coach is an expert and partner (social recognition and establishment of partnership); and (c) to learn about more general orientations of the athlete or coach (philosophy). All this information can contribute to establish social acceptance and promote teamwork.

In relation to the ethical issues discussed by Watson and Etzel (see chapter six), it is essential in professional sports for sport psychology practitioners, as well as for professional athletes, to develop an appropriate attitude and ethical understanding beyond the rules of the specific performance context in terms of a professional, moral approach. In some, or maybe most, sports, there is a high risk to hurt an opponent or to injure an adversary physically and psychologically, such as in boxing, soccer, and American football. A sport psychologist has to know not only about the rules of the specific sport, but also about strategies of how to stress the tolerated exceedance of the limits and the attitude behind it. Consider Schinke's chapter about professional boxing and strategies of how to implement lessons derived from an opponent's professional profile. Unlike amateur sport, performers, when necessary, must stretch the boundaries of what might be tolerable elsewhere in terms of psychological antics. The performance consultant must help the performer explore the morality surrounding these decisions so that psychological tactics remain within a morally acceptable standard, so as to augment the entertainment value without compromising one's own and another's health. There is also the broader quality of being an ethical professional. Confidences need to be maintained, and there must also be concern over the welfare and holistic development of the performer. A mentally healthy performer in everyday life has longevity, and also, with mental health, performers tend to enjoy what they do for longer periods of time. There needs to be meaning in the performance, and this meaning must be regarded as adding to the broader meaning in the performer's life.

The ethical practitioner must also see professional responsibilities as a necessary part of what one does. Sometimes these do not jibe with being popular, especially when one acts in the best interest of the client's long-term health. Each performer has a window when she/ he can, and then, no longer is able to perform safely at the appropriate level. In consequence, in professional performance domains and especially in professional sport, a sport psychologist has to consider both ethical guidelines (see e.g. Code of Ethics, Ethical Principles of the ISSP) as well as the moral guidelines (and potential deviations) in that sport. In the case of a conflict, the practitioner is morally bound to his or her ethical standards as well as the more formal ethical guidelines associated with accreditation. These standards are often clearly written, but they are much more challenging to apply when the performer relies on the capacity to perform in order to continue in a salaried position. There is also sometimes the competing pressure of a sport organization, where the focus is on entertainment and the performer's entertainment value over the performer's welfare. Both the performer and the organization are the practitioner's clients, and their immediate desires need to be weighed carefully, with the responsibility to the performer's long-term health being prioritized. Practitioners exist in complex professional performance contexts, and these contexts will inevitably challenge one's professional values and standards.

The consulting career and issues of expertise

Learning about the different and partially heterogeneous backgrounds and circumstances in becoming involved in professional performance by the colleagues contributing to the book, it is obvious that at present there is no standard procedure for psychologists and mental training consultants to become involved in their contexts. There are also no criteria for the attribution of being an accredited expert or a specialist for this action field. The term *mental coach* is unprotected and can be used by people who (try to) suggest that they are sport psychology experts but do not have any relevant education, professional training, and certification. The completion and implementation of certified courses and training papers, including confirmation by a well-known expert, could be of some help to overcome the risk of unqualified people in the field who might damage the reputation and image of sport psychology and also impede a performer's development and well-being. Supervision, consultation, accreditation, and then upgrading are relevant steps that will contribute to career development, especially for people who are committed to working in sport and performance psychology, such as those who are expanding a general psychology practice to include professional level clients. Supervised experience already is a requirement for certain certifications and accreditations (e.g. Accredited Sport and Exercise Scientist, BASES; Certified Consultant, Association for Applied Sport Psychology).

A practitioner working in almost any professional context is facing various special challenges, which may create difficulties, least of which include the ethical decisions mentioned above. Consultation, supervision, and continuing education can help practitioners to cope with problems induced by traveling with teams and athletes, consulting with coaches and athletes simultaneously, communicating frequently with clients over long distances, managing confidentiality in an athletic and professional system, and consulting with multiple professionals (e.g. physical trainers, physicians, physiotherapists, personal coaches) for service delivery. The authors in this book are predestined to serve as coordinators of these services, beyond their capacity toward analytics garnered from a scientific background. Furthermore, certifying organizations provide lists of those who have met certain requirements and are available to provide supervision (e.g. see http://www.appliedsportpsych.org/certified-consultants/become-a-certified-consultant/ for a list of AASP-certified consultants; www.BASES.org.uk for a list of BASES-accredited sport and exercise scientists in the UK).

The commitment to professional standards, common values of the professional community, and ethical standards or a code of ethics, as it was discussed, are of fundamental meaning with respect to deciding about scope of practice. In the case of mental training or clinical problems, it has to be decided by the practitioner him- or herself who is most competent based on formal training, and then afterward, contextual knowledge. When an athlete is suffering with a defined mental problem, he/she has to be regarded to be a patient. As such, a clinical approach and an expert in clinical psychology is best suited as the practitioner. When the task is to augment performance by psychological means, a sport/performance psychologist could be the appropriate expert. For a sport psychologist, it is characteristic to combine both competencies in psychology and sport science, such as with regard to motor performance, training, or exercise. In principle, this kind of expertise is needed for a transdisciplinary approach (organizational aspect) and interdisciplinary cooperation (subject relation) in this action field.

The authors have argued that success in relation to professional performance requires teamwork. Furthermore, many of the chapters discuss that the job of a practitioner encompasses performance lifestyle management, which then augments performance enhancement. With regard to special lifestyle issues, there are challenges for professional (tertiary) socialization, such as communication with sponsors, handling of media, and self-presentation in the public, which are decisive for professional success. In various contributions to the book, it becomes obvious that the sport/performance psychologist is playing a role as coordinator who facilitates communication and performance strategies in an interdisciplinary setting built up by experts with a heterogeneous background. She or he takes responsibility for tasks, such as helping to craft a working atmosphere, bettering a household climate, and crafting a positive living environment during a training camp. Hence, the sport psychologist must be able to demonstrate expertise that extends beyond mental skills and convince the athlete, and equally, the people around him or her, to commit to a synergistic performance environment. This form of craft necessitates emotional intelligence on the part of the practitioner.

Familiarity with the action field also means that beyond rational decision making, there is a basis for intuition, which is also a necessary professional requirement. Based on experiences and reflections, thinking and feeling are both valuable sources in the process of analysis and decision making (see Gigerenzer, 2007). Feelings are often neglected, underestimated, or mistaken with regard to their functional meaning. Between the lines in various contributions, it is proposed that especially in complex situations, a holistic signal like a feeling is of fundamental importance to be able to find a useful approach for sport psychology counseling or intervention. To develop or increase this valuable skill set, it is necessary to immerse in relevant action situations, to learn as much as possible from the action field, and to become actively involved. For a most effective functioning of action regulation, the interplay of cognitive and affective regulation/control with regard to performance and performance enhancement is essential. Piaget (1954) explained that affective and cognitive processes are complementary. This insight was neglected or ignored sometimes, especially by colleagues interested in decision making, not only in sport and performance psychology. In the elaboration of the concept of action regulation (Nitsch & Hackfort, 2016), it always was and still is a key issue associated with a functional analysis of the meaning of emotions and how affective processes contribute to achievement and success or what kind of interrelation between cognitive and affective, emotional, and motor processes (coordination) may be disturbing or even impede performance.

To ensure a sophisticated professional development and integration for young colleagues, mentoring and supervision would be most supportive. Perhaps the contributions to this book will motivate aspiring readers to contact such an expert, with skills and experience readily transferable to one's context of interest. There are already national organizations (e.g. the German Association for Sport Psychology, Association for Applied Sport Psychology) managing a database for experts in applied sport psychology. To be accepted and included in the database, applicants have to meet certain criteria to increase the likelihood that athletes, coaches, and clients looking for competent practitioners are protected against charlatanism. We foresee that the International Society of Sport Psychology will soon offer such a service via the homepage of its organization, though from the vantage point of regional practices that permit cultural safety beyond more general culture- and region-blind guidelines and standards.

Experts interested in providing their services by region will be asked to indicate their special competencies (supervision, mental training, goal-setting, etc.), field of expertise (sport), and some further information useful to prospective clients seeking their services for sport and performance support.

Last, but not least, it should be mentioned that sport and sport performance can be regarded to be a model for performance in a broad(er) scope of domains. There are typical characteristics which create the special feature of competition/performance requirement, most relevant in this context (professional sport and the performing arts). The characteristics are as follows:

1 There is only one chance (matchlessness), no further opportunity or second chance (no repeatability) for the athlete, as well as for the sport psychology practitioner, e.g. to create a first impression within the action field (i.e. context).
2 There is no safety net or second bottom, neither for the performer nor for the full-time practitioner. As such, practices need to be deliberate, useful, and efficient.
3 One's mistakes are noted in the public, by the media. As such, the accountability and one's (performer's as well as practitioner's) reputation are always at risk.
4 The practitioner is apt to work with a performer who runs the risk of committing damage to oneself due to the job commitment of having to perform.

In case of not being able to meet and cope effectively with these circumstances, the consequences in professional performance are severe and sometimes dramatic, and frequently not only for the performer but for the entire team around him or her. Beyond knowledge and skills, the sport/performance psychology practitioner needs to develop the appropriate attitude to meet and handle these situations. Most certainly, professional performance contexts will test not only one's knowledge base, but also how one acts and reacts in a pressure context where viability is contingent on yesterday's results.

References

Gigerenzer, G. (2007). *Gut feeling: The intelligence of the unconscious*. New York: Viking.

Hackfort, D. (2001). Experiences with application of action-theory-based approach in working with elite athletes. In G. Tenenbaum (Ed.), *The practice of sport psychology* (pp. 89–99). Morgantown, WV: Fitness Information Technology.

Hackfort, D. (2006). A conceptual framework and fundamental issues for investigating the development of peak performance in sports. In D. Hackfort & G. Tenenbaum (Eds.), *Essential processes for attaining peak performance* (pp. 10–23). Aachen, Germany: Meyer & Meyer.

Nitsch, J. R., & Hackfort, D. (2016). Theoretical framework of performance psychology: An action theory perspective. In M. Raab, B. Lobinger, S. Hoffmann, A. Pizzera & S. Laborde (Eds.), *Performance psychology: Perception, action, cognition, and emotion* (pp. 11–29). Amsterdam, The Netherlands: Elsevier.

Piaget, J. (1954). *Les relations entre l'affectivité et l'intelligence dans le development mental de l'enfant [The relation between affectivity and intelligence in the mental development of the child]*. Paris, France: Centre de documentation universitaire.

INDEX

Boldface indicates essential or most significant information (e.g., definitions).